The Sociology of Knowledge Approach to Discourse

The Sociology of Knowledge Approach to Discourse (SKAD) has reoriented research into social forms, structuration and processes of meaning construction and reality formation; doing so by linking social constructivist and pragmatist approaches with post-structuralist thinking in order to study discourses and create epistemological space for analysing processes of world-making in culturally diverse environments.

SKAD is anchored in interpretive traditions of inquiry and allows for broadening – and possibly overcoming – of the epistemological biases and restrictions still common in theories and approaches of Western- and Northern-centric social sciences. An innovative volume, this book is exactly attentive to these empirically based, globally diverse further developments of approach, with a clear focus on the methodology and its implementation. Thus, *The Sociology of Knowledge Approach to Discourse* presents itself as a research program and locates the approach within the context of interpretive social sciences, followed by eleven chapters on different cases from around the world that highlight certain theoretical questions and methodological challenges.

Presenting outstanding applications of *The Sociology of Knowledge Approach to Discourse* across a wide variety of substantive projects and regional contexts, this text will appeal to postgraduate students and researchers interested in fields such as Discourse Studies, Sociology, Cultural Studies and Qualitative Methodology and Methods.

Reiner Keller (Dr. phil.) is Professor of Sociology at Augsburg University, Germany.

Anna-Katharina Hornidge (Dr. phil.) is Professor of Social Sciences at the University of Bremen and heads Development & Knowledge Sociology at the Leibniz Centre for Tropical Marine Research (ZMT), Bremen, Germany.

Wolf J. Schünemann (Dr. phil.) is Junior Professor of Political Science with a focus on Internet and Politics at Hildesheim University, Germany.

Routledge Advances in Sociology

244 **Time and Temporality in Transitional and Post-Conflict Societies**
   Edited by Natascha Mueller-Hirth, and Sandra Rios Oyola

245 **Practicing Art/Science**
   Experiments in an Emerging Field
   Edited by Philippe Sormani, Guelfo Carbone and Priska Gisler

246 **The Dark Side of Podemos?**
   Carl Schmitt's Shadow in Progressive Populism
   Josh Booth and Patrick Baert

247 **Intergenerational Family Relations**
   An Evolutionary Social Science Approach
   Antti O. Tanskanen and Mirkka Danielsbacka

248 **Performing Fantasy and Reality in Contemporary Culture**
   Anastasia Seregina

249 **The Philosophy of Homelessness**
   Barely Being
   Paul Moran and Frances Atherton

250 **The Sociology of Knowledge Approach to Discourse**
   Investigating the Politics of Knowledge and Meaning-making
   Edited by Reiner Keller, Anna-Katharina Hornidge and Wolf J. Schünemann

251 **Christianity and Sociological Theory**
   Reclaiming the Promise
   Joseph A. Scimecca

For a full list of titles in this series, please visit www.routledge.com/series/SE0511

The Sociology of Knowledge Approach to Discourse

Investigating the Politics of Knowledge and Meaning-making

Edited by Reiner Keller,
Anna-Katharina Hornidge and
Wolf J. Schünemann

LONDON AND NEW YORK

First published 2018
by Routledge
2 Park Square, Milton Park, Abingdon, Oxon OX14 4RN

and by Routledge
711 Third Avenue, New York, NY 10017

Routledge is an imprint of the Taylor & Francis Group, an informa business

© 2018 selection and editorial matter, Reiner Keller, Anna-Katharina Hornidge and Wolf J. Schünemann; individual chapters, the contributors

The right of Reiner Keller, Anna-Katharina Hornidge and Wolf J. Schünemann to be identified as the authors of the editorial matter, and of the authors for their individual chapters, has been asserted in accordance with sections 77 and 78 of the Copyright, Designs and Patents Act 1988.

All rights reserved. No part of this book may be reprinted or reproduced or utilised in any form or by any electronic, mechanical, or other means, now known or hereafter invented, including photocopying and recording, or in any information storage or retrieval system, without permission in writing from the publishers.

Trademark notice: Product or corporate names may be trademarks or registered trademarks, and are used only for identification and explanation without intent to infringe.

British Library Cataloguing-in-Publication Data
A catalogue record for this book is available from the British Library

Library of Congress Cataloging-in-Publication Data
A catalog record has been requested for this book

ISBN: 978-1-138-04872-0 (hbk)
ISBN: 978-1-315-17000-8 (ebk)

Typeset in Baskerville
by Wearset Ltd, Boldon, Tyne and Wear

Contents

List of illustrations — vii
Notes on contributors — ix
Foreword — xiv
ADELE E. CLARKE

1 **Introduction: the sociology of knowledge approach to discourse in an interdependent world** — 1
   ANNA-KATHARINA HORNIDGE, REINER KELLER AND WOLF J. SCHÜNEMANN

2 **The sociology of knowledge approach to discourse: an introduction** — 16
   REINER KELLER

3 **Situating SKAD in interpretive inquiry** — 48
   REINER KELLER AND ADELE E. CLARKE

4 **The social construction of value: a comparative SKAD analysis of public discourses on waste in France and Germany** — 73
   REINER KELLER

5 **SKAD analysis of European multi-level political debates** — 91
   WOLF J. SCHÜNEMANN

6 **Legislation and discourse: research on the making of law by means of discourse analysis** — 112
   ANDREAS STÜCKLER

7 **A SKAD ethnography of educational knowledge discourses** — 133
   ANNA-KATHARINA HORNIDGE AND HART NADAV FEUER

Contents

8 Using SKAD to study Chinese contemporary governance: reflections on our research process   150
SHAOYING ZHANG AND DEREK McGHEE

9 Using SKAD to analyse classification practices in public health: methodological reflections on the research process   169
HELLA VON UNGER, PENELOPE SCOTT AND DENNIS ODUKOYA

10 Self-positioning of semi-skilled workers: analysing subjectification processes with SKAD   186
SAŠA BOSANČIĆ

11 Dangerous or endangered? Using the sociology of knowledge approach to discourse to uncover subject positions of sex workers in South African media discourse   202
CAROLIN KÜPPERS

12 Guidance on transitions: reconstructing the rationalities of the European discourse on career guidance services using the sociology of knowledge approach   223
INGA TRUSCHKAT AND CLAUDIA MUCHE

13 Using SKAD to investigate cooperation and conflict over water resources   237
TOBIAS IDE

14 Studying discourses ethnographically: a sociology of knowledge approach to analysing macro-level forces in micro-settings   254
FLORIAN ELLIKER

15 From analysis to visualisation: synoptical tools from SKAD studies and the entity mapper   274
ANNE LUTHER AND WOLF J. SCHÜNEMANN

Illustrations

Figures

5.1	Discourse Map – French referendum on the EU Constitutional Treaty 2005	98
5.2	Structural Scheme for the Dutch debate on the Constitutional Treaty in 2005	106
7.1	SKAD's discursive hierarchy	138
9.1	Arena map of social worlds focused on ethnicity classification in the health arena in the UK	174
9.2	Comparative study design: exploring four discourses over time	175
15.1	Policy publics on trash and recycling in Germany	279
15.2	Discourse map for the first Irish referendum debate on the Lisbon Treaty in 2008	282
15.3	Structural Scheme for the Dutch debate on the Constitutional Treaty in 2005	284
15.4	The public discourse arena (policy-specific) in Germany	285
15.5	Emerging Knowledge Age	286
15.6	Node-Link Network of data structure developed in Atlas.ti	287
15.7	Display of all entities	289
15.8	Display of codes and code families	290
15.9	Hovering over entities	292
15.10	Access to quotations	293
15.11	Paradigm Map	294

Tables

4.1	Example: phenomenal structure, French hegemonic discourse "socio-technological modernisation"	84
5.1	Arguments in EU referendum debates	100

5.2	Cumulative argumentatives yes-/no-discourse Ireland 2008 (selected arguments)	108
11.1	Number of published articles on sex work in South African print media 2010	209
13.1	Examples of open questions (narrative elements) in the guidelines for the semi-structured interviews	243
13.2	Example from the coding process	246

Contributors

Saša Bosančić (Dr. phil.) is Senior Researcher at Augsburg University. His fields of research are the Sociology of Knowledge and the Interpretative Paradigm of Sociology, Sociology of Work and Inequality, Discourse Analysis and Qualitative Methods. He authored several articles on subjectification processes and the discursive situatedness of human subjectivity. He is editor of the *Journal for Discourses Studies*.

Adele E. Clarke (PhD) is Professor Emerita of Sociology and Adjunct Professor Emerita of History of Health Sciences at University of California, San Francisco (UCSF). She grew up in New York, received a B.A. in sociology in 1966 from Barnard College and an MA in sociology in 1970 from New York University. She then taught women's studies at Sonoma State University (CA). In 1980, she selected the sociology program at the University of California, San Francisco for her PhD. She worked there with Anselm Strauss and Virginia Olesen, among others, and returned to UCSF as an Assistant Professor in 1989 after a Postdoctoral Fellowship at Stanford University. She was tenured in 1992 and promoted to Full Professor in 1998. Her research centres on social, cultural and historical studies of science, technology and medicine with emphases on biomedicalisation and common medical technologies for women such as contraception and the Pap smear.

Florian Elliker (PhD) is Senior Lecturer in Sociology at the University of St. Gallen (Switzerland) and Research Fellow at the Department of Sociology, University of the Free State (South Africa). His publications deal with populism, experiences of precarity and marginalisation in ethnically diverse societies, a sociology of knowledge approach to discourse and ethnography, and qualitative methods and methodology. He has recently co-edited a thematic issue of the *Journal for Discourse Studies* on "discourse ethnography" (3/2017).

Hart Nadav Feuer (Dr. agr.) is a junior associate professor in the Graduate School of Agriculture, Kyoto University. His current work encompasses broadly the importance of creativity and embeddedness in education systems, with a particular focus on passive development of soft skills for maintaining cultural food heritage and dietary balance. He is also concurrently studying the impact of new food transparency mechanisms (labelling, certification, awareness programs), and continuing an investigation into the history of smallholder rice intensification in Asia. Formerly, he researched education reconstruction in post-conflict areas, neo-liberalisation projects in higher education in Southeast Asia, and gender-related issues in agriculture in Jordan.

Anna-Katharina Hornidge (Dr. phil.) is Professor of Social Sciences in the Marine Tropics at the University of Bremen and Head of Department of Social Sciences and of the Working Group "Development and Knowledge Sociology" at the Leibniz Centre for Tropical Marine Research (ZMT), Bremen. Trained in Southeast Asian Studies and Sociology in Bonn and Singapore, Hornidge received a PhD in Sociology from the Technical University of Berlin in 2007 and finalised her habilitation in Development Research at the University of Bonn in 2014. Hornidge held the position of Professor and Director of Social Sciences at the Center for Development Research, University of Bonn from 2014 until leaving for Bremen in 2015. Ms Hornidge's research focuses on the social construction and materiality of (environmental) knowledges, sustainability futureing and knowledge discourses, as well as (im-)mobility based conceptualisations of space in the context of transformation processes. Her regional focus lies on Southeast Asia (Indonesia, Singapore, Philippines, Malaysia), with additional, partly collaborative, work in Central Asia, East and West Africa.

Tobias Ide (Dr. rer. nat.) is head of the Research Field Peace and Conflict at the Georg Eckert Institute for International Textbook Research in Braunschweig and an associated researcher in the Research Group Climate Change and Security at the University of Hamburg. Recently, he accepted a one-year fellowship at the School of Geography, The University of Melbourne. His research interests include peace and conflict, environmental security, climate change, critical geopolitics, discourse analysis and other research methods. He recently published in journals like *Global Environmental Change, Political Geography, Third World Quarterly,* and *Wiley Interdisciplinary Reviews Climate Change.*

Reiner Keller (Dr. phil.) is Professor of Sociology at Augsburg University (Germany) since 2011. He received a PhD in sociology in 1997 at the Technical University Munich and accomplished his habilitation in sociology in 2004 at Augsburg University. From October 2006 to September 2011 he was professor of sociology at Koblenz-Landau University. Currently, he is scientific director of the Jakob-Fugger Centre for Transnational Studies, Augsburg University, and, since 2015, member of the executive committee of the German Sociological Association. From

2010–2016, he headed its Sociology of Knowledge Section. His research centres on sociology of knowledge and culture, discourse studies, sociological theory, qualitative methods, risk and environment, politics of knowledge and knowing, and French sociology. He has published extensively on these areas.

Carolin Küppers (Dr. phil.) is a research associate at the Federal Foundation Magnus Hirschfeld in Berlin, Germany. Currently her research projects evolve around media discourses on queer refugees and on sex work in South Africa. Her research interests are feminist theory of science, discourse analysis, intersectionality as well as queer and postcolonial studies.

Anne Luther (PhD) is a researcher, arts manager and software developer whose work examines the contemporary art market and data visualisation in qualitative research. She received her PhD from Central Saint Martins College of Art and Design, London and is currently a researcher at the Department for Modern Art History at the Institute of Art Studies and Historical Urban Studies at TU Berlin and at The Center for Data Arts at The New School in New York. Her research is grounded in cultural studies, ethnography and art theory bridging an interdisciplinary approach to computer sciences, IT and design.

Derek McGhee (PhD) is Professor of Sociology, Dean of Research for Humanities and Social Sciences, and the Director of the Institute for Social Inclusion at Keele University. Previous to this he was the Head of Social Sciences at the University of Southampton. His research interests are primarily in migration, citizenship and governance. He has conducted research with a diverse group of communities and organisations, including recently European migrants to the UK and organisations that support asylum seekers. He has also started to develop research interests in China with co-author Dr. Shaoying Zhang on governance in China with regards to social and ethnic policy and also the impact of the anti-corruption campaign of the Chinese Civil Service.

Claudia Muche (Dr. phil.) is research associate at the Institute for Social and Organisational Pedagogy, University of Hildesheim. She finished a study programme of social work and a Master degree in Social and Organisational Pedagogy. In 2016 she completed her doctoral graduation about changing organisations in work with the handicapped. Her work priorities are social inclusion and organisation, transitions to work, organisations of social work, institutional change.

Dennis Odukoya (M.A.) is a research fellow and doctoral student at the Institute of Sociology, Ludwig Maximilians University (LMU) Munich, Germany. Initially trained as an anthropologist, his research interests include migration, public health and screening. From 2013 to 2015, he was a research fellow in the project "Changing Categories: Migrants in epidemiological, preventive and legal discourses on HIV and tuberculosis – A discourse analysis comparing Germany and the UK".

Penelope Scott (PhD) is a guest researcher at the Institute of Sociology, Ludwig Maximilians University (LMU) Munich, Germany. Her research interests include im/migrant and refugee health as well as migrants' right to health. From 2012 to 2015, she was research fellow in the project "Changing Categories: Migrants in epidemiological, preventive and legal discourses on HIV and tuberculosis – A discourse analysis comparing Germany and the UK".

Wolf J. Schünemann (Dr. phil.) is junior professor of Political Science with a focus on Internet and Politics at Hildesheim University. His research and teaching cover the fields of Internet Governance, International Relations and European Integration. After having studied political science, philosophy, German literature, and media at Kiel University and Sciences Po in Rennes, France, he worked as a research fellow and lecturer at the University of Koblenz-Landau. He received his doctoral degree with a comparative discourse study of referendum debates in France, the Netherlands and Ireland. Between 2013 and 2016 he worked as post-doc researcher at Heidelberg University. There he founded the Netzpolitik AG, an interdisciplinary group of researchers doing studies on online communication, Internet governance and cybersecurity. Moreover, he is part of the steering committee of Discourse Lab at Heidelberg University.

Andreas Stückler (M.A.) is doctoral candidate in the Department of Sociology at the University of Vienna. His research interests include the sociology of law, critical gerontology, men's studies, discourse studies and critical theory.

Inga Truschkat (Dr. phil.) is professor for social pedagogy and organisation studies at the University of Hildesheim. She finished her PhD in educational science in 2007 at the University of Göttingen. She worked as post-doc researcher at Humboldt-University in Berlin and the University of Koblenz-Landau. Her research interests and publications cover the topics of competence discourses, inclusive education and biography research. Her methodological focus is on Grounded Theory and Sociology of Knowledge Approach to Discourse.

Hella von Unger (Dr. phil.) is professor of sociology (Qualitative Methodologies) at Ludwig Maximilians University (LMU) Munich, Germany. She is executive board member of the section on qualitative methods at the German Sociological Association (DGS). Her research interests include qualitative methodologies, research ethics as well as studies in the sociology of health and illness, migration and ethnicity. From 2012 to 2015, she was principal investigator of the project "Changing Categories: Migrants in epidemiological, preventive and legal discourses on HIV and tuberculosis – A discourse analysis comparing Germany and the UK".

Shaoying Zhang (PhD) is currently an Associate Professor at Shanghai University of Political Science and Law. He is a Shanghai Young Eastern Scholar (2015–2017). He obtained his PhD in Sociology at University of Southampton in 2014. His area of interests lies in political sociology, governance in contemporary China and social science methodology. He also does empirical research on anti-terrorism and de-radicalisation in prisons. He is currently translating Reiner Keller's Book *Doing Discourse Research* into Chinese (first draft is completed).

Foreword

Adele E. Clarke

A good exemplar is worth 10,000 words. A bunch of them are worth a book! I began learning this crucial academic lesson in the early 1990s when Anselm Strauss, my advisor, asked to republish an article of mine that had just appeared in a new reader of grounded theory research papers he and Julie Corbin were preparing, *Grounded Theory in Practice* (Strauss and Corbin, 1997). I was deeply thrilled and honoured to be part of it (Clarke, 1990; 1997). I had recently joined the sociology faculty at the University of California, San Francisco, and begun teaching qualitative research methods – especially but not only grounded theory – to doctoral students. I waited impatiently for this reader to appear in order to assign it. Finally, it came out, sadly just after Anselm died in 1996, and became invaluable in teaching and mentoring.

By about 2010, the extension of grounded theory I subsequently developed, situational analysis (Clarke, 2005), was itself starting to have published exemplars as well. Then Norm Denzin invited me to organize a session of papers using situational analysis at the International Congress on Qualitative Inquiry for 2013. Aha, I thought, I can ask scholars who have used the method and published articles to present their reflections on actually using this method in the session. Four sets of authors presented and wrote up their exceptionally thoughtful reflections for publication as well. The time for a situational analysis reader had come, and Mitch Allen of Left Coast Press agreed. That remarkable session was the basis for *Situational Analysis in Practice* (Clarke, Friese and Washburn, 2015), borrowing from Anselm and Julie's pragmatist title.

In 2011, after a zillion emails, I finally met Reiner Keller who had arranged for me to present on situational analysis at the 7th Annual Berlin Meetings on Qualitative Research. He had also most generously organized a German translation of Situational Analysis (Clarke, 2012). And gradually I began to get to know Reiner's own impressive method, the Sociology of Knowledge Approach to Discourse (SKAD). Together we have presented on doing discourse analysis at several of the International Congresses in Illinois. Quite amazingly, despite being developed wholly separately in different countries by scholars from different generations, both our methods are based on essentially the same interpretive, pragmatist philosophical, interactionist, Foucauldian and constructivist sociology of knowledge groundings. Yet they are not at all the same, and I most enthusiastically urged him to use an International Congress session as the basis of generating a reader of SKAD works. It was also exciting to have a slew of German scholars on the great American prairie in Illinois (where the corn does grow as high as an elephant's eye) and to begin to see the breadth of applications of SKAD.

Having a bunch of excellent examples of using a particular research method all together in one volume is a great gift. The reader can grasp the range and scope of *possibilities* the method offers so much more easily. Significantly, good scholars also tend to be quite creative and to move the method forward in distinctive ways through their innovative approaches and applications of the method. Good users push the envelope. In a reader, one can come to appreciate how individual researchers do so, seeing how they thoughtfully fine tune a method to meet their specific goals for a particular project.

This SKAD reader exceeds all these goals for a great reader. First and foremost, the SKAD method itself invites users to be creative in using it – *explicitly* declaring its openness and flexibility for use in new and diverse research areas. And scholars using the method have in fact "run with it" – creating many new "epistemic friendships" between SKAD and other valuable approaches to research and theorizing. The range and innovation of the eleven SKAD case studies presented here are truly impressive and exciting. Like my own reader, this one too emerged through a session at the International Congress on Qualitative Inquiry (in 2014) and centres on users' thoughtful reflections on putting SKAD to work in very different projects. But most significantly, SKAD has already travelled the world and its career of transnational research adventures is ably presented in this volume by authors from several continents. This is assuredly a major accomplishment for a method less than twenty years old.

I have now practiced qualitative inquiry using exemplars for over thirty years. In terms of teaching and mentoring, the message is not "put your best foot forward", but "put your best exemplars forward". Happily, Anna-Katharina Hornidge, Reiner Keller and Wolf J. Schünemann have done precisely that in this exciting new contribution to the rapidly expanding SKAD library.

References

Clarke, A. E. (1990). A Social Worlds Research Adventure: The Case of Reproductive Science. In: S. Cozzens and T. Gieryn, eds. *Theories of Science in Society*. Bloomington: Indiana University Press, 23–50.
Clarke, A. E. (1997). A Social Worlds Research Adventure: The Case of Reproductive Science. In: A. L. Strauss and J. Corbin, eds. *Grounded Theory in Practice*. Thousand Oaks, CA: Sage, 63–94.

Clarke, A. E. (2005). *Situational Analysis: Grounded Theory After the Postmodern Turn*. Thousand Oaks, CA: Sage.

Clarke, A. E. (2012). *Situationsanalyse. Grounded Theory nach dem Postmodern Turn*. Hrsg. und mit einem Vorwort von Reiner Keller. Wiesbaden: VS-Verlag für Sozialwissenschaften. [Situational Analysis. Grounded Theory after the Postmodern Turn. German Translation. Edited and with an introduction by Reiner Keller.]

Clarke, A. E., Friese, C. and Washburn, R., eds. (2015). *Situational Analysis in Practice: Mapping with Grounded Theory*. Walnut Creek, CA: Left Coast Press; now London: Routledge.

Strauss, A. L. and Corbin, J., eds. (1997). *Grounded Theory in Practice*. Thousand Oaks, CA: Sage.

1 Introduction
The sociology of knowledge approach to discourse in an interdependent world

Anna-Katharina Hornidge, Reiner Keller and Wolf J. Schünemann

The Sociology of Knowledge Approach to Discourse (hereafter SKAD) has reoriented research on social forms, structurations, and processes of meaning construction and reality formation by linking social constructivist with post-structuralist thinking. It is especially well-suited for studying discourses and processes of sense-making in culturally diverse environments. SKAD offers a conceptual and methodological research program open to the pursuit of diverse research objects and issues. To do so, it allows issue-oriented modifications of its practices central to the specific questions of meaning-making, knowledge and knowledge society raised by a particular project. It thereby allows stretching and possibly overcoming the epistemological biases and restrictions still common in theories and approaches of Western- and Northern-centric social sciences. This book focuses precisely on such empirically based, globally diverse developments of the SKAD approach to date, providing clear articulation of the methodology and its implementation.

Studying discourses as world-making activity

In 2005, Adele Clarke stated in her book on Situational Analysis that today's world is "awash in seas of discourses" and pointed out the high degree in which social scientific inquiry around the world strongly needs elaborated methodologies of discourse research (Clarke, 2005: 145). At about the same time, social scientists from different disciplines and backgrounds were developing decisive steps towards discourse research, presenting their new approaches at conferences, in books, etc. (e.g. Keller *et al.*, [2001] 2011; Wetherell, Taylor and Yates, 2001; Jaworski and Coupland, 2002). What these new methodologies had in common was that they pioneered by going beyond the core linguistic issues and established discursive critiques of ideology characteristic of earlier approaches to discourses. Instead they argued for a legitimate social science and humanities space for research into questions of the social (discursive) making of realities.

A decade later, this pattern of innovation continues. The essential challenge posed to all such approaches concerns how to best proceed in an increasingly interdependent world. These challenges include the omnipresence of the Anthropocene era of human-made ecological and climatic risks in constant interplay with *knowledge societies*, and the mediatisation and digitalisation of social life, deeply reshaping both production and consumption patterns. These are accompanied by transnational or global circulations of knowledges, ideologies, religious belief systems and attached symbolisms. Such heterogeneous systems of meaning-making require theoretically and methodologically sound means of research to better grasp the complex discourses of our times.

Renewed conflicts between ideologies, religions and (scientific) claims to knowledge and symbolic ordering are occurring, especially in making sense of environmental, climatic and related socio-political processes of change on global to local scales. Such conflicts vividly illustrate the power of public discourses in shaping not only public opinion but, by means of guiding actors in their decision-making, also shaping everyday life. Social relations of knowledge and knowing, as well as politics of knowledge and knowing, are highly consequential structures and processes both within and between societies across the globe. In very fundamental ways, they shape the world and worlds, the "multiple realities" (Schütz, [1945] 1973) in which we dwell. In line with social constructivist theory, the discursive, communicative and social construction of reality can thus be *empirically* observed globally. Moreover, it needs to be *analytically* understood in its local to global workings of shaping social realities in a century of globally interdependent turmoil.

This edited volume addresses the methodological challenges ahead by diving into SKAD, an original social science approach to analysing discourse based on the sociological traditions of the interpretive paradigm, the sociology of knowledge and Foucauldian research. SKAD was established in Germany in the early 2000s in a series of well-received books and articles (e.g. Keller, 2005, [2005] 2011a, 2012, 2013, 2019; Keller and Truschkat, 2012; Keller, Knoblauch and Reichertz, 2013). It is now widely used across disciplines (e.g. see Herzig and Moon, 2013; Sommer, 2012; Gorr and Schünemann, 2013; Holmgren, 2013). While SKAD was initially taken up in Germany in the late 1990s (see references in Keller on SKAD, Chapter 2, this volume), there has been increasing transnational interest among scholars worldwide in recent years (e.g. Wu, 2012; Feuer and Hornidge, 2015; Hornidge, Oberkircher and Kudryavtseva, 2013; Hornidge, 2017).[1]

Demonstrating SKAD's transnational reach, this edited volume brings together empirically outstanding SKAD applications from a range of academic disciplines, geographic, socio-cultural and thematic contexts. The common aspects addressed in all the chapters include (1) using SKAD in generating the specifics of the research perspective and questions;

(2) presenting analytical categories taken from SKAD; (3) describing the data selection process and sampling; (4) illustrating the concrete application of SKAD in data analysis; (5) describing the issue-specific analytical framework developed and its relation to SKAD; (6) demonstrating the integration and presentation of empirical findings; as well as (7) noting potential contributions to the particular research area addressed.

In short, it is the aim of this volume to discuss SKAD and its further development through its recent implementation in highly varied research settings. SKAD is a global yet not hegemonic tool which becomes local in the process of being interpreted and adapted to the local context, theme, and the specific discourse at hand.

Methodology, not method. Frame, not recipe

In studying processes of the institutionalisation and transformation of symbolic orderings, SKAD adopts Berger and Luckmann's perspective on the dialectical relationship between *objective* and *subjective reality*. This is constructed through the employment of different knowledges, while additionally drawing on Foucault's call to regard discourses as practices of power/knowledge, discursive formations, statements, dispositifs and discursive battles. SKAD is in some ways close to certain ideas in social studies of sciences and technology (e.g. Law 1986, 1993, 2008). But instead SKAD brings to the fore the broad traditions of sociologies of knowledge and meaning, as well as poststructuralist Foucauldian perspectives. It argues for inquiry into the production, circulation and performance of processes of meaning making all across society and societies – far beyond the core science fields initially studied in Science and Technology Studies (STS) research.

SKAD offers a comprehensive conceptual and methodological framework, but no pre-defined, static or prescriptive set of methods to be implemented as part of the empirical and practical operationalisation of the research (Keller, [2005] 2011a; 2011b; Christmann and Mahnken, 2013; Hornidge, 2013). Instead, and in line with Berger/Luckmann's definition of knowledge as everything that is regarded as knowledge in and by society (1966/1984: 16), SKAD emphasises *context-specific conceptualisations of discourse*. Discourses are explicitly understood as historically established, identifiable ensembles of symbolic and normative devices, all of which are context- and case-specific in nature. They are performed through social actors' (often competing or conflictual) discursive practices, with high impacts on the reality of the world we encounter, see, and feel.

SKAD's implementation depends on the particular discourse being studied, its main advocates or contestants, the communication platforms housing it, its underlying rationalities, logics, languages and power structures. SKAD thus emphasises the importance of defining afresh the concrete methods for studying a particular discourse using SKAD as research lens on each occasion, while also reflecting on the positionality of the researcher in relation to the discourse itself (e.g. both emic and etic to the discourse itself).

Discourses socially construct, communicate, legitimate, and objectify structures of meaning which have social consequences for the institutional, organisational and social actors' levels. As detailed elsewhere in this volume (Chapter 2), Reiner Keller therefore stresses the study of discourses as knowledge/power complexes that exist through and in *practice(s)* and *dispositifs*. *Practices* are broadly defined as conventionalised patterns of action, based on collective stocks or repertoires of knowledge about *proper* ways of acting (Keller, 2011b: 55; [2005] 2011a: 255–257).

A *dispositif* is defined as an infrastructure established by social actors or collectivities in order to resolve a particular situation. A further distinction is also made between dispositifs of discourse production and dispositifs or infrastructures emerging out of a discourse (Keller, 2011b: 56; [2005] 2011a: 258–260). This distinction of discourses constituted in social practices as well as the resulting dispositifs also underlines the material and immaterial character of discourses, while bearing in mind the role of social actors in constructing and reconstructing *realities*. Therefore SKAD discourse research, according to its concrete purpose, makes use of textual analysis as well as ethnographic inquiry (see contributions to this volume).

Not for simple causal explanation

While SKAD can and must be adapted by every researcher wanting to use it, its adaptability is nevertheless limited. The choice of a discourse approach always implies the foregrounding of certain features while backgrounding others. The same is true for SKAD as it does not pretend to be an all-comprehensive strategy for discourse studies and should not be mistaken for a *one-size-fits-all* approach. First and foremost, integrating discourse as conceived by SKAD in any kind of causal-mechanic theoretical model makes no sense and would not work conceptually. In contrast, SKAD assumes that no single explanatory factor for social behaviour can be isolated from the complex processes of meaning-making through discourse. SKAD therefore refuses to include "*the* discourse" as another variable in a formula, which mainstream positivism might demand in taking discourse research seriously. Indeed, some social-constructivists or discourse-oriented scholars who attempt to seize "the middle-ground" try and fail to do this in hopes of fulfilling positivist demands.

As SKAD provides a theoretically grounded research methodology, it does not include any predefined schemes of explanation (see Keller on SKAD, Chapter 2 this volume). In particular, SKAD does not claim to be able to reveal any causal mechanisms for any empirically observable outcome. Nor does SKAD legitimate the application of a "hermeneutics of suspicion" (Ricœur, 1970; Keller and Clarke, Chapter 3, this volume). Applying SKAD is *not* about explaining certain outcomes by certain factors, but centres instead on reconstructing the dynamics of knowledge orders and revealing power/knowledge relations, processes and effects in sociohistorically specific settings.

What is true for SKAD in relation to mainstream social science can also be said in contrast to other discourse analytic approaches. While SKAD is theoretically grounded, it does not arrive (over-)loaded with theoretical baggage, instead remaining open to fruitful combinations with other substantive theories depending on the research object under study. Like interpretive research in general, SKAD suggests developing and adapting research strategies across the processes and progress of inquiry. If a researcher is seeking a quick empirical substantiation of certain claims and assumptions, then SKAD is probably a bad choice of method as it is intended for intensive, profound and detailed interpretive analysis of social communication. Such analyses are sorely needed and SKAD can help provide them.

SKAD for a glocal academy

Studying the interdependent discursivities[2] of our time entails crossing increasingly contested and renegotiated disciplinary and geographic boundaries. These include boundaries between so-called *systematic disciplines* focusing on the *Global North* and OECD-world,[3] and *Area Studies* or *Postcolonial Studies* focusing on the *Global South* including so-called "developing" and transforming countries. Today, the greater or lesser global interdependence of discourses, their circulations and translations into manifold contexts challenge our existing methodological and analytical lenses. They emphatically do *not* remain in the traditional disciplinary and geographic container spaces of the traditional Western science system.

SKAD enthusiastically takes on these challenges, offering a guiding methodological and analytical frame, while intentionally leaving ample room for local, context-, theme- and discourse-specific further development and additions. This volume was designed to present a broad range of such contextualisations and operationalisations of SKAD. Foucault's critical ontology of the present as well as more current challenges to the *intellectual dominance* of the West, legitimised through colonial histories, voiced by colleagues such as Stuart Hall (1997), Gayatri Spivak (1999), and Dipesh Chakrabarty (2000) have encouraged and informed SKAD to seek engagement with the politics of power/knowledge and the work they do within and between societies. Examples can be found in the chapters here by Zhang and McGhee, and Küppers.

SKAD heeds Walter Mignolo's plea to study the social starting from *many worlds* and thereby diversity, rather than from one assumed *universal,* reference frame. Mignolo called this concept "pluriversality" (2007: 453,

2011: 2). It captures and further encourages the intention of SKAD to support study of the manifold discursivities of our times in their own right, according to their own logics, in their own languages and cultural and socio-political contexts. We will not be able to understand the interdependent social and discursive worlds of today if the tools we use are developed based only on limited empirical realities, everyday experiences, ways of knowing and ways of explaining, rather than the full array. SKAD offers a conceptual and methodological frame for studying the everyday workings of discourse in a wide variety of academic disciplines and studies, geographic, socio-political, cultural or thematic contexts.

It is precisely on this point that SKAD as a proposed epistemological frame interlinks and is inspired by recent discussions regarding rethinking Area Studies. In *Area Studies at the Crossroads* (Mielke and Hornidge 2017), authors from five different continents reflect on the *how* of decolonising the academy requisite for *understanding*, in Max Weber's terms, social reality on this planet. The authors argue for the need (1) to develop conceptual approaches and methodologies for *empirically* assessing social reality in its dynamic, constantly changing forms based on local empirical contexts, by and with local researchers at local research institutes; and (2) to contribute to the nurturing of critically thinking minds and high degrees of reflexivity in local epistemic cultures and knowledge systems. To accomplish these goals, the authors reject the often cited divide between so-called *systematic disciplines* and Area Studies and instead strongly argue for their mutual enrichment and reciprocal further development. Several of the chapters in Mielke and Hornidge's (2017) book illustrate the empirical and analytical strength, but also substantial challenges and limits, of linking conceptual thought of *systematic* social science disciplines with area studies' language, cultural and local expertise (see e.g. Mielke, and Hornidge, 2017). In addition, these chapters clearly illustrate the challenges and limits of conceptually and methodologically strong, locally embedded empirical social science and humanities research practiced by researchers socialised into diverse systems of science at research institutions located on several different continents. What does *conceptually and methodologically strong*, while empirically based in local contexts, languages etc. actually mean? Which quality criteria are applied? Which epistemes gain authority over others, to use Gieryn's (1999) terms? And where do *epistemic privilege* and *epistemic oppression* lead to *epistemic injustice* in Fricker's understanding (1998, 2007)?

While the answers provided in the chapters here cannot fully do justice to these questions, they actively contribute to a global yet local discussion and the mutual development of a pluriversal rather than hegemonic methodology and conceptual frame for discourse research. Distinctive reflexivities are requisite to jointly developing such a methodological and conceptual frame further and contributing to the decolonising of discourse research. Both a) the researcher's reflexivity, and b) SKAD's own reflexivity as a method are called into play. With regard to the researcher, this entails conscious and continuous reflection on her/his own position in relation to the discourses under study and their discourse carriers, the research subjects. With regard to SKAD as a methodological and conceptual frame with affinities with interpretive methods, the distinctive reflexivity entails its constant further development based on the empirical realities encountered in the research process. This further development of both the method and the project through the actual doing of discourse research is part of the agenda of this book.

Organisation of the book

The book gathers a number of exemplary studies by researchers working in various fields and disciplines internationally. They have entered a reciprocal relationship, or epistemic friendship, with SKAD – for the study of a particular discursivity, and in turn they have developed SKAD further in that particular context. In thirteen chapters, the volume presents basics of doing SKAD research along with different ways of operationalising the approach in a broad variety of research projects. The regional contexts range from Europe, to Asia, North-America and Africa.

What all chapters have in common is that the authors shed light on their particular use of SKAD, including their conceptual considerations as well as the methodological implications drawn, and finally the modifications and additions to the method they have made. Thus, the main focus of all chapters lies on methodological questions and applications in relation to a common heuristics and hence to each other. The main questions are: How is the sociology of knowledge approach to discourse used to generate the research perspective and questions? Which analytic categories of SKAD are applied and how? How have data corpuses been built? Which more specific analytical frameworks are developed inspired by or in relation to SKAD? How have the results and findings been integrated and presented? Finally, how does this project contribute to and engage with a particular research area?

To critically reflect on and advance SKAD based on very different empirical contexts, the book begins with an outline of the core conceptualisation and aim of SKAD by *Reiner Keller*. This chapter introduces the basic theoretical groundwork, central concepts of and arguments for SKAD, followed by a short discussion of methodological aspects and methods for empirical research. The chapter explains SKAD's understanding of discourses and dispositifs, and lays out the basic framing for the contributions that follow.

In the next chapter, co-authored by *Reiner Keller* and *Adele E. Clarke*, SKAD is situated within both the history and current scope of qualitative inquiry and vis-à-vis discourse research in sociology and related disciplines. This chapter explores SKAD's embeddedness within the interpretive paradigm, as well as its affinities with ethnographic work, analysis of meaning making and the sociology of knowledge. Much like situational analysis developed by Clarke, SKAD argues for the urgent need for inquiry into processes of discursive construction and world making.

Following these foundational chapters on SKAD as conceptual frame and methodology, the reader is invited to dive into the intricacies of empirical research, data collection and analysis inspired by SKAD. This empirical part of the book begins with a chapter by *Reiner Keller* on the social construction of value. Household waste and waste policies are high on the public agendas of wealthy countries around the globe – important issues in the Western world at least since the 1960s. Waste is an interesting topic for socio-cultural analysis as it encompasses structures of production and consumption as well as resource exploitation, environmental pollution and social norms of valuation and de-valuation. The chapter presents a comparative SKAD investigation into public waste discourses and policies in France and Germany from 1970 to 1995. What Keller finds is that the symbolic reality of waste mastery in both countries is considerably different. While German discourses were stimulated by protracted warnings of a coming catastrophe, the hegemonic discourse on waste in France repeatedly performed an ever-failing but still reassuring proclamation about civilisation's victory over the threats of waste production.

From France and Germany, it is only a small step to the analytic focus of *Wolf J. Schünemann* on political debates in the EU multi-level system. Drawing upon his comparative study of EU treaty referendum discourses in France, the Netherlands and Ireland, Schünemann introduces SKAD as a research program useful in the analysis of political debates in general and referendum debates in particular. To date, EU referendum research has largely sought universal explanatory models of electoral behaviour – why people voted as they did, how campaigns affected voting behaviour, and why referenda failed or succeeded. Instead, SKAD offers assistance in reconstructing the structures of political meaning-making deeply embedded in the respective socio-cultural settings. In addition, the chapter describes important modifications and adaptations of SKAD for use in political research.

The next chapter, contributed by *Andreas Stückler*, takes us from politics to policy. He analyses law-making processes in the amended Penal Procedure Code in Austria using a SKAD-inspired exploration of how different discourses construct victims' rights. In order to reconstruct the historical processes of discursive construction of the "victim" as a new category in criminal procedure law, the case study then explores different victim discourses circulating in the law-making process as well as victim-related patterns of interpretation constitutive of those discourses. Stückler used official documents from the legislative process (draft laws, minutes of parliamentary sessions, etc.). His analysis demonstrates how the Austrian reform of penal procedure was framed through the competition between two essentially different victim discourses in law ("injured person" vs. "victim").

Interested in SKAD's potential in non-European empirical contexts, *Anna-Katharina Hornidge* and *Hart Nadav Feuer* then invite the reader to Southeast Asia. Their chapter is based on SKAD inspired research pursued since 2005 on different discourses of knowledge and their action guiding potential in the region vis-à-vis higher education. The authors argue that the triad of cooperation, international exchange and standard-setting among institutions of higher education has become a dominant framework for fostering strong transnational ties of *knowledge societies*. Hornidge and Feuer discuss how SKAD can help guide ethnographic research methods on both theoretical and practical levels and how SKAD itself becomes a heuristic tool in subsequent analyses. Specifically, they reflect upon and widen the SKAD tradition of ethnographic methods for long-term empirical field research, while also bringing in an approach to using traditional discourse fragments and quantitative data (e.g. on capital investments, graduation rates, publications and international agreements) for triangulation purposes.

From the landscape of Southeast Asia, SKAD next travels further North to China with *Shaoying Zhang* and *Derek McGhee*. They reflect on using SKAD in their explorations of the three-fold relationship between discourses and actors as a paradigm to understand Communist officials as *both* governing agents *and* governed subjects within the Communist Party of the People's Republic of China. The authors demonstrate how both the dynamic political situation in China and the individual's distinctive political situations together guided the recruitment of participants for this research. Interestingly, the interviewees used their research participation as an opportunity for risk-sharing and speaking the truth in hopes that the research would subsequently influence the Chinese government. The interviews thus became political theatre – an instrument wherein communist officials took risks to become specific intellectuals through practicing what Foucault called Parrhessia [speaking truth to power]. Referencing Stenson's "governing from below" (1998) and Buzan and colleagues' "securitization" (1998), the authors succeed in making the complex power relations in Chinese contemporary governance more visible. Further, within the analytical framework of SKAD, they found that every step of reflection is a paradigm-seeking process. Numerous "stories" developed in space and time were collected during the research, and informed the authors' analyses and narratives.

The politics of classification stand at the centre of the next chapter by *Hella von Unger, Penelope Scott* and *Dennis Odukoya*. Employing SKAD, the authors compared changes in the categorisation and classification of im/migrants and ethnic groups in public health reporting in Germany and the UK. They sought to shed light on the genesis and power effects of classification systems and the underlying acts of categorisation as discursive practices within specific socio-historical contexts, specifically health reporting on HIV/AIDS and tuberculosis since the 1980s. Here their analysis focuses on methodological aspects of the study design and the challenges they encountered in the research process. The authors argue that the heuristic framework of SKAD allows the productive integration of elements from neighbouring methodologies such as grounded theory and its more poststructural version, situational analysis.

At a historical moment when the constantly accelerating flows of goods, people, viruses, symbols and systems of ordering have become constitutive of every day social realities, both classification and categorisation relate closely to important questions of identity and identity politics. Moreover, this topic is inherently built into SKAD as a methodological and conceptual frame via its focus on the discursive formations of both subject and speaker positions.

Continuing in this vein with reference to the German labour market, *Saša Bosančić* assesses the increasing cultural and economic marginalization of unskilled work. With reference to SKAD, Bosančić argues that in addition to being formed in the lifeworld and through biographical events, identities are shaped and reshaped by discourses as well as by one's position in the social structure. *All* have major impacts on the self. The methodological groundings for his underlying research design derive from the concept of subjectification located in the SKAD frame of reference. The author proposes that it is necessary to extend and adapt the actor categories of SKAD in order to fully examine the discursive situatedness of human subjectivities.

Carolin Küppers offers further insights into the SKAD-inspired assessment of subject positions. She studied national and international media reports, especially newspaper articles, leading up to the Soccer World Cup 2010 in South Africa. Her focus is on which subject positions of sex workers were employed by these media and how they reflected the political intentions of the various authors and media outlets studied. Küppers argues that three subject positions were repeatedly deployed: the "magosha" ("whore"), the "victim" and the "mother". In further reflections, Küppers combines SKAD with scholarly work from queer, postcolonial and intersectional theories. She argues that the three subject positions must be understood within the context of heteronormative, postcolonial and intersectional power relations in South Africa. With regard to SKAD, Küpper's work illustrates the openness and integrative nature of the conceptual and methodological frame, allowing adaptation based upon the empirical and field context-specific realities of the research.

The following chapter brings us back to Europe. *Inga Truschkat* and *Claudia Muche* studied support systems for handling major transitions in the life course, and how they may be enhanced and enlarged. Today such so called "career guidance services" are increasingly offered in quite different social sites and for an increasing array of life events. The authors focus on how they developed their research questions according to SKAD and how SKAD guided their research interests, as well as on their strategy of data collection. They discuss their use of the strategy of theoretical sampling in detail, and present an exemplary analysis of a short section of the data.

Tobias Ide next presents his research in progress, insights from research practice, and his reflections on using SKAD. In recent years, potential links between environmental stress, natural resource scarcity and (violent) intergroup conflict have attracted much academic and political attention. Drawing upon his case study of the Israel-Palestine water conflict, Ide examined the assessment of intersubjective dimensions of socio-environmental conflicts. In contrast to many empirical projects, this chapter is sensitive to the intersubjective construction of conflict identities, threat perceptions and environmental assessments, as well as the relevance of these constructions for human agency. The author applies SKAD in order to dissect and better understand these intersubjective dimensions of socio-environmental conflict and cooperation. Thus the chapter introduces SKAD as a helpful theoretical-methodological approach to make sense of the *simultaneity* of both conflict and cooperation about water between Israel and Palestine.

Florian Elliker applies SKAD to racial diversity in South African student residences. Starting from SKAD arguments for an ethnography of discursive production and discursive intervention into fields of practice, the author sought a new way to study local settings (such as student residences) in combination with analyses of discourses – phenomena and processes on the so-called macro-level of analysis. From this, Elliker develops a sociology of knowledge approach to discourse ethnography and discusses its strengths. This case study helps us to understand how an ethnographic study may contribute to a differentiated understanding of how discourses are entangled with local contexts and how such entanglements are implied in structuring social action.

The volume ends with a contribution focused on the "how" of visualising qualitative data by *Anne Luther* and *Wolf J. Schünemann*. Qualitative researchers in general and discourse analysts in particular are regularly challenged when it comes to the visualisation of empirical findings. In contrast with quantitative investigations that successfully integrate complex information and facts into accessible graphs and tables, a synoptical reduction of complexity using visual tools in qualitative research often fails, or is not even attempted, given the complexity of the objects and empirical approaches. The authors critically reflect on these challenges and are particularly aware of the temptations of so-called "creeping quantification" they see in many works that rely on ready-made tools available in QDA-software packages. As an alternative, they argue for independent and creative visualisation and present some illustrative examples from selected SKAD works. The chapter also introduces the Entity Mapper, an open source software tool for visualising qualitative data and the results of qualitative analysis.

The book's history and a word of gratitude

This edited volume emerged from a panel entitled *Spotlight: The Sociology of Knowledge Approach to Discourse*, chaired by Reiner Keller at the Tenth International Congress of Qualitative Inquiry, organised by Norman K. Denzin and team at the University of Illinois in Urbana-Champaign in 2014. Five of the thirteen chapters were initially presented and jointly discussed at that Congress. At that time, SKAD was just beginning to expand beyond the borders of the German speaking academic world where it had continuously gained ground for over a decade. We therefore decided to prepare this edited volume for an international audience with a focus on how to apply SKAD to very different research objects and in quite different national and regional contexts. Fortunately, Routledge was delighted with our proposal.

Many people have supported this project over the years of its creation. First, we would like to thank Norman Denzin and Adele E. Clarke for their unrelated but equally crucial, support, conceptual inspiration and platform for debate, prerequisite to the volume as given. Further, we thank all the authors for their interest in SKAD and their willingness to publish their work in this compendium, offering an internationally visible platform for SKAD. We thank them as well for their patience with us, the editors, in finally making it happen. We also extend deep thanks to the anonymous reviewers of the original proposal for their encouragement and helpful comments. Last but far from least, we especially thank Elena Chiu and Emily Briggs at Routledge who patiently accepted our delays and answered our questions during the entire process in a highly competent and considerate manner. Finally, we would like to thank the many helping hands, the crucial support in proofreading and editing all chapters, checking diagrams and tables, compiling CVs and abstracts. Here in particular we would like to thank Julia Franz at Hildesheim University, Philip Schenck and Lucas Barning at the Leibniz Centre for Tropical Marine Research (ZMT) in Bremen and Cathrin Tettenborn at Augsburg University.

Notes

1 See the references in Keller on SKAD, Chapter 2, as well as references on SKAD studies in other languages: http://kellersskad.blogspot.de (last accessed 1 March 2018).
2 By discursivity we refer to the complexity and interwovenness of discourses and processes of discursive construction.
3 OECD-world refers to member countries of the Organisation for Economic Co-operation and Development (OECD).

References

Berger, P. L. and Luckmann, T. (1984). *Die gesellschaftliche Konstruktion der Wirklichkeit – Eine Theorie der Wissenssoziologie*. Frankfurt a. M.: Fischer Taschenbuch Verlag. [The Social Construction of Reality: A Treatise in the Sociology of Knowledge.]

Berger, P. L. and Luckmann, T. (1966). *The Social Construction of Reality: A Treatise in the Sociology of Knowledge*. Garden City: Doubleday.

Buzan, B., Wæver, O. and De Wilde, J. (1998). *Security: A New Framework for Analysis*. Boulder: Lynne Rienner Publishers.

Chakrabarty, D. (2000). *Provincializing Europe: Postcolonial Thought and Historical Difference*. Princeton and Oxford: Princeton University Press.

Christmann, G. and Mahnken, G. (2013). Raumpioniere, stadtteilbezogene Diskurse und Raumentwicklung. Über kommunikative und discursive Raum(re)konstruktionen. In: R. Keller and I. Truschkat, eds., *Methodologie und Praxis der Wissenssoziologischen Diskursanalyse. Band 1: Interdisziplinäre Perspektiven*. Wiesbaden: Springer, VS Verlag. 91–111. [Pioneers of Space, Urban Quarter specific Discourses and Spatial Development. Communicative and discursive (Re-)constructions of Space. In: Methodology and Practice of SKAD research. Vol. 1: Interdisciplinary Perspectives.]

Clarke, A. E. (2005). *Situational Analysis: Grounded Theory after the Postmodern Turn*. Thousand Oaks, CA: Sage.

Feuer, H. and Hornidge, A.-K. (2015). Higher Education Cooperation in ASEAN: Building Towards Integration or Manufacturing Consent? *Comparative Education*, 51(3), 327–352.

Fricker, M. (1998). Epistemic Oppression and Epistemic Privilege. *Canadian Journal of Philosophy*, 25, 191–210.

Fricker, M. (2007). *Epistemic Injustice: Power and the Ethics of Knowing*. Oxford: Oxford University Press.

Gieryn, T. F. (1999). *Cultural Boundaries of Science*. Chicago: University of Chicago Press.

Gorr, D. and Schünemann, W. J. (2013). Creating a Secure Cyberspace – Securitization in Internet Governance Discourses and Dispositives in Germany and Russia. *International Review of Information Ethics*, 20(12), 37–51.

Hall, S. (1997). The Centrality of Culture: Notes on the Cultural Revolutions of our Time. In: K. Thompson and Open University, eds., *Media and cultural regulation*. London: Sage and The Open University Press, 207–238.

Herzig, C. and Moon. J. (2013). Discourses on Corporate Social Ir/responsibility in the Financial Sector. *Journal of Business Research*, 66(10), 1870–1880.

Holmgren, S. (2013). REDD+ in the Making: Orders of Knowledge in the Climate-deforestation Nexus. *Environmental Science and Policy*, 33, 369–377.

Hornidge, A.-K. (2013) 'Knowledge', 'Knowledge Society' and 'Knowledge for Development': Studying Discourses of Knowledge in an International Context. In: R. Keller and I. Truschkat, eds., *Methodologie und Praxis der wissenssoziologischen Diskursanalyse, Band 1: Interdisziplinäre Perspektiven*. Wiesbaden: Springer VS Verlag, 397–424.

Hornidge, A.-K. (2017). Mid-Range Concepts—The Lego Bricks of Meaning-Making: An Example from Khorezm, Uzbekistan. In: K. Mielke and A.-K. Hornidge, eds., *Area Studies at the Crossroads: Knowledge Production after the Mobility Turn*, New York: Palgrave Macmillan, 213–230.

Hornidge, A.-K., Oberkircher, L. and Kudryavtseva, A. (2013). Boundary Management and the Discursive Sphere – Negotiating 'Realities' in Khorezm, Uzbekistan. *Geoforum*, 45, 266–274.

Jaworski, A. and Coupland, N., eds. (2002). *The Discourse Reader*. New York: Routledge.

Keller, R. (2005). Analysing Discourse. An Approach from the Sociology of Knowledge. *Forum Qualitative Sozialforschung/Forum: Qualitative Research*, [online] 6(3). Available at: www.qualitative-research.net/index.php/fqs/article/view/19/41 [Accessed 7 March 2018].

Keller, R. ([2005] 2011a). *Wissenssoziologische Diskursanalyse. Grundlegung eines Forschungsprogramms*. 3rd edn. Wiesbaden: Springer VS Verlag. [The Sociology of Knowledge Approach to Discourse. Grounds for a Research Agenda.]

Keller, R. (2011b). The Sociology of Knowledge Approach to Discourse (SKAD). *Human Studies*, 34, 43–65.

Keller, R. (2012). Entering Discourses: A New Agenda for Qualitative Research and Sociology of Knowledge. *Qualitative Sociology Review*, VIII(2), 46–55.

Keller, R. (2013). *Doing Discourse Research. An Introduction for Social Scientists*. London: Sage.

Keller, R. (2019). *The Sociology of Knowledge Approach to Discourse. Grounds for a Research Agenda*. New York: Springer [forthcoming].

Keller, R., Hirseland, A., Schneider, W. and Viehöver, W., eds. ([2001] 2011). *Handbuch Sozialwissenschaftliche Diskursanalyse Bd. 1: Theorien und Methoden*. 3rd edn. Wiesbaden: VS-Verlag. [Handbook for Discourse Analysis in the Social Sciences: Vol. 1: Theories and Methods.]

Keller, R., Knoblauch, H. and Reichertz, J., eds. (2013). *Kommunikativer Konstruktivismus: Theoretische und empirische Konturen eines neuen wissenssoziologischen Ansatzes*. Wiesbaden: Springer VS Verlag. [Communicative Constructivism: Theoretical and Empirical Contours of a new Knowledge Sociological Approach.]

Keller, R. and Truschkat, I., eds. (2012). *Methodologie und Praxis der Wissenssoziologischen Diskursanalyse*. Band 1: Interdisziplinäre Perspektiven. Wiesbaden: Springer VS. [Methodology and Practice of the Sociology of Knowledge Approach to Discourse. Volume 1: Interdisciplinary Perspectives.]

Law, J., ed. (1986). *Power, Action and Belief: A New Sociology of Knowledge*. London: Routledge.

Law, J. (1993). *Organising Modernity: Social Ordering and Social Theory*. Oxford: Blackwell Publishers.

Law, J. (2008). Actor-network Theory and Material Semiotics. In: B. S. Turner, ed., *The New Blackwell Companion to Social Theory*. 3rd edn. Oxford: Blackwell, 141–158.

Mielke, K. and Hornidge, A.-K., eds. (2017). *Area Studies at the Crossroads: Knowledge Production after the Mobility Turn*. New York: Palgrave Macmillan.

Mignolo, W. D. (2007). Delinking: The Rhetoric of Modernity, the Logic of Coloniality and the Grammar of De-coloniality. *Cultural Studies*, 21(2/3), 449–514.

Mignolo, W. D. (2011). Geopolitics of Sensing and Knowing: On (de)coloniality, Border Thinking, and Epistemic Disobedience. *European Institute for Progressive Cultural Policies*, 9, 1–8.

Ricœur, P. (1970). *Freud and Philosophy: An Essay on Interpretation*. New Haven: Yale University Press.

Schütz, A. ([1945] 1973). On Multiple Realities. In: A. Schütz, *Collected Papers I: The Problem of Social Reality*. M. Natanson, ed. The Hague: Nijhoff, 207–259.

Sommer, V. (2012). The Online Discourse on the Demjanjuk Trial. New Memory Practices on the World Wide Web? *ESSACHESS. Journal for Communication Studies*, 5(2), 133–151.

Spivak, G. C. (1999). *A Critique of Postcolonial Reason: Toward a History of the Vanishing Present*. Cambridge, MT and London: Harvard University Press.

Stenson, K. (1998). Beyond Histories of the Present. *Economy and Society*, 27(4), 333–352.

Wetherell, M., Taylor, S. and S. Yates, eds. (2001). *Discourse Theory and Practice: A Reader*. London: Sage.

Wu, A. X. (2012). Hail the Independent Thinker: The Emergence of Public Debate Culture on the Chinese Internet. *International Journal of Communication*, 6, 2220–2244.

2 The sociology of knowledge approach to discourse
An introduction
Reiner Keller

Introduction

In one of his less recognised books, Michel Foucault discusses the Pierre Rivière murder case (Foucault, 1982). Rivière, a young man from the French region of Normandy, had killed his mother, sister and younger brother. After wandering around in the woods for a few days, he was caught by the police. Weeks later, a trial took place, involving different kinds of experts (psychologists, doctors, a judge, policemen). Rivière had confessed to the murders once he was caught: yes, he had killed them. During his time in prison, waiting for the trial to take place, he wrote a lengthy text explaining why he had done what he did. He pronounced himself guilty and stated that he wanted to be sentenced to death. Consequently, the defence case focused on a slightly different, but linked question: given that he was the doer of the deed, was he really responsible for what he had done? Should he be considered sane or insane? This question became the crux of the case. If he was sane, then that implied full responsibility and thus the death sentence; if he was insane, then that implied limited or even a complete lack of responsibility and therefore the asylum. Rivière made strong arguments for the soundness of his reasoning and full responsibility. And medical, psychological and police experts confirmed his sanity. Yet others did not. One particular expert in psychology stated that there were obvious signs of insanity in his report of the crime, in his confession and in his childhood behaviour (based on testimonies from people in his village). The arguments of this particular expert determined the outcome: Rivière was declared insane and sent to an asylum.

Foucault refers to this story in order to reveal discourses as core structuring elements in discursive battles and conflicts. In the Rivière example, the case was fought on the basis of different competing discourses. Their struggle consisted of what we can call the *definition of the situation* (an old term from pragmatist and symbolic interactionist sociology, established by William I. Thomas and Dorothy Thomas). This definition was highly consequential, as we have seen. If we look closer at the situation, we can identify different actors engaged with the case: Rivière, some policemen, a medical doctor, several psychologists, a judge and others. These participants collected data (medical data, police data, psychological data, etc.). They wrote reports. They argued in front of the judge. Crucially, they assembled different kinds of knowledge and rival ways of knowing in their presentation of different perspectives on the case. Moreover, they did not act as individuals; rather, they performed discursive expertise. That is, in their role as actors or agents of a particular type of expertise, they drew upon established and institutionalised practices of discursive meaning making. Discourse here does not mean simply *using language, speaking to each other*, or *engaging in communication and interaction*. Here, *discourse* is used to identify specific instances of communication as being articulations, parts or expressions of particular patterns of serious speech and sign-using acts which derive from a home base in, for example, academic institutions of psychological knowledge production. Foucault (2010) uses the term "discourse" to refer to complexes of serious, regulated statement practices which constitute the objects they are dealing with (that is, referring to) in a particular way, for example a particular scientific discipline, a religious belief system, or a political ideology.

Conflicts over the definition of situations likewise occur in quite different areas and arenas. In fact, they are a basic feature of the collective human struggle with the world, its existence and resistances, with unfolding events, catastrophes, action choices, evaluations and all kinds of corresponding ways of problem solving. Events, problematisations and their actors who are engaged in the politics of knowledge and knowing, that is, in meaning/world making: these are the core drivers of discursive struggles (and social transformation). To illustrate, consider a society which has invented individual cars for moving around, going to work or to places for leisure. And this society also has invented alcoholic drinks for the purpose of promoting good feelings now and again. Here again a core question of responsibility emerges. If alcohol consumption affects human perception and hence bodily reaction time, then a drunken driver might be a danger for others on the streets. Much like the Rivière case, this too is a situation where different experts and discourses can jump in. First, statistics can show whether there are more or worse accidents when drunken drivers are involved. Medical experts provide evidence of bodily perception and reaction to dangerous driving situations. Religious movements see a chance of supporting a ban on alcoholic beverages, that devil's brew. Other organisations mobilise other knowledge in order to show that drivers under the influence of alcohol drive much more slowly and therefore are less dangerous than other drivers. Public transport lobbyists pick it up as a chance to establish better public transportation systems. They all will look for evidence, refer to normative and/or factual evaluations and contribute all kinds of performances in a struggle for a collective definition of the situation. This is exactly what Joseph Gusfield (1981) investigated in his analysis of *The Culture of Public Problems*. Other symbolic interactionists were interested in similar cases, as was Foucault, for example when he researched madness, the medical gaze, the order of things, the new regimes of disciplining and punishing and the social ordering of sexual relations (see Keller, 2017a). The very same core ideas are present in *Orientalism* by Edward Said (1978) and *Policing the Crisis* by Stuart Hall et al. ([1978] 2013). These authors practiced in different ways discourse research on scientific and public meaning making and reality construction. Ulrich Beck (2008: 24–46), in his works on world risk society, suggested the concept of "relations of definition as relations of domination" in order to explore the social hierarchies and processes which account for a situation of ecological or technological risk, threat, or danger. SKAD expands this concept, applying it to the idea of social relations of knowledge and knowing, and the politics of knowledge and knowing, which occur throughout all social fields and concerns. This is what Foucault called regimes of power/knowledge. This is what SKAD is all about.[1]

Discourses as objects of inquiry

SKAD proposes a conceptual frame of its object (discourses and dispositifs), a corresponding methodology to approach that object and concrete methods or techniques for collecting and analysing data.[2] As human beings, we live in particular, sometimes rather limited, sometimes quite large and comprehensive symbolic universes. SKAD, as a research agenda, is interested in the events, actors and processes that establish, shape and transform such universes via discursive structuration, that is through social relations of knowledge and knowing, and competing politics of knowledge and knowing – what Foucault called regimes of power/knowledge, or what Stuart Hall referred to as the "centrality of culture".[3] Social relations of knowledge are complex socio-historical constellations of production, stabilisation, structuration and transformation of symbolic orders that link agency, practices and objects within a variety of social arenas. These constellations imply hierarchies, domination, exclusion, compliance, conflict, resistance and competing ways of accounting for what is "real": a concern, a problem, the right way to evaluate factual and moral evidence and how to act. SKAD is a sociology of knowledge-based perspective on what Linda Tuhiwai Smith addressed in her path-breaking work, *Decolonizing Methodologies*: SKAD aims to provoke thinking "about the roles that knowledge, knowledge production, knowledge hierarchies and knowledge institutions play in [...] social transformation" (Smith 2012: XII). It is about what feminist theories call the situatedness of knowledges (Haraway, 1988), its effects and dynamics. Such arguments resonate strongly with basic sociology of knowledge arguments established by Alfred Schütz, Karl Mannheim, Ludwik Fleck, Peter Berger, Thomas Luckmann and many others (see Keller, 2011a, 2011b, 2019). The term knowledge herein refers not only to what counts as socially recognised and confirmed positive knowledge. It refers to the totality of all social systems of signs, and in so doing, to the symbolic orders and stocks of knowledge constituted by these systems which mediate between human beings and the world they thereby experience through the pragmatic reference function of signs. Included among these are such things as religious doctrine, sociological theory, interpretive knowledge about social situations, wider theories of globalisation, freedom, sustainability and so on:

> The cultural archive [...] should be conceived of as containing multiple traditions of knowledge and ways of knowing. Some knowledges are more dominant than others, some are submerged and outdated. Some knowledges are actively in competition with each other and some can only be formed in association with others. Whilst there may not be a unitary system, there are 'rules' which help make sense of what is contained within the archive and enable 'knowledge' to be recognized. These rules can be conceived of as rules of classification, rules of framing and rules of practice.
>
> (Smith, [1999] 2012: 45)

Discourses become real through the actions of social actors, who supply specific knowledge claims and contribute to the reproduction, liquefaction and dissolution of the institutionalised interpretations and apparent unavailabilities. Discourses crystallise and constitute themes in a particular form as social interpretation and action issues. The concept of discourse is well suited to the analysis of social processes, practices and politics of knowledge in and between contemporary societies. SKAD states that the discursive construction of realities is *one* form of the "social construction of reality" (Berger and Luckmann, 1966), but one of the most influential and basic ongoing activities, on local as well as regional, national, transnational and even global scales, as well as in between such layers. It is the particular form which can be addressed as *discourse(s)*. We cannot see discourses in the way we see, for example, a piece of cake, a building, or even a concrete set of social interactions. *Discourse* is not an ontological entity per se. In the empirical world, we have ongoing series of small discursive events: minor and major texts, leaflets, reports, written or spoken expertise, speeches, pictures, figures, numbers, and so on, produced, performed and challenged by concerned and committed social actors. In order to analyse discourses, we can only collect such disparate elements or utterances, occurring at different points in time and in different social as well as geographical spaces. *Discourse* is a heuristic device for ordering and analysing data, a necessary hypothetical assumption in order to start research. It assumes that particular documents or pieces of data are performed according to the very same principles or rules of ordering, while other documents of sign usage will differ from that. Discursive orders are the results of a continuous communicative production which, however, is not understood as spontaneous or chaotic, but rather occurs within interwoven, structured practices which relate to one another. Discourses are realised through the communicative actions of social actors. A pamphlet, a newspaper article, or a speech within the context of a demonstration actualises, for instance, an environmental policy discourse in differing concrete forms and with differing empirical scope. The materiality of discourses simply refers to the way discourses exist in societies, how they become *real* in what potentially could be used as *possible empirical data*. A discourse can be defined as *a regulated practice of statement formulation responding to some problem, urgency or need for action*, including *knowing something*, defining a situation and *perpetuating or transforming a given order* as such problems for action. Empirically, it is manifest as a sequence of concrete utterances, which are bound together or assembled by the very same logic of regulation and formation. Discourse as structuration offers

- normative orientations and rules for the performance of speech acts (e.g. established genres),
- rules of signification for the constitution of meaning,
- social and material resources for action (actors, dispositifs).

In performing their articulations, social actors draw upon the rules and resources that are available via the present state of a given discursive structuration. This is not a deterministic rule or regulation – rather, such a given and performed structuration works as instruction, which implies some freedom of application on the actor's side. Research into discourse must take account of the social actors' agency if it is to consider the creativity, shift, or transformation in discursive meaning making over time. Social actors are socially configured incarnations of agency, according to the socio-historical and situational conditions. When performing discursive statements, they participate in a crossfire of multiple and heterogeneous, perhaps even contradicting discourses, trying to negotiate the situations and *real world* problems they meet.

Discursive construction is different by its forms and means from other processes of social construction such as personal talk and private interaction or some instrumental activity. It implies diverse materialities, practices, relations – what Foucault referred to as dispositifs. SKAD conceives of this form as existing within the broader framework of sociology of knowledge established by Peter Berger and Thomas Luckmann (1966) and their predecessors. Such a re-embedding of discourse research allows for a direct link with the qualitative and interpretive research methodologies of the social sciences. Building upon arguments from pragmatist and symbolic interactionist traditions, the sociology of knowledge and Foucauldian analysis, SKAD argues that each of these traditions has something important to offer for discourse research. In the following, SKAD's basic understanding of discourses as objects of inquiry will be further outlined.

Sociology of knowledge approach to discourse 21

(1) Conceiving of discourses as practices of sign usage implies social actors who take up the role of speakers articulating, realising and performing a particular discourse in a given, that is (to be) defined situation. This idea holds for written and spoken utterances, visualisations and other micro-events of discursive production, for example in climate-change discourses or in academic (scientific) or religious discourses. Actors/speakers perform a particular discursive structuration in order to respond to some urgent need for action. Such an urgency can be located in an epistemic endeavour (as in producing scientific knowledge), in educational purposes (as in teaching sociology), or reacting to some event in the outside world (such as a nuclear catastrophe, a situation of poverty, a court case, a *social problem*) or similar. Such a performance requires skilled actors, that is, human beings able to handle symbols and larger sign systems in general, as well as the more specific sign systems and sign relations established in a particular process of discursive structuration, which in itself can be considered a longer or shorter process of historical institutionalisation through continual permutations of (inter)action.[4] According to pragmatist philosophers of mind and language, such a competence builds upon the basic social processes of communication which take place in a given "universe of discourse", that is in a symbol or sign system, which has been established by some collective around a common concern:

> This universe of discourse is constituted by a group of individuals carrying on and participating in a common social process of experience and behavior, within which these gestures or symbols have the same or common meanings for all members of that group, whether they make them or address them to other individuals, or whether they overtly respond to them as made or addressed to them by other individuals.
>
> (Mead, [1934] 1963: 89–90)

Although this concept of discourse is somewhat broader than that suggested by Michel Foucault, such an idea holds true for everyday existential life in a social community as well as for more specialised fields of (discursive) action (such as an academic discipline, or poetry, or a religion). In order to become a competent symbol user and a participant within a pre-established collective and field of such an action, you have to undergo a process of socialisation. Only then can you perform a discursive practice which fits into the given discursive universe. Communicational events are not a direct effect of structural regulation, but the effect of the way social actors actively articulate, interpret and deal with a given discursive formation in a given situation.

(2) Building upon what has been said in the preceding paragraph, one has to state that the individual mind's capacity for symbol usage is somehow an effect of social structuration. Using signs and symbols allows

our embodied minds to transform sensual experience into conceptual experience.[5] What our bodies perceive on a sensual level (light, sound, smells, tactility, temperature, etc.) in their permanent pre-reflexive state of existence gets transformed in our minds through an ongoing flux of "typifications". Our consciousness can be considered an ongoing process of "typifying", which means that we use (in a mostly non-reflected way) interpretive schemes to identify elements of a situation and their supposed qualities. Thinking here is the outcome of a permanent *doing relations* between our body/mind and some "object" it is concerned with (whether it is material or ideal, living or not living and so forth, including the fact that our embodied mind might turn to itself as such an object, for example when thinking: "I know what kind of statement to make in this situation"). This point is crucial in understanding the practice of sign usage behind discursive performances – here as well it presupposes a perceived and more or less ordered situation as a situation where this or that discourse I might be able to perform applies (and others not). When you as a reader, here and now, of this text perceive and identify black and white lines and spots, and your mind combines such perceptions into letters, words and sentences which you read as written signs of a particular language in a particular setting of reading (your office, your apartment, in a train, or wherever), with a particular meaning and reference to something beyond these pure signs, you are performing this process. Schütz ([1932] 1967) called such a complex interplay between body, mind and signs in the common adult person with quite common skills the *constitution of the world* in the individual embodied consciousness. Such a constitution performs a particular ordering of the world, for example as a moment of reading a book here and now, as being this or that kind of situation, as articulating this or that discursive structuration (a religious confession, a sociological argument in a discussion and so forth). This allows human beings to act in and interact with the world, its materiality or existence, including other individuals in this world, and including producing fragments or pieces of discourse. In some rare occasions, an individual will have to invent, or try to invent, a particular new sign in order to deal with a "new" experience, situation, or problem. This happens for example when someone invents a new word for a machine she or he has just created. There is a basic capacity and freedom of sign creation and interpretation of a present situation inherent to the human condition. But most of the time, individuals use established signs, or what Schütz called "types" and "interpretive schemes" out of the social and collective, historically established stocks of knowledge at hand (Schütz and Luckmann, 1973; Schütz, 1973a). Talking about the constitution of the ordered (or disordered) world in the individual body/mind therefore does not imply that this is a process outside the social, not deeply shaped by social means. On the contrary, it is the socio-historical embeddedness of human beings which allows for such a constitution. This happens when we classify black from white, letters from pictures, books from texts, people from apes, a rock from a rose. One could say that in most of the situations we have to deal with, society has already done the interpretation and classification, the basic ordering of the world. We do not have to invest much energy into navigating that – our bodies/minds just do it. We then can focus on more particular elements and handlings of small and large situations.

According to Schütz, such processes ground the very basic matrix of the everyday life world of humans in which we all live, eat, drink, make love, run, sleep, care for others and so forth. And it applies for particular sub-universes of meaning which are ordered along particular ways of experiencing (like dreams or fantasies) or particular ongoing concerns. Consider the case of a scientist entering the field of mathematics and starting to work in it. S/he, as an embodied mind, constitutes this situation in a particular way which implies a given pre-structuring of what to do, to write, to tell:[6]

> [...] the scientist enters a pre-constituted world of scientific contemplation handed down to him by the historical tradition of his science. Henceforth, he will participate in a universe of discourse embracing the results obtained by others, methods worked out by others. This theoretical universe of the special science is itself a finite province of meaning, having its peculiar cognitive style with peculiar implications and horizons to be explicated. [...] Any problem emerging within the scientific field has to partake of the universal style of this field and has to be compatible with the pre-constituted problems and their solution by either accepting or refuting them. Thus the latitude for the discretion of the scientist in stating the problem is in fact a very small one.
>
> (Schütz, [1945] 1973b: 250–256)

These particular universes of discourse have their own social histories. Take mathematics as an example: it emerged out of the social practices of calculation and reflexivity, which became formalised and institutionalised, as all other scientific disciplines. In the process of socio-historical and interactive institutionalisation, the means and resources for performing mathematical discourse are established, including the constitution of actors capable of producing the statements of mathematics and able to control each other in such a production. This holds for public discourses, too, although in lesser degrees of discipline and structuration. One might be able to perform basic arguments from climate change discourses without being a climate researcher. Therefore, public discourses involve heterogeneous actors and statements which are not related to each other by a discipline or religious world view but by the performance of particular definitions of a situation. In order to articulate "climate change as a human made threat" in a given discursive event, you have to combine certain elements of meaning making while excluding others.

Following Schütz and Luckmann (1973) and Berger and Luckmann (1966), we use "knowledge" to mean all kinds of types (signs and meaning/reference) and incorporated ways of action people use in general and particular ordering of situations.[7] Knowledge refers to entities that some kinds of people suppose to exist. These entities can be "classes" for sociologists, angels for children, a heaven for Christians, or life on Mars for some musicians. Knowledge is not a term reduced to the factual given, but to phenomena assumed (by some) to exist. Language/meaning is a social reserve for knowledge. The social construction of reality implies dealing with materiality as well as with the effects, resistances, or agency of such materiality: "Knowledge about society is thus a realization in the double sense of the word, in the sense of apprehending the objectivated social reality, and in the sense of ongoingly producing this reality" (Berger and Luckmann, 1966: 84).

Talking about "social construction" does not imply some architect's master plan for constructing something. Certainly, there are historical situations of collective institutional design making (as in revolutions and religions). But as a whole, social construction can be considered rather an ongoing historical process which emerges out of the interwoven interactions of social actors and the material conditions they live in. Society becomes objective reality through historical processes of interaction with others and with our material world, through human interpretation of this world and comprehensive processes of institutionalisation. As objectivated reality it exists, whether we want it to or not, as long as material conditions for existence stand, as long as it is produced by human action and its objectifications – allowing, shaping and constraining our thinking, feeling and acting. In ongoing processes of socialisation and internalisation, elements of such a historical *social construction of reality* become our "subjective reality", that is the ground for the body/mind based *constitution* of the world in everyday life which allows us to define situations, to use some vocabulary of motives and to interact with others. Berger and Luckmann (1966: 172) emphasised especially the role of language and the daily conversation machinery for the construction of a shared social reality:

> The most important vehicle of reality-maintenance is conversation. One may view the individual's everyday life in terms of the working away of a conversational apparatus that ongoingly maintains, modifies and reconstructs his subjective reality. [...] It is important to stress, however, that the greater part of reality-maintenance in conversation is implicit, not explicit. Most conversation does not in so many words define the nature of the world. Rather, it takes place against the background of a world that is silently taken for granted. Thus an exchange such as, 'Well, it's time for me to get to the station', and 'Fine, darling, have a good day at the office', implies an entire world within which these apparently simple propositions make sense. By virtue of this implication the exchange confirms the subjective reality of this world.

The same argument holds for a discursive statement such as "Sociology deals with social structures (like class, race and gender-based inequalities) and processes (like socialization or habitus formation) which shape individual action."

(3) The points made so far are important to understand the basic condition for discourses to come into existence in a longer or shorter process of socio-historical emergence and structuration as well as for their transformation and perhaps disappearance. Discursive events and practices, in order to be performed, need skilled actors capable of using particular combinations of symbols, capable of defining situations. Discourses exist as series or assemblages of such performances which all together make up their empirical reality and existence. This account is not only valuable for the discourses and discursive conflicts we research. It is also valuable for our own analytical work as discourse researchers. We too are performers of discourses about discourses. There is no escape.

Discourses, as a particular way of constituting specified meaning, emerge around some concern or problem requiring action and thinking, more or less in competition with or opposed to other ways or modes of meaning making. These can be issues of knowing something (for instance about *nature, god, the nation*) or of dealing with small events (like a court case) or big events (like sustainability, migration, global interconnection, a disaster). They are the emergent effects of historically-situated collective action and interaction. Think about the evolution of competing religious worldviews or of highly specialised sciences. They do not simply show up all of a sudden. They develop their concrete Gestalt through concrete socio-historical processes. Like everything human made, they are the historical products of human interaction with the world. To talk about a *discourse X* or a *discourse Z* is just a shortcut for all those permutations of action and actors interplaying, adjusting and disciplining themselves by commenting on what meaning patterns or tools to use, judging good from bad, correct from incorrect performances and so on. Such an account holds true for comprehensive and long lasting historical discursive formations like Catholicism or the social sciences. It holds true too for more hybrid public discourses with shorter spans of existence, like those arising around and competing with regard to a current matter of public concern such as Brexit, affirmative action, gay and lesbian rights issues, economic intervention into markets, the post-colonial condition or ecological disaster, to name only a few. Most current discourse research is interested in cases such as these, their causes, dynamics and effects. Often we identify such discourses (competing or not, conflictual or not) by their theme or concern: energy transition, climate change, bioengineering, biodiversity, drug addiction, human trafficking, health insurance issues, European integration, refugee crisis and so on. We have to be very precise about our point of entry into their analysis. Climate change discourse, one of the most researched discursive processes, is in fact plural: such discourses differ according to national and linguistic contexts, to the level of political action in a given case, to the speakers involved and so forth. We never find THE discourse, but instead particular discourses on their concrete levels of singularity and appearance.

Discourses, according to Foucault, can be analysed by considering given and collected fixed speech acts (textual, visual, oral), performed and accessible utterances which follow a particular set of rules governing their production.[8] We can refer to this as a co-constructive relationship between a discourse and a given discursive event within this discourse. Actors perform discourses in a process of realisation (in the sense of Berger and Luckmann) or articulation of a discursive structuration. They actualise them and thereby bring them into the situation here and now. And they are sometimes able to shape or even transform them, for example when adapting them to new purposes and problems. In most of the cases, established discursive regulation grounds the coherence of dispersed discursive events as being elements or fragments of one discourse, and not of another. Therefore, discourse is the name we give to an amount of empirically accessible data (pieces of text, reports, books, lectures, leaflets, etc.) which have a concrete materiality as discursive practices and effects of such practices. The research interest in discourses then can take rather different shapes. A very basic distinction is an interest in the *internal* historical genealogy or emergence of *one* or several discourses and the power/ knowledge work they do (for example religious or scientific discourses). This was Foucault's interest in his study of the order of things (in academic discourses), the medical gaze, or the history of madness. Such discourses (like sociology and psychology) differ in their vocabulary and in the meaning making patterns and strategies they use, in the reference claims they perform, in the objects and in the speaker positions they establish. Their evolution is shaped by internal as well as by external forces, including sometimes oppression, control and censorship by religious or political powers. The concrete shape of such processes has to be identified in empirical analysis of given cases of interest. Said's work in *Orientalism* as well as Hall's *et al.* in *Policing the Crisis* are cases in point.

A different question would address the participation or involvement of discourses in ongoing (conflictual) definitions of situations, events and needs for action, as in the examples given at the beginning of this text. Then SKAD discourse research focuses on that situation or a series of such situations and the performativity of involved discourses: What knowledge and moral claims do they make? How do they account for factual evidence and aesthetic or moral evaluation? What resources do they draw upon? How do they relate to each other, and with what effects for the definition of the situation?

Whether you are interested in the historical emergence of one discourse or a set of discourses in a particular field, or in discursive conflicts upon matters of concern, SKAD argues for a perspective on discursive patterns of meaning making (the *content side* of discourse which will be discussed in the next paragraph) and on the concrete materialities of discourses. It addresses their materiality through the concept of the *dispositif*. Here again, Foucault introduced some key arguments. Dispositif refers to a complex of heterogeneous but related elements such as actors, texts, laws, buildings, practices, legal and procedural measures, objects – in short: sayings, doings, artefacts and materiality – assembled to deal with an "urgency": some problem, identified via occurring processes of problematisation.[9] SKAD's usage of the dispositif concept refers to two dimensions of discursive world making. First, it permits addressing the concrete *infrastructure of discourse production*, that is the symbolic and material resources which allow for a discourse to articulate discursive events, to perform a particular discursive practice. Sociology, as a discourse, needs qualified speakers and positions in academia; it needs devices to research, write and publish. It needs funding to produce statements and so on. Exactly the same thing holds for social movement actors or NGOs which perform a counter-discourse in a concrete case of problematisation. The infrastructures may differ considerably, but any particular discourse produced requires some kind of infrastructure – otherwise it just would not happen.

SKAD's usage of dispositif, moreover, refers to a second element, the *infrastructures of discursive intervention*: discourses and discursive conflicts produce highly diverse outcomes like laws, rules, judgments, evaluations, classifications, new human actors, practices and artefacts, which address the mastery of an empirical concern. Consider the case of inequality in education (following the PISA-rankings). Governmental action which tries to improve national performances will set up whole packages of intervention into schooling and pre-school education, for example by devices for classification of *weak* pupils and measures for teachers' empowerment. Such measures intervene into a given field of practice; their effects then might re-enter discursive meaning making. In fact, discourses and dispositifs are closely related, interwoven, or interconnected.

SKAD's methodology and conceptual tools

SKAD is not a method but rather a research agenda and a theory-methodology-methods package aiming to examine the discursive construction of realities in social relations of knowledge and knowing and in the social politics of knowledge and knowing. Such a perspective implies that discourse research is not about applying a given theory (like Bourdieu's field theory) to a concrete case. On the contrary, it conceives of research as experimentation in the sense of Michel Foucault (see Foucault, 1991 and Keller, 2017a). Such a stance allows for surprises and new conceptual thinking and theorising stimulated by the empirical case and its analysis. SKAD is concerned with analysing the processes, causes, dimensions, dynamics and effects of discursive construction in whatever area of society you are interested in. Even in experimentation, researchers need heuristic concepts which allow them to proceed, to decide what to look for and what to neglect. Therefore core elements of SKAD's conceptual framework will be presented in the following. These imply a comprehensive range of possible questions to be asked. It is important to keep in mind that in a concrete research, no one can address the totality of given discourses, possible questions and tools at hand. SKAD proposes a toolkit; for a concrete research purpose you will have to make your own choices regarding questions, concepts and proceedings. As the contributions in this volume show, researchers will focus for example on the meaning making side of competing discourses via the analysis of texts and documents, or inquire into the dispositifs of intervention via ethnographic research. In concrete research, you choose which SKAD concepts suit your research interests and you might introduce new concepts from other methodologies if necessary, as far as they integrate into the basic SKAD framework of sociology of knowledge.[10]

Research questions

Discourses are situated in time and in social as well as geographical space. The analysis of a concrete discourse or discursive conflict might start from general research interests, current theoretical and empirical concerns in your discipline, your interest in a particular phenomenon, or similar. It then addresses questions ranging from micro-levels of concrete and situated discursive practices to issues about the dynamics of discursive structuring of symbolic orders and to wide-ranging reflections on the relationship between discourse, extra-discursive events and social change. A given theoretical problem or discussion in a field as well as a concrete interest in a particular object[11] might serve as the origin of one's investment in a precise question. Therefore you will have to adapt the following general questions to your specific purpose:

- What is the historical trajectory (the emergence, presence and disappearance) of discourses and the way they change through time and space?
- What is their unfolding structuration of meaning, their impact and the knowledge work they do in given social contexts? What kind of definitions do they perform in collective struggles for an issue of concern and with what effects?
- How are they located in a current power/knowledge regime or field and its stabilisation or transformation?
- What are the social actors, practices, means and resources involved in discursive conflicts and meaning making in a public or specialised

arena of a given concern? Are there excluded or marginalised voices? Who is allowed to speak and define what?
- How do discourses sustain or challenge established values, norms and factual statements?
- What is the role of (key) events in discursive conflicts? Are there major changes, and how do they occur?
- How do available dispositif infrastructures of discourse production shape the dynamics of discursive meaning making?
- What kind of dispositif intervention infrastructures are established, and with what effects?
- How do particular discursive formations or discursive conflicts relate to other dimensions of social structuration? How do they establish and shape phenomena like "interests" or "motives"?
- What are the social consequences or the power/knowledge effects of discourses as they relate to fields of social practice and everyday life, action and interpretation?

Such questions can be addressed in different kinds of case studies, on different levels of the social, and with a broad range of applications to concrete research issues. The contributions in this volume give some examples of that. Since real world empirical research in the social sciences always is subjected to restrictions of wo/menpower, time and money, it is not feasible to address all such questions at once. Therefore a concrete study of discourse must select a research interest to focus upon.

Interpretive analytics and co-construction

SKAD discourse research involves a process of empirical *reconstruction* of power/knowledge regimes and their dynamics. The aim is to understand and thereby explain them, and to make visible the contingencies in the work they do. This kind of reconstructive analysis requires data. Written texts (like newspaper coverage, scientific reports, books, expertise, leaflets, advertisements), orally performed speeches (like lectures, TV debates, parliamentary debates, interviews), visual (like graphs, figures, tables, maps, photos, paintings) and other artefacts (like books as material devices, a building, a digital website device, etc.) and observable practices can become such data, when approached via research (or produced by research). Using data in an analytically sound way implies that such information functions as a corridor of resistance, in the sense that you have to ground your arguments in reference to that data. You cannot say or write anything you want about a given document. Its material and symbolic qualities allow you to make certain statements, but not others. To put it very simply: the present book cannot be considered a biomedical sciences document; it would be hard to argue that, given the current nature of that discipline. The relationship of data to the research is addressed in the term co-construction. Co-construction means that you work with the help of data. Nevertheless, it is you, the analyst, who starts with questions and looks for responses in the documents. Different questions will lead to quite different responses, and sometimes, there may be no response at all. In that case you have to retrace the document and case inspiring and guiding you in order to rethink and pose different questions.

Finally, this kind of case study work is an exercise in interpretive analytics. Here I refer to two major arguments. First, a piece of data has to be split up, to be divided into its diverse elements and dimensions (some might call that the element of deconstruction in SKAD). In contrast to most interpretive research, such a document cannot be considered per se as being a document of just one discourse. Instead, it may appear as an arena for various and heterogeneous discourses. Consider a long article in a high quality newspaper assembling different points of view about a given concern. This does not make it a document of a single discourse, but rather a discursive micro-arena in itself. Furthermore, such a text usually performs only elements or fragments of particular discourses. Discourse research therefore is an art of combination: the analyst has to put together pieces of a discursive puzzle in order to reconstruct the whole discursive structuration, which then can provide grounds for a more theoretical or critical diagnosis (for example with emerging concepts like *bio-power* – this was Foucault's approach in his empirical work).

Second, all this work is profoundly shaped by continual interpretation of signs, symbols, practices and situations. The analyst simply cannot escape such processes of interpretation:

> The basic problem for the sociological researcher when he or she is reflecting upon his/her work, is making it transparent for him- or herself and for others how (s)he understands that which (s)he believes to understand, and how (s)he knows what (s)he thinks (s)he knows. [...] Their claim entails absolutely stripping the basic operations in sociological research and theory construction of their epistemological naïveté, to reconstruct them and elucidate them.
>
> (Hitzler and Honer, 1997: 23–25)

As was argued above, every human definition of a situation is an interpretive process. This holds true for discourse research too. The analyst interprets both the research situation and the research case; in working through concrete data a continual interpretation of signs and symbols is always involved. Therefore, hermeneutics, the methodology of interpretation, plays an important role in discourse research. This is not about hermeneutics in the older sense of unmasking a hidden economical or ideological force behind the present data, or of revealing what some author intended to say by what she or he wrote. Rather it can be considered a hermeneutics of surfaces, which allows for making sound arguments about given and created data. There are different options for such a hermeneutics, and some SKAD ideas about it will be presented below.

SKAD, much like all approaches in the field of discourse studies, is characterised by a high degree of self-reflexivity. SKAD reconstruction work is also inevitably construction work. It is a discourse about discourses which follows its own discourse production rules, ways of enabling and disciplining. Therefore it does not allow for an objectivist account of a given research case, but a situated analysis which tries to argue its case not in an arbitrary way, but in a conceptually and methodologically sound way. Its results then can be discussed and related to other work using different approaches (see Zhang and McGhee, Chapter 8, this volume).

Analysing discursive meaning making, knowledge and knowing: some concepts

As we have seen above, SKAD has a theory and methodology with regard to its research objects (discourses, dispositifs, their relations, confrontations and effects) and to its own analytical procedure. This theoretical grounding explains the conditions of possibility of discursive processes. It is not an explanatory device which identifies *ex ante* a few causal factors then used to explain given discursive issues of interest. Instead, it suggests a conceptual toolbox and a methodology for heuristic purposes. This means that diverse elements of such a toolbox can be used in concrete research in order to analyse, to establish questions with which to approach data and, one hopes, get some answers. Not all of these resources will be employed in every study. And other conceptual tools might be added, if necessary.

Utterances and statements

The first and most important conceptual distinction was established by Michel Foucault in his work in *The Archeology of Knowledge* (Foucault, [1969] 2010). This distinction addresses the core discursive effect of producing or organising meaning and thereby, based on the referential function of signs and symbols and the resistance corridors of the world, the reality of the phenomenon a discourse deals with. "Utterance" refers to the concrete given and ever singular micro-discursive event which allows us to analyse discourses: a speech, a printed text, a unique result of a concrete discursive practice, a historical individuality. Even two versions of the very same newspaper article have distinct concrete materialities resulting from the atoms and molecules constituting them. If you consider their symbolic content, made out of a particular arrangement of signs and symbols, the appresentation of meaning which they perform, they already appear less singular. So a book might sell a million copies, each of which has its own material structure, but all perform the same arrangements of signs and symbols. This too is a kind of singularity. As Foucault argued, discourse research has to use such data, but it is not interested in their material but rather their symbolic singularity. He introduced the concept of "statement" (and statement formation) in order to label what such research should be interested in. Statement refers to typical patterns, to the rules and regulations which give coherence to a given piece of data as being a performance of this discourse rather than of a different one. This seemingly complex idea is in fact rather simple. Consider how you would identify a sociological text from a psychological one, or from a religious or a political one. Such texts differ by the elements they use to address issues in different ways. Such elements are more than vocabularies and rhetorical devices. They include patterns of relating some elements rather than others, and in particular ways. Therefore, discourse research has to look for statement patterns, not for the concreteness of utterances – the latter ones being only points of entry for analysis. This implies that the very same statement can be made in very different utterances and situated forms; it might even exist as text, image, graph, or audio-visual data. In his book *The Order of Things* ([1966] 2001), Foucault identified such statement patterns as "epistemes" (e.g. the episteme of similarity between entities, organizing relational knowledge in academia for some centuries). SKAD suggests using five analytical concepts deriving from general sociology of knowledge in order to analyse patterns of statement production: (1) interpretive schemes, (2) argumentation clusters, (3) classifications, (4) phenomenal structures and (5) narrative structures (plots). Taken together, these elements form the "interpretative repertoire" (Wetherell and Potter, 1988) by which a discourse performs its symbolic structuring of the world.

(1) *Interpretive schemes:* The term interpretive scheme (in German: *Deutungsmuster*) denotes social/collective meaning and action-organising schemata, which are combined in and circulated through discourses (see Keller on waste, Chapter 4, this volume; Truschkat and Muche, Chapter 12, this volume). The concept is close to the idea of "frame" and "framing" as used in symbolic interactionist social movement and social problems research. But it does not imply any reference to cognition or intentional use. It is a concept applied to knowledge patterns in the social stocks of knowledge established by situated groups and societies in order to deal with some constellation of the world ("romantic love" is an example of such a pattern, related to emotional relations between two people; "technology is always a risk" might be a pattern in a quite different field which organise how some technological concern is presented). Such interpretive schemes can organise rather different kinds of phenomena or events, and indeed, they do undergo historical and social transformations. Discourses differentiate in the way they combine such frames in specific interpretive frameworks. They are able to generate new interpretive schemes and ways

of positioning them within the social agenda. This concept has a particular importance for the relation between discourses and our everyday practices and self-understanding, e.g.: Are we really in love? Is this technology safe? Shall we run to improve our health? What is it like to be a good father or mother – what do I have to do?

(2) *Argumentation clusters:* Schünemann (see Chapter 5, this volume) introduced the concept of typified argumentation clusters as another helpful category. A strong interest in argumentation goes hand in hand with a focus on political issues. Argument, as conceived here, is defined as appearing at the intersection of a discourse strand (as for example the macroeconomic discourse strand in a given society) and the strategic orientation and calculations of actors in a political conflict or campaign situation. Arguments thus emanate from a discourse strand and most likely develop in different strategic directions. Consequently, the concept is not to be conflated with rationalist or deliberative notions of the *good, better, bad* or *worse* argument. It refers to particular clusters of *if A, then B* relations which organise a particular set of statements in discourses.

(3) *Classifications:* A third element in the content-focused analysis of discourses is the exploration of classifications (and therefore qualifications) of phenomena which are performed within them and by them (see Unger, Scott and Odukoya, Chapter 9, this volume). According to the long history of sociology of knowledge, classifications are a highly effective form of social typification processes (Keller, [2005] 2011b, 2019). Like every form of symbolising, sign usage in discourses classifies the worldly given into particular entities (for the classifier) which provide the basis for its conceptual experience, interpretation, and way of being dealt with. Competition for such classifications occurs, for example, between discourses about what "groups at risk" should be identified for medical health purposes, what kind of substances should be considered drugs, what category of people should be attributed what kind of rights and duties, or what kind of behaviour should be considered "normal" or "deviant". Classifications have significant impacts on action. The interest in classificatory devices and classifications is due to their constitutive role for symbolic ordering in discourse and practical action as an effect (see Bowker and Star, 2000).

(4) *Phenomenal structures:* The concept of phenomenal structure does not refer to some kind of ontological entity that is supposed to be behind representations, or to some essential qualities of a phenomenon. Rather, it assumes that the so-called Gestalt of a phenomenon of concern at a given socio-cultural and historical moment, is constituted by discursive action and meaning making *within* a concrete discourse. Competing discourses and discourse coalitions set up competing phenomenal structures. Such meaning making establishes phenomenal dimensions and their concrete qualification (see Ide, Chapter 13, this volume; Keller on waste, Chapter 4, this volume; Truschkat and Muche, Chapter 12, this volume). For instance, constructing a theme as a problem on the public agenda

requires that the protagonists deal with the issue in several dimensions. They have to refer to argumentative, dramatising and evaluative statements; the determination of the kind of problem or theme of a purpose for action, the definition of characteristics, causal relations (cause-effect) and their link to responsibilities, identities of involved actors and non-humans, values, moral, aesthetic, and factual evaluation and judgments, consequences, possible courses of action, forms of self-positioning and othering, etc. In such processes, *different, heterogeneous or hybrid forms of knowledge and claim making* might be involved (as referring to scientific evidence, to morality, to religious cosmologies, or political programmes), or competing forms of *futurising* (like prognosis, scenario, oracle) and "historising" (narratives about the past and its implications for the present). The concept of phenomenal structure addresses these kinds of considerations and links them to the fact that discourses, in the constitution of their referential relation (their *theme*), designate different elements or dimensions of their topic and link them to a specific filler (an interpretive scheme, an argumentative pattern, a classification pattern, etc.) Both the dimensional structure of phenomena and their concrete implementation have to be depicted out of empirical data – there is no pre-established dimensional matrix to apply (although there are some common patterns in problem definition, like causation, evaluation and solution which might occur often in given cases). Identifying particular phenomenal structures, their presence and transformation through time, and analysing how they relate to phenomenal structures performed by opposing discourses is one of the core analytical processes in researching discursive conflicts. You should be aware that reconstructing such a structure at a given moment in discursive processes is like taking a snapshot – they change over time and in discursive competition. Indeed, they are always situated snapshots, even if they might be stable for a certain period and discursive context. Looking for the events, actors, processes and knowledges which intervene and cause them to change from a situation X to a situation Y is one of the core tasks of discourse analysis.

(5) *Narrative structures:* The structuring moments of statements and discourses, through which various interpretive schemes, classifications and dimensions of the phenomenal structure (for example, actors or problem definitions) are placed in relation to one another in a specific way, can be described as narrative structures. Narrative structures are not simply techniques used to combine linguistic elements, but a *mise en intrigue* (Paul Ricoeur's "emplotment"), a configurative act which links disparate signs and statements in a particular form (Ricoeur, 1984: 5). Narrative structures integrate the various statement patterns of a discourse into a coherent and communicable form. They provide the acting scheme for the narration with which the discourse can address an audience in the first place and with which it can construct its own coherence over the course of time. These may be stories of progress or decline, of true or false

knowledge, of religious empowerment and belief or established facts, of heroes or criminals, of upcoming disasters or much better and equal societies and futures (see Keller on waste, Chapter 4, this volume; Truschkat and Muche, Chapter 12, this volume).

Social actors, speakers, subject positions, subjectification

SKAD starts with a sociological concept of (individual or organisational) *social actors* and their constituted agency in a social context. Such actors are related to discourses in different ways. The first and most obvious relation is that of actors becoming *speakers* in discursive affairs. This might happen by their being socialised within a particular universe of discourse (such as mathematics or psychological expertise) for example through university education and careers and institutional role taking. This might happen also by just starting to engage for organisational or private reasons with an issue of public concern (like poverty, human rights, or ecological transformation). It is important to see that assuming a particular speaker position in a given situation might not result in a stable or permanent engagement. Some collective actors (like political parties and their representatives) can switch and even take opposing speaker positions at the same moment, depending on the trajectory of a discursive conflict. So discourse research should look carefully at how speakers relate to discursive positions taken, and how this might change. To insist on a general category of social actors is helpful then in order to look for invisible speakers, implied speakers, excluded speakers or "silent voices", that is, actors you might expect to show up, but who don't – which can become a matter for your analysis. Finally, social actors bring in their economic, symbolic, social, cultural and knowledge resources in a discursive structuration. This can have significant impacts on the discursive processes of interest.

The category of *speakers* is rather simple. They are those producers of discourse who perform the utterances mentioned above. They might draw upon different resources in order to authorise their contribution (like scientific expertise or personal experience, religious spirituality, or success in elections and so forth). SKAD discourse research is not about the unmasking of a hidden agenda or intent of real speakers, but about the way statements are legitimised by certain categories of speakers rather than by others. SKAD assumes that actors and speakers have a more or less complex set of interests (like making money, performing a "good show" etc.) and use strategic action. There are highly diverse drivers for action and engagement. But according to SKAD the interesting point is their legitimation as speakers, the kind of knowledges they use in order to articulate their statements, and the effects resulting from this.

Subject positions refer to identity and action templates for subjects or role models constituted in discursive meaning making (see Küppers, Chapter 11, this volume; Stückler, Chapter 6, this volume). A good example is the eco-citizen, the friend of the environment who in principle does not take the airplane, reduces water consumption, has a bike instead of a car, works to lower her/his carbon footprint and so on. Often, there are negative subject positions too, that is positions which have to be educated, disciplined, punished, excluded, like the ecologically irresponsible type who isn't concerned about questions of climate change and such. A third variation here are the implicated subjects, that is actors (groups) which are referred to as being the core concern of a discursive structuration. One example would be the case of "the possible users of this or that technology with this or that need – we are doing what we can for them". Aspects of such subject positions are positioning processes such as othering (the capitalists, the oriental people) and "selfing" (we the people, we the west, we the good versus them, the bad and the ugly). Another variation might be the evocation of non-human speakers like ghosts, angels and gods as having made this or that speech, order, or statement. In such cases these non-human speakers are represented by other speakers (such as believers of all kinds) who perform their speech acts as a kind of ventriloquism in order to make them real and empirically accessible.

Subject positions can be core instances of the interpellation processes that discourses perform. But we should not confuse discursive templates with occurring processes of *subjectification*, for example in organisations or in everyday life. If we are addressed as entrepreneurial subjects or ecologically friendly subjects, we have a capacity for manoeuvring such interpellations, ignoring them, refusing them or giving them a most personal shape (see Bosančić, Chapter 10, this volume). Dispositifs play a central role here, such as in institutional and organisational infrastructures that offer concrete situational settings for the corresponding programming efforts in the form of buildings, trainers, seminars, technologies of the self, codes of practice, laws, participants and so forth.

Discursive fields, discursive coalitions

SKAD describes discursive fields as being social arenas, constituting themselves around contested issues, controversies, problematisations and truth claims in which discourses are in reciprocal competition with one another. Such arenas can be public, as in most mass mediated controversies, or more closed for particular publics (such as scientific discourses). In the processing of discourses, discourse coalitions might emerge by effect – different and sometimes even opposing actors might use overlapping forms of statement production which serve to add to each other's power in a given case. These coalitions can be established intentionally too, certainly.

Practices

The term *practice(s)* depicts very generally conventionalised action patterns which are made available in collective stocks of knowledge as a repertoire for action, that is, in other words, a more or less explicitly known, often incorporated script about the *proper* way of acting. *Discursive practices* are the communication events which realise a discursive statement production in a concrete situation. They can be observed and described as typical ways of acting out statement production whose implementation requires interpretive competence and active shaping by social actors. The social processing of discourses also takes place through ways of acting which do not primarily use signs, but which are essential for the statements of a discourse (for example, the construction or assembly of measuring instruments in order to prove specific statements about environmental pollution, or the collection of waste in order to measure its components). We can call them discourse related non-discursive practices. And finally, there are practices which are only loosely related to particular discourses, like taking a train or producing energy. Although they might be closely linked to certain discourses (like energy transition), they might be much less related to other discourses (like drug addiction). Nevertheless they are important in order to allow for scientists to meet and books to be published and so on. SKAD here again differentiates between the latter and between *model practices* generated in discourses, that is, exemplary patterns (or templates) for actions which are constituted in discourses for their addressees. For example, in environmental discourses, this might include recommendations for eco-friendly behaviour (turning the shower off while you shampoo your hair, using your bike, or preparing slow food).

Dispositifs of discourse production and world intervention

The social actors who mobilise a discourse and who are mobilised by discourse establish a corresponding infrastructure of discourse production and problem solving which can be identified as a dispositif. Consider the state's need to get some *money of its own*: financial laws, administrative regulation, tax authorities, tax assessment, tax investigators all together, mixed up with texts, objects, actions and persons, constitute the dispositif in question. SKAD distinguishes between *dispositifs as infrastructures of discourse production* and *dispositifs as infrastructures of intervention and implementation emerging out of a discourse* (or out of several discourses) in order to deal with the real world phenomena addressed by discourses. Consider the issue arena of *the refugee crisis*: with reference to the discourse (re-)production level, these include the discursive interventions of the various managements, spokespersons, NGOs and press committees as well as the research centres which produce, diffuse and legitimise specific "problem statements", brochures and so on. With regard to implementation one could include among these, for example, the legal regulation of responsibilities, formalised proceedings, specific objects, technologies, sanctions, courses of study, personal and other phenomena produced to intervene in this case of *urgency* (like the Mediterranean sea watch and border control boats).

SKAD therefore is not just textual analysis of signs in use, communication, textual or image research. It can be simultaneously case study, observation and even a dense *ethnographic description and analysis*, which considers the link between statement events, practices, actors, organisational arrangements and objects such as historical and far-reaching sociospatial processes (see Hornidge and Feuer, Chapter 7, this volume; Elliker, Chapter 14, this volume).

Doing SKAD: about methods

SKAD research, like other research in social sciences and the humanities, has to be led by a research interest or concern. Such a concern can be informed by a diverse range of motives: a comprehensive reading of literature, a theoretical interest, a curiosity about a particular event or process of problematisation, an engagement with power/knowledge regimes, their effects and their transformation. This has to be translated into more concrete questions referring to empirical cases for research and thereby leads to reflections about data collection and data analysis. Following a given research interest, such data might consist of highly diverse textual and visual documents, including sometimes media coverage and social media utterances, scientific reporting and publications, expert interviews (see Zhang and McGhee, Chapter 8, this volume) or group discussion; other cases will prefer ethnographic observation and so forth.

Foucault stated in one of his interviews that he does not establish a pregiven data corpus but preferred to be informed and guided by data and analysis, from one piece of data/step of analysis to the next one according to his results, upcoming new questions and other indications given by such data. This is close to the idea of theoretical sampling as formulated by grounded theory. Theoretical sampling implies reflecting upon and arguing good points for the entrance and continuation of research. Why might this piece of data be interesting to start with? Then, do the analysis and think about the next piece of data to look for. Given first results, what kind of data could be interesting for a next moment of analysis? According to your research interest, you might be able to identify big events (like scandals, disasters, manifestations, law making, parliamentary debate, a scientific invention or whatever), or moments of a major discursive conflict, or a minor struggle about the definition of the situation as a point of entry. A useful strategy is to look for comparative cases or longer time spans (if you are interested in a more genealogical perspective). How was a problem conceived of in the 1960s? What about ten years later? Had any changes occurred? If not, then what about another ten years later? Yes? Then try to identify the phase of transformation and start from that in order to identify (new) involved actors, knowledges, events and discursive meaning making. According to grounded theory vocabulary, this can be called a strategy of minimal and maximal contrasting: For the latter, look for most different data in order to explore the broad range of a discursive structuration and then decide, if some document still performs the very same or rather a different, competing, opposing discourse? Use minimal contrasting, that is the most similar pieces of data in order to explore discursive elements more deeply. Criteria like "similarity at first glance" or "complete difference at first glance" are very useful to develop precise reconstruction of core elements, the latter being helpful to explore the range of heterogeneities in a discourse or discursive field. Use ethnographic approaches if you are interested in the situatedness and the work of dispositifs in discourse production and world intervention. Since today more and more discourse data are available as digitalised data, it becomes easier to work with computer-aided qualitative data analysis and software tools for documenting analysis. But one should keep in mind that, given that such programmes at hand are useful tools to organise research and data analysis, they do not replace the researchers' tasks and interpretive strategies (see Luther and Schünemann, Chapter 15, this volume). And there is a growing risk of working only with *easy-to-access* data, and of no longer taking the time and pains to do archive research. The range of data to consider and the places or sites to look for them depend on your research interests. You will have to decide when enough is enough, when you will no longer find any new, interesting details or aspects. But be aware that analysis is never complete in an objectivist sense of *having it all.*

Close or deep readings of collected data (*natural* texts and audio-visual data, conducted interviews, etc.) imply two strategies. First, close reading serves as information gathering in order to get just *information* out of the data: information about involved actors in a given case of concern, about important events, artefacts, documents, knowledges, relation building, whatever. Mapping such information again and again can help you in pursuing, reflecting on and developing your research.[12] And mapping is useful for presenting results (see Keller, Chapter 2, this volume; Luther and Schünemann, Chapter 15, this volume). A different kind of analytical reading takes place when you work on the reconstruction of statement patterns like interpretive schemes, argument clusters, classifications, phenomenal structures, or narratives, as discussed above. Here you can start with a careful analysis of the document as document (see Prior, 2003): What does or should it perform, in which context? What are the general features of such documents? Then SKAD, like other qualitative approaches, favours sequential analysis of textual or visual data, a step by step elaboration of categories which give labels to patterns of meaning making (interpretive schemes, classifications, narratives), dimensions and fillers of phenomenal structures, involved forms, legitimations and hierarchies of knowledge etc., much like the Foucauldian labelling of three different epistemes mentioned above (see Foucault, [1966] 2001). This step is about reconstructing the rules of discursive production in a given case of interest (see Keller, Chapter 4, this volume).

SKAD is not interested in the *consistency of meaning* inherent to *one* particular document of discourse per se – most speech acts humans perform are not really consistent (why should they be?). Therefore, it assumes that such data articulates some (not all) heterogeneous elements of discourse or that perhaps a piece of data is a crossing point of several discourses (as in many books or newspaper articles). So discourse research has to break up the surface unity of utterances. The mosaic of the analysed discourse or discourses in conflict and competition evolves incrementally out of this process. Writing research memos helps in reflecting on, readjusting, integrating and rethinking analysis (see Strauss, 1987).[13]

Please be aware that a sound analysis of data is the driver of empirical research, but in itself usually cannot be considered a successfully accomplished research project. During research you should not forget your questions or the theoretical concerns and discussions in the field you are working in. So try to include reflections on the question. What is my case a case of? What can I conclude from this case for a broader discussion or field of research? What has my research contributed to more general interests and discussions beyond the given case? What does it tell us about power/knowledge regimes, their dynamics and effects? Such reflections and their translation into theorising contribute to the lasting success of works in discourse research.

Outlook

SKAD theory, methodology and methods have been presented here in a condensed way. More detailed argumentation can be found in the references given and in the empirical case studies which constitute this volume. These studies account for SKAD's coherence as an analytical framework, as well as for the need to adapt it to the diversity of given research interests and concerns. Current challenges (not only) for SKAD research include a more detailed account of the role of visualisation in discursive meaning making, emotional and affective dimensions of discourses, and a closer look at the materialities which are involved in discursive performance and discursive world intervention. Recent contributions from New Materialism and the affective turn have again placed a range of stimulating ideas on the agenda of the social sciences. But contrary to some arguments levelled against social constructivism in such work, SKAD assumes that its approach to discourse research can deal very effectively with such issues. There is no need to move beyond discourse analysis. Instead, its capacity promises productive exploration in the years to come.[14]

Notes

1 The Sociology of Knowledge Approach to Discourse (SKAD) has been developed by the author since the late 1990s in Germany (see Keller 2005; 2011a; 2011b; 2012; 2019). The label was fixed in 2000 for a presentation in the first *German Handbook on Discourse Research in the Social Sciences* (Keller et al., [2001] 2011). A follow-up book, *Doing Discourse Research* (Keller, 2013), introduced readers to different perspectives in discourse analysis, including several chapters presenting core SKAD research methodology. The theoretical ground and conceptual framework were designed in *The Sociology of Knowledge Approach to Discourse. Grounds for a Research Agenda* (Keller, [2005] 2011b), including a comprehensive discussion of the history of the sociology of knowledge and approaches to discourse research across disciplines. An English translation will be published in 2019. Articles and edited books as well as conference series followed, which further elaborated elements of SKAD. I refer readers to this work for a broader discussion of SKAD's methodology and relation to other approaches in the field of discourse research.

Meanwhile SKAD has spread widely into discourse analysis in German social sciences and related disciplines (consider for example the list of SKAD work at the end of this article). I used SKAD in work on public discourses around waste policies (see Keller, Chapter 4, this volume), in research on sociological knowledge production via qualitative methods in Germany and France, in a study of the legal regulation of prostitution in Germany, and in comparative studies on Hydraulic Fracturing and shale gaze controversies or energy transition in Germany, France, and Poland. Supervised SKAD PhD work includes studies on language politics in Kazakhstan, the new eugenics after World War II in Germany, democracy building in Bulgaria, making futures in risk conflicts, and many others. Regular SKAD workshops in German and English are held at Augsburg University each year, as well as at other places around the world. Please refer to Keller's SKAD-Blog (see http://kellersskad.blogspot.de) or www.diskurswissenschaft.de for updated information.

2 SKAD can be considered a theory-methods-package much like grounded theory. That is, theory in SKAD does not refer to a system of cause-effect explanatory devices, but rather to what could be called in the English-speaking world a research agenda and a corresponding research methodology.

3 It is not by chance that the original SKAD book from 2005 started with a Stuart Hall quote:

> Recent commentators have begun to recognize not only the real breaks and paradigm-shifts, but also the affinities and continuities between older and newer traditions of work; for example, between Weber's classical interpretative 'sociology of meaning' and Foucault's emphasis on the role of the 'discursive'.
>
> (Hall, 1997: 224)

In his text titled "The Centrality of Culture" Hall suggested a definition of discourse related to knowledge and culture, quite close to SKAD. Later cultural studies did not pick up this definition but used discourse in a way closer to Critical Discourse Analysis work (Barker and Galasiński, 2001).

4 This refers to Anselm Strauss ([1993] 2008). For pragmatist philosophy see works by John Dewey and George Herbert Mead (on mind, action, and communication) and Charles S. Peirce (on signs) as well as early Chicago-school sociology.

5 This is a meeting point between pragmatist philosophy and social phenomenology as elaborated by Alfred Schütz ([1932] 1967) and his subsequent work in

the 1940s and 1950s (see Schütz, 1973a; Schütz and Luckmann, 1973), where he develops his own theory of signs in dialogue with pragmatism and language philosophies.
6 This is what Schütz wrote in 1945 on the existence of "multiple realities". Such a statement is close to Foucauldian ideas about discursive formations (see below).
7 In English-language research communities, sociology of knowledge today is still mainly reduced to the sociology of the construction of scientific knowledge or STS. Such a shortcut ignores the historical tradition and range or scope of sociology of knowledge in classical French and German sociology.
8 Foucault held different ideas about the interests of discourse analysis (see Keller, 2008, 2017a).
9 The term *dispositif* is common in French; it refers to an ensemble of measures that is made available for a specific purpose, such as for a political, economic, or technical undertaking. In this, it is close to the English word *device*, but implies a more complex arrangement of elements in order to address a purpose. Such a complex constellation of relations is not the result of a social actor's master plan, but the effect of an accumulation of diverse strategies. The common English translation as "apparatus" implies a much too machine-like view of such a constellation.
10 STS scholars have produced a large number of concepts (like boundary object, blackboxing, inscription) which can be very useful for SKAD research. For example arguments from material semiotics as established by John Law (2008) and from situational analysis by Adele Clarke (Clarke, Friese and Washburn, 2017) can be related to SKAD.
11 Foucault was interested in the analysis of the historical emergence of the modern subject in different fields of knowledge and politics. Most of his concrete research can be closely linked to his own life experiences (being born into a family of surgeons, working in asylums, being homosexual in a heteronormative social order, etc.).
12 See especially Clarke, Friese and Washburn (2017) on mapping.
13 To be clear: SKAD, unlike classical Grounded Theory, does not aim to explore particular "situations and (inter)actions" and their basic social processes, but ongoing discourses in social arenas. It is therefore closer to Situational Analysis (Clarke, Friese and Washburn, 2017).
14 See e.g. the response to affect theory by discourse analyst Margaret Wetherell (2012) or Keller (2017b) on Latour's critique of discourse oriented work.

References

Barker, C. and Galasiński, D. (2001). *Cultural Studies and Discourse Analysis. A Dialogue on Language and Identity*. London: Sage.

Beck, U. (2008). *World at Risk*. 2nd edn. Cambridge: Polity Press.

Berger, P. L. and Luckmann, T. (1966). *The Social Construction of Reality*. New York: Anchor Books.

Bowker, G. C. and Star, S. L. (2000). *Sorting Things Out. Classification and Its Consequences*. Cambridge, Mass.: The MIT Press.

Clarke, A., Friese, C. and Washburn, R. (2017). *Situational Analysis: Grounded Theory After the Interpretive Turn*. 2nd edn. Thousand Oaks: Sage.

Foucault, M. (1982). *I, Pierre Rivière, Having Slaughtered my Mother, My Sister, and My Brother: A Case of Parricide in the 19th Century*. Lincoln: Univ. of Nebraska Press.

Foucault, M. (1991). *Remarks on Marx: Conversations with Duccio Trombardori*. New York: Semiotexts.

Foucault, M. ([1966] 2001). *The Order of Things: An Archaeology of the Human Sciences*. 2nd edn. London: Routledge.

Foucault, M. ([1969] 2010). *The Archaeology of Knowledge and The Discourse on Language*. New York: Vintage Books.

Gusfield, J. (1981). *The Culture of Public Problems*. Chicago: University of Chicago Press.

Hall, S. (1997). The Centrality of Culture: Notes on the Cultural Revolutions of our Time. In: K. Thompson and Open University, eds., *Media and Cultural Regulation*. London: Sage and The Open University Press, 207–238.

Hall, S., Critcher, C. and Jefferson, T. ([1978] 2013). *Policing the Crisis. Mugging, the State and Law and Order*. 2nd edn. London: Palgrave.

Haraway, D. (1988). The Science Question in Feminism and the Privilege of Partial Perspective. *Feminist Studies*, 14(3), 575–599.

Hitzler, R. and Honer, A. (1997). Einleitung: Hermeneutik in der deutschsprachigen Soziologie heute. In: R. Hitzler and A. Honer, eds., *Sozialwissenschaftliche Hermeneutik. Eine Einführung*. Opladen: Leske & Budrich (UTB), 7–27. [Introduction: Hermeneutics in current German Sociology. In: Social Sciences Hermeneutics. An Introduction.]

Keller, R. (2005). Analysing Discourse. An Approach from the Sociology of Knowledge. *Forum Qualitative Sozialforschung /Forum: Qualitative Social Research*, [online] 6(3), Art. 32, Available at: http://nbn-resolving.de/urn:nbn:de:0114-fqs0503327 [Accessed 20 February 2018]

Keller, R. (2008). *Michel Foucault*. Konstanz: Universitätsverlag Konstanz.

Keller, R. (2011a). The Sociology of Knowledge Approach to Discourse (SKAD). *Human Studies*, 34(1), 43–65.

Keller, R. ([2005] 2011b). *Wissenssoziologische Diskursanalyse. Grundlegung eines Forschungsprogramms*. 3rd edn. Wiesbaden: VS-Verlag. [The Sociology of Knowledge Approach to Discourse. Grounds for a Research Agenda.]

Keller, R. (2012). Entering Discourses: A New Agenda for Qualitative Research and Sociology of Knowledge. *Qualitative Sociology Review*, VIII(2), 46–55.

Keller, R. (2013). *Doing Discourse Research*. London: Sage.

Keller, R. (2017a). Michel Foucault. In: R. Wodak and B. Forchtner, eds., *The Routledge Handbook of Language and Power*. London: Routledge, 67–81.

Keller. R. (2017b). Has Critique Run Out of Steam? On Discourse Research as Critical Inquiry. *Qualitative Inquiry*, 23(1), 58–68.

Keller, R. (2019). *The Sociology of Knowledge Approach to Discourse. Grounds for a Research Agenda*. New York: Springer [forthcoming].

Keller, R., Hirseland, A., Schneider, W. and Viehöver, W., eds. ([2001] 2011). *Handbuch Sozialwissenschaftliche Diskursanalyse Bd. 1: Theorien und Methoden*. 3rd edn. Wiesbaden: VS-Verlag. [Handbook for Discourse Analysis in the Social Sciences: Vol. 1: Theories and Methods.]

Law, J. (2008). Actor-network Theory and Material Semiotics. In: B. S. Turner, ed., *The New Blackwell Companion to Social Theory*. 3rd edn. Oxford: Blackwell, 141–158.

Mead, G. H. ([1934] 1963). *Mind, Self and Society*. Chicago: University of Chicago Press.

Prior, L. (2003). *Using Documents in Social Research*. London: Sage.

Ricoeur, Paul (1984). *Time and Narrative, Volume 1*. Chicago: University of Chicago Press.

Said, E. W. (1978). *Orientalism.* New York: Vintage Books.
Schütz, A. ([1932] 1967). *The Phenomenology of the Social World.* Evanston: Northwestern University Press.
Schütz, A. (1973a). *Collected Papers Vol. I-III.* M. Natanson, ed. Den Haag: Nijhoff.
Schütz, A. ([1945] 1973b). On Multiple Realities. In: A. Schütz, *Collected Papers I: The Problem of Social Reality.* M. Natanson, ed. Den Haag: Nijhoff, 207–259.
Schütz, A. and Luckmann, T. (1973). *Structures of the Lifeworld. Vol. 1 and 2.* Evanston: Northwestern University Press.
Smith, L. T. ([1999] 2012). *Decolonizing Methodologies: Research and Indigenous Peoples.* 2nd edn. New York: Zed Books.
Strauss, A. L. (1987). *Qualitative Research for Social Scientists.* Cambridge: University Press.
Strauss, A. L. ([1993] 2008). *Continual Permutations of Action.* Chicago: University of Chicago Press.
Wetherell, M. (2012). *Affect and Emotion: A New Social Science Understanding.* London: Sage.
Wetherell, M. and Potter, J. (1988). Discourse Analysis and the Identification of Interpretative Repertoires. In: C. Antaki, ed., *Analysing Everyday Explanation.* London: Sage, 168–183.

Studies using SKAD include:

English

Herzig, C. and Moon, J. (2013). Discourses on Corporate Social Ir/responsibility in the Financial Sector. *Journal of Business Research,* 66(10), 1870–1880.
Holmgren, S. (2013). REDD+ in the Making: Orders of Knowledge in the Climate-Deforestation Nexus. *Environmental Science and Policy,* 33, 369–377.
Hornidge, A.-K. (2013). 'Knowledge', 'Knowledge Society' and 'Knowledge for Development'. Studying Discourses of Knowledge in an International Context. In: R. Keller and I. Truschkat, eds., *Methodologie und Praxis der Wissenssoziologischen Diskursanalyse, Band 1: Interdisziplinäre Perspektiven.* Wiesbaden: Springer VS Verlag, 397–424.
Hornidge, A.-K., Oberkircher, L. and Kudryavtseva, A. (2013). Boundary Management and the Discursive Sphere – Negotiating 'Realities' in Khorezm, Uzbekistan. *Geoforum,* 45, 266–274.
Lippert, I. (2014). Studying Reconfigurations of Discourse: Tracing the Stability and Materiality of "Sustainability/Carbon". *Zeitschrift für Diskursforschung,* 2(1), 32–54.
Paukstat, A. and Ellwanger, C. (2016). "Wir sind das Volk" – Narrative Identity and the Other in the Discourse of the Pegida Movement. *Contention: The Multidisciplinary Journal of Social Protest,* 4(1–2), 93–107.
Sommer, V. (2012). The Online Discourse on the Demjanjuk Trial. New Memory Practices on the World Wide Web? *ESSACHESS. Journal for Communication Studies,* 5(2), 133–151.
Wu, A. X. (2012). Hail the Independent Thinker: The Emergence of Public Debate Culture on the Chinese Internet. *International Journal of Communication,* 6, 2220–2244.

German

Alber, I. (2016). *Zivilgesellschaftliches Engagement in Polen. Ein biographietheoretischer und diskursanalytischer Zugang.* Wiesbaden: Springer VS. [Civil Society Contributions in Poland. An Approach Using Biographical Theory and Discourse Analysis.]

Bechmann, S. C. (2007). *Gesundheitssemantiken der Moderne. Eine Diskursanalyse der Debatten über die Reform der Krankenversicherung.* Berlin: Sigma. [The Semantics of Health in Modernity. A Discourse Analysis on the Debate Regarding Health Insurance Reform.]

Biermann, A. (2014). *Das diskursive Verschwinden der Religionsfreiheit. Der Moscheebau zu Köln-Ehrenfeld im Spiegel der politischen Kultur.* Wiesbaden. VS-Verlag. [The Discursive Disappearance of Religious Freedom. The Cologne-Ehrenfeld Mosque Construction Process Through the Lens of Political Culture.]

Bosančić, S. (2014). *Arbeiter ohne Eigenschaften. Über die Subjektivierungsweisen ungelernter Arbeiter.* Wiesbaden: VS-Verlag. [Workers Without Qualities. The Subjectivation of Unskilled Labourers.]

Bosančić, S. and Keller, R., eds. (2016). *Perspektiven wissenssoziologischer Diskursforschung.* Wiesbaden: Springer VS. [Current Perspectives in the Sociology of Knowledge Approach to Discourse.]

Brunner, C. (2010). *Wissensobjekt Selbstmordattentat. Epistemische Gewalt und okzidentalistische Selbstvergewisserung in der Terrorismusforschung.* Wiesbaden: VS-Verlag. [Suicide Bombings as Knowledge Objects. Epistemic Violence and Occidentalist Self-reassurances in Terrorism Research.]

Christmann, G. B. (2004). *Dresdens Glanz, Stolz der Dresdner. Lokale Kommunikation, Stadtkultur und städtische Identität.* Wiesbaden: VS-Verlag. [Dresden's Glory, Dresden's Pride. Local Communication, City Culture and Urban Identity.]

Elliker, F. (2013). *Demokratie in Grenzen. Zur diskursiven Strukturierung gesellschaftlicher Zugehörigkeit.* Wiesbaden. VS Verlag [Bounded Democracy. The Discursive Structuration of Social Affiliation.]

Fegter, S. (2012). *Die Krise der Jungen in Bildung und Erziehung. Diskursive Konstruktion von Geschlecht und Männlichkeit.* Wiesbaden, VS Verlag. [The Crisis of Boys in Education. The Discursive Construction of Gender and Masculinity.]

Hamborg, S. (2018). *Lokale Bildungslandschaften auf Nachhaltigkeitskurs. Bildung für nachhaltige Entwicklung im kommunalpolitischen Diskurs.* Wiesbaden: Springer VS. [Local Education Sets a Course for Sustainability. Sustainable Development Education in Municipal Policy Discourses.]

Hofmann, U. (2011). *Sexueller Missbrauch in Institutionen: Eine wissenssoziologische Diskursanalyse.* Saarbrücken: Pabst. [Sexual Abuse in Institutions: An Analysis using the Sociology of Knowledge Approach to Discourse.]

Hövelmann, S. (2015). *Deutungskämpfe mit ungleichen Chancen? Der Konflikt um die Umbenennung der ‚Mohrenstraße' in Berlin Mitte.* Augsburg: Unv. Masterarbeit. [Unequal Opportunities for Influencing Contested Meanings? The Conflict Surrounding the Renaming of "Mohrenstraße" in Central Berlin.]

Keller, R. ([1988] 2009). *Müll – Die gesellschaftliche Konstruktion des Wertvollen.* 2nd edn. Wiesbaden: Springer VS. [Waste – The Social Construction of Value.]

Keller, R. and Poferl, A. (2016). Soziologische Wissenskulturen zwischen individualisierter Inspiration und prozeduraler Legitimation. Zur Entwicklung qualitativer und interpretativer Sozialforschung in der deutschen und französischen

Soziologie seit den 1960er Jahren. *Forum Qualitative Sozialforschung/Forum: Qualitative Social Research,* [online] 17(1), Art. 14. Available at: http://nbn-resolving. de/urn:nbn:de:0114-fqs1601145 [Accessed 02 March 2018]. [Sociological Cultures of Knowledge from Individualized Inspiration to Procedural Legitimation. On the Development of Qualitative and Interpretive Social Research in German and French Sociology Since the 1960s.]

Keller, R. and Truschkat, I., eds. (2012). *Methodologie und Praxis der Wissenssoziologischen Diskursanalyse. Band 1: Interdisziplinäre Perspektiven.* Wiesbaden: Springer VS. [Methodology and Practice of the Sociology of Knowledge Approach to Discourse. Volume 1: Interdisciplinary perspectives.]

Kessler, S. (2017). *Die Verwaltung sozialer Benachteiligung. Zur Konstruktion sozialer Ungleichheit in der Gesundheit in Deutschland.* Wiesbaden: VS-Verlag. [Administrating Social Disadvantage. The Construction of Social Inequality Through Health in Germany.]

Klinkhammer, N. (2014). *Kindheit im Diskurs. Kontinuität und Wandel in der deutschen Bildungs- und Betreuungspolitik.* Marburg: Tectum. [Childhood in Discourse. Continuity and Change in German Educational and Care Policy.]

Kurath, N. (2016). *Nichtwissen lenken. Nanotechnologie in Europa und den Vereinigten Staaten.* Baden-Baden: Nomos. [Governing ignorance. Nanotechnology in Europe and the United States.]

Lönnendonker, J. (2018). *Konstruktionen europäischer Identität – Eine Analyse der Berichterstattung über die Beitrittsverhandlungen mit der Türkei 1959–2004.* Köln: Herbert von Halem Verlag. [European Identity Constructions – An Analysis of Media Coverage on Turkey's Accession Negotiations 1959–2004.]

Madeker, E. (2007). *Türkei und europäische Identität: Eine wissenssoziologische Analyse der Debatte um den EU-Beitritt.* Wiesbaden: Springer VS. [Turkey and European Identity: A Sociology of Knowledge Analysis of the Debate Surrounding EU-accession.]

Rausch, S. (2015). *Lernen regierbar machen. Eine diskursanalytische Perspektive auf Beiträge der Europäischen Union zum Lebenslangen Lernen.* Wiesbaden: Springer VS. [Making Learning Governable. A Discourse Analysis Perspective on the EU's Contributions to Lifelong Learning.]

Renoult, G. (2015). *Wissen in Arbeit und in Bewegung. Aktuelle Strategien von „Lebenskünstlerinnen" in Kreativarbeit und zeitgenössischem Tanz.* Wiesbaden: VS-Verlag. [Knowledge in (the) Work(s) and in Motion. Current Strategies of "LebenskünstlerInnen" (Bohemian Subculture) in Creative Work and Contemporary Dance.]

Roslon, M. (2017). *Spielerische Rituale oder rituelle Spiele. Überlegungen zum Wandel zweier zentraler Begriffe der Sozialforschung.* Wiesbaden: VS-Verlag. [Playful Rituals or Ritual Play. Considerations on the Development of Two Central Concepts of Social Research.]

Sander, E. (2012): Vitamin (D)emographie für die Personalpolitik? In: M. Göke and T. Heupel, eds., *Wirtschaftliche Implikationen des demografischen Wandels.* New York: Springer, 301–317. [Vitamin (D)emography for Human Resource Policy? In: Economic Implications of Demographic Change.]

Schmied-Knittel, I. (2008). *Satanismus und ritueller Missbrauch. Eine wissenssoziologische Diskursanalyse.* Würzburg: Ergon. [Satanism and Ritual Abuse. A Sociology of Knowledge Approach to Discourse Analysis.]

Scholz, S. and Lenz, K. (2013). *Ratgeber erforschen. Eine Wissenssoziologische Diskursanalyse von Ehe-, Beziehungs- und Erziehungsratgebern.* Bielefeld: transcript. [Research

with Self-help Literature. A Sociology of Knowledge Approach to Discourse Analysis of Self-help Guides to Marriage, Relationships, and Parenting.]
Schübel, T. (2016). *Grenzen der Medizin. Zur diskursiven Konstruktion medizinischen Wissens über Lebensqualität.* Wiesbaden: VS-Verlag. [The Limits of Medicine. The Discursive Construction of Medical Knowledge on Quality of Life.]
Schünemann, W. J. (2014). *Subversive Souveräne. Vergleichende Diskursanalyse der gescheiterten Referenden im europäischen Verfassungsprozess.* Wiesbaden: Springer VS. [Subversive Sovereigns. A Comparative Discourse Analysis of Failed Referendums in the E.U. Constitutional Process.]
Schwarz, N. (2016). Die Total-Kontroverse oder das Scheitern eines Rassismus-Diskurses. In: R. Keller and J. Raab, eds., *Wissensforschung – Forschungswissen.* Weinheim: BeltzJuventa, 94–105. [The "Total" Controversy or How a Discourse on Racism Failed. In: Researching Knowledge and the Knowledge of Researching.]
Sitter, M. (2016). *PISAs fremde Kinder. Eine diskursanalytische Studie.* Wiesbaden: VS-Verlag. [PISA's Foreign Children. A Discourse Analysis.]
Traue, B. (2009). *Kompetente Subjekte: Kompetenz als Bildungs- und Regierungsdispositiv im Postfordismus.* Wiesbaden: Springer VS. [Competent Subjects: Competency as an Educational and Government Dispositif in Post-Fordism.]
Truschkat, I. (2008). *Kompetenzdiskurs und Bewerbungsgespräche. Eine Dispositivanalyse (neuer) Rationalitäten sozialer Differenzierung.* Wiesbaden: VS-Verlag. [Competency Discourses and Job Interviews. A Dispositif Analysis of (New) Rationalities of Social Differentiation.]
von Unger, H., Odukoya, D. and Scott, P. (2016). Kategorisierung als diskursive Praktik: Die Erfindung der „Ausländer-Tuberkulose". In: S. Bosančić and R. Keller, eds., *Perspektiven Wissenssoziologischer Diskursforschung.* Wiesbaden: Springer VS, 157–176. [Categorization as a Discursive Practice: The Invention of "Foreigner's Tuberculosis". In: Perspectives of Sociology of Knowledge Based Discourse Studies.]
Wundrak, R. (2010). *Die chinesische Community in Bukarest. Eine rekonstruktive diskursanalytische Fallstudie über Immigration und Transnationalismus.* Wiesbaden: VS-Verlag. [The Chinese Community in Bucharest. A Rekonstructive Discourse Analysis Case Study on Immigration and Transnationalism.]
Zimmermann, C. (2010). *Familie als Konfliktfeld im amerikanischen Kulturkampf. Eine Diskursanalyse.* Wiesbaden: VS-Verlag. [The Family as a Field of Conflict in the American Culture War.]

3 Situating SKAD in interpretive inquiry

Reiner Keller and Adele E. Clarke

Introduction

We use the term interpretive inquiry to refer to traditions in sociological and social science methods more broadly which insist that human beings must make sense out of the situations they confront by defining them, granting them meaning, and thereby deciding what is going on, and what to do next based on those interpretations. In this sense, interpretation is at the very heart of human life. Further, interpretation most often just happens to us rather than our consciously exercising control or mastery over it. As pragmatist philosophy informed us, only situations of rupture – strangeness or irritation, absolute newness or unknown problems – transform such ongoing routine interpretation into a more seriously reflexive process. This holds true in everyday life as well as in sociological research.

However, despite making such a general claim, we must also assume that sociological interpretation is, by definition, a different process from interpretation in everyday life due to its specific disciplinary means and modes of reflection. Although there is no, in principle, difference between everyday life experimentation (the way we try to figure out what works in a situation) and analysis of what is going on, sociological (and other scientific/academic) analysis creates an artificial setting which allows us to pose questions about everyday routine action. Normal meaning making has to be suspended in order to pursue sociological analysis. According to Alfred Schütz, academic life and research life take different stances toward their objects of inquiry, adopting different systems of relevance when doing research (see Schütz, 1973b).

Interpretation, as we use it here, points to the basic procedure through which we approach and analyse data, some piece of reality *out there* that we consider in the process of our research-based questions and arguments. Interpretation begins from the moment we have to define a document in the world in order to transform it into data for us, for a particular project. Later we have to define procedures which help us make statements about such documents. Such procedures, including for example line by line sequential analysis of a given text, or collective brainstorming, or whatever, are pursued to stimulate ideas about what is going on in the data at hand (as a document of a real world event) and to ground analysis, by giving it *some* particular explanatory powers – and not others.

This view of qualitative, or as we prefer here interpretive, research is anchored in *social science traditions of hermeneutics*, considered, at least in German contexts, *the arts and methodologies of interpretation*. Included in such arts of interpretation are those approaches in qualitative inquiry which do not simply assume that you directly perceive the content of a given document or scene in which you are participating. Rather you must stop and reflect upon your own thinking and analysis during the process of inquiry, including the micro-situation of analysing a piece of data, in order not to simply impose your own pre-given assumptions upon it. This is what Hitzler and Honer (1997) called the basic purpose of social science hermeneutics.

Some approaches in such a hermeneutics are quite close to classical perspectives from philosophy or humanities-based traditions of past centuries. They might aim at using a text as a document of some individual's mind, in the sense of deriving from a text or interview what some author really intended in producing it. Or one might adapt a variation of "hermeneutics of suspicion" (Ricoeur, 1970) as in Marxist or psychoanalytic traditions, assuming that some given document (an interview, a group discussion) is a product of a deeper, hidden *underlying structure*.

In contrast, other approaches, such as those used in German traditions of the sociology of knowledge, in Foucauldian discourse research, or in Straussian grounded theory, can instead be considered hermeneutics of the given (Keller, 2015). They begin from the document and its performance in order to understand a social phenomenon. Again, *interpretation* here is used in the sense of accounting for the basic capacity and concrete procedures we must use in order to analyse data. It does not refer to the process of *big meaning making* by producing a formal theoretical diagnosis for a comprehensive, completed research project. In fact, this is how Dreyfus and Rabinow (1983) discussed interpretation in Michel Foucault's work, thereby addressing the world famous concepts such as bio-power or governmentality with which Foucault theorised his findings. We agree that interpretive research needs such conceptual elements to account for its results. Such Interpretation (with a capital I) makes cases interesting, resonates with other cases and creates awareness for broader audiences.

But big I Interpretation is not our primary concern here. Rather, our concern is interpretation with a small i as present in the procedures Anselm Strauss described in his book on qualitative methods for social scientists (Strauss, 1987). Here, for example, line-by-line analysis was used in order to analyse an ill woman's account of her suffering and pain in taking a shower. It was used to provoke both creativity and adequacy in conceptual category building.[1]

In this chapter, we situate the Sociology of Knowledge Approach to Discourse (SKAD), developed by Reiner Keller, in the history and contemporary field of social research methodologies. SKAD is a research agenda and methodology,[2] which includes a conception of its object – both reflection *about* the methodology and reflexive awareness of analysing discourses by using particular discourses (those of sociology and SKAD), and concrete research methods (see Keller, Chapter 2, this volume, on SKAD). Its objects include discourses and dispositifs, the discursive construction of realities, social relations of knowledge and knowing and the politics of knowledge and knowing. SKAD methods include strategies for *data collection* (including textual data and artefacts produced in the field of research itself – sometimes referred to as *natural* data, in contrast to data produced by more obvious interventions of researchers, such as interviewing, group discussion, participation and observation in the field), *data documentation* (including archiving, recording, writing field-notes and memos) and *data analysis* (including sequential interpretation, coding and/or categorising) as well as more comprehensive accounting for *what's going on* by theorising and more conceptual diagnoses.

A very short history of classical interpretive inquiry

We cannot provide a comprehensive account of the complex history of methods in sociology (much less the social sciences more broadly) here. Such a task is vast and complex, considering the heterogeneity of developments in different countries and language regions around the world. We therefore focus only on French, German and US-based traditions. There was, in fact, considerable exchange between German and US philosophy and social science at the turn of the twentieth century, most often via US scholars travelling to Germany to study.[3]

Ethnography, the name under which most early qualitative inquiry was pursued, has a long history, extending back centuries. It was deeply stimulated and shaped by European colonialism and linked to emerging interest in *Others* from the sixteenth century onwards, including Western travellers' historical accounts of non-Western locales and their peoples (e.g. Pratt, 1992).

Within Europe, processes of industrialisation, urbanisation and enlightenment as well as the expansion of the public sphere were based on the capacity to read and discuss texts. These were also accompanied not only by statistical studies of populations and their qualities (e.g. Engels, [1845] 2009) but also by inquiries into folk life and reports on ordinary (poor and marginalised) people's situations and miseries as well. French writers of the nineteenth century such as Honoré de Balzac, Emile Zola and Gustave Flaubert were especially interested in researching real life situations of people and describing them in their novels. These can be viewed as pre- or proto-sociological projects in micro and macro-perspectives (e.g. Zola's novel *Germinal* about coal mine workers in Northern France, published in 1885; see Zola, 2004). Documenting workers' living conditions as well as accounting for vanishing rural and feudal ways of life in the processes of modernisation were part and parcel of art and fiction in this era, as well as being taken up in more journalistic and scholarly modes of reportage.

Although such realism was most prominent in France, similar projects of social reporting were undertaken by artists and scholars in other European countries as well. American sociologists in the pragmatist tradition drew on such ideas starting in the early twentieth century, adapting them to their interests in urban life and the effects of immigration on the US as well as on immigrants (e.g. *The Polish Peasant in Europe and America* by William I. Thomas and Florian Znaniecki, 1918). Their courses included sociological works by Georg Simmel and Max Weber, both of whom pointed to the importance of meaning-making for individual and collective action. Further inflected with additional focus on communication processes and interaction, much of this early US sociological work emerged from the University of Chicago and became known as Chicago School. It included early sociological manuals on field research (Palmer, 1928) and the core organising idea of the Thomas-theorem (Thomas, [1923] 1978; Thomas and Thomas, [1928] 1970). This proto-constructivist "theorem" asserted in the 1920s that if situations are believed to be or interpreted as real, they are real in their consequences. Such early sociological work raised important civic issues of concern to democracy including how marginalities, ethnicity and race and class differences "matter" when racial and ethnic segregation were very much the norm if not the law.

Another historically emerging interest is notable here. Changing ways of both living and thinking became topics of interest in academia due to thousands of years of contact and relations between societies, influenced by early colonialism, and given the long history of philosophy as well as the philosophy of enlightenment. Today we call this area of study "systems and practices of knowledge, representation and meaning making" (see Keller, [2005] 2010, 2011, [2005] 2019). French scholars initiated general inquiries into ideologies as consistent systems of categories in the eighteenth and early nineteenth centuries. These were later transformed into the Marxist analysis of base and superstructure (Marx and Engels, [1846] 2011), and in the 1920s, reframed by Karl Mannheim (1936, [1922–24] 1980; [1925–24] 1986) as his standpoint theory of milieu-driven ideologies in competition. Mannheim was one of the classic founders of the sociology of knowledge, pointing to the situated experiences and mental representations generated by members of particular social categories and groups (for example, those of conservative milieus, specific generations, men versus women, village versus urban people, etc.).[4]

Moreover, Mannheim (1952) developed a particular method which he called "the documentary method of interpretation" for data analysis linked to his research interests. Here the core idea was to analyse a given piece of data as a document representing the expression of a particular standpoint, or describing a larger cultural frame and situation. This analytic strategy later became a basic approach in Harold Garfinkel's ([1967] 1984) *Studies in Ethnomethodology* in the US (Coulon, 1995: 32), in Pierre Bourdieu's ([1979] 2010) sociology of habitus in France, and in Ralf Bohnsack's (2014) "documentary method approach" in Germany.

Other classical sociologists also expressed interest in questions of knowledge. For example, starting in the 1830s, Auguste Comte ([1830–42] 1989) was interested in human history as the evolution of knowledge systems. Emile Durkheim ([1912] 2008) and Marcel Mauss (Durkheim and Mauss [1903] 1963) pursued research on the social origins and histories of systems of representation around the turn of the twentieth century. Ludwik Fleck ([1935] 1981) presented detailed sociological work on the genesis and development of *scientific facts*. Michel Foucault's interests in the "history of systems of thought" (the title of his chair at the Collège de France) and power/knowledge regimes are later manifestations of this as well (Foucault, 1980; Keller, 2017b).

But perhaps closest to current interests in discourse research was Max Weber's analysis of the Protestant ethic which can certainly be considered an early exemplar of discourse research. Weber ([1904/1905] 2002) used documents from religious contexts in order to make his arguments about a particular organisation of everyday life and work which, as he stated, was so congruent with organising capitalism that it precisely accounted for many of the astonishing historical conditions of Western capitalist expansion. In fact, sociology itself was conceived by Weber ([1904] 1949) as "Kulturwissenschaft" (cultural studies) which deal with the meanings human societies and individual beings attribute to the chaos of "the worldly given". C. Wright Mills (1940) referred back to Weber in his significant later argument for an analysis of *social vocabularies* of motives for action (rather than motives per se). Alfred Schütz ([1932] 1967), who was interested in the "methodology of understanding", further developed the concept of a *collective* social stock of knowledge from which acting agents obtain blueprints or repertoires for their actions and interpretations of (and in) the world and for its reality to them (see Schütz and Luckmann, 1973).

In sum, there was extensive and ongoing interest in what we now call the sociology of knowledge and discourse studies in the social sciences and their predecessors.

The interpretive paradigm after World War II

Since the mid-1930s and 1940s, social research in the US has been dominated by quantitative approaches using statistical procedures, and interest in mass media communication including their content analysis. But during the 1950s a new generation of Chicago scholars (including Howard

Becker, Anselm Strauss, Blanche Geer, Erving Goffman, Rue Bucher and many others) began to come to the fore. They actively re-explored and discussed strategies for seriously pursuing qualitative inquiry, including methods for field research and interviewing.

In Europe, after the disasters and closures of social science departments during World War II, French and German sociologies were partially renewed in quite different ways, both influenced by US scholars again travelling to Europe to do research and to help rebuild academia. French and German scholars also went to the US during this era to learn about American sociology. In both France and Germany, the concept of "qualitative methods" was introduced via these exposures in and to the US, mainly with reference to an article on "Some functions of qualitative analysis in social research" by Barton and Lazarsfeld (1955)[5] and qualitative content analysis of mass media and communications research as presented by Bernard Berelson (1952: 114). By the end of the 1950s, scholars in both countries had developed their own fields of qualitative and interpretive research methods in quite different ways (see Keller and Poferl, 2016).

In France, post-World War II academic sociology liberally made use of different approaches to field work. The situation was one where curious intellectuals with no training in sociology or in any academic discipline became interested in the transformation of work life and in the modernisation of French rural societies and pursued research in these areas. French anthropology added to these kinds of methods, and field work and observation became influential approaches. But "qualitative research methods" per se never became an important label or identity marker in France. Rather, as Pierre Bourdieu and some of his colleagues stated in the late 1960s, in France, the opposition between qualitative and quantitative research was considered to have had its historical moment but no longer really mattered (Bourdieu, Chamboredon and Passeron, [1968] 1991).

French researchers subsequently elaborated their own individual approaches, based on the distinctive concerns, skills and competencies of the researcher. These were rarely organised into broader schools or traditions of qualitative inquiry. Since the end of the 1990s, a deeper interest in ethnography seems to be the main feature of the French qualitative landscape, which fits well with the rather individualistic French approach to research methodology. This interest includes the strong presence of US sociologist Howard Becker as one inspiration for such work, amongst others from the French tradition. There was also a brief flurry of interest in Anselm Strauss occasioned by the French translation of his *Mirrors and Masks* (Strauss, [1959] 1997), but this seems not to have extended to grounded theory.

In Germany in the 1950s and 1960s, returning critical theorists introduced group discussion, their documentation and textual analysis as one major strategy for understanding the ongoing transformations of German society. This so called Frankfurt "group experimentation" (Gruppenexperiment) was financed by the "US High Commissioner for Germany" and consisted of 121 formalised "group discussions" with different groups of workers (e.g. from coal mining, farmers), based on a methodology imported from the US market research. Very much like today's focus group methodologies in market research, a small sample of workers from similar backgrounds was assembled to discuss some current issues. The aim was to analyse their assumed milieu-bounded "mentalities" and "political orientations". Mangold (1960) developed a systematic approach from this method as qualitative research, using additional resources from earlier Chicago School group research. Horkheimer and Adorno (1960), in their preface to Mangold's book, insisted on the scientific quality of such a method and argued that it should be further elaborated (see Keller and Poferl, 2016).

German critical theorist and philosopher Jürgen Habermas introduced basics as well as logics of interpretive inquiry in Germany in his most influential 1967 book on the *Logics of the Social Sciences* (Habermas, [1967] 1988). Some translations of US-based qualitative approaches were also published 1970 in German, and visits by German scholars to the US were undertaken, as well as the other way round. During the 1970s, fundamental identity-building around a qualitative research paradigm emerged. This subsequently resulted in the ongoing presence of qualitative and interpretive research emphases across German sociology *and* in its institutions. In contrast to the US, much of this research was oriented towards textual analysis of interview data and group discussion. For an example of analysis of biographical narratives or narrative accounts of situations, experiences and interactions, see Fritz Schütze's writings in methodology and empirical work on soldiers, or the lived experiences of people growing up in East Germany in the Soviet era (e.g. Schütze, 2008a, 2008b; the special issue on Schütze in Qualitative Sociological Research, 2014).

With deep historical reference to German hermeneutical traditions (e.g. Wilhelm Dilthey, 1989; see Soeffner, 2004), several qualitative approaches (including objective hermeneutics, reconstructive hermeneutics in the sociology of knowledge, the documentary method of interpretation, conversational analysis close to the US model, narrative interview analysis, etc.) were established in Germany based on different modes of sequential analysis in order to follow quite diverse interests in social research (e.g. Wernet, 2014). What they all shared was a strong focus on line by line analysis of textual documents (mostly interviews and documents of verbal interaction) and a strong urgency to demonstrate one's argument through textual materials (see, e.g. contributions from German scholars in Flick, 2014). Ethnographic work could not keep up with such demands and has remained at the margins of German qualitative inquiry. Later, grounded theory was seen to fit comfortably with the textual analytics characteristic of German qualitative inquiry, and it has become the most prominent import from the US and a frequently used methodology.

The US has experienced rich and diverse developments in qualitative research as well. One important strand, deriving from Chicago School sociology and American pragmatist philosophy, was *symbolic interactionism*, the name coined by Herbert Blumer in 1937 (Blumer, 1969: 1). Throughout the 1960s and 1970s, interactionism offered a very lively defence of interpretive research, largely against American structural functionalism and survey research. It also sustained Chicago School engagements with diversity, marginality and racism (e.g. Reynolds and Herman-Kinney, 2003), and some works are considered prescient of postmodernist and poststructuralist developments.

The second enduring strand of anti-scientism in American social science that seriously nurtured interpretation was C. Wright Mills' (1959) more critical approach as manifest in his *The Sociological Imagination*, also with deep roots in American pragmatist philosophy. The third was *ethnomethodology* (Garfinkel, [1967] 1984), very much inspired by Alfred Schütz and his work on *social phenomenology* (e.g. Schütz, [1932] 1967, 1973a). Symbolic interactionists largely used ethnographic approaches as well as interviewing and field observations in research pursuits. In contrast, ethnomethodology insisted on more detailed and precise line-by-line analysis of smaller pieces of data, and rejected more general theoretical concepts such as social class or social structure.

Fundamental to the coming qualitative renaissance, explicit social constructivism was triggered in the US in 1966 by Berger and Luckman's (1966) classic *The Social Construction of Reality: A Treatise in the Sociology of Knowledge*, based on a quite different reading of Schütz. This constructivism assumes that people (including researchers) construct or interpret the realities in which they participate through their own situated perspectives and with the help of their repertoires of social knowledge and meaning making. Such repertoires emerge from historical processes of institutionalisation and change performed by human beings dealing with their existential affairs. They become a socio historical a priori – taken for granted as *reality as it is for us here and now*.

Blumer's (1969) *Symbolic Interactionism: Perspective and Method* was another US sociological "manifesto" for constructivism and the interpretive turn. In anthropology, Geertz (1973) *The Interpretation of Cultures* provoked similar debates. But in terms of research methods, it was *The Discovery of Grounded Theory*, the manifesto for qualitative research by Glaser and Strauss (1967) that became the most influential document of the qualitative renaissance for many decades. Denzin and Lincoln's (1994) *The Sage Handbook of Qualitative Research* can be considered the next major milestone intervention in US qualitative inquiry, serving as a broad and inclusive umbrella for a wide array of interpretive approaches. Significantly, its impacts were felt across multiple disciplines, specialties and even the professions, widening perspectives and widely introducing new theoretical and epistemological worlds of interpretive research.

Closely linked to symbolic interactionist writing, ethnographic field work and interviewing, a broader interest in *public discourses* and *collective struggles* over the definitions of situations also emerged in the US during the 1970s. Some Chicago scholars such as Herbert Blumer (1933) had begun analysing movies and their influence on youth behaviour in the 1930s. Again Blumer (1958) pointed to the highly consequential public construction of ethnic or racial categories and their shifting consequences. Other interactionist work focused on social problems, deviance, the careers of public issues and the reformist campaigns of "moral entrepreneurs" (e.g. Becker, 1963). With a background in early pragmatist arguments about "universes of discourse" and the core role of communication in society as well as about "the public and its problems" (Dewey, 1927; Mead, 1934), scholars started investigating public discourses as conflictual processes of defining situations between competing organisational actors (see Gusfield, 1981; Hilgartner and Bosk, 1988). Social movement research, picking up on Erving Goffman's (1974) work on frame analysis, began analysing strategic campaigns (Benford and Snow, 2000) and mass media coverage of public concerns, moving from qualitative exploratory research to quantified coding of framing processes in public debates (e.g. Gamson and Modigliani, 1989; for a critical discussion: Ulrich and Keller, 2014).

Grounded theory too became a more complex family of approaches or tradition in its "second generation" (Morse *et al.*, 2009). In 1990 and 1998, Anselm Strauss and Juliet Corbin (1990, 1998) published the first two editions of *The Basics of Qualitative Research: Grounded Theory Procedures and Techniques*, essentially a "how to" textbook largely in the interactionist tradition which became extremely popular. Glaser (1992) soon actively distanced his own approach to GT from that of Strauss. Then, at the turn of this century, Charmaz (2000, 2006, 2014) argued for a new and more fully *constructivist interpretive GT* that emphasised reflexivity and theorised analysis rather than generating formal theory. This was soon followed by Clarke's (2005) cartographic extension of GT, *Situational Analysis* (SA), explicitly including analysis of extant discourse materials found in the situation under study. SA's perspective on situations as co-defined by the observer and the observed led GT further around postmodern and poststructural turns, towards more reflexive theorising of complexities and ecological relations in the situation, also eschewing formal theory (see Clarke and Keller, 2014; Clarke, Friese and Washburn, 2015, 2018).

Providing a more panoramic view, Keller (2012) framed the major strands of interpretive research as "the interpretive paradigm", using Thomas P. Wilson's term (Wilson, 1970). In an article on "Qualitative Methods in Europe", Knoblauch, Flick and Maeder (2005: §5) stated that this paradigm is:

based on theories like symbolic interactionism, phenomenology, hermeneutics, ethnomethodology etc. – positions that stress the importance of investigating action and the social world from the point of view of the actors themselves. In a Kuhnian sense, this interpretive paradigm was supposed to substitute for the 'normative paradigm', represented by structural functionalism or Rational Choice theories.

Thus qualitative research today is both supported by and dependent upon approaches oriented towards meaning, context, interpretation, understanding and reflexivity.

The interpretive turn and its receptions

Let us first clarify more specifically here what we mean by the interpretive turn, and then discuss its varied receptions in our three focal countries. Since the 1960s, theoretical and methodological shifts in direction and emphasis have commonly been referred to as "turns" (e.g. see Bachmann-Medick, 2006). To make a long story short, the *interpretive turn* (Rabinow and Sullivan, 1987a) – which is central to SKAD – has deep roots in (German) European traditions from Friedrich Nietzsche via Wilhelm Dilthey to Max Weber, and their welcoming reception in US pragmatism, as well as pragmatism's later welcoming reception in French post-structuralism.[6] The interpretive turn became a cultural force in the late 1960s and early 1970s through some important books and extended far beyond our core field of sociology. These works demonstrated new philosophical interest in language and speech acts (e.g. Rorty, [1967] 1992), and major anthropological debates about what constituted "good" interpretive ethnographic work (e.g. Geertz, 1973; Clifford and Marcus, 1986; and Rosaldo, 1989). In the late 1970s, Paul Rabinow and William M. Sullivan, ([1979] 1987b) had predicted a general turn towards a more interpretive social sciences and presented a collection of core articles on such a turn. Anthropologist Geertz' call for "thick description" was echoed by interactionist sociologist Denzin's (1989: 52) call for "thick interpretation" in his *Interpretive Interactionism* which innovatively interwove interactionism and poststructuralisms (see also Fontana, 2005).

The interpretive turn built upon several foundational assumptions:

- Meaning is re-located from *reality out there* to *reality as experienced by the perceiver*;
- An observer is assumed to inevitably be a participant in what is observed;
- Interpretations are not assumed to be universal but situated – emerging from some specific place, time and social space;

- Cultures are best understood as changing networks of distinctive symbols and signifying practices, and therefore interpretation per se is conditioned by cultural perspectives and mediated by symbols and practices.

Thus the interpretive turn asserts an interesting relation between what those researched do (their own situated interpretations), and what researchers do (situated interpretations of others' situated interpretations).

To pursue research, social science inquiry must directly engage with this condition of the interpretation of interpretations. Social scientists must provide some account of what is being done and why. In these postpositivist times, if you do not wish to proceed by blurring boundaries and combining different genres or forms of relating to the real such as those used in art (novels, documentary photography, painting, etc.) or journalism, then you need to account for your use of one or several particular methodologies in doing your research.

For example, attending to the complexities in case study research today (such as studying a situation or a discourse, see Clarke and Keller, 2014) is not inquiry "after method" (see Law, 2004). Rather, it needs to be conducted with the accountability called for by an ethics of reflexivity. That is, we do not believe "anything goes" methodologically. Instead we are asserting that the researcher must account for what they have done, and moreover, do so reflexively. Regardless of earlier critiques of methods development, social science research still has to clarify what makes it valuable as a contribution to knowledge production.

Certainly and perhaps for good reason, one can advocate the blurring of genres and a general queering of disciplines as well as methods. But while there may be gains through such a stance, there may also be some important losses in terms of the analytic reach and richness of research. This is why we are insisting here on the need for methodologies in discourse research which *neither* fall into the trap of pure positivism *nor* accept the myth of pure artistic production and creativity. We are both, in our distinctive ways, attempting *not* to throw the social science research baby out with the bath water, however murky the latter may be. Sensitive, critical interpretive methodologies are and will continue to be useful in social science – and other – research (see Clarke, Friese and Washburn 2015, 2018; Keller, [2005] 2019).

The receptions with which the interpretive turn and its sub-turns were met varied tremendously. As we have seen, the dynamics of qualitative research development had already unfolded in quite different ways in the three countries in focus here. French research communities, at least in sociology, had generated rather individualistic approaches to qualitative perspectives, with different ethnographic perspectives as well as some influence of interactionism, narrative analysis and individualised method making. Germany followed a more institutionalised pattern wherein qualitative inquiry became a kind of identity anchor for a broad and established research community subdivided into an array of different competing and sometimes conflictual specific approaches and interests. In both France and Germany, some facets of the interpretive turn were taken up and others not.

In sharp contrast, in the US and UK contexts, by the late twentieth century, a deep and serious fissure had developed *within* worlds of qualitative inquiry essentially in reaction to postmodern and post-structural theories and their research implications essentially captured as "the interpretive turn". Those who largely eschewed the interpretive turn continued to advocate more "classical and scientific" approaches to qualitative research often with positivist tendencies, while others, more experimental, constructivist and critical in their perspectives, more enthusiastically advocated that turn, pursuing an array of new directions. They were varyingly inspired by social movements and political engagement with issues of race, gender, Indigenous rights and concern about participatory, decolonising and democratising potentials of research methods and orientations. The International Congress of Qualitative Inquiry, a highly international organization based in Urbana-Champaign, Illinois and initiated by critical interactionist Norman Denzin, became one haven for such interests (see Denzin, Lincoln and Smith, 2008). To date, and for many reasons, in both Germany and France there has been much less impact of such more political forms (discussed next) of the interpretive turn on research methodologies. There have also been some subsequent turns following the interpretive turn. Most were articulated by Anglo-American scholars and are referred to as the *visual turn* (e.g. Jay, 2002), the *body turn* (e.g. Gugutzer, 2006), the *affective turn* (e.g. Clough and Halley, 2007) and most recently, the *material turn* (e.g. Mukerji, 2015). Those turns can be seen as objections and corrections to a certain textual bias in research questions, research objects, data collection and analysis which have characterised qualitative and interpretive social research for quite some time. But given the interpretive turn's argument that *there is no escape from interpretation*, in considering affect, for example, you must *define* something as affect. Moreover, it must be defined as something different from, for example, calculated action. You classify, and in the very act of doing so, you therefore perform an interpretation.

At this historical point, these subsequent turns can be considered helpful suggestions about where to look next in research, possible turns ahead, or what else you might consider taking into account, methodologically. But they do not replace the basic arguments of interpretive research and methods. Moreover, this holds true for a quite different turn too which we might call the *political turn*, which centres on the challenging and sometimes existential question of *why we do research, for whom and with what (hoped for) benefits*. Again this political turn is having very different impacts in different countries, due to historical contexts, political developments and situations and many other factors. To date, its impact on qualitative methods in sociology beyond the core academic culture of various specialised "studies" (such as feminist and queer studies, disability studies, postcolonial studies, etc.) is rather low in Germany and France and other European contexts. In sharp contrast, impacts seem rather high in the US and in many countries in the southern hemisphere whose scholars are increasingly participating in transnational conversations about social science methodologies.

The political turn includes engagements by feminist, civil rights, anti-racist, queer, post- and decolonial, Indigenous and related scholars. Critiques of *both* qualitative and quantitative research in the U.S. since at least the 1980s have included, for example, having sexist, racist, classist, elitist, homophobic and/or voyeuristic colonialist tendencies. The feminist adage that "the personal is political", or "lived experience matters", was a key early generator of feminist research issues as well as the central tenet of consciousness-raising. Sociologist Patricia Hill Collins (1990) published perhaps the major anti-racist feminist statement as *Black Feminist Thought: Knowledge, Consciousness, and the Politics of Empowerment* still echoing loudly across the social sciences and humanities and increasingly around the world. The feminist anthropologists' response to the almost complete absence of women's voices in Clifford and Marcus's (1986) edited volume was *Women Writing Culture*, edited by Behar and Gordon (1995). Visweswaran's (1994) brilliant *Fictions of Feminist Ethnography* then integrated postcolonial, cultural and discourse concerns. More recently Phellas (2012) and others have attended to *Researching Non-Heterosexual Sexualities*. More broadly, there has been a spate of new books on critical research (e.g. Cannella, Pérez and Pasque, 2015; Denzin and Giardina, 2015), including critical auto-ethnography (e.g. Boylorn and Orbe, 2014) and critical interactionism (Jacobsen, 2019). There is even discussion of post-qualitative research (e.g. Lather and St. Pierre, 2013). How, when and where these will manifest next remains to be seen (see e.g. Denzin and Lincoln, 2018).

SKAD discourse research and the disciplines

Discourse means different things in different languages (for the following see Keller, 2013). In German, the word did not exist but was introduced centuries ago from other languages (most importantly Latin). Its newer usage was mainly influenced by German philosopher Jürgen Habermas and his "ethics of discourse" paradigm which refers to a normative setting of well-organised processes of discussion about conflictual issues (such as consensus-conferences or environmental mediation). Habermas' approach is linked to the idea that better arguments win, or at least prepare the ground for consensus-building between stakeholders in conflictual situations.

In English and French, the meanings of this term have been quite different. In everyday English, discourse simply means a conversation, a verbal interaction between people or a debate in the public sphere. In French (or Latin and related languages) *discours* (or *discorso*) is the usual term for a comprehensive serious speech act, such as a lecture, a treatise, a sermon, a presentation and more. "Public discourses" here also refers to debates in the public sphere, mediated by mass media.

The contemporary transnational and transdisciplinary field of discourse research contains a multiplicity of research methodologies and interests, influenced by traditions from linguistics, the humanities and the social sciences.[7] In sociology and the social sciences (including Birmingham Cultural Studies), interest in discourse research questions has been articulated throughout their history (as we noted above regarding Max Weber and the classics of the sociology of knowledge). But except for certain ideas in the works of Michel Foucault since the 1960s, and contributions from social movement research in symbolic interactionism in the 1970s also noted above, there has been little work on a methodology of discourse research for the social sciences. The major exception is the broad use of the concept of discourse for studying processes of "social construction" (see Hacking, 2000) via collective meaning making.

Here SKAD, much like situational analysis in a different realm, is an intervention which aims to strengthen social science interest in discourses as power/knowledge regimes, and discursive constructions of reality as major sites of current and ongoing highly consequential meaning making. In contrast to perspectives in discourse theory and research which pose a strong explanatory intent on the one hand (such as work inspired by Ernesto Laclau and Chantal Mouffe, see Howarth, Glynos and Griggs, 2016), and a rather narrow or loose usage of term on the other (see the discussion in Leipold, 2014), SKAD proposes a heuristics of discourse research based in the interpretive traditions of sociology and linked to methods.

So what then is the place of SKAD in the broader field of discourse research? In American structural and distributional linguistics, Zelig Harris (1952) initially introduced the term "discourse analysis" to characterise a precise structural-grammatical analysis of Native American languages. Here "discourse" referred to distinctive linguistic structures. Harris's approach became a source of inspiration for *quantitative* analyses of major text corpora in linguistics, including in France in the late 1960s, making interconnections between linguistics and history. In contrast, linguistic pragmatics is concerned with *language in use*, and has inspired conversational analysis since the 1960s, as well as "discourse analysis" as analysis of verbal interaction or textual genres (like news, media commentary, etc.) still lively today. Here the core focus is on micro-processes and structured patterns of language usage, verbal interaction and textual organisation or features of distinctive textual genres.

Another very influential intellectual tradition was initiated by Swiss linguist Ferdinand de Saussure ([1916] 1977) centred on his theory of language as sign system where each sign/meaning-relation depends on the particular position of this combination within a broader comprehensive system of signs. This theory was inspired by sociologist Emile Durkheim and his ideas about institutions as historically created social facts. Saussure became very influential in French structuralist philosophy and anthropology (e.g. in the work of Claude Lévi-Strauss) and eventually provoked post-structuralism as a counter-movement in philosophy and beyond.

Yet another thread of discourse research drew upon the pragmatist concept of "universes of discourse" as systems of shared symbols and meaning, especially in the work of George Herbert Mead (1934) and the linguistic theory established by Charles S. Peirce (1994; see Cefaï, 2016). In the 1930s and 1940s, Charles Morris (1946) presented a conception of different sub-universes of discourse within societies (such as fiction, mathematics, religion) which presaged later usages by French philosopher Michel Foucault.

Today, the most influential thinker in discourse research is Michel Foucault.[8] Across his career he moved from a more structural perspective centred on discourses as comprehensive formations or systems of meaning making, to a more pragmatist and poststructuralist view. In his later more pragmatist post-structural tradition, one asks: What do discourses and actors do in conflictual situations? How is meaning performed, made, and used in concrete discursive practices? While Foucauldian structuralism understood and investigated discourses as regulating systems, his post-structuralism turned attention to the interactions between (abstract) symbolic orders and the concrete use of language or signs, that is, the relationships among various structures and events (mostly linguistic actions or social practices).

Through Foucault's own empirical work and its reception in cultural studies, his ideas became the most influential usage of "discourse" today, probably around the globe, despite having a rather black-boxed methodology or, according to some, lacking a discernible one. In the British Birmingham cultural studies tradition, with Stuart Hall as a leading figure, Foucault was combined with interpretive, culturalist sociology from Weber to Gramsci, to symbolic interactionism. A variety of integrations of Foucault with other approaches has also occurred. "Discourse" here is used as a concept to analyse comprehensive processes of institutional or organisational meaning-making and knowledge production, as well as to inquire into current conflictual processes of discursive construction of realities.

Since the late 1980s and 1990s, a broad array of research approaches to discourse has emerged and many new methods have become established, demonstrating quite different interests and disciplinary backgrounds.

These approaches range from large corpus-based linguistics via pragmatics of language usage, to Critical Discourse Analysis (CDA) with its interest in unmasking ideological and discriminatory language usage, to Essex School interest in populist movement mobilisation and other political science concerns with arguing as political process, to social science analyses of world making via studies of knowledge production, public mobilisation, domination and other performances of symbolic universes (see Keller, 2013; Jaworski and Coupland, 2002; Wetherell, Taylor and Yates, 2001).

It seems to us that besides linguistic concerns, CDA (e.g. Fairclough, 2010) is currently the most prominent version of discourse research in Anglo-American contexts. In France, for example, despite the world wide success of Foucauldian thinking, and despite some experimentation between history and linguistics using particular versions of discourse analysis (e.g. Guilhaumou and Maldidier, 1995) there have not been any major developments in social sciences discourse research. Inquiry into discourse largely remains a linguistic domain, specifically within corpus linguistics and pragmatics (Maingueneau, 2017). In French sociology, research on environmental conflicts, known as a sociology of controversies, can be considered closer to interests in discursive meaning making as approached here (e.g. Chateauraynaud, 2011).

Since the 1990s, German linguistics as well as the social sciences more broadly have seen a proliferation of debates, development and discussion of newer approaches to discourse research. In fact, these maybe the most lively sites of discourse research development today (e.g. see Keller *et al.*, [2001] 2011; and the *Journal for Discourse Research/Zeitschrift für Diskursforschung*, established in 2013).

SKAD was introduced into this lively field in Germany in the late 1990s as an approach which, by integrating different theoretical traditions, seeks to provide a heuristics for a methodologically sound way of approaching discursive meaning making and discursive constructions of realities. SKAD argues for using research strategies and tools from the interpretive sociological tradition, especially from the sociology of knowledge, pragmatism and Foucault. Significant here, SKAD does *not* presuppose or imply a general and explanatory theory of what discourses are and how they perform the work they do in the world. Moreover, it does *not* seek to generate such a theory through the analytic work it does. Instead SKAD takes a case study approach, insisting that each case we deal with is *a case of its own sui generis*, or at least has to be approached as such, via a *heuristics of research* which ultimately provides some theorisation about that case, but does not offer a definite causal theory.

In this regard, SKAD has deep affinities with situational analysis (hereafter SA) as conceived by Adele Clarke as an extension of grounded theory at the turn of this century (see Clarke 2003, 2005; Clarke, Friese and Washburn, 2015, 2018). In fact both approaches were developed very much in parallel, but without being aware of the other for quite a while.

With pragmatist and interactionist roots through grounded theory, SA sought to move grounded theory fully around the postmodern and poststructural turns, explicitly integrating the analysis of discursive materials. SA also attends to the significance of nonhuman elements in situations, and attends assiduously to the relational ecologies of the situation.

SKAD sought to move the sociology of knowledge and interpretive research in German (and Anglo-American, etc.) contexts towards an interest in the work discourses do in contemporary societies. Such a move can be pursued using a methodology of discourse research designed for social science questions about discursive meaning making. SKAD argues for a re-orientation of discourse research toward questions of power/knowledge regimes, their processing through time, space and people and their actual impacts on fields of practices. As sociology of knowledge based research, it also has affinities with some social studies of science work. But distinct from some of its threads, SKAD insists that performances of knowledge and meaning making are present not only in science and technology fields, but can and must also be traced throughout societies and their heterogeneous fields of practices. Thus it may be useful to clarify the contingencies of relations of knowledge and knowing, and the politics of knowledge and knowing, as well as their effects in our current moment. Again SKAD is situated close to Foucauldian ideas of experimentation and critique (see Keller, 2017a, 2017b).

Outlook

In a millennial review, two main themes in current qualitative inquiry in Europe were discerned by Knoblauch, Flick and Maeder (2005): *diversity* manifesting in an array of new approaches, and *unity* through sharing the interpretive paradigm. They also remind us that qualitative inquiries are "imprinted by cultures ... their surrounding institutions, traditions and political as well as economic contexts" (Knoblauch, Flick and Maeder 2005: §4). But today's pressures for using English as a common language in academia risks our ending up with a rather hegemonic constellation of Anglo-American traditions and approaches. We risk ignoring or excluding rich traditions from *out there* or *down there* due to the fact that they are based in different epistemological cultures or emerge from other continents, despite the efforts of some handbook projects to try to make them more visible (e.g. from Germany to the Anglo-American public, see Flick, 2014; for Indigenous methodologies, see Denzin, Lincoln and Smith, 2008).

There are today more intentionally transnational venues for publication about research, such as the new *International Review of Qualitative Research* and *International Journal of Social Research Methodology*, but still in English. The *Journal for Discourse Studies* (edited by Reiner Keller, Werner Schneider and Willy Viehöver) was founded in 2013 and publishes articles from authors all over the world in either German or English. The online journal *FQS: Forum: Qualitative Social Research/Sozialforschung* innovatively offers abstracts of everything in English while articles may be in some other languages, allowing much broader access for scholars not from the West but from what Stuart Hall (1996) called "the rest".

While some have lamented the profusion of new approaches in qualitative inquiry (e.g. Hammersley, 2008: 181), in contrast, we agree with political scientists Yanow and Schwartz-Shea (2006: 390): "If knowledge is power, then methodological pluralism disperses that power, whereas 'one best way' concentrates it. Reembracing interpretive approaches as a legitimate scientific undertaking, then, strengthens both the human sciences and democracy". Using interpretive qualitative inquiry to strengthen democracy is a critical and increasingly urgent task for decades to come all over the planet.

Notes

1 One of us, Adele Clarke, was fortunate to take part in the group discussions the book refers to. The other of us, Reiner Keller, was trained in similar procedures but much later and in quite different contexts.
2 It can be seen as a theory-methods package, according to the terms Susan Leigh Star (1989) applied to grounded theory.
3 E.g. both Robert E. Park and Talcott Parsons earned their PhDs in Germany; other pragmatist philosophers and sociologists also studied and travelled in Germany in the early twentieth century.
4 We can see echoes of this in feminist standpoint epistemologies (e.g. Sandra Harding, 2003) and theories of situated knowledge (e.g. Donna Haraway, 1988).
5 Ironically, this was a contribution to a Festschrift for critical theorist Max Horkheimer.
6 In 2005, the original SKAD book had carefully noted the affinities between Michel Foucault and pragmatism (Keller, [2005] 2010: 150; see in addition Keller 2008, 2017b). Richard Rorty (1982) and Nancy Fraser (1997) had made similar arguments. On pragmatism and French post-structuralism today, see e.g. Bignall, Bowden and Patton (2014), and the Special Issue of *Foucault Studies* (2011) on Foucault and Pragmatism, especially Koopman (2011a, 2011b).
7 This includes discursive psychology, argumentative discourse analysis, critical discourse analysis, discursive institutionalism, Essex school discourse research, corpus linguistics, pragmatics and many others. A more detailed discussion of the area of discourse research, including full references, is given in Keller (2013).
8 See Keller (2017b) and Keller on SKAD (Chapter 2, this volume) for a summary discussion and further references.

References

Bachmann-Medick, D. (2006). *Cultural Turns. Neuorientierungen in den Kulturwissenschaften.* Reinbek bei Hamburg: Rowohlt. [Cultural Turns. New Orientations within Studies of Culture.]

Barton, A. H. and Lazarsfeld, P. F. (1955). Some Functions of Qualitative Analysis in Social Research. In: T. W. Adorno and W. Dirks, eds., *Sociologica. Aufsätze, Max Horkheimer zum sechzigsten Geburtstag gewidmet. Frankfurter Beiträge zur Soziologie Bd.*

1. Frankfurt am Main: Europäische Verlagsanstalt, 321–361. [In: *Sociologica. Festschrift for Max Horkheimer's 60th birthday.*]

Becker, H. S. (1963). *Outsiders: Studies in the Sociology of Deviance.* New York: The Free Press.

Behar, R. and Gordon, D. A. (1995). *Women Writing Culture.* Berkeley: University of California Press.

Benford, R. D. and Snow, D. A., eds. (2000). Framing Processes and Social Movements: An Overview and Assessment. *Annual Review of Sociology*, 26, 611–639.

Berelson, B. (1952). *Content Analysis in Communication Research.* New York: Hafner.

Berger, P. and Luckman, T. (1966). *The Social Construction of Reality: A Treatise in the Sociology of Knowledge.* Garden City, NY: Doubleday.

Bignall, S., Bowden, S. and Patton, P., eds. (2014). *Deleuze and Pragmatism.* London: Routledge.

Blumer, H. (1933). *Movies and Conduct.* New York: The McMillan Company.

Blumer, H. (1958). Race Prejudice as a Sense of Group Position. *Pacific Sociological Review*, 1, 3–8.

Blumer, H. (1969). *Symbolic Interactionism: Perspective and Method.* Englewood Cliffs, NJ: Prentice Hall.

Bohnsack, R. (2014). Documentary Method. In: U. Flick, ed., *The SAGE Handbook of Qualitative Data Analysis.* London/Thousand Oaks: Sage, 217–233.

Bourdieu, P. ([1979] 2010). *Distinction.* London: Routledge.

Bourdieu, P., Chamboredon, J.-C. and Passeron, J.-C. ([1968] 1991). *The Craft of Sociology: Epistemological Preliminaries.* Berlin: de Gruyter.

Boylorn, R. M. and Orbe, M. P., eds. (2014). *Critical Autoethnography: Intersecting Cultural Identities in Everyday Life.* Walnut Creek, CA: Left Coast Press.

Cannella, G., Pérez, M. and Pasque, P., eds. (2015). *Critical Qualitative Inquiry: Foundations and Futures.* Walnut Creek, CA: Left Coast Press.

Cefaï, D. (2016). Social Worlds: The Legacy of Mead's Social Ecology in Chicago Sociology. In: H. Joas and D. Huebner, eds., *The Timeliness of G. H. Mead.* Chicago: University of Chicago Press, 164–184.

Charmaz, K. (2000). Grounded Theory: Objectivist and Constructivist Methods. In: N. Denzin and Y. Lincoln, eds., *Handbook of Qualitative Research.* 2nd edn. Thousand Oaks, CA: Sage, 509–536.

Charmaz, K. (2006). *Constructing Grounded Theory: A Practical Guide Through Qualitative Analysis.* London: Sage.

Charmaz, K. (2014). *Constructing Grounded Theory: A Practical Guide Through Qualitative Analysis.* 2nd edn. London: Sage.

Chateauraynaud, F. (2011). *Argumenter dans un champ de forces. Essai de balistique sociologique.* Paris: Edition Petra.

Clarke, A. E. (2003). Situational Analyses: Grounded Theory Mapping After the Postmodern Turn. *Symbolic Interaction*, 26(4), 553–576.

Clarke, A. E. (2005). *Situational Analysis: Grounded Theory After the Postmodern Turn.* Thousand Oaks, CA: Sage.

Clarke, A. E. and Keller, R. (2014). Engaging Complexities: Working Against Simplification as an Agenda for Qualitative Research Today. *FQS Forum: Qualitative Social Research*, [online] 15(2), Art.1, available at: www.qualitative-research.net/index.php/fqs/article/view/2186/3667 [Accessed 06 March 2018].

Clarke, A. E., Friese, C. and Washburn, R., eds. (2015). *Situational Analysis in Practice: Mapping Research with Grounded Theory.* Walnut Creek, CA: Left Coast Press.

Clarke, A. E., Friese, C. and Washburn, R., eds. (2018). *Situational Analysis: Grounded Theory After the Interpretive Turn.* 2nd edn. Thousand Oaks, CA: Sage.
Clifford, J. and Marcus, G. (1986). *Writing Culture: The Poetics and Politics of Ethnography.* Berkeley: University of California Press.
Clough, P. and Halley, J., eds. (2007). *The Affective Turn: Theorizing the Social.* Durham NC: Duke University Press.
Collins, P. H. (1990). *Black Feminist Thought: Knowledge, Consciousness, and the Politics of Empowerment.* Boston: Unwin Hyman.
Comte, A. ([1830–42] 1989). *Cours de philosophie positive [Première et Deuxième leçons].* Paris: Nathan.
Coulon, A. (1995). *Ethnomethodology.* London: Sage.
Denzin, N. (1989). *Interpretive Interactionism.* Newbury Park, CA: Sage.
Denzin, N. (2001). *Interpretive Interactionism.* 2nd edn. Newbury Park, CA: Sage.
Denzin, N. and Lincoln, Y. S., eds. (1994). *The Sage Handbook of Qualitative Research.* Thousand Oaks, CA: Sage.
Denzin, N., Lincoln, Y. and Tuhiwai Smith, L., eds. (2008). *Handbook of Critical and Indigenous Methodologies.* Thousand Oaks, CA: Sage.
Denzin, N. K. and Giardina, M. D., eds. (2015). *Qualitative Inquiry—Past, Present, and Future: A Critical Reader.* London: Routledge.
Denzin, Norman K. and Lincoln, Yvonna S. (2018). *The SAGE Handbook of Qualitative Research.* 5th edn. Thousand Oaks, CA: Sage.
Dewey. J. (1927). *The Public and its Problems.* New York: Henry Holt.
Dilthey, W. (1989). *Selected Works Volume 4. Hermeneutics and the Study of History.* R. A. Makkreel and F. Rodi, eds. Princeton: Princeton University Press.
Dreyfus, H. L. and Rabinow, P. (1983). *Michel Foucault. Beyond Structuralism and Hermeneutics.* 2nd edn. Chicago: The University of Chicago Press.
Durkheim, E. ([1912] 2008). *The Elementary Forms of Religious Life.* Oxford: Oxford University Press.
Durkheim, E. and Mauss, M. ([1903] 1963). *Primitive Classification.* Chicago: The University of Chicago Press.
Engels, F. ([1845] 2009). *The Condition of the Working Class in England.* London: Penguin.
Fairclough, N. (2010). *Critical Discourse Analysis: The Critical Study of Language.* 2nd edn. London: Routledge.
Fleck. L. ([1935] 1981). *Genesis and Development of a Scientific Fact.* Chicago: University of Chicago Press.
Flick, U., ed. (2014). *The SAGE Handbook of Qualitative Data Analysis.* London/Thousand Oaks, CA/Dehli: Sage.
Fontana, A. (2005). The Postmodern Turn in Interactionism. *Studies in Symbolic Interaction,* 28, 239–254.
Foucault, M. (1980). *Power/Knowledge: Selected Interviews and Other Writings, 1972–1977.* New York. Vintage.
Foucault Studies (2011). *Foucault and Pragmatism,* Special Issue: Pragmatism, 11.
Fraser, N. (1997). Structuralism or Pragmatics? On Discourse Theory and Feminist Politics. In: Nicholson, Linda, ed., *The Second Wave: A Reader in Feminist Theory.* New York: Routledge, 379–395.
Gamson, W. A. and Modigliani, A. (1989). Media Discourse and Public Opinion on Nuclear Power: A Constructionist Approach. *American Journal of Sociology,* 95(1), 1–37.

Garfinkel, H. ([1967] 1984). *Studies in Ethnomethodology.* Cambridge: Polity Press.
Geertz, C. (1973). *The Interpretation of Cultures: Selected Essays.* New York: Basic Books.
Glaser, B. G. (1992). *Basics of Grounded Theory Analysis: Emergence Versus Forcing.* Mill Valley, CA: Sociology Press.
Glaser, B. G. and Strauss, A. L. (1967). *Discovery of Grounded Theory: Strategies for Qualitative Research.* New York: Aldine.
Goffman, E. (1974). *Frame Analysis: An Essay on the Organization of Experience.* Cambridge, MA: Harvard University Press.
Gugutzer, R., ed. (2006). *Body Turn: Perspektiven der Soziologie des Körpers und des Sports.* Bielefeld: transcript. [Body Turn: Perspectives in Sociology of the Body and of Sports.]
Guilhaumou, J. and Maldidier, D. (1995). *Discours et archive: Expérimentations en analyse du discours.* Liège: Mardaga.
Gusfield, J. (1981). *The Culture of Public Problems.* Chicago: University of Chicago Press.
Habermas, J. ([1967] 1988). *On the Logic of the Social Sciences.* Cambridge, MA: MIT Press.
Hacking, I. (2000). *The Social Construction of What?* Cambridge, MA: Harvard University Press.
Hall, S. (1996). The West and the Rest. In: S. Hall, D. Held, D. Hubert and K. Thompson, eds., *Modernity: An Introduction to Modern Societies.* Malden, MA: Blackwell, 184–201.
Hammersley, M. (2008). *Questioning Qualitative Inquiry: Critical Essays.* London: Sage.
Haraway, D. (1988). Situated Knowledges: The Science Question in Feminism and the Privilege of Partial Perspective. *Feminist Studies,* 14(3), 575–599.
Harding, S., ed. (2003). *The Feminist Standpoint Theory Reader: Intellectual and Political Controversies.* London: Routledge.
Harris, Z. S. (1952). Discourse Analysis. *Language,* 28(1), 1–30.
Hilgartner, S. and Bosk, C. L. (1988). The Rise and Fall of Social Problems: A Public Arenas Model. *American Journal of Sociology,* 94(1), 53–78.
Hitzler, R. and Honer, A. (1997). Einleitung: Hermeneutik in der deutschsprachigen Soziologie heute. In: R. Hitzler and A. Honer, eds., *Sozialwissenschaftliche Hermeneutik. Eine Einführung.* Opladen: Leske and Budrich (UTB), 7–27. [Introduction: Hermeneutics in Current German Sociology/In: Social Sciences Hermeneutics. An Introduction.]
Horkheimer, M. and Adorno, T. W. (1960). Vorwort. In: W. Mangold, *Gegenstand und Methode des Gruppendiskussionsverfahrens. Aus der Arbeit des Instituts für Sozialforschung.* Frankfurt/M.: Europäische Verlagsanstalt, 5–8. [Preface/In: The method and subject matter of group discussions. From the ongoing work of the Institute for Social Research (Frankfurt).]
Howarth, D, Glynos, J. and Griggs, S. (2016). Discourse, Explanation and Critique. *Critical Policy Studies,* 10(1), 99–104.
Jacobsen, M. H., ed. (2019). *Critical and Cultural Interactionism.* London: Routledge.
Jaworski, A. and Coupland, N., eds. (2002). *The Discourse Reader.* New York: Routledge.
Jay, M. (2002). That Visual Turn. *Journal of Visual Culture,* 1, 87.
Keller, R. (2008). *Michel Foucault.* Konstanz: Universitätsverlag Konstanz.

Keller, R. ([2005] 2010): *Wissenssoziologische Diskursanalyse. Grundlegung eines Forschungsprogramms*. 3rd edn. Wiesbaden: Springer VS. [The Sociology of Knowledge Approach to Discourse. Grounds for a Research Agenda.]

Keller, R. (2011). The Sociology of Knowledge Approach to Discourse (SKAD). *Human Studies*, 34(1), 43–65.

Keller, R. (2012). *Das interpretative Paradigma*. Wiesbaden: VS-Verlag für Sozialwissenschaften. [The Interpretive Paradigm.]

Keller, R. (2013). *Doing Discourse Research: An Introduction for Social Scientists*. London: Sage.

Keller, R. (2015). Weber und Foucault. Interpretation, Hermeneutik und Wissenssoziologische Diskursanalyse. In: R. Keller, W. Schneider, W. Viehöver, eds., *Diskurs – Interpretation – Hermeneutik. 1. Beiheft der Zeitschrift für Diskursforschung*. Weinheim: Beltz Juventa, 173–210. [Weber and Foucault. Interpretation, Hermeneutics and the Sociology of Knowledge Approach to Discourse. In: *Discourse – Interpretation – Hermeneutics. 1st supplement to the Journal for Discourse Studies*.]

Keller, R. (2017a). Has Critique Run Out of Steam? On Discourse Research as Critical Inquiry. Printversion. *Qualitative Inquiry. Special Issue: Challenges for a New Critical Qualitative Inquiry*, 23(1), 58–68.

Keller, R. (2017b). Michel Foucault. In: R. Wodak and B. Forchtner, eds., *The Routledge Handbook of Language and Power*. London: Routledge, 67–81.

Keller, R. ([2005] 2019). *The Sociology of Knowledge Approach to Discourse. Grounds for a Research Agenda*. New York: Springer [forthcoming].

Keller, R., Hirseland, A., Schneider, W. and Viehöver, W., eds. ([2001] 2011). *Handbuch Sozialwissenschaftliche Diskursanalyse Bd. 1: Theorien und Methoden*. 3rd edn. Wiesbaden: VS-Verlag. [Handbook for Discourse Analysis in the Social Sciences: Vol. 1: Theories and Methods.]

Keller, R. and Poferl, A. (2016). Soziologische Wissenskulturen zwischen individualisierter Inspiration und prozeduraler Legitimation. Zur Entwicklung qualitativer und interpretativer Sozialforschung in der deutschen und französischen Soziologie seit den 1960er Jahren. *Forum Qualitative Sozialforschung /Forum: Qualitative Social Research*, [online] 17(1), Art. 14, Available at: http://nbn-resolving. de/urn:nbn:de:0114-fqs1601145 [Accessed 01 March 2018]. [Epistemic Cultures in Sociology between Individual Inspiration and Legitimization by Procedure: Developments of Qualitative and Interpretive Research in German and French Sociology since the 1960s.]

Knoblauch, H., Flick, U. and Maeder, C. (2005). Qualitative Methods in Europe: The Variety of Social Research. *FQS Forum: Qualitative Social Research*, [online] 6(3), Art. 34. Available at: www.qualitative-research.net/index.php/fqs/article/view/3/8 [Accessed 06 March 2018].

Koopman, C. (2011a). Foucault and Pragmatism: Introductory Notes on Metaphilosophical Methodology. *Foucault Studies*, 11, 3–10.

Koopman, C. (2011b). Genealogical Pragmatism: How History Matters for Foucault and Dewey. *Journal of the Philosophy of History*, 5, 533–561.

Lather, P. and St. Pierre, E. A. (2013). Post-Qualitative Research. *International Journal of Qualitative Studies in Education*, 26(6), 629–633.

Law, J. (2004). *After Method: Mess in Social Science Research*. London: Routledge.

Leipold, S. (2014): Creating Forests with Words – A Review of Forest-related Discourse Studies. *Forest Policy and Economics*, 40, 12–20.

Maingueneau, D. (2017). *Discours et analyse du discours: Une introduction.* Paris: Armand Colin. [Discourse and Discourse Analysis. An Introduction.]

Mangold, W. (1960). *Gegenstand und Methode des Gruppendiskussionsverfahrens. Aus der Arbeit des Instituts für Sozialforschung.* Frankfurt/M.: Europäische Verlagsanstalt. [The Method and Subject Matter of Group Discussions. From the Ongoing Work of the Institute for Social Research (Frankfurt).]

Mannheim, K. (1936). *Ideology and Utopia.* London: Routledge.

Mannheim, K. (1952). On the Interpretation of Weltanschauung. In: K. Mannheim, *Essays in the Sociology of Knowledge.* London: Routledge & Kegan Paul, 33–83.

Mannheim, K. ([1922–24] 1980). *Structures of Thinking.* London: Routledge & Kegan Paul.

Mannheim, K. ([1925] 1986). *Conservatism. A Contribution to the Sociology of Knowledge.* London: Routledge & Kegan Paul.

Marx, K. and Engels, F. ([1846] 2011). *The German Ideology.* Eastford: Martino Fine Books.

Mead, G. H. (1934). *Mind, Self, and Society: From the Standpoint of a Social Behaviorist.* Chicago: University of Chicago Press.

Mills, C. W. (1940): Situated Actions and Vocabularies of Motive. *American Sociological Review,* 5(6), 904–913.

Mills, C. W. (1959). *The Sociological Imagination.* New York: Oxford University Press.

Morris, C. W. (1946). *Signs, Language and Behavior.* New York: Prentice-Hall.

Morse, J., Stern, P. N., Corbin, J., Bowers, B., Charmaz, K. and Clarke, A. E. (2009). *Developing Grounded Theory: The Second Generation.* Walnut Creek, CA: Left Coast Press.

Mukerji, C. (2015). *The Material Turn. Emerging Trends in the Social and Behavioral Sciences: An Interdisciplinary, Searchable, and Linkable Resource,* 1–13.

Palmer, Vivien M. (1928). *Field Studies in Sociology.* Chicago: University of Chicago Press.

Peirce, C. S. (1994). *Peirce on Signs: Writings on Semiotic.* J. Hoopes, ed. Chapel Hill, North Carolina: University of North Carolina Press.

Phellas, C. N., ed. (2012). *Researching Non-Heterosexual Sexualities.* Farnham, UK: Ashgate.

Pratt, M. L. (1992). *Imperial Eyes: Travel Writing and Transculturation.* London: Routledge.

Qualitative Sociology Review (2014). *Special Issue: 70th Jubilee of Professor Fritz Schütze.* [online] 10(1). Available at: www.qualitativesociologyreview.org/ENG/volume28.php [Accessed 06 March 2018].

Rabinow, P. and Sullivan, W. (1987a). The Interpretive Turn: A Second Look. In: P. Rabinow, and W. Sullivan, eds., *Interpretive Social Science: A Second Look.* Berkeley: University of California Press, 1–32.

Rabinow, P. and Sullivan, W., eds. ([1979] 1987b). *Interpretive Social Science: A Second Look.* 2nd edn. Berkeley: University of California Press.

Reynolds, L. and Herman-Kinney, N., eds. (2003). *Handbook of Symbolic Interactionism.* Walnut Creek, CA: AltaMira Press.

Ricoeur, P. (1970). *Freud and Philosophy: An Essay on Interpretation.* New Haven: Yale University Press.

Rorty, R. (1982). *Consequences of Pragmatism.* Minneapolis: University of Minnesota Press.

Rorty, R., ed. ([1967] 1992). *The Linguistic Turn.* 2nd edn. Chicago: University of Chicago Press.
Rosaldo, R. (1989). *Culture and Truth: The Remaking of Social Analysis.* Boston: Beacon.
Saussure, F. de ([1916] 1977). *Course in General Linguistics.* Glasgow: Fontana/Collins.
Schütz, A. ([1932] 1967). *The Phenomenology of the Social World.* Evanston: Northwestern University Press.
Schütz, A. (1973a). *Collected Papers Vol. I-III.* M. Natanson, ed. The Hague: Nijhoff.
Schütz, A. (1973b). Common-Sense and Scientific Interpretation of Human Action. In: A. Schütz, *Collected Papers Vol. I.* M. Natanson, ed. The Hague: Nijhoff, 3–47.
Schütz, A. and Luckmann, T. (1973). *Structures of the Lifeworld. Vol. 1 and 2.* Evanston: Northwestern University Press.
Schütze, F. (2008a). Biography Analysis on the Empirical Base of Autobiographical Narratives: How to Analyse Autobiographical Narrative Interviews. Part 1. *European Studies on Inequalities and Social Cohesion,* [online] 1/2, 153–242. Available at: www.profit.uni.lodz.pl/pub/dok/6ca34cbaf07ece58cbd1b4f24371c8c8/European_Studies_2008_vol_1.pdf [Accessed 06 March 2018].
Schütze, F. (2008b). Biography Analysis on the Empirical Base of Autobiographical Narratives: How to Analyse Autobiographical Narrative Interviews. Part 2. *European Studies on Inequalities and Social Cohesion,* [online] 3/4, 6–77. Available at: www.profit.uni.lodz.pl/pub/dok/6ca34cbaf07ece58cbd1b4f24371c8c8/European_Studies_2008_vol_2.pdf [Accessed 06 March 2018].
Soeffner, H.-G. (2004). *Auslegung des Alltags – Der Alltag der Auslegung. Zur wissenssoziologischen Konzeption einer sozialwissenschaftlichen Hermeneutik.* Konstanz: UVK/UTB. [Interpreting the Everyday – Everyday Aspects of Interpretation. On Sociology of Knowledge Conceptualization of Hermeneutics in Social Sciences.]
Star, S. L. (1989). *Regions of the Mind: Brain Research and the Quest for Scientific Certainty.* Stanford, CA: Stanford University Press.
Strauss, A. L. (1987). *Qualitative Research for Social Scientists.* Cambridge: University Press.
Strauss, A. L. ([1959] 1997). *Mirrors and Masks: The Search for Identity.* London and New York: Routledge.
Strauss, A. L. and Corbin, J. (1990). *The Basics of Qualitative Research: Grounded Theory Procedures and Techniques.* Newbury Park, CA: Sage.
Strauss, A. L. and Corbin, J. (1998). *The Basics of Qualitative Research: Grounded Theory Procedures and Techniques.* 2nd edn. Newbury Park, CA: Sage.
Thomas, W. I. ([1923] 1978). The Definition of the Situation. In: R. Farrell and V. Swigert, eds., *Social Deviance.* Philadelphia: Lippincott, 54–57.
Thomas, W. I. and Znaniecki, F. (1918). *The Polish Peasant in Europe and America.* Chicago: University of Illinois Press.
Thomas, W. I. and Thomas, D. S. ([1928] 1970). Situations Defined as Real Are Real in Their Consequences. In: G. P. Stone and H. A. Farberman, eds., *Social Psychology Through Symbolic Interaction.* Waltham, MA: Xerox College Publishing, 154–155.
Ulrich, P. and Keller, R. (2014). Comparing Discourse Between Cultures. A Discursive Approach to Movement Knowledge. In: B. Baumgarten, P. Daphi and P. Ulrich, eds., *Conceptualizing Culture in Social Movement Research.* Hampshire: Palgrave, 113–139.

Visweswaran, K. (1994). *Fictions of Feminist Ethnography.* Minneapolis: University of Minnesota Press.

Weber, M. ([1904] 1949). *On the Methodology of the Social Sciences.* Illinois: The Free Press of Glencoe.

Weber, M. ([1904/1905] 2002). *The Protestant Ethic and the "Spirit" of Capitalism and other Writings.* London: Penguin.

Wernet, A. (2014). Hermeneutics and Objective Hermeneutics. In: U. Flick, ed., *The SAGE Handbook of Qualitative Data Analysis.* London/Thousand Oaks, CA/ Dehli: Sage, 234–246.

Wetherell, M., Taylor, S. and Yates, S., eds. (2001). *Discourse Theory and Practice: A Reader.* London: Sage.

Wilson, T. P. (1970). Normative and Interpretive Paradigms in Sociology. In: J. D. Douglas, ed., *Understanding Everyday Life: Towards a Reconstruction of Sociological Knowledge.* Chicago: Aldine Publishing, 57–70.

Yanow, D. and Schwartz-Shea. P. (2006). *Interpretation and Method: Empirical Research Methods and the Interpretive Turn.* New York: Routledge.

Zola, E. ([1885] 2004). *Germinal.* London: Penguin.

4 The social construction of value
A comparative SKAD analysis of public discourses on waste in France and Germany

Reiner Keller

Introduction

In December 1971, a letter to the German weekly *DER SPIEGEL* stated that as in former times when people had to be taught about basic ethical rules and personal hygiene, the moment had arrived when they had to be educated in the control of their waste-production (*DER SPIEGEL*, No. 51, 13.12.1971). This somehow signalled the beginning of a long struggle concerning ecological citizenship, responsible consumption, ecological modernisation, waste reduction, separation, recycling and waste-related policies, which has continued ever since. Right now, we are still producing rubbish, litter, garbage, waste, trash and detritus not only in household consumption, but in resource extraction and the production and distribution of goods. And don't forget journalistic and academic processes of waste production, where the leitmotifs "bring new facts" and "innovate" serve to devalue yesterday's truths. It cannot be avoided: all that is solid thereby melts into the air, or ends up in a disposal. The social destruction of values is a well-established historical process inherent to the core dynamics of (plural, entangled) modern societies. It might be considered the hidden driver of capitalist economics, cultural enlightenment, acceleration and "progress". The discursive construction of value in waste policies and ecological discourses in general is one counterattack to this storm which blows us into the future (to paraphrase Walter Benjamin's interpretation of Paul Klee's "Angel of history", which, to be honest, had a much more terrible background and reference):

> A Klee painting named "Angelus Novus" shows an angel looking as though he is about to move away from something he is fixedly contemplating. His eyes are staring, his mouth is open, his wings are spread. This is how one pictures the angel of history. His face is turned toward the past. Where we perceive a chain of events, he sees one single catastrophe which keeps piling wreckage upon wreckage and hurls it in front of his feet. The angel would like to stay, awaken the dead, and make whole what has been smashed. But a storm is blowing

from Paradise; it has got caught in his wings with such violence that the angel can no longer close them. This storm irresistibly propels him into the future to which his back is turned, while the pile of debris before him grows skyward. This storm is what we call progress.

(Benjamin, [1940] 1969: 257–258)

The present contribution resumes a sociology of knowledge approach to discourse (SKAD) study of public debates and policies on household waste in France and Germany conducted by the author (Keller, [1998] 2009). During a three-year period, it dealt with twenty-five years of public debate on disciplining household waste production. As such, that research can be considered the starting point of what is now established as the sociology of knowledge approach to discourse (e.g. Keller, 2011, 2012, 2019).

The study of waste discourses and policies originally started with a frame analytical approach informed by social movement research, especially Gamson and Modigliani (1989) and related texts and arguments, but for several reasons (see Ulrich and Keller, 2014) I soon moved away from that towards an interpretive approach based on the sociology of knowledge and Michel Foucault (Keller, 2018). The research covered public discourses about waste problems, "good" waste policies, problems of waste management technology, the value of goods and nature, the scarcity of raw materials and the dynamics of consumer society and solutions to linked problems in France and Germany. Its primary concern was the interpretive schemes and meaning-making processes of involved speakers and in institutional structures, that is orders of discourse, apparent in those countries between 1970 and 1995 (Keller, [1998] 2009). As do the other examples presented in this book, it represents one way of making use of SKAD. It is not the only, or necessarily the best way of doing it. Other research interests and questions need designs of their own, proceedings adapted to their proper purpose. That research was part of a larger research network interested in ecological communication and discourses in Germany and several European countries (France, Ireland, Italy and Spain). As SKAD theory and methodology are presented in some detail in earlier chapters in this book, the following text focuses on the concrete way of doing a SKAD analysis: (1) starting with questions, (2) setting the scene, (3) collecting data, (4) analysing the data and (5) telling a story.

Starting with questions

As has been explained in the initial chapters of this book, SKAD establishes a research programme which is interested in the social relations of knowledge and the social politics of knowledge as they are manifest in the discursive construction, transformation, stabilisation and destruction of realities. It therefore supplies research with a theory of its object (discourses) and the conditions for existence of such an object. It further provides a reflexive methodology of interpretation which accounts for its basic condition of producing a discourse about discourses. And it offers various methods or strategies for sampling and analysing data and telling a story about the object of inquiry (Becker and Keller, 2016). Therefore the core questions of a SKAD project are directed towards the specific object of inquiry: what kind of discursive processes and spheres can be observed? Who is speaking and who is not? What kinds of argument and legitimation are in play? What kinds of phenomena are established through discursive meaning making? How do they relate to each other? How do they emerge, stabilise and change over time? Are there competing problematisations? What is the role of actors and events in such processes of discursive structuration? What resources are in play? What effects can be observed? And so on.

These are very general questions, which can be addressed to rather different issues. But concrete research needs some more concrete questions, too, in order to choose and work upon its subject. In the present case, my research interests were based on several elements:

- the just-mentioned research context of studying ecological communication in European countries, which is based on the observation of sharply contrasting environmental protest movements and their impacts in different European countries;
- my language skills in French coupled with my interest in French sociology and "French ways of life" led me to argue against social science research which assumed, at the time given, that "different national mentalities" in both countries – a "Cartesian mentality" in France and a "Romantic spirit" in Germany – accounted for the differences;
- an interest in the social processes that create, evaluate and destroy the value of ideas, men, practices, objects and "nature", combined with a certain scepticism towards public, state and organisational rituals of ecological performance;
- an interest in the sociological debates on "Risk Society" (Beck, 1992) and "reflexive modernization" (Beck, Giddens and Lash, 1994) and their empirical evidence.

The assumption that environmental debates and ecological conflicts are the ways in which ecological issues are performed as and through discourses does not ignore the role of "real problems" or "real facts and events". Instead it fully acknowledges that the reality of a problem is constituted via discursive meaning making and how such meaning making reacts to the worldly given, which by itself can be considered the effect of previous discursive meaning making, human action and non-human involvements, institutions and materiality. Such an approach rejects the pure influence of "the given" factual problems, political systems, national and cultural traditions as explanatory factors for differences in ecological mobilisation and communication. It accordingly enquires into the discursive performances which establish and sometimes transform such "givens" through time, space and social settings.

The basic research design was developed in late 1992 and early 1993. Following on from the events of the 1980s, there was at that time considerable evidence of the rather different ways that ecological concerns and risk issues were resonating in France and Germany. Germany was experiencing an extremely high degree of environmental-movement mobilisation against the risks of nuclear energy usage, dying forests, air pollution and whatever. France, in contrast, had seen far less of this kind of mobilisation, except for some intensive protests against nuclear energy plants in the 1970s. I spent the first half of 1986 in France, where I learned, via the French press and government releases after the Chernobyl catastrophe, that the Germans once again had been taken over by their irrational "Angst" and that, no matter what had happened, there were no effects of radiation in France (decades later, the French government had to acknowledge that it simply lied about that).

If we do not take for granted that such differences are due to some "factual evidence", then the collective definition of the situation, that is, the impact of discourses, comes into play. A comparative study of those two countries as sites or arenas for discursive production must not be regarded as a return to methodological nationalism. On the contrary, there are still good arguments for such comparative work. First, even taking into account a wider European Union framework for environmental regulation, both countries have been (and still are) the political sites for decision making about waste policies concerning their territory and resource management (incoming and outgoing flows and the regulation of pollution and of technical devices in waste treatment and so forth). Second, according to Foucault, we can understand a state or a nation as a permanent performative outcome of discursive meaning making, institutionalised practices and their integration and transformation via contestation, conflict, or adaptation to new situations.

Concerning waste in both countries, especially household waste, there was a common point of departure, without which such a study could not have been developed: these countries are not only neighbours, they are similar in terms of wealth, population, industrial structures and consumption schemes. In both France and Germany, waste had become an issue, a problem to deal with, simply as a result of the fact of growing wealth and changing patterns of consumption after World War II, and more precisely, since the early 1960s, with the arrival of supermarkets, plastics, one-way usage packaging and discussions about planned obsolescence. In both countries since the mid-sixties, local administrations have had to seek new and larger sites of waste disposal. Both countries since the 1970s have enacted several federal laws and other regulations in order to "govern" waste making. When my research started in 1993, household waste was, as a result of then-current law making, a hot topic on the public and political agendas in France and in Germany. At that time the research addressed the following core questions:

- Are there any differences between public discourses and policies on household waste issues? How are waste problems constructed in discursive processes, with what resources and what effects and by which actors and responsibilities? Which interpretive schemes appear and how do they perform the discursive construction of household waste in order to present it as a matter of urgency that must be dealt with, or as simply another example of "fake news"?
- How can any differences (or similarities) be accounted for?
- How can such results be interpreted against the theories of reflexive modernisation and risk society, or other current theoretical debates in sociology?

Setting the scene

In preparing and doing the research, I read a considerable amount of academic literature on waste, capitalism, consumption and the social meaning of things (objects), such as Thompson's theory of rubbish published in 1979 (Thompson, 2017). Moreover, I read about political institutions, structures and processes, mass media arenas, mass media communication, public relations and environmental issues in the countries I was interested in. I added technological instruction books to that, and even fiction, for there is lot of literary fiction dealing with waste. I went to sites of waste performances, such as expositions, conferences and industrial fairs, and I talked to a variety of rather different experts. I was nosing around in both countries to get a feeling for my object of inquiry. Some basic insights came out of this investigation, which constitute the early chapters of the book, preparing the analysis as well as its later presentation: first, modern affluent societies with capitalist market economies are based on a permanent drive, or staging, to innovate and to replace, both in the realm of ideas and in the realm of objects. The life cycle and replacement routines of nowadays smartphone production are a case in point. They are built up on mountains of waste, and their fuel is simply this: to transform objects into waste in order to replace them with new ones. Throughout history, societies of economic scarcity, resulting from less developed technologies and modes of production or from war, have developed sophisticated practices of waste separation and recycling, mostly by man- and woman-power. Modern capitalist societies use cheap resources and a cheap workforce. Therefore, as long as resources are cheap, recycling lacks a given inherent economic driver. Out of sight, out of mind, is the corresponding social regime of practices. Buying new is cheaper and more convenient.

Waste discourses are attempts to change the definition of this situation, to construct values to oppose the social destruction of values. Second, I learned from media and communication studies about the production of news in the mass media, especially about gate keeping, news values and selection, public agenda setting and public relations. If discourse analysts are going to deal with mass media texts, digital data and audio-visuals, then they should know about the production of such data. And they can "learn" from German media studies in the 1980s and early 1990s, that conservative analysts claimed there was too much reporting on environmental damage in Germany, given that we had such a high standard of living, whilst left-wing inspired studies argued that there was too little, as the real situation was much worse than the "ideologically biased" mass media systems reported. A third element concerned the development of modern technical infrastructures of waste treatment in both countries. Modern city governing of waste collection and transportation in France and Germany was established basically in the 1850s. It implied a destruction of the existing practices of recycling and the social groups making their living from it. New knowledge concerning hygiene, city planning and increasing city populations led to new classifications, norms of behaviour and technical standards in waste treatment. As new incineration technologies developed and were promoted from the late nineteenth century on, profound conflicts developed between "burners", "recyclers" and "friends of disposal sites". After a few failed trials of mostly war-scarcity-driven recycling economies, on-site waste disposal and (to a lesser degree) incineration became the dominant technologies in use in the first half of the twentieth century. Their domination continued after World War II, with different economic structures and technical coverage in Germany and France (middle-sized business in the former, a few big companies in the latter). During the golden 1960s, economic growth, increasing wealth in French and German households and new economic strategies for selling goods led to the above-mentioned problems of waste disposal in local communities – here and there, they had to look for new sites, and they confronted citizens complaining about negative side effects: rats, smells, water pollution, aesthetics. Following that, various laws or minor legislation passed in both countries' national assemblies; new devices or dispositifs (to use a Foucauldian and SKAD term) of waste treatment were developed and a new figure and role model for current governmentality appeared prominently on the stage: the ecological citizen. And certainly, there was now a new villain too: the one who ignores his duties as fellow citizen. Interestingly, as my research showed, such figures entered the drama of waste discipline only after the failure of more structural regulation and agreement on national levels.

The social construction of value 79

Collecting data

As already mentioned above, the empirical study was informed by various strategies to get a "feeling" for the issues at stake. This implied participation and observation in different French and German sites where waste technology presentation occurred, as well as in public-political conferences and artistic performances. But it was not designed as ethnography. Instead, empirical data collected and used for analysis were basically texts – all kind of texts: leaflets, 1,000-page long scientific reports, brochures, transcriptions of political debates in the national assemblies and working groups, articles in general newspapers and weekly periodicals, special interest media produced by NGO-activists or business organisations, press releases, non-fiction books and expert interviews. Because in those days I worked in a mainly pre-digital world, I had to do archive work in libraries and darkened storage rooms in strange buildings. Such archive work should not be abandoned – there is a tendency nowadays to work just on digital data which is easily at hand and to avoid other strategies of data collection. I did some brainstorming about the arena of concern and its principal actors (most of whom you would know from public discourses and careful information extraction), mapped it and wrote to them in order to get their statements. I asked different kinds of experts for interviews – from environmental movement organisations to academic economists, business organisations and high state officials. I conducted fifteen interviews in France and four in Germany. I was able to make additional use of eight interviews in France and eleven in Germany which I obtained from colleagues working on similar topics. I learned from all that about what was happening in my field of concern, and whose contributions I needed to consider. And I asked press services for help, for example the French ministry of environmental affairs and the French state waste information system run by an organisation named ADEME. Regarding the German case, I specifically asked the press and archive services of the German Federal Government for help. Such organisations hold comprehensive press archives on political issues and were able to organise press samples for scientific or other purposes. I gave them key words for query (such as "household waste", "waste", "recycling", "deposit", "incineration", "waste & regulation") and they provided me with documents. Using such different providers, I was able to cross-check by comparing material they provided me with. And I spent weeks and weeks in public libraries, running through the weekly *DER SPIEGEL* from early 1950s to today, in order not to miss some important event. Data collection was informed by several concerns:

- I was interested in the national levels of household waste conflicts (which in fact only cover a minor amount of today's waste production) and corresponding political debates, not in local Not In My Backyard issues or other short news coverage, nor in cultural essays (such as "waste is a metaphor for the universe") and summer time page fillers (like the regularly recurring news about "poor Egyptian children making their living on Cairo's disposal sites").

- I decided to concentrate on a time span from the late 1960s (in fact starting with 1970) to 1995. The former corresponded to the emergence of waste as a "national policy issue" in both countries resulting from economic growth and changing patterns of production, distribution and consumption. This implied that I should start at a particular moment in the post-war history of waste treatment, with already existing infrastructures, technologies, administrative responsibilities and business structures. In both countries, national regulation efforts started around 1969/1970 and accordingly entered mass media agendas. 1995 was a crucial year for a definite settlement of waste policies – at least it was presented as *definitive* by both governments who had just passed their newest waste and recycling legislations, and promised that now at last, all waste problems had been definitely mastered, and we would enter the time of circular economies ("Kreislaufwirtschaft").

- I included documents concerning all kinds of involved stakeholders, except for films, TV news and other audio-visual data (there was no digital world yet).[1] For press coverage, I focused on "serious" mainstream daily and weekly media texts from the right (conservative) via the centre to the left (progressive). But note that this was just a way to organise data collection. As I will discuss later, I didn't assume that a newspaper considered to be "left leaning" (in the sense of European political spheres) would publish "left leaning" articles or different positions per se.[2] If you learn from media and communication studies that up to 80 per cent of newspaper articles consist of only slightly modified press releases and organisations' public agenda setting (including government and administrations as major players, but also economic actors or Non-Governmental Organisations like, in my case, Greenpeace) then you no longer wonder why such texts so often look so similar, aside from investigative journalism.

- One major point has to be added. If you do a software-based keyword search in order to get frequencies of word usage, for example of a particular term throughout a given time period, you will end up with a series of ups and downs, with high peaks and drop-offs in coverage. You can use this information for the selection of points of entry. But in fact, mass media coverage of debated or conflictual issues simply follows events – it is high when laws are debated in the congress, or when there is a manifestation, a catastrophe, or some other event "worthy of reporting"; and it is low when nothing much happens. In my case this implied that I ignore the highs and lows and follow political regulation debates. These became my main entry points in order to sample data: two weeks before and after a national parliamentary debate, a high impact manifestation of anti-waste movements, or a pertinent legislative procedure proved to be a useful formula. Such newspaper and weekly coverage became the main data for my analysis.

The core German sample then contained around 700 articles out of general public media from 1970–1972 (first federal state law on waste management), 1975 (governmental programme on waste economies), 1985–1986 (remaking of waste management law), 1989–1995 (regulation of one-way packaging systems law for circular economy); with an additional 40 articles originating in the ecological movement context, and 30 from the economic and engineering press. The French sample (620 articles) was constructed around the period from 1972–1975 (the first of the newer French waste management law decisions), 1989/1990 (French national plan for the environment) and 1992 (French one-way package legislation and waste management law). For each country, the complete lists of ministerial reports, scientific reports and other general political reports on household waste problems were added.

Analysing data

I made a threefold use of collected data. First, the data supplied me with information about the various actors involved who speak, are addressed, or decide issues about waste, thus making it a matter of concern. It provided me with the material necessary to map the scenes and their changes over time.[3] The data likewise told me about upcoming events in the waste domain (such as scandals, laws and other legal regulation, manifestations and critical events). The data made me aware of the rather similar textual production in different social arenas (public, political, scientific) and document types. Most certainly, genre matters. A newspaper commentary differs from a scientific report. But both of them might perform the same "statement" (in Foucault's sense) by using the very same interpretive scheme. Second, the data allowed me to develop a permanent contextualisation of what was going on, an account of the unfolding scene and its different shapes along the twenty-five year period covered. And third, I used a particular selection of data as the basis for detailed, finely-tuned analysis of waste statement production.

The comprehensive original samples came into existence following a couple of theoretical criteria outlined above. But a total of 1,320 newspaper articles and a mountain of additional documents from each country could not be analysed according to strategies of interpretive research in sociology. I therefore proceeded with further selections in order to establish a final core data sample for sequential analysis. Accordingly I used the following guidelines:

- Look for coverage of all the core events identified in waste management policies in each country, from two weeks before to two weeks after the event.
- Make sure that the sample includes texts from the whole range of serious newspapers and weeklies.
- Look for similar genres of texts and for references to events (using comprehensive reporting in preference to short news items focused on the same issue).

The final sample then contained forty articles from the mass media of each country and a complementary sample of documents from related spheres (such as governmental reports, statements by business organisations, NGOs and scientific advisory boards). I read them very carefully again, and I made short descriptions of their content. I added a deconstructive reading which accounted for textual structure, fragmentation and oppositions in the given document (which often was an arena of discourse in itself rather than just a performance of only one discourse), speakers that appeared, subjects introduced, the positioning of actors, the presence of arguments and rhetorical devices and the obvious elements of phenomenal structures (What causes the problem? What kind of problem? What solutions? What obstacles?, and so forth). I identified core paragraphs of interest, that is those textual sequences which referred to the core issue that was presented, excluding the usual media strategies designed to attract readers' attention (such as the "people from the street have lived through this or that" short story which is often used as an opener). Using sequential analysis, I reconstructed interpretive schemes as core statement practices. Sequential analysis meant that I analysed such paragraphs on a line-by-line basis, according to the idea that there are marked turning points in textual reporting, where new content sequences start (which can be a new paragraph, or somewhere in the middle of a paragraph and so on – such turning points do not simply follow formal structures). In a process of coding I created categories out of this material which later became the labels for the ever-repeating interpretive schemes I identified. In fact, the reconstruction of phenomenal structures and interpretive schemes reveals their deep entanglement. Interpretive schemes fill up the dimensions which make the structural pattern of a given phenomenal structure. Or it can be put the other way round: they perform the dimensions which can then be identified as part of such a structure. All such elements taken together were summed up in the concept of interpretive repertoire. A final step beyond the analysis of singular fragments of data then was the reconstruction of story lines which made up a "story to tell" between all the different statement elements and across time. Again I have to add an important point: in order to do such a deep sequential analysis, you need questions. Texts don't explain just themselves; rather, they respond to your questions and research interests. Different questions lead to different codes and categories.

Here is one example (a quote) of a core interpretive scheme taken from the German debates. I identified it as part of a particular discursive structuration which I labelled "cultural critique":

> Branded as the most modern waste incineration device in Germany, if not in the world, a plant in Augsburg costing more than 900 million marks underwent a 'warm start-up' in the autumn of last year. Last week the trial run came to an abrupt end. In connection with this, words were used that newspaper readers know only in reference to nuclear reactors: cracks in a steam pressure-pipe, leaks in water pipes, quick shutdown. And of course: the legally permitted pollution output into the environment was not exceeded. One should not forget: all technology is subject to breakdowns – and the more complex it is, the greater the likelihood of breakdowns – a truism.
>
> (*Süddeutsche Zeitung*, 5.5.1994, my translation)

I used the category "(technological) risk" scheme to name such statements. They are widely used in technical controversies and state an inherent and uncontrollable tendency of complex technologies to fail at some point and thereby to create damage, pollution and the like. This is easy to see: imagine for yourself a talk or text about genetically modified organisms, nano-technologies, nuclear energy, or fracking – using such a risk frame is very common today. Sometimes, the term "risk" even shows up in the data. Of course, one might choose a slightly different word to label this statement, so long as it holds for the same idea. "Technological risk" entered German waste debates in the early 1980s with reference to carcinogenic air pollution from incineration plants or water pollution caused by disposal sites. Before that time, waste had been considered an issue of resource management (avoid plastics and one-way packages) and finding landfills. But when risk statements started appearing, such matters became a real public concern. The text presented above shows only one way of manifesting such a statement. It is also performed, for example, as visual graphs (showing incinerations sites all over Germany, imitating campaigns from the anti-nuclear movement) or as sidelong reports on the dangers of pollution presented by scientific expert councils. The risk scheme was part of the opposing counter-discourse, widely present in German public debates at that time. It was performed in combination with other patterns, such as the "scarcity of nature (as resource and receptive container)" scheme, a "society controls economy" scheme, an "ethics of responsibility against profit making interests" and a few more.

A different scheme may illustrate the French hegemonic discourse, the only one present in the public space (the mass media). I named it "socio-technical control and civilisational mastery":

84 *Reiner Keller*

Finally clean waste. No more yellowish trails of smoke, which came out of the old chimneys. Long live the ultramodern incineration plant, which remediates without contaminating and which has the advantage of converting the content of a trash bag into a source of energy. Industrial reliability, environment protection, a high level of utilization regarding the retrieval of energy, this bet has been won by the engineers and architects who were able to work together in such a way that the performance merges with the beauty of shape and pattern.

(*Humanité*, 4.7.1990, my translation)

Here again, we see a pattern that showed up in very different ways, and it was part of a larger arrangement which constituted a particular discursive structuration of statements, performed predominantly by French state officials and related actors.

I used other concepts from SKAD methodology as well in order to account for the statement dimension of discourses: phenomenal structure, story line and interpretive repertoire. For reasons of space, I cannot provide details on all of them here. However, based on my empirical data, as a result of such reconstructions I established specific phenomenal structures: two competing ones in the German case and one dominant structure in the French case. I did this in a rather static way in order to account for their appearance in the early to mid-1990s, close to the final data present in my sample. Today I would do it in a much more procedural and dynamic way. In fact, phenomenal structures change over time, due to discursive events and practice, and discourse analysis should account for such transformations. In the French case, I identified only one phenomenal structure in public debates, with slight variations. In the early 1990s, it looked as follows:

Table 4.1 Example: phenomenal structure, French hegemonic discourse "sociotechnological modernisation"

Dimensions	Realisation
Causation	• Waste as "sanitary issue"; discrepancy between amount produced and disposal or recycling infrastructure • Wealth growth, economic and technical advances, consumption needs of the consumers → rise in waste produced • Waste as a problem of deficient waste disposal at landfills • Waste as a problem of a lack of citizen responsibility and discipline • Waste as a problem of national payments balance/usage of raw materials • Waste as a problem of international competitive conditions • → *waste as a "quasi-natural" by-product of progress and wealth*

The social construction of value 85

Dimensions	Realisation
Responsibilities	• Politics/government/national administration (must develop and enforce a waste policy framework programme in coordination with the economy) • Regional corporations, economy (individual responsibility for the implementation of the political specifications) • Citizens/Society (giving up irrational fears and selfish denials; taking over responsibility for waste; acceptance of the technologies)
Need for action/ problem-solving	• Low problem level; technical mastery of the waste issue is possible through recycling and elimination → *nature is governable* • Large-scale technological expansion and optimisation of the disposal and recycling infrastructure → *interpretative pattern of socio-technical mastery* • Obtaining acceptance of removal infrastructure through the use of communication und participation • Comprehensive mobilisation of citizens' responsibility (local authorities, economy, consumers) for the *national interest in resource importation reduction*
Self-positioning of speakers	• Representatives of scientific-technical, economic and pragmatic reason, of civil (socio-cultural/socio-technical) progress • Government as the administrator of the collective interest • → *French state as representing civilisation, its modernity and progress in behaviour and technology, as incorporating pragmatic reasoning*
Othering	• French civil actors (regional corporations, economy, citizens) show a *lack of consciousness for their responsibility as citizens of France* • Irrationalism and fundamentalism of German waste politics, disguise for economic protectionism
Thing culture	• Not a topic of the waste discussion; follows seemingly "sacrosanct" modernisation dynamics and market rationalities • Material model of affluence; freedom of needs (production and consumption)
Values	• Government secures collective interests (affluence, progress, modernity) • (Actual and moral) cleanliness of the public space • Nature as (scarce national) resource, whose usage can be optimised • *Society as it is right here and now as realisation of "good life"*

Please note two points here: the dimensions in the left column are not pre-established and then used for whatever discourses are to be analysed. I identified them as core dimensions in *my* work, in the discourse I was analysing, and with regard to the questions I was interested in. On the right, you see some typical arguments that refer to those dimensions. The words in italics point to the more general interpretive patterns I reconstructed out of the data, those elements which make up the basic statements of this particular discursive production.

In working through these detailed analytical steps, I again followed the ideas of theoretical sampling, here applied to the sequences of data to be considered. Maximal and minimal contrasting proved to be particularly helpful in this analysis. During this ongoing process, I established (via reflection and decision) relations between dimensions of phenomenal structures and corresponding interpretive schemes. I followed, according to my interest in the relations of knowledge and the politics of knowledge, the genres and spheres of argumentation which were used to account for such dimensions (such as risk evaluation, proof of evidence of security standards, moral appeals and so forth). I looked for the entanglement between document production in other places (as in governmental advisory boards, expert reports, etc.) and mass media reporting. I discovered how environmental movement actors established "counter-knowledge" about recycling, for example by proving with empirical evidence that recycling refrigerators is both possible and rather cheap (something industry had denied before). I did mappings of actors present in both public arenas and fixed them in their particular place in the discursive space of meaning making. I reconstructed discursive structuration in France and Germany as ideal-types in the sense of Max Weber, which means that concrete documents contain only elements of it, in a more or less pure way (sometimes very pure, sometimes mixed up with other things, or just in particular variations). I identified two competing discourses in the German case and one hegemonic discourse in the French case, with an excluded and marginalised counter-discourse outside the media sphere. Such discourses changed over the course of the twenty-five years under scrutiny; new elements (such as risk evaluation) were added in statement production over time and in relation to major discursive events; speakers appeared and disappeared and so on.

Telling a story

For reasons of space, I present only a few findings here. First, I would like to differentiate between the core discourse analysis and its results that is the reconstruction of discursive structuration, its patterns for statement production, its speakers, its dynamics, resources and effects. And second, I will give a more theoretically informed interpretation of what has happened in these waste conflicts, with reference to theories of risk society

The social construction of value 87

and reflexive modernisation and the initial interest in German-French differences.

For the German part I identified a highly conflictual competition between two discourses which I labelled "structural-conservative" (because it insisted on the established capitalist market economy as a core principle) and "cultural critique" (because it argued for new social structuration on the basis of a different cultural setting of needs and consumption). I identified six main interpretive schemes for each of those discourses (for example, structural-conservative discourse: core scheme: autonomy of the economic sphere is the higher good; linked schemes: problem naturalisation (more goods, more waste: it's unavoidable), ongoing progress and modernity (no need for change, we are on the best way forward), technological and administrative control (engineering and administrative skills combined with safe technology is the solution at hand), nature is a cornucopia with never-ending resources (there is no scarcity of resources), we follow an ethics of responsibility (not an ethics of good intentions which doesn't take care of its consequences). This discourse told a story of ongoing process, economic growth, welfare and technological control. It was contested by a counter discourse which insisted on the social control of economy, the scarcity of nature as a resource, the principal risks of technology (from the mid-1980s on) and the need for a huge cultural turn against economic profit making through externalisation of costs. Concrete law making and waste policies could be seen as an effect of this conflictual constellation; the more conservative discourse was forced to move along and to shift some of its basic assumptions in order to get legislation passed and protest subsided. On the French side, I identified a single hegemonic discourse of civilisational mastery, which promoted recycling for reasons of national interests concerning import reduction and ritualistically repeated again and again that French state authority and French experts were in control of whatever might happen – the only worry was that French civil society actors might ignore what the good state provided and what state reason claimed. I already mentioned another marginal counter-discourse similar to its German counterpart. Whilst German discourses focused on the pros and cons of an announced catastrophic collapse of its modes of consumption with unavoidable pollution and risk, the hegemonic French discourse performed the ritual of regularly repeating the state's civilisational mastery over nature and risk.

In addition to this reconstruction of meaning making through statement production, I did mappings of speakers in the arena of public waste discourses in order to represent the situation around 1990. Their position on the map refers to the strength or clarity of their promoting discursive statements in relation to the general discursive patterns identified (the more to the left or right of the column, the "purer" the position).[4]

A model of the "public spheres of waste discourses" established for both countries accounted for the ways of addressing other actors and the public in this particular, contested-issue arena. In France mass media reporting was interpreted as setting a stage so that the French state officials could address, critique and appeal to French civil society (including business actors and municipalities) to follow the state's instructions and to believe in the state's rituals of performance. Besides this I could observe a well-established practice of consulting and close relations between the state administration and business actors as well as environmental NGOs, which identified themselves as the "state's little helpers". In Germany, the mass media arena looked more like a battlefield where two discourses met and fought against each other. State officials were divided, for example due to the complicated German political arrangements between the federal state level and the German Länder. The political culture of waste issues was conflictual both in the public sphere and in the huge amount of produced scientific expertise, and the media were just the playground. Besides this, both formal and informal practices of consultation could be observed, with a particular bias favouring economic actors with direct access to governmental institutions; actors of the counter-discourse had much less chance to get direct access. The political outcome of this was different in both countries: the conflictual and much more dynamic development in Germany led to higher technical standards in waste treatment plants and sites, as well as a quota for household waste recycling. But the French public "rituals of household waste mastery" were accompanied by rather strict policies concentrating on other organisational sites of waste production (for example industrial and commercial sites) and therefore nevertheless resulted in high recycling performances as well (compared to Germany), but not in the domain of household waste.

The second part of accounting for my results referred to theoretical debates and reflections. Again, I will point to only a few issues. I identified a process of *individualisation* of ecological responsibilities throughout these debates: the ecologically aware citizen became a dominant subject position, charged with solving the problems of waste through responsible consumption and disciplined waste separation, in place of more structural solutions. I identified *risk schemes* as a major driver in the German debate, which did not show up in France. Therefore, I argued that the French development corresponded to what Ulrich Beck called "linear modernisation", and the German debates could be considered a case in point of "reflexive modernisation" during the very same period. And, to name just one last argument, I concluded, against theories of cultural mentalities and so forth, that current discursive performance and institutional structuration account for the major observable differences. These performances pointed to questions regarding a collective shame shared by everyone and a joint responsibility as drivers, in the German case, and to a public ritual of state performance and civilisation, in the French case. A quote from an Austrian newspaper, *Die Presse*, covering a waste management technologies trade fair in Vienna, nicely illustrates this kind of *cultural* difference:

Munich openly embraces all that trash and presents containers packed full of the corpus delicti. The annual amount of refuse produced by one family decorates the fair stand. Paris, however, feels that it is 'clean' and is committed to technological achievements. In addition to a prototype of the 'Dogofant', a motorcycle which collects dog excrements, the French present their newest incineration plant – and an antique desk.

(*Die Presse*, 5.10.1989; my translation)

That is, discourses are the means of establishing such differences, making them durable, moving them and melting them down again. In connection with an insight of Joseph Gusfield, who stated that institutions and structures can be seen as processes frozen in time, I would add discursive processes, frozen in time, and thawed, from time to time:

> At any moment the "structure" itself may be fought over as groups attempt to affect the definitions of problems and authority to affect them. [...] Structure is process frozen in time as orderliness. It is a conceptual tool with which we try to make that process understandable. What is important to my thought here is that all is not situational; ideas and events are contained in an imprecise and changing container.
>
> (Gusfield, 1981: 5–7)

Notes

1 Germany: NGOs such as Greenpeace, BUND, Robin Wood, The Better Waste Policy; the Ministry for Environmental Affairs; political parties CDU, SPD and the Greens; the Association of German Industrials, the Association of Waste Business Companies, the Federal Expert Council on Environmental Issues and others; France: NGOs including France Nature Environment, Friends of the Earth, Greenpeace; parties such as the Greens; the Ministry of Environmental Affairs; the Association of French Majors; ADEME; the Association of Waste Economy Businesses, etc.
2 More details (such as names) on the chosen newspapers and weeklies from the "serious" national press arena (not including yellow press) are given in the book (see Keller, [1998] 2009).
3 I learned from this sampling for example that Greenpeace France had translated from German Greenpeace some expertise on waste issues and promoted a waste policy very similar to its German counterpart, but unlike German Greenpeace, without any presence in French mass media coverage.
4 Please see the contribution by Luther and Schünemann (Chapter 15) for some of my maps presenting the public sphere of waste discourses and the arenas/landscapes of discursive positioning.

References

Beck, U. (1992). *Risk Society. Towards a New Modernity*. London: Sage.
Beck, U., Giddens, A. and Lash, S. (1994). *Reflexive Modernization. Politics, Tradition and Aesthetics in the Modern Social Order*. Redwood City, CA: Stanford University Press.
Becker, H. S. and Keller, R. (2016). Ways of Telling About Society. Howard S. Becker in Conversation With Reiner Keller. *Forum Qualitative Sozialforschung/ Forum Qualitative Social Research*, [online] 17(2), Art.12. Available at: http://nbn-resolving.de/urn:nbn:de:0114-fqs1602122 [Accessed 13 October 2017].
Benjamin, W. ([1940] 1969). Theses on the Philosophy of History. In: ibid., *Illuminations*, trans. Harry Zohn. New York: Schocken Books, 253–264.
Gamson, W. A. and Modigliani, A. (1989). Media Discourse and Public Opinion on Nuclear Power. A Constructionist Approach. *American Journal of Sociology*, 95, 1–73.
Gusfield, J. (1981). *The Culture of Public Problems*. Chicago: University of Chicago Press.
Keller, R. ([1998] 2009). *Müll – Die gesellschaftliche Konstruktion des Wertvollen*. 2nd edition. Wiesbaden: Springer VS. [Waste – The Social Construction of Value.]
Keller, R. (2011). The Sociology of Knowledge Approach to Discourse (SKAD). *Human Studies*, 34(1), 43–65.
Keller, R. (2012). *Doing Discourse Research. An Introduction for Social Scientists*. London: Sage.
Keller, R. (2018). Foucault. In: R. Wodak and B. Forchtner, eds. *The Routledge Handbook of Language and Politics*. 1st edn. London: Routledge, 67–81.
Keller, R. (2019). *The Sociology of Knowledge Approach to Discourse*. New York: Springer (in preparation).
Thompson, M. (2017). *Rubbish Theory. The Creation and Destruction of Value*. 2nd edn. Chicago: University Press.
Ulrich, P. and Keller, R. (2014). Comparing Discourse Between Cultures. A Discursive Approach to Movement Knowledge. In: B. Baumgarten, P. Daphi and P. Ulrich, eds. *Conceptualizing Culture in Social Movement Research*. 1st edn. Hampshire: Palgrave, 113–139.

5 SKAD analysis of European multi-level political debates

Wolf J. Schünemann

EU referendums and the question of knowledge

Long before the British referendum on EU membership in June 2016 (the so-called Brexit referendum), EU referendums have been particularly disturbing events in European integration (Schünemann, 2017). Given mainstream support for the European project across Europe, at least until recent crises, referendum results that countered further EU integration have regularly caused irritation among proponents of the respective treaty reform and most political elites. For many cases in former times and still for the Brexit referendum, the intuitive reactions of commentators of all sorts have tended to doubt the sufficient knowledge or capacity of the voters, at least the ones that followed the advocacy of the opposite camp. Questions came up as to whether voters actually voted on the treaty at hand or were influenced by other issues having nothing to do with the matter of the referendum. Much was attributed to irrational motivations, fear and blind refusal (in younger times: fake news etc.) instead of informed consideration of the issue. For example, the Green Party fraction in the European Parliament commented on the failed referendums on the Constitutional Treaty in France and the Netherlands in 2005 as follows: "[I]t is evident that this No is not a real No against the constitution but a clear vote of protest against the internal policies of the national governments of France and the Netherlands" (in Furedi, 2005). While such an explanation would rather not convince in the case of the Leave/Remain-question in the Brexit referendum of 2016, pointing to the irrationality and misinformation of the Brexiteers was nevertheless one of the most obvious strategies of making sense of the result for disappointed EU adherents and commentators.

So is knowledge the key to understanding the failure (in the sense of EU supporters) of EU referendums? The answer is yes and no. No, because the integration-affirmative assumption of a lack of knowledge that causes rejection so widely shared in empirical referendum research is simplistic and heavily biased towards an elitist mainstream attitude regarding European integration. Moreover, it does not live up to reality when we look, for instance, at how the French were much better informed on the EU's constitutional treaty in 2005 (when their referendum failed) than the Germans across the border, who were not engaged in a referendum debate but had a super-majority of parliamentarians voting the reform treaty through without much public attention. Especially given the intensity of a referendum debate as a manifest conflict of political meaning-making (see Schünemann, 2016), it does not make much sense to start from a lack-of-knowledge assumption anyhow, because there is always knowledge circulating in a given society and social communication. Then it is not really the question of *if* but *what* knowledge is present and processed in a given society and situation and how it is linked by campaign actors to the issue at hand in a referendum or another political conflict situation. Thus, yes, knowledge is key to understanding the campaigns and, indirectly, the results of EU referendums. However, the knowledge elements must be analysed in their complexity and specificity. This is where SKAD steps in.

The approach is based on the so-called interpretive paradigm in social sciences, which in recent years has become more and more established in political theory and policy studies. It still needs to be systematically transferred to politics and campaign studies. This chapter shall serve as a contribution in this sense. The chapter is on methodology, but as the illustration includes cases to study, it is important to highlight the limitations that come along with SKAD for political research. First and foremost, the approach is focused on the referendum debates and not on the outcomes. That is to say that it does not make any claims regarding the definite reasons for the outcome of a single referendum or a more general explanatory model of voting behaviour in EU referendums. Instead, the primary goal of this chapter is not to explain why the referendums failed, but to better understand what the different groups discussed and how they talked when they debated the issue in question.

After having shortly exemplified how knowledge matters and plays out in a referendum debate (and how it does not), in the remainder of the chapter I present how a tailor-made SKAD can be used to analyse political debates in general and the European multi-level polity in particular. Theoretical grounds are laid out in section two. Section three then illustrates the essential preparatory step of text selection and presents the different sets of speakers in a first comparative synopsis. Section four gives some insight into the practice of discourse analysis and exhibits some illustrative examples from each debate, comparing them to each other. The final section gives a short conclusion.

Reading referendums: a discourse analytical framework

As illustrated above, one of the key questions in referendum research so far is about knowledge or information. Many commentators, EU elites and scholars alike consider citizens as lacking the necessary sophistication in EU issues to vote on a reform treaty (Leduc, 2002: 727; Laffan and O'Mahony, 2008: 263–264; more nuanced Hobolt, 2009b: 48–53). An extension of this opinion even leads to a frequently purported positive relation between knowledge and support, giving rise to the hypothesis that more knowledge on EU issues would lead to more support towards EU integration or a treaty in a referendum (Marsh, 2009: 188; Lubbers, 2008: 64; Millward Brown, 2008: 16; Sinnott et al., 2009: 19).

For the purpose of this study, any positivist knowledge hypothesis must be challenged on fundamental grounds, mainly for two reasons. First, the supposed knowledge-support-relation constitutes an unresolved endogeneity problem. The causal assumption that more knowledge about the EU would lead to more support for European integration is highly contestable. Indeed, the relation could be exactly the other way around (critical analysis also in Mößner, 2009). Second, it is questionable whether any single fact, any element of information per se, on a reform treaty for instance, can result in higher support for it or the EU as a whole. From this perspective, the double majority as a central reform provision, for example, could be interpreted either as a necessary reform in order to increase efficiency in EU decision-making or as a *power-grab* by the big states introducing a population-based mechanism in order to increase their own power position in relation to smaller member states. Adopting one of these interpretive schemes (or frames) arguably has more effect on voting behaviour, one way or the other, than the mere information about double majority itself.

Assuming that all of these diverging interpretations do derive from election campaigns led by the social actors engaged in the debate, framing processes become particularly relevant. The framing concept has already been applied to many studies on political communication and, more specifically, also on campaigning in EU referendums (Hobolt, 2009a; De Vreese and Semetko, 2004). However, many scholars tend towards a strategic concept of framing, regarding frames as a sort of manipulative tool strategically deployed by elite actors in order to influence citizens' opinion (see Hobolt, 2009a: 5). Thus, frames are understood as campaign instruments available for the discretionary use of actors. This concept needs to be challenged, not on the grounds that there was not any possibility for strategic frame selection by election campaigners, but that their choice is principally limited by the discursive formation in which a debate takes place as well as the single actor's social position within this discursive formation. Hence, it is one of the principal assumptions of this chapter that frames derive from discourse in which knowledge is socially constructed and in which frames are received, reproduced and only from time to time even produced by social actors engaged in debate (see also Donati, 2006). Therefore, although this study is far from being able to answer the question of knowledge effects on voting behaviour, it finally leads me to the discourse analytical framework proposed in this chapter, because as Foucault (1981: 260) puts it: "there is no knowledge without discursive practice". Whereas this qualitative approach thus cannot contribute to the prevalent attempts at ex post-rationalisation of referendums, it shall offer some guidance on how to read them.

There is not just one way of performing discourse analysis. During the last decades, several varied approaches have been introduced into social sciences in general, political science in particular and even European Union studies. This research design builds upon the Sociology of Knowledge Approach to Discourse. Its main advantage, especially for the analysis of politics, would be that SKAD brings "the actors back into focus" (Keller, 2005: 5), proposing a methodology which is highly sensitive to the actor or speaker positions in a given discursive formation. According to SKAD, discourse is to be understood as a material manifestation and circulation of knowledge (Keller, 2008: 97; also Konersmann, 2007: 80). Transferred to the issue at hand, the referendum campaigns, this would be the knowledge of European integration, the European Union as a political institution, the national state, knowledge of different policy fields such as foreign, social or environmental policies and, finally, knowledge of broader concepts such as constitution, sovereignty, neo-liberalism, globalisation etc.

The discourse-analytical framework

First, building upon the theory of Foucault, the main theoretical assumption of SKAD is that discourses can be analysed in a systematic manner by exposing the recurrent statements that are materialised through different forms (written or non-written, verbal or non-verbal) and an approximately infinite amount of so-called utterances. This makes particular reference to Foucault's important distinction between utterances and statements. Whereas the total amount of utterances (*énonciations*) produced, for instance, during a referendum campaign may tend towards infinity, the total number of materialised and recurrent statements (*énoncés*) is principally finite (Foucault, 1981: 115ff.). By using the vocabulary of language philosophy, statements can thus be seen as the *types* and utterances as the *tokens* of discursive practice.

At least for studies of political debate, I would propose avoiding any kind of inconsistency of the term by defining discourse as abstractly as possible. Thus, discourse itself is understood as a social process of text production that needs further specifications to be appropriately defined. Accordingly, for Keller (2005: 6) discourse may not be seen as "an ontological entity" but as "a theoretical device for ordering and analysing data, a necessary hypothetical assumption to start research". Therefore, although discourse is real and can be empirically analysed, *the discourse* does not *exist*. For this chapter on referendums, a special and rather broad discourse term is chosen. It relies on the particular logic of referendums with a binary decision option. Thus, every statement relevant for this study would either explicitly or implicitly reflect its persuasive intention, be it towards yes or no. For discourse analysis, this means that the very basic first distinction between a yes-discourse and a no-discourse directly derives from the bipolar structure of persuasion given in a referendum debate. Whereas the former would include statements consisting of reasons to vote yes, the latter would comprise statements uttered in order to provoke a no vote. From this, it follows that every single statement relevant for this study has either the explicit form or the implicit character of an argument on how to vote. Each would give a potential answer to the question of "Why to vote yes/no?". So, for every referendum debate we would expect a finite set of statements/arguments that can be traced through analysis.

The most important addendum of this SKAD method of analysing political debates is the argument as an overarching analytical category that is not part of the original SKAD terminology. Arguments are topic-related and strategically directed ensembles of statements. Campaign actors form arguments in the run-up to an election or referendum by taking up socioculturally specific discourse threads and transforming them into a reason to vote yes or no, to vote for party x or party y, or in a more general sense: to support or oppose a political reform proposal. The argument, conceived in this way, provides for the connectivity with the study of political debates as well as different kinds of rhetorical research. Regarding the issue at hand, referendum debates on EU treaty reforms, one can further divide arguments into more narrowly issue-oriented treaty-arguments and meta-arguments, wherein the reasoning goes well beyond the issue at hand. Finally, one finds counter-arguments – sets of statements that do little more than negate what the other camp has claimed beforehand.

In order to better understand the logic of the proposed analytical framework, two frequently uttered arguments of the debate, both of which can be traced from each of the cases, shall serve as illustrations. First, the so-called Democracy Argument (DemA) constitutes a very prominent yes-side argument. The DemA can be condensed to the core statement: *Vote yes because the treaty makes the EU political process more democratic.* Second, a universal example from the no-side would be the Militarisation Critique (MilC) with its core statement: *Vote no because the treaty leads to further militarisation of the EU.* Of course, other arguments like these were to be found on both sides (see Table 5.1 on p. 100). Nevertheless, the resulting main catalogue of arguments is not sufficient. The analysis should go at least one level deeper, so to speak. Being confronted with the DemA, one would probably ask again: why? Why does the EU become more democratic through the treaty? Every potential answer to this question would belong to a second level of persuasion. Thus, we can dissect statements again. In our typology, these statements shall be classified as sub-arguments, such as: *The EU becomes more democratic because the European*

Parliament will get more powers (see articles x, y and z). Another sub-argument of DemA would be: *... because a Citizen's initiative is to be introduced (article x).* On the other hand, thus for the MilC, a possible (and observable) statement of this sort would be: *The treaty militarises the EU because a European Defence Agency is established (article x),* or: *... because member states are obliged to increase their military budgets (article y).*

The social constructivist perspective

As mentioned above, SKAD comes with a strong analytical interest in social actors. Individual actors are not to be seen as unimportant speakers and materialisation *machines* uttering structurally determined statements per se. Structures predispose, but do not totally determine actors' discursive behaviour (Diez, 1999: 611). At this point, social constructivism comes into play. Thus, individual actors can be seen as deeply embedded in social contexts that provide them with collective stocks of knowledge which they can appropriate. In this way, this social construction of reality constitutes an ongoing process in which the actor serves as recipient and co-producer of a socially constructed reality. From a SKAD perspective, individual actors are of interest in their function as speakers for collective actors (be it a political party, a permanent association or interest group or any sort of ad-hoc campaign organisation) in a given campaign or another communicative process. Social actors maintain so-called speaker positions in a given discursive formation (Diez, 1999: 603). Thus, by representing a social actor, every individual speaker can be assigned to such a position, and all speakers are expected to derive their subjective knowledge on the issue in question through the social construction processes going on in their respective social settings.

Another important and helpful insight concerning actors' options in discursive practice is that they coalesce into so-called *discourse coalitions*. What Keller (2008: 253–255) defines as discourse coalition can be better understood as coalitions mainly and, often enough, unintentionally achieved by actors through discursive practice. In the case of referendum debates, discourse coalitions must be differentiated from any form of intended campaign co-operation. Therefore, in the referendum debates I studied, it was possible and indeed observable that even though there was no intended campaign co-operation between the no-camps of the far left and far right, they were bound together through discursive practice and factually *clustered* in unintended discourse coalitions that allowed for their main ideological differences but still offered a number of commonly acceptable statements.

What to read? – Building comprehensive text samples

Three national referendum debates constituted the object of previous research that I use in this chapter to illustrate how to apply SKAD to political debates in general and EU referendum debates in particular. Each debate lasted for several weeks or even months and involved a huge amount of persuasive texts, be they written or verbal, produced by a wide range of authors, the so-called speakers active during the campaign. A first step in the research was the identification of social actors who have been engaged in the debate on the national level and approached the public with a clearly persuasive intention towards yes or no. Therefore, media coverage was examined and half-standardised expert interviews with twenty-nine politicians from the three states, all of them active speakers in one of the debates, had been conducted. Time ranges for every campaign were defined in order to reduce the amount of texts to be included. For each case a representative sample of written or transcribed texts (F: 620, NL: 294, IRL: 528) has been composed, thereby primarily relying on the online material and news archives available on the websites of the respective social actors or campaigns. The texts included in the sample can all be regarded as natural data, for they were produced exclusively in the real socio-historical contexts of the respective referendum debates which were to be analysed.

Obviously, text selection cannot be separated from speaker analysis, since the researcher already has to be informed about the set of speakers active during the campaign before setting up text samples. Therefore, the combined speaker and text selection process already constitutes the first part of the analysis. The leading questions for this part are:

- Which speakers participate in the national debate?
- Which speaker positions are identifiable? Which collective actors are engaged in the national debate?
- Where are speaker positions located in the general political sphere?
- Do social actors co-operate (campaign co-operation)?
- Are there collective actors split by discursive borders?

Figure 5.1 is a simplified illustration of speaker positions in the French debate on the EU constitutional treaty in 2005. It is oriented along a rough left-right spectrum (criteria being socio-economic and/or socio-ethical attitudes) of the respective political spheres.

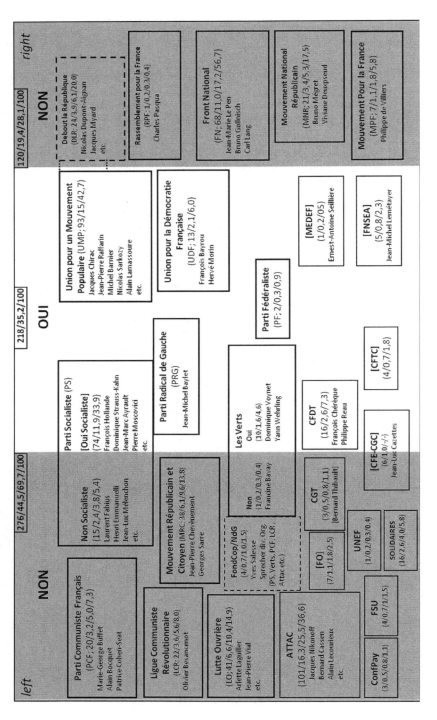

Figure 5.1 Discourse Map – French referendum on the EU Constitutional Treaty 2005.

How to read? – The interpretive analysis

The second part of the analysis consists of reading. This is the main part of discourse analysis. The leading questions for this step are: first, which main arguments can be found in the referendum debate? Second, of which statements and sub-arguments are the main arguments composed? Third, how can arguments be classified (treaty-argument, meta-argument, counter-argument)? Fourth, which interpretive schemes, narratives, classifications, subject positions are observable?

Based on the theoretical framework laid out above, it becomes clear that discourse analysis is certainly interpretive work and, thus, must be carried out using a qualitative methodology. All the texts of the respective samples have been read in a first round. A sequential analysis has been carried out, meaning a detailed analysis of all the texts in the respective samples, sentence by sentence, paragraph by paragraph. Accordingly, interpretive codes have been assigned to sequences following the qualitative research practice of Grounded Theory (cf. Strauss, 1998). This process has been effectuated with software support (MaxQDA) in order to obtain the results and have easy access to all codings later on. Since the set of interpretive codes was further developed during the first reading procedure, all codings had to be re-read in a second round in order to apply the definite interpretation scheme to all texts.

Table 5.1 presents the set of main arguments that can be found – to a greater or lesser extent – in each of the cases analysed. Although the finding of broad commonalities at this level of persuasion would suggest a certain similarity between the cases, at the deeper level, namely as regards sub-arguments, the debates show quite divergent patterns of argumentation which in this chapter can only be illustrated by giving some examples (main arguments marked with bold font in Table 5.1).

Legend
"PCF: Parti communiste français; LCR: Ligue communiste révolutionnaire; LO: Lutte ouvrière; PT: Parti des travailleurs; MRC: Mouvement républicain et citoyen; FO: Force ouvrière; CGT: Confédération générale du travail; Attac: Association pour la taxation des transactions financières et pour l'action citoyenne; FondC: Fondation Copernic; ConP: Confédération paysanne; PS: Parti socialiste; UMP: Union pour un mouvement populaire; PRG: Parti radical de gauche; ParF: Parti fédéraliste; UDF: Union pour la démocratie française; CFDT: Confédération française démocratique du travail; CFTC: Confédération Française des Travailleurs Chrétiens; UNSA: Union nationale des syndicats autonomes; FNSEA: Fédération nationale des syndicats d'exploitants agricoles; MEDEF: Mouvement des entreprises de France; FN: Front na-tional; MPF: Mouvement pour la France; MNR: Mouvement national républicain; RPF: Rassemblement pour la France; CPNT: Chasse, pêche, nature et traditions.

The political parties are marked by bold frames, parties in development by bold dashed frames, permanent interest groups by narrow frames, finally ad-hoc campaign organisations by narrow dashed frames.

Table 5.1 Arguments in EU referendum debates

Argument	Core statement
YES ARGUMENTS – Vote Yes to the treaty because …	
Charter Argument (ChartA)	… it guarantees the protection of fundamental rights.
Consequentialist Argument (ConsA)	… voting no will have bad consequences for our country.
Democratic Argument (DemA)	… it makes the EU political process more democratic.
Development Policy Argument (DPA)	… it strengthens the commitment to EU development policy.
Ecological Argument (EcoA)	… it lays the grounds for better environmental protection.
Economic Argument (EA)	… ratification is good for economic development.
Foreign Policy Argument (FPA)	… the EU can play a greater role in the world then.
Historical Argument (HistA)	… our country has benefitted from EU membership.
Institutional Argument (InstA)	… it makes EU institutions work more efficiently.
Security Argument (SecA)	… it promotes judicial and police cooperation in the EU.
Social Policy Argument (SPA)	… it promotes EU social policy.
NO ARGUMENTS – Vote no to the treaty because …	
Critique of the Democratic Deficit (DDC)	… it does not remedy the democratic deficit/even increases it.
Economic Critique (EconC)	… it is bad for our economic development.
Influence Argument (InflA)	… it reduces our country's power in EU decision-making.
Militarisation Critique (MilC)	… it leads to a further militarisation of the EU.
Critique of Neoliberalism (NeoC)	… it is a manifest of neoliberal ideology.
Plan B Argument (PlanB)	… there is a better option/a Plan B available.
Sanction Vote-Argument (SVA)	… it damages our national government.
Socio-ethical Critique (SEC)	… it endangers our national values.
Sovereignty Argument (SovA)	… it brings a further loss of national sovereignty.

Yes-arguments

a Consequentialist argument (ConsA)

The Consequentialist Argument is one of the most frequently uttered arguments in the yes-discourses of all referendum debates. It is a clear meta-argument since it does not refer to any concrete treaty content or even specific articles, but rather reflects on the character of the vote as a collective performative act and a chance to affirm commitment to the common EU project. The many articulations of ConsA can therefore be condensed to the core statement that voting no will have bad consequences for our country. In all three cases, there are many articulations of ConsA wherein similar interpretive schemes can be found. For example, in all three debates treaty apologists caution the public against isolation on the European scene. Thus, a no-vote in the referendum has often been framed as turning our backs on Europe. For instance, the Irish Foreign Minister alerted in a public address given in February 2008 that "[i]t would not make sense for us to turn our backs on Europe" (Ahern, 2008). The then leader of the Dutch Liberal Party (VVD) and former Foreign Minister Jozias van Aartsen (2005) used almost the same phrase while also combining his warning (as many Irish apologists likewise did) with a reminder of the economic prospect of the country as a small open economy:

> Weet u dat wij wereldwijd de zesde afzetmarkt van China zijn. De zesde afzetmarkt! Omdat wij de poort naar Europa zijn. Wij moeten dus niet met onze rug naar Europa gaan staan.[1]

Finally, in a public declaration of the French UDF-leader Bayrou, the same pattern can be traced in a statement on the importance of the EU. Therein he stated: "Il n'est aucun domaine [...] où nous puissions envisager de tourner le dos à l'immense entreprise européenne" (Bayrou, 2005).[2]

b Historical argument (HistA)

The story of European integration has often been framed using a "progressive narrative" of the EU as the institutional result of a peace project and an unmatched success story (Gilbert, 2008). It is basically this narrative that can be traced in the Historical Argument. The HistA is also a common meta-argument observed in all three cases, but there are evident differences in how the success story is told. In the French and Dutch cases, the underlying narrative is a continental European story of peace and stability after centuries of conflict and war between European nation states. In this sense, the French PS politician and former Prime Minister Pierre Mauroy (2005) named peace as the primary reason to vote yes on the treaty in a Senate intervention and referred to the founding fathers of the Communities: "Le premier objectif de ceux qui, au lendemain de la Seconde guerre mondiale, ont engagé la construction européenne a été de faire la paix".[3] The HistA in the Dutch yes-discourse follows the same pattern (see for example Veld, 2005).

In contrast, with some remarkable exceptions the continental European story of peace and stability cannot be found in the Irish yes-discourse. It was instead dominated by another country-specific success story, namely the story of the miraculous transformation of Ireland from the *poor man of Europe* to its *shining light*, which is to be called the *Celtic Tiger narrative*. In this dominant country-specific narrative, Europe is not so much seen as a success story for itself, but rather as a catalyst and facilitator of the country's own development: "EU membership has been pivotal to Ireland's success story" (Kenny, 2008).

c Foreign Policy Argument (FPA)

The Foreign Policy Argument is a frequently uttered treaty-argument that can be found in the yes-discourses of all debates. Its core statement is that with the treaty enacted, *the EU can play a greater role in the world*. The FPA did refer to some treaty details. For the more general argument, these were the new or enforced functions of a permanent president of the European Council and primarily the new post of a *Foreign Minister*, as it was called in the Constitutional Treaty but not in the Lisbon Treaty. In any case, the general statement that these reforms, including the establishment of a European External Action Service, would facilitate the EU playing a more powerful role and being more visible on the global stage can be found in all debates.

A remarkable difference at the sub-argument level is that French and Dutch treaty apologists also highlight the reforms and new provisions in the field of European Security and Defence Policy. In effect, the French UMP politician Lellouche (2005), for example, pointed out that the treaty would introduce a mutual defence clause for the first time: "La Constitution introduit en effet une clause de défense mutuelle (article I-41 para. 7)".[4] Conversely, in the Irish debate the newly codified solidarity clauses and other provisions for a stronger military and defence policy were rather topics of the treaty opponents and the no-discourse (MilC), whereas the treaty apologists in neutral Ireland tried to play down the new provisions for ESDP.

No-arguments

a Critique of Neo-liberalism (NeoC)

The Critique of Neo-liberalism can be considered the dominant argument in the French no-discourse, and it also played a major role for the argumentation of treaty opponents on the left in the Netherlands and Ireland. In this argument, the treaty is evaluated as *a manifesto of neoliberal ideology*. Most sub-arguments of the NeoC clearly refer to different treaty articles. One of the most important sub-arguments of the NeoC was that the treaty would make *free and undistorted competition* a fundamental value of the Union.[5] For instance, it was written in a pamphlet of *Non Socialiste* (Non Socialiste, 2005a): "Le principe de « concurrence libre et non faussée » est la clé de voûte de ce texte et tout en découle".[6] The Irish *People Before Profit Alliance* (People before Profit, 2008) claimed throughout the campaign that "[t]he EU is increasingly dominated by large corporations who use its institutions to impose their policies on national governments". A very important sub-argument of the NeoC was against the supposed attacks on public services contained in the treaty. Thus, the Dutch Socialist Party (SP, 2005b) claimed that saying yes to the treaty would be like saying yes to market competition even in the public education and care sectors. Despite all similarities, however, there is a remarkable divergence between the Dutch and the French no-discourses on the one hand and the Irish one on the other. Whereas in both continental states the warning against so-called fiscal dumping, meaning detrimental inner-European competition via tax systems, was one of the sub-arguments of NeoC, this point was not addressed by even a single treaty opponent in the Irish debate.

b Militarisation Critique (MilC)

Another important argument for treaty opponents in all three referendum debates was the Militarisation Critique. Its core statement is that the treaty would lead to a further militarisation of the EU. They substantiated their main claim through different sub-arguments, each referring to one of the new elements of ESDP contained in the treaty, namely the member states' obligation to increase their military capabilities, the establishment of a European Defence Agency, the possibility of Permanent Structured Cooperation as well as the mutual defence and solidarity clauses. In their main leaflet on the military development of the EU, the Dutch SP (SP, 2005a) warned, for example, against a new arms race facilitated through the treaty provisions: "Deze sterke focus op militarisering van Europa kan leiden tot een nieuwe wapenwedloop".[7]

In the Irish no-discourse, the MilC was directly connected to the national position of military neutrality, which is widely accepted as an important part of the collective identity and was presented as being existentially endangered by the proposed integration steps in the field of security and defence policy. Accordingly, the Irish version of MilC was integrated into a broad country-specific narrative telling the story of the traditional value of military neutrality which has become more and more jeopardised by European integration: "Lisbon Treaty will end any pretence of Irish neutrality" (Horgan, 2008). By contrast, such a principled pacifistic opposition was very rare in the French debate and of course not related to any sense of neutrality. Instead, treaty opponents, like the apologists, generally showed a strong commitment to a concept of *Europe Puissance*, but they criticised ESDP provisions for their supposed submission to a NATO- and thus US-driven global order of international security policy:

> L'OTAN est incompatible avec l'existence d'une défense européenne indépendante ayant pour but la protection de son territoire et de ses citoyens. L'Europe ne se construit évidemment pas contre les Etats-Unis, mais elle ne doit pas non plus se construire sous la domination des Etats-Unis.[8]
>
> (Non Socialiste, 2005b)

c Sovereignty Argument (SovA)

A last example present in all three no-discourses is evidently the very broadly applicable *Sovereignty Argument*. Its core statement is the self-evident diagnosis that *the treaty brings a further loss of national sovereignty*. In all cases this central fear was most clearly expressed by the common interpretive scheme of the EU as a super-state, with the treaty at hand accomplishing the federalist move that subsequently undermined national autonomy, thereby finally transforming the member states into provinces of this new federal state. Unsurprisingly, the SovA was the dominant argument for treaty opponents on the far right. For instance, the leader of the French *Front National*, Jean-Marie Le Pen (Le Pen, 2005), derived the supposed super-state quality of the new union directly from its constitutional symbolism: "Une Constitution est l'acte fondateur d'un Etat [...] la Constitution européenne est donc bien l'acte fondateur d'un super-Etat européen".[9]

This common interpretive scheme was also used by the Dutch right-wing populist Geert Wilders, who, after splitting from VVD, campaigned in his newly founded *Groep Wilders* against ratification of the Constitutional Treaty. He said during a talk:

> De Europese Grondwet schaft het beginsel van het primaat van de nationale democratie en politieke onafhankelijkheid van de lidstaten af. Zowel juridisch als politiek wordt Nederland een provincie van een Europese superstaat.[10]
>
> (Wilders, 2005)

Similarly, in Ireland the fear of a European super-state was often combined with or upgraded by the warning against a new empire oppressing the young Irish nation. For example, PANA-speaker Cole (Cole, 2008) said: "Of course Ireland was part of a militarised, centralised, neo-liberal

Superstate before, it was called the British Union and Empire". In a public meeting of the *People's Movement*, the speakers additionally stated: "Ireland would become a province, not a nation, once again" (McKenna and Bree, 2008), thereby referring to the famous Irish rebel song "A nation once again".

Synoptical instruments

Having presented a tool for the illustration of speakers and speaker positions in a referendum debate with the discourse map (Figure 5.1), in this section I introduce some synoptical tools for the comparative discourse analysis as well. This is important, as it can be seen as one of the major challenges of discourse analytical research to find ways of presenting the results of such empirical work in an accessible manner, ideally without filling volumes exclusively with documentation in the form of quotations (see Chapter 15). First, a detailed discourse analysis allows for complexity reduction by mapping as well. Thus, as done before for the speakers, Figure 5.2 proposes a spatial visualisation for all the arguments of both camps in the Dutch referendum campaign of 2005, including the respective sub-arguments. While it is not the aim of this chapter to introduce any meaningful quantification into qualitative discourse analytical research, the size of the labels does nonetheless depend on the frequency of codings for the respective category.

Second, each argument has been somewhat condensed in the sections above. In the more detailed analysis, sub-arguments have to be taken into account; thus, core statements needed to be re-formulated, making the great variation between national cases visible. To present a substantial but still easily readable synopsis of the results, I propose a so-called Cumulative Argumentative for each discourse or camp identified in a political debate (see Table 5.2).

Cumulative Argumentatives are particularly helpful for international comparisons, as argumentatives for the same camp in different countries can be cross-read. This makes similarities and differences easily recognisable.

Finally, if the extended versions of Cumulative Argumentatives still fill too much space, one could also choose an abbreviated form, as in a formula, for more schematic illustrations. In this example (see below), short labels replace the core statements. For the order of appearance, one can again follow the number of respective codings, starting with the most frequent argument.

> Yes Discourse France: SPA + ConsA + DemA + InstA + FPA + HistA + ChartA + EA + SecA + EcoA;
> Yes Discourse NL: DemA + InstA + SecA + EA + FPA + SPA + ConsA + ChartA + EcoA + HistA;

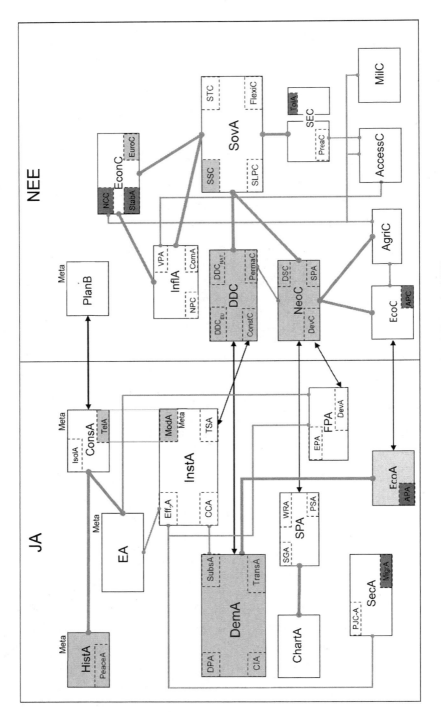

Figure 5.2 Structural Scheme for the Dutch debate on the Constitutional Treaty in 2005.

Yes Discourse IRL: HistA + EA + FPA + ConsA + InstA + DemA + EcoA + ChartA + SPA + SecA;
No Discourse F: NeoC + DDC + EconC + PlanB + SovA + MilC + AccessC + SEC;
No Discourse NL: SovA + DDC + EconC + NeoC + InflA + SEC + AccessC + PlanB + EcoC + MilC + AgriC;
No Discourse IRL: SovA + NeoC + DDC + MilC + PlanB + InflA + EconC + AgriC + SEC.

Conclusion

Section four could only give some superficial insights into the interpretive results of discourse analysis. However, the main aim of this chapter was to present a SKAD-oriented research approach for the study of political debates in general and referendum research in particular. This can be considered a new and complementary discourse analytical framework for referendum studies and the study of political debates in general. Therefore, sections one to three laid out in detail the theoretical and methodological groundwork.

In different sections of the chapter, especially in section five, synoptical tools for the integration and visualisation of empirical findings have been presented. For the speaker analysis, this was the discourse map, which brings together all the collective actors engaged in a debate and positions them along a rough political left-right-spectrum. For the interpretive analysis several options have been presented, including a table of all main arguments, a mapping of arguments and the formulation of a cumulative argumentative. This methodological chapter can hopefully help establish SKAD in political science and beyond as a suitable approach for the qualitative analysis of political debates. Some thoughts and tools presented above might be helpful for further work in this tradition, and there remains much more to be developed from here.

Legend

"Sub-arguments: APA: Animal Protection Argument; APC: Animal Protection Critique; CCA: Competence Catalogue Argument; ChartA: Charter Argument; CIA: Citizen Initiative Argument; ComA: Commission Critique; ConstC: Constitutional Critique; DevA: Developmental Argument; DevC: Developmental Critique; DPA: Democrati-sation and Politicisation Argument; DSC: Dumping Social Critique; Eff2A: Effectivity and efficiency Argument; EPA: Europe Puissance Argument; EuroC: Euro Cri-tique; FlexiC: Flexibility Critique; IsolA: Isolation Argument; MigrA: Migration Argument; ModA: Modernisation Argument; NCC: Net Contributor Critique; NPC: New Posts Critique; PeacA: Peace Argument; PermaC: Permanency Critique; PJC-A: Police and Justice Cooperation Argument; PreaC: Preamble Critique; PSA: Public Services Argument; SGA: Social Goals Argument; SLPC: Supremacy and Legal Personality Critique; SPA: Services Publics Argument; SSC: Super State Critique; StabA: Stability Argument; STC: Sovereignty Trasfer Critique; SubsA: Subsidiarity Argument; TelA: Teleological Argument; TolA: Tolerance Argument; TransA: Transparency Argument; TSA: Treaty Simplification Argument; VPA: Voting Power Argument; WRA: Workers' Rights Argument.

Table 5.2 Cumulative argumentatives yes-/no-discourse Ireland 2008 (selected arguments)

Yes discourse (HistA, FPA, ConsA)	No discourse
|HistA| European integration for 35 years has been pivotal to the successful development of the country. For recent progresses in integration have helped the economic success story of Ireland. Moreover, it was EU membership that brought real economic independence of Ireland towards its British neighbour. The EU also contributed to the peaceful resolution and management of the conflict in Northern Ireland. [...] |FPA| The treaty improves the power and effects of EU foreign policy. The capacities of the Union for peacekeeping missions and humanitarian interventions will be enhanced. As a small nation, Ireland needs multilateral cooperation for its visibility and activities on the international scene. The Treaty enforces the commitment and the leverage of the EU in the fields of development policy and poverty reduction. Finally, only a reformed EU can cope with the manifold challenges of globalisation, that no single country is able to deal with effectively by itself. |KonsA| A rejection of the Treaty would be detrimental for Ireland and the Community. Because Ireland would put its so valuable reputation with international investors at risk as well as its political position in the heart of the community. It would risk being isolated on the international scene. The European Union as unique peace project would be damaged as well, if its necessary constitutional progress was hampered. [...]	|SovA| The Treaty means a further substantial loss of national sovereignty and the end of independence as a country. The EU develops into a federation. The country, in contrast, will be degraded to the state of a province. For the treaty includes further substantial transfers of sovereignty towards the community. It codifies the legal personality of the Union as well as the supremacy of its law. Moreover, majority voting is introduced in political key areas and national veto options are reduced. Finally, the Treaty includes flexible mechanisms for the modification of primary law beyond member states' control. |NeoC| With the ratification of the Treaty, neoliberal ideology would finally prevail in EU politics. For a radically market-driven economic order would be codified. The privatisation of public goods and services would be further promoted. The deregulation of national labour markets would be accelerated by a competitive race to the bottom. The commitment to price stability and the mechanisms of the Stability and Growth Pact would further limit the leverage of member states in steering their economies. Finally, the Treaty confirms the negative role of the EU in an exploitative global trade order. |MilC| The Treaty promotes the militarisation of the European Union and thus endangers the Irish tradition of military neutrality, which has become precarious already. For the spectrum of military operations will be extended and will include even the fight against terrorism. With its new assistance and solidarity clauses, the Union will be transformed into a system of collective defence. The Treaty codifies a requirement for military armament and the activities of the European Defence Agency. Both would serve the interests of the weapon lobby. The provision of Permanent Structured Cooperation would allow the formation of mini alliances with only some member states on board that have higher ambitions in military cooperation.

Notes

1 "Do you know that we are the sixth largest sales market of China. The sixth largest! Because we are the harbor to Europe. Hence, we must not turn our back on Europe."
2 "There is no domain where we could ever imagine to turning our backs on the immense European project."
3 "The primary objective of those men who immediately after the end of World War II have been engaged in the construction of Europe was to bring peace to the continent."
4 "The Constitution effectively introduces a mutual defence clause (article I-41 para. 7)."
5 "After the failure of the Constitutional Treaty the strong commitment to a *free and undistorted competition* has been removed from the main document so that in the Lisbon Treaty it is only contained in a protocol."
6 "The principle of 'free and undistorted competition' is the key element of this text and everything else derives from it."
7 "This strong focus on militarisation from Europe can lead to a new arms race."
8 "The NATO is not suited to the existence of an independent European defence policy aiming to protect its own territory and its own citizens. Europe is evidently not constructed against the United States, but it must not be constructed under the domination of the United States either."
9 "A constitution is the founding act of a state [...] thus the European Constitution is the founding act of a European super-state".
10 "The European Constitution abolishes the principle of primacy of national democracy and political independence of the member states. Both legally and politically, the Netherlands became a province of a European super-state".

References

van Aartsen, J. van (2005). *Speech Jozias van Aartsen tijdens de Algemene Ledenvergadering in Groningen op vrijdag 27 mei 2005*. [online] Available at: http://nederland.archipol.ub.rug.nl/content/vvd/20050607/www.vvd.nl/privatedata/DocUpload/40/Speech%20Jozias%20van%20Aartsen%20ALV%20Groningen.doc [Accessed 15 October 2010].

Ahern, D. (2008). *Address by the Minister for Foreign Affairs, Dermot Ahern, T.D., to the Institute of European Affairs*. [online] Available at: www.dfa.ie/home/index.aspx?id=41229 [Accessed 26 January 2010].

Bayrou, F. (2005). Déclaration de M. François Bayrou, président de l'UDF, sur la campagne de l'UDF pour le "oui" au référendum sur la Constitution européenne. [online] Available at: http://discours.vie-publique.fr/notices/053000762.html [Accessed 13 August 2010].

Cole, R. (2008). *Partnership Europe or Imperial Europe*. [online] Available at: www.pana.ie/idn/240408.html [Accessed 26 November 2009].

Diez, T. (1999). Speaking "Europe". The Politics of Integration Discourse. *Journal of European Public Policy*, 6(4), 598–613.

Donati, P. R. (2006). Die Rahmenanalyse politischer Diskurse. In: R. Keller, A. Hirseland, W. Schneider and W. Viehöver, eds., *Handbuch Sozialwissenschaftliche Diskursanalyse – Band 1: Theorien und Methoden*. 2nd edn. Wiesbaden: VS-Verlag, 147–177.

Foucault, M. (1981). *Archäologie des Wissens*. Frankfurt am Main: Suhrkamp.

Furedi, F. (2005). To Say or Imply that the Public is Too Stupid to Grasp the High-minded and Sophisticated Ideals of the Advocates of the EU is to Express a Profound Sense of Contempt Towards Ordinary People. *New Statesman*, 13 June.

Gilbert, M. (2008). Narrating the Process: Questioning the Progressive Story of European Integration. *Journal of Common Market Studies*, (3), 641–662.

Hobolt, S. B. (2009a). Framing Effects in Referendums on European Integration: Experimental Evidence. In *EUSA Eleventh Biennial Conference*. Los Angeles.

Hobolt, S. B. (2009b). *Europe in Question: Referendums on European Integration*. Oxford: Oxford University Press.

Horgan, E. (2008). *Lisbon Treaty Will End any Pretence of Irish Neutrality*. [online] Available at: www.caeuc.org/index.php?q=node/146 [Accessed 26 November 2009].

Keller, R. (2005). Analysing Discourse. An Approach From the Sociology of Knowledge. *Forum: Qualitative Social Research* (FQS), 2005(3), 32.

Keller, R. (2008). *Wissenssoziologische Diskursanalyse Grundlegung eines Forschungsprogramms*. 2nd edn. Wiesbaden: VS-Verlag.

Kenny, E. (2008). *Europe: Let's Be At The Heart Of It*. [online] Available at: www.finegael.org/news/y/1009701/article/ [Accessed 19 November 2009].

Konersmann, R. (2007). Der Philosoph mit der Maske. Michel Foucaults L'ordre du discours. In: M. Foucault, *Die Ordnung des Diskurses*. Frankfurt am Main: Suhrkamp, 51–94.

Laffan, B. and O'Mahony, J. (2008). *Ireland and the European Union*. Basingstoke: Palgrave.

Le Pen, J.-M. (2005). Intervention Parlement Européen. Strasbourg. [online] Available at: www.frontnational.com/doc_interventions_detail.php?id_inter=34 [Accessed 09 January 2007].

Leduc, L. (2002). Opinion Change and Voting Behavior in Referendums. *European Journal of Political Research* 2002, 711–732.

Lellouche, P. (2005). L'*Europe* contre la tentation de la neutralité. *Le Figaro*, 17 May.

Lubbers, M. (2008). Regarding the Dutch 'Nee' to the European Constitution. A Test of the Identity, Utilitarian and Political Approaches to Voting 'No'. *European Union Politics*, 9(1), 59–86.

Marsh, M. (2009). Voting Behaviour. In: J. Coakley and M. Gallagher, eds., *Politics in the Republic of Ireland*. 5th edn. Abingdon: Routledge, 168–197.

Mauroy, P. (2005). *Intervention de Pierre Mauroy: révision constitutionnelle*. [online] Available at: http://web.archive.org/web/20050524180334/www.ouisocialiste.net/article.php3?id_article=358 [Accessed 21 July 2017].

McKenna, P. and Bree, D. (2008). *OSCE Requested to Carry out Election Assessment Mission of Lisbon Treaty Referendum*. [online] Available at: www.people.ie/press/080529.pdf [Accessed 13 October 2012].

Millward Brown, I. M. S. (2008). *Post Lisbon Treaty Referendum. Research Findings*. Dublin: Millward Brown IMS.

Mößner, A. (2009). Cognitive Mobilization, Knowledge and Efficacy as Determinants of Euroscepticism. In: D. Fuchs, R. Magni-Berton and A. Roger, Antoine, eds., *Euroscepticism. Images of Europe Among Mass Publics and Political Elites*. Opladen: Budrich, 157–173.

People before Profit (2008). *Vote 'No' to the Lisbon Treaty*. [online] Available at: www.people-before-profit.org/taxonomy/term/24 [Accessed 29 November 2009].

Schünemann, W. J. (2016). Manifeste Deutungskämpfe: Die wissenssoziologisch-diskursanalytische Untersuchung politischer Debatten. In: S. Bosancic and R. Keller, eds., *Perspektiven Wissenssoziologischer Diskursforschung*. Wiesbaden: Springer VS, 29–51.

Schünemann, W. J. (2017). *In Vielfalt verneint: Referenden in und über Europa von Maastricht bis Brexit*. Wiesbaden: Springer VS.

Sinnott, R., Elkink, J. A., O'Rourke, K. and McBride, J. (2009). *Attitudes and Behaviour in the Referendum on the Treaty of Lisbon*. Dublin: UCD Geary Institute.

SP (2005a). *Als je JA zegt tegen deze Europese grondwet, zeg je JA tegen een peperduur Europees leger*. [online] Available at: http://nederland.archipol.ub.rug.nl/content/sp/2005 0607/www.sp.nl/nieuws/actie/grondwet/ja7.html [Accessed 05 October 2010].

SP (2005b). *Als je JA zegt tegen deze Europese grondwet, zeg je JA tegen meer marktwerking, ook in zorg en onderwijs*. [online] Available at: http://nederland.archipol.ub.rug.nl/content/sp/20050607/www.sp.nl/nieuws/actie/grondwet/ja3.html [Accessed 05 October 2010].

Strauss, A. L. (1998). *Grundlagen qualitativer Sozialforschung. Datenanalyse und Theoriebildung in der empirischen soziologischen Forschung*. 2nd edn. München: Fink.

in 't Veld, S. (2005). *Waarom ik voor de Europese Grondwet stem*. [online] Available at: www.d66.nl/europa/nieuws/20050521/congrestoespraak_sophie_in_t_veld?ctx=vhopg90lkduz [Accessed 01 September 2010].

De Vreese, C. H. and Semetko, H. A. (2004). *Political Campaigning in Referendums Framing the Referendum Issue*. London: Taylor & Francis.

Wilders, G. (2005). *Eerste Openbare Speech Geert Wilders Sinds de Moord op Theo van Gogh*. [online] Available at: http://web.archive.org/web/20050314020628/www.groepwilders.nl/ [Accessed 15 October 2010].

6 Legislation and discourse
Research on the making of law by means of discourse analysis

Andreas Stückler

Introduction

Legislation represents a research field widely neglected in the sociology of law. Only once, in the 1960s and 1970s, the study of legislative procedures – in terms of a systematic analysis of the course of concrete law-making processes, the role of players involved, as well as of societal (particularly economic and political) interests expressed in the legislative process – experienced a certain *boom*. Furthermore, this boom was rather limited on studies in criminology and criminal sociology, thus research was primarily performed from a criminal law perspective.[1] Since the middle of the 1980s at the latest, research on the making of (criminal) law has been practically ceased. Only recently – albeit still only occasionally – there seems to be a reinforced focus on issues of legislation and law-making (see Hebberecht, 2010; Helmke, 2011; Fuchs, 2014; Hammel, 2014).

The strikingly low sociological research activity in the area of legislation may arise from various causes. A main reason for this is most probably the fact that legal sociologists usually are jurists themselves or at least attached to a law faculty and, therefore, operate from a primarily legal point of view.[2] However, the decisive reason might be a much more basic, epistemological one. Obviously, it is due to law itself – namely to the legal form, that is, to law as a capitalist social form hived off to an autonomous and independent legal system and reifying law to a property of society per se (Buckel, 2007: 242). Exactly the fact that society and law today cannot be thought without each other any longer provides a remarkably protective and durable immunity of law against the intellectual insight into its social construction.

In this respect, a social-theoretical approach seems to be necessary that allows for approaching law as a product of social action. As is argued in the following, theoretical and methodological frameworks related to the sociology of knowledge and, particularly, discourse analytical approaches prove to be very useful, since they draw attention to the social dependence and construction of social entities and thus to law as a continually contested formation of knowledge.

This contribution, therefore, attempts to briefly present a discourse analytical approach to the making of law. It is intended to show that the use of a discourse analytical framework, due to its focus on the analysis of competing social knowledge orders, facilitates new and additional insights into the dynamics of law-making processes. Moreover, such an approach might promote the study of legislative processes insofar as the making of law may be profiled as a relevant research field of currently flourishing discourse studies.

Law, legislation, and discourse

With respect to the "discursive construction of reality" (Keller *et al.*, 2005) – as the main focus of discourse studies in the tradition of Michel Foucault – law has to be regarded as having a very important role to play. Finally, it is law defining what is justice and un-justice or, with particular regard to criminal law, what is normal and deviant behaviour. It was precisely this critical insight marking the starting point of the before-mentioned law-making studies of the 1960s and 1970s that crime is a social construction, a label being attributed to certain actions and, consequently, certain persons. Crime, in the first instance, only exists as a product of a certain world view, always tied up with specific interests and values, that is legally enshrined and – in the true sense of the word – codified as *legitimate* reality.[3] It is law that provides these reality constructions and world views and their underlying claims to power with legitimacy and, if necessary, makes them compulsory enforceable. Therefore, law can be regarded as a formation of knowledge defining "forms of knowledge, and, consequently, relations between man and truth" (Foucault, 2000: 4). It makes a claim to truth and by this means exercises power by disqualifying other forms of knowledge, experience and world views (Buckel, 2007: 203). By defining justice and injustice, law produces "subjugated knowledges" (Foucault, 2003: 7). However – and this is decisive – this definition of justice and injustice is not a priori given by law. The law does not determine by itself what justice and injustice is, this is the result of discursive struggles in which social players seek to enforce their particular world views against each other by legal legitimation. In this discursive struggle, law works as a sort of consensus technology providing for the universalisation of certain interests and world views. The universalisation of particular world views can be regarded as the main function of law as a governmental technology of power allowing social players to employ "law as tactics" (Foucault, 2007: 99) in antagonistic struggles for power and social influence.

The discourse analytical approach to law-making to be sketched in the following therefore considers legislation and the making of law as a discursive procedure of construction and definition. It is an antagonistic process involving several social players with different world views, correspondingly various interests as well as different (power) resources. Consequently, legislation represents a very conflict-prone power process in which different discourses, in terms of institutionally stabilised knowledge orders, clash and compete with each other – that is, a process in which various players seek to enforce their perspectives, ideologies and interests against other players and to universalise them through law. Legal norms, in this respect, are effects of discursive struggles for power of definition and interpretation, at the end of which certain discourses are superior over other discourses and a specific world view, a certain knowledge prevails and dominates.

Thus, the aim of law-making studies by means of discourse analysis is to reconstruct and describe different discourses competing in the law-making process and to analyse their effects on the concrete form and the contents of laws (Stückler, 2014b).

Law-making research by means of SKAD

The Sociology of Knowledge Approach to Discourse (SKAD) provides a particularly suitable approach for the discourse analytical study of law-making processes, in several respects. First of all, its explicit action-theoretical, social constructivist perspective allows for approaching law as a result of human action. SKAD regards social actors not simply as bearers of societal knowledge orders but rather as active producers and recipients of discourses. This action-theoretical approach is what SKAD distinguishes from many other discourse analytical approaches. From this perspective, laws are not simply created within or by an abstract and anonymous legal discourse. But law is made by acting people who are, however, determined by their social position and institutional affiliation as well as corresponding interests and world views.[4]

At the same time – in addition to this action-theoretical dimension – SKAD-based analyses, due to the integration of discourse theoretical insights, are always focused on the meso and macro level of institutions and organisations which is exactly the societal level on which law-making processes occur. Law, in particular, represents a social sphere that cannot be immediately accessed by people's (everyday) action. It is made within institutional fields such as jurisprudence, justice and politics. By using SKAD, therefore, collective structures of action, perception and thought as well as institution-specific constellations of interest enter into the research focus. These specific interests are represented by the different actors involved in the legislative process and become manifest in their discursive practices and the discursive strategies they deploy.

Another strength of SKAD finally consists in providing a number of analytic concepts from the sociology of knowledge that can be used for an in-depth analysis of the contents-related structuring of discourses (for example, analysis of interpretive schemes). The analysis of the contents-related structuring of discourses is also, as for the action-theoretical orientation of SKAD, a main characteristic of SKAD-based discourse analyses. SKAD is based on the presumption that discourses do not only have a manifest but also a latent level, that is, they consist of mainly latent interpretive schemes and patterns of thought that are linked in a specific manner and, in so doing, bond together to a certain discourse. Discourses, from this point of view, most of all produce and process interpretive frameworks that finally constitute reality in a specific way (Keller, 2011: 72). Not least due to this focus on the contents-related structuring of discourses, as to be shown in this contribution, SKAD proves to be a highly promising theoretical and methodological approach regarding the discourse analytical study of law-making processes.

A discourse analysis of the Austrian reform of criminal procedure and the codification of victims' rights

In the following, this SKAD-based discourse analytical approach to law-making is illustrated by a case study on the development of victims' rights during the Austrian reform of criminal procedure in 2008 (Stückler, 2010). This reform – as well as several other recent reforms of criminal procedure in Europe – was particularly characterised by demands for victim protection and the greater consideration of interests of crime victims in criminal proceedings. Traditionally, crime victims had not been involved in criminal proceedings and thus criminally marginalised. It was not until the end of the 1970s that a reintegration process began, continually enhancing the standing of victims in criminal cases (Stangl, 2008). The increasing reintegration of victims in criminal proceedings can be regarded as the result of a general "'victimological' turn in criminal law" (Boutellier, 1996: 16).[5] The 2008 reform of criminal procedure in Austria, in this respect, represents a new and temporary peak of these criminal legal developments.

Research issue

A significant innovation of the reform is, above all, the definition of the crime victim itself, that is, the concept of the *victim* as legal term of the Austrian Code of Criminal Procedure. It is exactly this definition-related aspect that is particularly interesting from a discourse analytical perspective and that suggests an investigation by means of discourse analysis. The hypothesis of the study was that the reform process involved many different institutional actors – from ministerial bureaucrats and jurists to representatives of the legal authorities such as lawyers, judges and defence lawyers, to politicians and several other stakeholders (for example, victim protection organisations) – taking divergent positions with regard to the criminal proceeding and, therefore, not only showing different approaches to victims' rights but also having different understandings and conceptions of crime victims in general. Thus, it was assumed that there were various victim discourses, in terms of victim-related knowledge orders, that could be identified in the legislative process. Consequently, the law-making of the amended Code of Criminal Procedure was interpreted as a process of discursive construction and definition, in the context of which with the concrete definition and implementation of victims' rights a certain victim-related pattern of thought prevails and thus becomes legally fixed and binding. At the same time, this victim-related knowledge order is produced during the legislative process and the symbolic figure of the *victim* discursively constructed. This process of discursive construction of the victim should be reconstructed and its impact on the development and codification of victims' rights be determined.

Data and methods

The discourse analysis primarily drew on documents of the legislative process of the reform. Law-making processes usually progress through different stages that can extend over several years, producing a variety of written material – from statements and expertises of diverse institutions involved, different reports, to minutes of parliamentary sessions and committee meetings, finally draft laws. This has provided the compilation of a comprehensive corpus of data, including the *ministerial draft*, the *government bill*, *fifty expert opinions of the expert procedure*, *six protocols of meetings of the parliamentary justice commission*, *the justice committee's report* as well as *two minutes of parliamentary sessions in the National Council* (Nationalrat) *and the Federal Council* (Bundesrat). The data material covers a time period of about three years, from the ministerial draft submitted in April 2001 to the enactment of the law by the Austrian parliament in February/March 2004.[6]

The collected data and documents have finally been analysed by means of coding techniques developed in the context of *Grounded Theory* (Strauss and Corbin, 1990; Strauss, 1987) as well as *sequential analytical interpretation strategies* used in the hermeneutic sociology of knowledge (Hitzler and Honer, 1997).[7] Using these techniques, a category system was compiled from the documents, in terms of an overview on the particular text structure (issues addressed, concepts used etc.) as well as on the phenomenal structure constructed in the texts. Based on that category system, discourse-specific narrative patterns and interpretive schemes were reconstructed and analysed in-depth. Particularly with regard to the analysis of interpretation schemes, being main elements of the discourses' contents-related structuring, sequential analytical interpretation strategies are predestined due to the extensive interpretation of data targeted by sequential analysis. The principle of sequential analysis consists of formulating as much variant readings of particular text passages or sentences as possible, which are discussed, maintained or dismissed in the further course of analysis until an interpretation arises that explains the text or a specific text passage best.

The objective of analysis was (1) to identify and reconstruct different victim discourses competing in the legislative process and (2) to examine their contents-related structuring, that is, which victim-related interpretive schemes those different discourses are fundamentally based on – or in other words: what the different social actors in the legislative process actually talk about when talking about the *victim*. Finally – and on that basis – it was to be analysed (3) what material effects the dominance (or the marginalisation) of certain victim discourses has on the course of the lawmaking process, that is, how victim discourses impact on the concrete formulation of victims' rights.

The discursive construction of the victim

As already mentioned before, the Austrian reform of criminal procedure is particularly interesting from a discourse analytical perspective, since one of the main issues of discussion about victims' rights during all stages of the legislative process was a primarily semantic one. That is, the discussion essentially focused on the question how crime victims had to be defined in the amended Code of Criminal Procedure. As the data analysis shows, this discussion was characterised by the clash of two different concepts competing for juridification – the *injured person* and the *victim*.

Competing victim discourses: victim versus injured person

The concept of *injured person* primarily appeared in the ministerial draft and the government bill, thus in an early phase of legislation. In these draft laws the *victim* concept did not occur – or to put it more succinctly: they dispensed with it and favoured instead the uniform term *injured person* (Federal Ministry of Justice, 2001: 111f.). One could even say the *victim* concept was avoided due to a potential "emotionalization" of crime cases and – as stated in a footnote in the explanatory notes of the ministerial draft – to its "symbolic character" (ibid.). It was argued that the participation of crime victims in criminal procedures may indeed be interpreted as an expression as well as recognition of particular affectedness, but often crime victims would in the first place pursue the goal to enforce their private rights in criminal cases (ibid.: 115). In this respect, the term *injured person* was considered more suitable.[8]

This stance taken by the ministerial draft and the government bill was heavily criticised by victims' rights representatives (especially the victim protection organisation *Weisser Ring*). They argued that the concept of *injured person* is terminologically associated with *injury* and thus reducing crime victims to civil law claims. As a consequence, crime victims would be systematically excluded as far as they do not want or are not able to enforce such claims, although they have been nevertheless victimised by a criminal act. This would be particularly the case with victims of violence and sexual offences. In turn this would mean to minimise and trivialise the understandable need of crime victims for satisfaction. Therefore, the concept of *victim* should be preferred to the *injured person*, since it emphatically refers to a trauma resulting from the experience of victimisation (Justice Committee, 2003b: 5f., 19). According to victims' rights representatives, the main concern of crime victims is to be recognised as a victim. Compensation and even punishment of offenders are only of secondary importance (Justice Committee, 2003a: 57). Moreover, they called attention to the Council Framework Decision of 15 March 2001 imposing binding requirements on any European Union member state with regard to the improvement of the standing of crime victims in criminal procedures and itself using the term *victim* (Council of the European Union, 2001). Finally, after long and hard discussions during the justice committee meetings, victims' rights representatives prevailed and the concept of *victim* was implemented instead of the term *injured person*.

The semantic difference between *injured person* and *victim* reflecting in these discussions is very instructive insofar as, at closer analysis, it reveals quite divergent conceptions and imaginations of a person being victimised by a crime. From a discourse analytical point of view, one can speak of two completely different and competing victim discourses. These discourses, moreover, are based on very different victim-related interpretive schemes.

On the one hand, there is a discourse primarily practiced by judicial actors, particularly by the leading legislators in the Ministry of Justice that is constituted around the concept of the *injured person*. The *injured person*, once again, is terminologically associated with *injury*. Generally, injury involves a material and quantifiable damage that allows for deriving and enforcing compensation claims. Hence, in this imagination constructed by the discourse of the *injured person* the crime victim is considered as a rationally acting person taking decisions autonomously and pursuing his/her particular interest. When becoming a victim of a crime, the *injured person* joins the criminal proceeding as a private party in order to make civil law claims. He/she calls for admission of evidence, inspects criminal case records, applies for continuation of proceedings in case the criminal procedure has been closed – in short: the *injured person* plays a quite active role in criminal proceedings.

In the *victim* discourse, mainly represented by victim protection organisations, the imagination of the crime victim is completely different from the *injured person* and even its absolute opposite. Unlike the term *injured person*, the *victim* concept is semantically associated with *trauma*. Trauma emphasises the personal affectedness of crime victims, the particular emotional stress and the lasting negative effects caused by victimisation. The *victim* experiences violation of his/her physical or even sexual integrity, also indirect violence such as in the form of dangerous criminal threats, and as a consequence suffers from psychological destabilisation. Thus, the injury the *victim* suffers is of a primarily immaterial nature. To be sure, this does not mean that a *victim* could not suffer material injury too. But it is not this material injury defining the *victim* as is the case with the *injured person*. The essence of the *victim* imagination is the trauma caused by the crime, the victimisation as a sort of experience of contingency: victimisation means the loss of confidence in the continuity of everyday life. The victim's sense of security is lastingly affected, the *victim* psychologically destabilised, afflicted by general fears and, in the worst case, suffering from post-traumatic stress disorders.

Accordingly, the *victim* is characterised by interests and needs completely different from those represented by the *injured person*. As victims' rights representatives stress, the *victim* first of all wishes to be recognised as a victim. His/her trauma caused by the crime should not be ignored but the victim's suffering should be taken seriously. Whereas the *injured person* pursues a (primarily material) interest of compensation and restoration, the *victim* rather strives for satisfaction. He/she wants to be recognised as a victim and expects a criminal law reaction to the crime he/she suffered, a confirmation that he/she is a victim before the law and the offender is an offender and, therefore, what has happened to him/her was injustice. At the end, restitution payments by the offender might play a role too, however first of all the *victim* aims for recognition.

Compared to the *injured person*, the *victim* is described as a person being characterised by emotional affectedness rather than by rational and autonomous agency. On the contrary, the trauma constitutive for the *victim* concept contains almost irrational aspects. And a quality definitely *not* represented by the *victim* is autonomy. Rather, the *victim* loses all his/her rationality and autonomy due to the experience of victimisation. Hence, he/she is not able to achieve that active and strong role attributed to the *injured person*. For the *victim* the criminal procedure, in the first instance, means a threat and potentially further victimisation. Thus, the *victim* cannot pass through the criminal proceeding as confident as the *injured person*, but rather needs protection and respect in order not to be revictimised by the criminal procedure. Whereas the *injured person* is strong, autonomous and rational, the *victim* is virtually the weak, emotional and needy counterpart. From this weakness and helplessness of the *victim* a special need for protection is derived referring to two aspects: On the one hand, it refers to a psychological impairment and a special emotional burden as a consequence of victimisation. On the other hand, it refers to particularly physical disadvantages being associated with a higher probability of victimisation. Finally, the victim's need for protection results from the combination of both victim-specific deficiencies. Particularly in need of protection are those victims generally least able to defend against violence and crime and who, therefore, are severely affected by the consequences of a crime.

The victim in need of protection and the entitled victim

After the *victim* concept had prevailed against the *injured person*, due to the insistence and assertion of victims' rights representatives, the debate primarily focused on how to take adequate account of the victim's special need for protection and which legal regulations had to be provided in this respect. Here, again, two different discourses can be identified arising from the discourses discussed above – both *injured person* and *victim* – and conveying divergent expectations regarding the final form and the range of victims' rights.

On the one hand, there is a discourse that can be subsumed under the term *need of protection*. This discourse in principle represents a sub-discourse or a sort of extension of the *injured person* discourse and is particularly practiced by the same institutional actors – that is, judicial authorities, legislators as well as, at the political level,[9] the conservative People's Party (ÖVP) and the right-wing populist Freedom Party (FPÖ), jointly forming the Austrian government at that time and also initiating (and finally passing) the Austrian reform of criminal procedure. As already discussed, the crime victim concept dominant in these institutions regards crime victims as rationally and autonomously acting persons whose interests in criminal proceedings are practically merged in the compensation and restoration of a (primarily material) injury caused by the crime. However, the special need for protection of certain groups of victims is at least in principle recognised, and in the end the *victim* concept being rather contested in these organisations was accepted and integrated into the legislative text. With regard to the concrete consideration of the victim's specific need for protection, this discourse aims at the most considerate and respectful interaction with crime victims possible in criminal proceedings. To this end, a number of measures to protect victims should be implemented in order to avoid revictimisation – but always under the premise that these measures do not conflict with the primary purpose of criminal proceedings, consisting in the determination of truth, and that criminal proceedings are not excessively complicated. Thus, the aim is to enable crime victims to pass the trial without further traumatisation and victimisation. For example, one such measure being targeted at the protection of crime victims is the possibility of a separated contradictory examination for particularly traumatised crime victims (especially victims of violence), as vehemently called for by victim protection organisations and finally implemented by the lawgiver. This allows for the hearing of crime victims in a separate room without being directly confronted with the accused person and therefore minimising the burden for the victim, while at the same time video conferencing makes it possible for other parties to follow the hearing from another room and the immediacy of the criminal proceeding is maintained to the best possible degree.

Another discourse opposed to the discourse on the *victim in need of protection* is practiced and represented both by victim protection organisations and opposition parties (notably the Green Party). This discourse can be summarised under the term *entitlement*. It is also, in the first instance, based on the assumption of the victim's particular vulnerability and need for protection – after all, nobody gives greater emphasis on the trauma and the resulting need for protection than victims' rights representatives. But as a distinct discourse clearly different from the *need for protection* discourse, this discourse is characterised precisely by the fact that it is not simply reduced to the protection of victims but in principle goes far beyond. According to the *entitlement* discourse, the victim is not simply in need of protection but first and foremost of legal framework conditions enabling victims to participate actively in criminal proceedings. Thus, the vulnerability and the victim's need for protection should translate into concrete procedural rights allowing the victim not only for passive sufferance, but particularly for active participation in criminal proceedings and for pursuing his/her specific interests. In this respect, the *entitled victim* is substantially more than just a witness in need of protection making his/her contribution to ascertaining the material truth in the most considerate environment possible. Whereas the *victim in need of protection* is actually a better treated piece of evidence, the *entitled victim* is practically a privileged crime victim, a subject of criminal proceedings willing to claim his/her particular interests. Hence, this discourse is also, but not exclusively, concerned with victim protection. Its main focus is on autonomisation, on the release of the victim from his/her victim role. The victim should not remain imprisoned with victimhood, but instead regain his/her autonomy and capacity to act that have been impaired due to victimisation. Looking back at the semantic difference between *injured person* and *victim*, one could perhaps even say: the *victim* should finally ascend to the *injured person*, overcome his/her trauma and pass through the criminal procedure as actively as it is attributed to the *injured person*. The *victim* has to be enabled to defend himself/herself and emerge strengthened from the criminal proceeding. Therefore, in the discourse of *entitlement* a rather emancipatory aspect appears. It is emphatically focused on the empowerment of crime victims. The most relevant legal right in this context codified in Austria's amended Code of Criminal Procedure is represented by the so-called *process support* (*Prozessbegleitung*). This is a professional, both legal and psychosocial support service for crime victims during criminal proceedings (see Haller and Hofinger, 2008). It works as a sort of link between victim protection on the one hand and an enhanced standing of victims in criminal proceedings on the other hand.

Quite in contrast to this emancipatory oriented *entitlement* discourse, in the discourse on *need for protection* the victim's vulnerability and weakness are ultimately perpetuated. Placing oneself under the protective mantle of the constitutional state means, in the first instance, a loss of equality and self-determination. Protection has to be bought by being available for the state as a means of evidence. In all of this, however, the victim remains fixated in the victim role – finally the victim remains weak and in need of protection.

Incidentally, an interesting version of the *need for protection* discourse can be found in the party political discourse of the Freedom Party that, in habitually populist manner, knew to combine the demands for better victim protection with the call for a harder line with criminals ("victim protection instead of protection of perpetrators"). The discursive link between victim protection and a more repressive attitude towards criminals appears to reflect the above mentioned punitive tendencies being criticised by critical criminologists as increasingly determining current developments in criminal law. As Garland (2001) states, the new victim orientation in criminal law represents a main characteristic of what he calls a criminal-political strategy of "punitive segregation":

> The need to reduce the present or future suffering of victims functions today as an all-purpose justification for measures of penal repression, and the political imperative of being responsive to victims' feelings now serves to reinforce the retributive sentiments that increasingly inform penal legislation.
> (Garland, 2001: 143)

Thus, the rather conservative victim discourse seems to give some indication that the *victimological turn* in criminal law effectively tends to go hand in hand with or at least promote a (once again) more repressive and punitive criminal-law policy.

Feminisation of the victim as a discursive strategy

In the end, the victim discourse practiced by victims' rights representatives proved superior over the conservative discourse of the legislator. They succeeded in asserting many of their demands and particularly their imagination of *victim*: The term *victim* was introduced into the legislative text, the *process support* implemented, several rights and entitlements to information and participation codified, and a number of further victims' rights and measures to protect victims during criminal proceedings (for example, the separated contradictory examination for particularly traumatised crime victims) extended to a wider group of entitled victims. In this respect, the 2008 reform of criminal procedure in Austria can be regarded as a great success of victims' rights representatives.

The discourse analytical approach applied here finally allows one to study their *secret of success* by reconstructing and analysing in-depth their discursive strategies employed in the reform process. For this purpose, all those analytical concepts from the sociology of knowledge being made fruitful by SKAD for the analysis of the contents-related structuring of discourses and their latent structures of meaning (e.g. interpretive schemes) have proved particularly useful.

For instance, an essential pattern can be identified drawing through all statements and comments of victims' rights representatives throughout the entire legislative process, particularly with regard to the way they laid emphasis on the victim's vulnerability and need for protection. As the analysis shows, victims' rights representatives talk in this respect exclusively about women. At the very centre of their victim discourse is the woman as victim of male violence, particularly in the intimate social environment (domestic violence). In several example cases drawn from the daily professional practice of victim protection organisations the special situation and the suffering of victims of violence is extensively depicted. The example cases particularly tell about marital rape and violent (ex) partners. By this means, they attempted to illustrate the drastic effects of lacking recognition during criminal proceedings for victims of violence, and to emphasise the importance of clear and enforceable victims' rights.

This pattern is, furthermore, not restricted to this special type of victims but appears to be a more general victim-related pattern of interpretation. Even beyond this typical victim of male violence, in the narrations of victim protection organisations crime victims are primarily described as women and, thus, evidently thought of as female. For example, they do not simply talk about victims of robberies but especially about older women as severely traumatised victims of bag snatching (Justice Committee, 2003b: 7). If they refer to victims of burglaries, they cite the example of a female doctor who is in psychotherapy after the traumatic experience of criminal intrusion into her private sphere (ibid.). Hence, even in crime constellations that do not necessarily presuppose the assumption of a female victim, narrations nonetheless exclusively concern women. In any case they do not concern male victims. There is no single statement dealing with a male crime victim or with the particular emotional strain of a man being victimised by a crime, and postulating his special need for protection. Quite the contrary, when a person of the male sex is mentioned in the data, he is almost exclusively mentioned as offender.

This phenomenon might be called a *discursive feminisation of the victim* (Stückler, 2014a). In all the different statements and case examples used to raise awareness of the special situation of crime victims this happens solely by example of women. Statements and case examples primarily refer to domestic violence, rape and criminal dangerous threats. Where that is not found to be the case and statements differ from that type of description, the victim is nonetheless described as female, that is, there is a narrative being about a woman who becomes the victim of a crime. The victim's need for protection and particularly the associated weakness appear in the statements of victims' rights representatives as a quality especially associated with femininity, if not to say a quality of genuinely female nature.

Initially, this suggests a quite conservative and patriarchal image both of women and victims being deeply rooted in modern culture. In modern societies it is particularly women and children who are recognised as weak and vulnerable and, as it were, *innocent victims* which is a cultural understanding containing a rather patriarchal motive. According to this understanding, both women and children due to their weakness are in need of protection by a *strong man* represented by the constitutional state (Steinert, 1998).

On closer analysis it turns out that all those numerous narrations about female victims and that conspicuous discursive feminisation of the victim in the case examples of victim protection organisations mainly might have fulfilled a highly strategic function, in terms of an emphatic and finally successful appeal to such a patriarchal motive of protection, by exploiting a conservative cultural image of victims in order to enforce victims' rights. This patriarchal image is particularly characteristic for the judicial field since the prevailing unease concerning the *victim* concept seems to result exactly from all the associated female connotations. Traumatisation, emotionality and all the other qualities represented by the *victim* are categories tending to be culturally associated with women and femininity, and as such they are obviously hardly compatible to the legal system. The common crime victim concept in the judicial field, as has been shown above, is embodied by the *injured person*, being thought as an autonomous and rationally acting person who has been injured by a crime and now calls for justice and satisfaction. In the light of the gendered or rather feminised construction of the *victim* the concept of *injured person* might be interpreted, in some way, as the male version of a crime victim. This would finally explain what the unease about the vulnerability of the victim is due to: It is exactly the *unmanly* character of the *victim* that makes it that hard for the inherently androcentric legal system to operate with it. Following this androcentric logic, the *victim* is no thinkable subject of criminal proceedings, and as such it can only be placed under the protection of the *supreme patriarch*, the constitutional state.

Exactly this patriarchal image of the victim is referred to by victims' rights representatives during the legislative process. Therefore, it is anything but a coincidence that the two competing victim discourses reconstructed above have many similarities with regard to the victim-related interpretive schemes they are based on. Both *need for protection* and *entitlement* discourse are constituted by the imagination of a weak and vulnerable (female) victim. How they differ from each other and what finally makes them two disparate discourses, however, is the way those similar patterns of interpretation are linked. In the *entitlement* discourse of victims' rights representatives the emphasis on the victim's need for protection is even considerably stronger than in the conservative *need for protection* discourse. There the call for victim protection and victims' rights takes on an almost aggressive dimension. But above all, from the victim's need for protection a legal entitlement is derived: The victim *must* have a statutory entitlement to protection to be demanded from the state. The victim *must* be strengthened and enabled to escape victimhood and to pursue his/her interests and get justice. By means of discursive feminisation of the victim, the androcentric patriarchal social order together with its dominant victim imagination has been taken at its word and practically exploited – in order to overcome it and liberate the weak and vulnerable victim (particularly the woman as a victim of male violence) with the help of the constitutional state from the victim role and to form an autonomous and strong victim.

The decisive factor for the successful enforcement of victims' rights during the Austrian reform of criminal procedure, therefore, was the interlinking of the victim discourse with a criminal legal gender discourse focusing on the protection and the empowerment of women. The discursive problematisation of the women's situation as victims of domestic violence finally proved to be a suitable vehicle for leading a tactical struggle for the recognition of traumatisation and vulnerability of crime victims in general. To be sure, the development of victims' rights was also positively influenced by the Council Framework Decision on the standing of crime victims in criminal proceedings that explicitly used the term *victim* itself and that was continually referred to by victims' rights representatives in their chain of argumentation. Generally, the importance of the enforcement of the *victim* concept for the further course of the reform can hardly be overestimated since its underlying victim imagination might have had a positive impact on the negotiations in a way that was particularly favourable for reaching further enhancement of the victim's standing in criminal proceedings. Last but not least it might have been helpful too that victim protection proved to be a politically exploitable issue also for rather conservative parties (see for example the populistic discourse of the Freedom Party). But particularly with regard to the enforcement of the *victim* concept the strategic discursive feminisation of the victim concept by victims' rights representatives and the resulting instrumentalisation of patriarchal motives of protection was probably the determining factor in the debate on victims' rights. This instrumentalisation and the related recourse to a superordinate gender discourse allowing for the combination of the empowerment of crime victims with the empowerment of women finally was crucial for the success of victims' rights representatives in the legislative process. Some of the new victims' rights would otherwise not have been achieved, but at least the enhancement of the victim's standing in criminal proceedings would have been much more modest. In this respect, the 2008 reform of criminal procedure in Austria provides an impressive illustration of current tendencies in criminal law with regard to the power and the impact of *victimistic* as well as gender discourses on present developments in criminal law.

Conclusion

This contribution was intended to roughly sketch a discourse analytical approach to law-making. This approach regards legislative processes as antagonistic, discursive struggles, in which several social players with different interests, world views and, therefore, divergent discursive practices encounter. By means of an analysis of such discourses clashing and competing with each other in the law-making process, the course of the legislative process is reconstructed and the impact of those discourses on the concrete form and the contents of laws determined.

This discourse analytical approach to the making of law was illustrated by a study on the development and the codification of victims' rights during the 2008 reform of criminal procedure in Austria. First, it was shown that the reform process was strongly characterised by the competition between two different victim discourses – a competition finally ending in favour of a victim concept particularly represented by victims' rights representatives thinking crime victims as vulnerable and in need of protection. On the material level of law, this was reflected in the implementation of the term *victim* in the code of criminal procedure.

Furthermore, two other discourses arising out of this competition were identified, primarily differing with regard to what consequences are considered to be drawn from the victim's need for protection and how this need for protection should be adequately taken into account in criminal proceedings. On the one hand, a rather conservative discourse particularly practiced within the judicial field was focused in the first place on the most considerate and respectful interaction with crime victims possible in criminal proceedings (*need for protection*). The second discourse represented by victims' rights representatives, on the other hand, derived from the victim's need for protection a special legal entitlement. Not only protection, but the strengthening of crime victims by adequate legal framework conditions was their primary objective (*entitlement*). As with the *victim* discourse, victims' rights representatives were also widely successful with their *entitlement* discourse. This was reflected in a number of new victims' rights and victim support measures such as the so-called *process support*.

As an essential and for their success perhaps most decisive discursive strategy of victims' rights representatives finally the interlinking of their victim discourse with a criminal legal gender discourse focusing on the better protection of women against male violence could be determined. This interlinking mainly found its expression in the discursive feminisation of the victim and the victim concept, serving as the preferred means for the construction of victim-related vulnerability. In so doing, they succeeded in raising the legislator's willingness to implement victims' rights and victim protection measures by appealing to patriarchal motives of protection inherent in modern governmental and legal institutions. These patriarchal motives of protection were exploited by victims' rights representatives in order to enforce more rights for crime victims.

Particularly with regard to the discursive feminisation of the victim, the selected discourse analytical approach of SKAD with its various knowledge-sociological concepts proved very useful. It was especially the analysis of interpretive schemes that provided valuable and additional insights into the contents-related structuring of victim discourses competing in the legislative process.

Last but not least, a main aim of this contribution was to profile and open up law-making as a relevant field of discourse research. Considering the fact that legislation and law-making practically mark a *blank spot* in the sociology of law, discourse studies might give some impetus for a desirable (re)animation of sociological perspectives on law-making by shifting the focus on law as a continually contested formation of knowledge and thus on the social construction of law.

The relevance and *added value* of discourse analytical approaches (particularly of SKAD) is, of course, not limited to research on legislation and the making of law but applies also to other legal fields. In comparison to many other research areas, the use of discourse analytical frameworks is rather scarce in the legal studies up to now. This might be at least partly due to the fact that law in Foucault's works and particularly in his numerous discourse analyses in principle has never been dealt with extensively and generally had the status of a "particular object" (Foucault, 1989: 415). Moreover, his theoretical perspective on law can definitely be qualified as rather ambivalent throughout his whole work (see Hunt and Wickham, 1994; Biebricher, 2009).

Relevant legal fields and research themes for discourse analyses might be (and occasionally already are), for instance, discursive practices in the entire field of crime, punishment, criminalisation and social control. Criminal law and social control represent the legal field with the highest amount of discourse analytical research activity by now. Discourse analyses are able to show the decisive role of discursive knowledge for the constitution of deviance and social control (Althoff and Leppelt, 1990; Singelnstein, 2010). In the criminal legal context, research might particularly focus on current tendencies with regard to neoliberal restructurings such as criminal political security discourses framing the state as permanently threatened by (organised) crime, terrorism and other social conflicts. These discursively constructed threat scenarios finally provide the basis for legitimacy for the tightening and the creation of new criminal law norms as well as of measures of social control (Kunz, 2005; Singelnstein and Stolle, 2006). Closely related to such developments are increasing repressive tendencies in criminal law, as already mentioned earlier, including a substantial increase in criminalisation, an increase of convictions and incarceration rates and a directional switch from the social rehabilitation to mere detention of criminals (Garland, 2001; Krasmann,

2003; Wacquant, 2009). The study of criminal political discourses, being at the same time a requirement and result of such societal developments, of their emergence and their concrete material effects can provide valuable insights into the mechanisms of neoliberal government and the specific role as well as the change of criminal law in this social transformation process. Böhm (2011), for example, analyses an ongoing discursive switch of criminal law from "crime" to "risk" and from "the criminal" to "the potential attacker", materialising in criminal legal measures such as preventive detention.

Thus, criminal law alone opens up a wide field for discourse research. There are many other legal areas relevant for the study of law as a specific formation of knowledge ranging from environmental law to migration law. Lange (2011), for instance, applies a discourse analytical approach in order to analyse the EU authorisations for transgenic agricultural products. Buckel (2013) provides an analysis of the juridical discourse on transnational social rights and the juridification of sea borders in the context of European migration management. Another relevant subject of legal discourse analysis can be (and increasingly is) found in issues concerning law and gender. In this respect, research might focus, from a criminologist perspective, on gender discourses and their effects on law and legislation (as has been shown above, gender discourses had a crucial impact on the codification of victims' rights in Austria), as well as from a feminist perspective on the discursive construction of gender in legal texts, for example in criminal legal discourses, in marriage law etc. (Temme and Künzel, 2010; Voithofer, 2013). In any case, law represents a social sphere that is definitely worth investigating by means of discourse analysis – both with regard to the discursive construction *of* law in legislative processes and the discursive, reality-constituting effects produced *by* law.

Notes

1 See, e.g. Becker, 1963; Gusfield, 1963; Chambliss, 1964; Quinney, 1970; Pilgram and Steinert, 1975; Blankenburg and Treiber, 1975; Turk, 1976; Hepburn, 1977; Haferkamp, 1980; Scheerer, 1982; Stangl, 1981.
2 The fundamental difference between sociological and genuinely legal perspective has been already stressed by Max Weber ([1913] 1985: 439f.).
3 For discourse analytical studies on crime and criminalisation, see, for instance, Althoff and Leppelt (1990) and Singelnstein (2010). Foucault himself has dealt with the problem of crime and the genealogy of modern criminal justice in his famous work *Discipline and Punish* (Foucault, 1979).
4 Such an approach basically also allows a different conceptual view on legislation as usual in other theoretical contexts, in which laws are approached, for example, as products of a self-referential legal system, as a consequence of systemic reduction of complexity (Luhmann, 1993; Teubner, 1989), or as mere reflections of societal (capitalist) relations of production (Marx).
5 By critical criminologists and legal sociologists the increasing victim orientation in criminal law is occasionally also referred to as "victimism" (Klimke, 2008; Cremer-Schäfer and Steinert, 1998). They particularly criticise that the focus on

crime victims implies a fundamental perturbation of principles of criminal law traditionally focusing on the punishment of perpetrators. It is feared that this fundamental shift might finally undermine the protective function of the constitutional state (Haffke, 2005). For example, it is argued that the victim orientation in criminal proceedings conflicts with the legal principle of presumption of innocence since the offender as well as the victim is determined only by the legal force of a judgment (Pollähne, 2012; Schünemann, 2009). Another criticism is that the increasing *victimistic* criminal policy would be immediately accompanied by punitive tendencies, that is, the criminal legal focus on crime victims would promote a more repressive policy against criminals through the tightening and expanding of criminal laws and an increase in criminalisation (Garland, 2001; Jung, 2000; Hassemer and Reemtsma, 2002, Rzepka, 2004). Thus, the reintegration of crime victims in criminal proceedings was (and is to this day) rather controversial.

6 It is important to note that the analysis presented here focuses on the parliamentary legislation process in the narrow sense. Ideally, the analysis of law-making processes would also include the entire (and occasionally many times more extensive) preliminary stages of legislation. With regard to the Austrian reform of criminal procedure, its preliminary stages extend far back to the 1980s. This is also the time period in which the whole discussion about victims' rights has arisen. Therefore, an analysis setting in at an earlier stage might provide some further insights since it would have to reconstruct in a historical perspective the emergence of the criminal legal victim discourse being already strongly institutionalised and differentiated at the time the here discussed study sets in.

7 SKAD itself does not represent a specific method of data analysis but a theoretical and methodological approach. Concrete methodical procedures regarding data analysis always have to depend on the scope and the research question of a study. Both Grounded Theory coding techniques and sequential analysis, however, are frequently applied in research projects based on SKAD, particularly with regard to the contents-related structuring and the analysis of interpretation schemes used in specific discourses.

8 It is worth mentioning that the term *injured person* was taken from civil law.

9 For the political discourse, see in particular the parliamentary sessions in the National Council (2004) and the Federal Council (2004).

References

Althoff, M. and Leppelt, M. (1990). Diskursive Praxis und Kriminalisierung. *Kriminologisches Journal*, 22(3), 170–184.

Becker, H. S. (1963). *Outsiders: Studies in the Sociology of Deviance*. London: Free Press.

Biebricher, T. (2009). Macht und Recht: Foucault. In: S. Buckel, R. Christensen and A. Fischer-Lescano, eds., *Neue Theorien des Rechts*. Stuttgart: Lucius & Lucius.

Blankenburg, E. and Treiber, H. (1975). Der politische Prozeß der Definition von kriminellem Verhalten. *Kriminologisches Journal*, 7(4), 247–280.

Böhm, M. L. (2011). *Der 'Gefährder' und das 'Gefährdungsrecht'. Eine rechtssoziologische Analyse am Beispiel der Urteile des Bundesverfassungsgerichts über die nachträgliche Sicherungsverwahrung und die akustische Wohnraumüberwachung*. Göttingen: Universitätsverlag Göttingen.

Boutellier, H. (1996). Beyond the Criminal Justice Paradox: Alternatives Between Law and Morality. *European Journal on Criminal Policy and Research*, 4(4), 7–20.

Buckel, S. (2007). *Subjektivierung und Kohäsion: Zur Rekonstruktion einer materialistischen Theorie des Rechts.* Weilerswist: Velbrück Wissenschaft.

Buckel, S. (2013). *Welcome to Europe: Die Grenzen des europäischen Migrationsrechts: Juridische Auseinandersetzungen um das Staatsprojekt Europa.* Bielefeld: transcript.

Chambliss, W. J. (1964). A Sociological Analysis of the Law of Vagrancy. *Social Problems,* 12(1), 67–77.

Cremer-Schäfer, H. and Steinert, H. (1998). *Straflust und Repression: Zur Kritik der populistischen Kriminologie.* Münster: Westfälisches Dampfboot.

Council of the European Union (2001). *Council Framework Decision of 15 March 2001 on the Standing of Victims in Criminal Proceedings* (2001/220/JHA): OJ L 82 of 22. 3. 2001.

Federal Council (2004). *Stenographisches Protokoll: 706. Sitzung des Bundesrates der Re-publik Österreich,* 11 März 2004, 109–175.

Federal Ministry of Justice (2001). *Entwurf eines Strafprozessreformgesetzes (214/ME): Part 1: Gesetzestext, Part 2: Erläuterungen.* Vienna: BMJ.

Foucault, M. (1979). *Discipline and Punish: The Birth of the Prison.* Harmondsworth: Penguin Books.

Foucault, M. (1989). What our Present is. In: S. Lotringer, L. Hochroth and J. Johnston, eds., *Foucault Live: Interviews 1961–1984.* New York: Semiotext(e), 407–415.

Foucault, M. (2000). Truth and Juridical Forms. In: J. D. Faubion, ed., *Essential Works of Michel Foucault 1954–1984, Vol. 3.* New York: New Press, 1–89.

Foucault, M. (2003). *Society Must be Defended: Lectures at the Collège de France 1975–76.* New York: Picador.

Foucault, M. (2007). *Security, Territory, Population: Lectures at the Collège de France 1977–78.* London: Palgrave Macmillan.

Fuchs, W. (2014). Die Normgenese des Unternehmensstrafrechts: Eine Fallstudie anhand des österreichischen Verbandsverantwortlichkeitsgesetzes (VbVG). *Zeitschrift für Rechtssoziologie,* 34(1 and 2), 51–89.

Garland, D. (2001). *The Culture of Control: Crime and Social Order in Contemporary Society.* New York: Oxford University Press.

Gusfield, J. R. (1963). *Symbolic Crusade: Status Politics and the American Temperance Movement.* Urbana: University of Illinois Press.

Haferkamp, H. (1980). *Herrschaft und Strafrecht: Theorien der Normentstehung und Strafrechtsetzung.* Opladen: Westdeutscher Verlag.

Haffke, B. (2005). Vom Rechtsstaat zum Sicherheitsstaat? *Kritische Justiz,* 38(1), 17–35.

Haller, B. and Hofinger, V. (2008). Die Begleitung von Gewaltopfern durch das Strafverfahren – das österreichische Modell der Prozessbegleitung. *Neue Kriminalpolitik,* 1/2008, 19–22.

Hammel, A. (2014). Who Writes Criminal Laws? Actors, Values, and Institutions in Criminal Law-Making. *Zeitschrift für Rechtssoziologie,* 34(1 and 2), 91–124.

Hassemer, W. and Reemtsma, J. P. (2002) *Verbrechensopfer: Gesetz und Gerechtigkeit.* Munich: Beck.

Hebberecht, P. (2010). Kapitalismus, Staat, Zivilgesellschaft und Strafgesetzgebung in der Spätmoderne. *Kriminologisches Journal,* 42(2), 129–142.

Helmke, N. (2011). *Der Normsetzungsprozess des Stalkings in Kalifornien (USA) und in Deutschland.* Hamburg: Verlag Dr. Kovac.

Hepburn, J. R. (1977). Social Control and the Legal Order: Legitimated Repression in a Capitalist State. *Contemporary Crises,* 1(1), 77–90.

Hitzler, R. and Honer, A. (1997). *Sozialwissenschaftliche Hermeneutik*. Opladen: Leske and Budrich.
Hunt, A. and Wickham, G. (1994). *Foucault and Law: Towards a Sociology of Law as Governance*. London: Pluto Press.
Jung, H. (2000). Zur Renaissance des Opfers – ein Lehrstück kriminalpolitischer Zeitgeschichte. *Zeitschrift für Rechtspolitik*, 33(4), 159–163.
Justice Committee (2003a). *Beratungen des Unterausschusses des Justizausschusses betreffend Strafprozessreformgesetz*, 1/AD, 15. Mai 2003: Auszugsweise Darstellung.
Justice Committee (2003b). *Beratungen des Unterausschusses des Justizausschusses betreffend Strafprozessreformgesetz*, 3/AD, 17. September 2003: Auszugsweise Darstellung.
Keller, R. (2011). *Diskursforschung: Eine Einführung für SozialwissenschaftlerInnen*. 4th edn. Wiesbaden: VS.
Keller, R., Hirseland, A., Schneider, W. and Viehöver, W., eds. (2005). *Die diskursive Konstruktion von Wirklichkeit*. Konstanz: UVK.
Klimke, D. (2008). *Wach- & Schließgesellschaft Deutschland: Sicherheitsmentalitäten in der Spätmoderne*. Wiesbaden: VS Verlag für Sozialwissenschaften.
Krasmann, S. (2003). Punitivität als Regierungstechnologie. In: W. Stangl and G. Hanak, eds., *Innere Sicherheiten*. Baden-Baden: Nomos, 81–89.
Kunz, T. (2005). *Der Sicherheitsdiskurs: Die Innere Sicherheitspolitik und ihre Kritik*. Bielefeld: transcript.
Lange, B. (2011). Foucauldian-inspired Discourse Analysis: A Contribution to Critical Environ-mental Law Scholarship? In: A. Philippopoulos-Mihalopoulos, ed., *Law and Ecology: New Environmental Foundations*. Abingdon: Routledge, 39–64.
Luhmann, N. (1993). *Das Recht der Gesellschaft*. Frankfurt am Main: Suhrkamp.
National Council (2004). *Stenographisches Protokoll: 551. Sitzung des Nationalrates der Re-publik Österreich:* XXii. Gesetzgebungsperiode, 26. Feber 2004, 33–106.
Pilgram, A. and Steinert, H. (1975). Ansätze zur politisch-ökonomischen Analyse der Strafrechts-reform in Österreich. *Kriminologisches Journal*, 7(4), 263–277.
Pollähne, H. (2012). „Opfer" im Blickpunkt – „Täter" im toten Winkel? In: H. Pollähne and I. Rode, eds., *Opfer im Blickpunkt – Angeklagte im Abseits? Probleme und Chancen zunehmender Orientierung auf die Verletzten in Prozess, Therapie und Vollzug*. Berlin: LIT, 5–19.
Quinney, R. (1970). *The Social Reality of Crime*. Boston: Transaction Publishers.
Rzepka, D. (2004). Punitivität in Politik und Gesetzgebung. *Kriminologisches Journal* 36(Supplement 8), 136–151.
Scheerer, S. (1982). *Die Genese der Betäubungsmittelgesetze in der Bundesrepublik Deutschland und in den Niederlanden*. Göttingen: Schwartz.
Schünemann, B. (2009). Risse im Fundament, Flammen im Gebälk: Die Strafprozessordnung nach 130 Jahren. *Zeitschrift für Internationale Strafrechtsdogmatik*, 5(10), 484–494.
Singelnstein, T. (2010). Diskursives Wissen als Grammatik sozialer Kontrolle: Zur Rolle von Diskursen bei der Konstituierung von Abweichung und Kontrolle. *Kriminologisches Journal*, 42(2), 115–128.
Singelnstein, T. and Stolle, P. (2006). *Die Sicherheitsgesellschaft. Soziale Kontrolle im 21. Jahrhundert*. 3rd edn. Wiesbaden: VS Verlag für Sozialwissenschaften.
Stangl, W. (1981). *Die Strafrechtsreform in Österreich 1954–1975: Rechtliche und soziale Voraussetzungen und Auswirkungen*. Vienna: Ludwig-Boltzmann-Institut für Kriminalsoziologie.

Stangl, W. (2008). Die Reintegration von Opfern in das Strafverfahren. *Neue Kriminalpolitik*, 10(1), 15–18.

Steinert, H.-J. (1998). Täter-, Opfer- oder andere Orientierungen in der Kriminalpolitik? *Sozialarbeit und Bewährungshilfe*, 20(3), 12–22.

Strauss, A. L. (1987). *Qualitative Analysis for Social Scientists.* Cambridge: Cambridge University Press.

Strauss, A. L. and Corbin, J. M. (1990). *Basics of Qualitative Research: Grounded Theory Procedures and Techniques.* Newbury Park, CA: Sage.

Stückler, A. (2010). *Zur diskursiven Konstruktion des Straftatopfers: Das Opfer und seine Rechte im Strafprozessreformgesetz.* Master's thesis, University of Vienna.

Stückler, A. (2014a). Die Feminisierung des Opfers als diskursive Strategie im Kampf um Opferrechte: Eine wissenssoziologisch-diskursanalytische Annäherung an den Prozess der Rechtsentstehung am Beispiel der Opferrechte im österreichischen Strafprozessreformgesetz. *Zeitschrift für Rechtssoziologie* 34(1 and 2), 183–203.

Stückler, A. (2014b). Diskursanalytische Rechtsnormgeneseforschung: Zur diskursanalytischen Untersuchung von Rechtsentstehungsprozessen. *Zeitschrift für Diskursforschung*, 2(3), 287–315.

Temme, G. and Künzel, C., eds. (2010). *Hat Strafrecht ein Geschlecht? Zur Deutung und Bedeutung der Kategorie Geschlecht in strafrechtlichen Diskursen vom 18. Jahrhundert bis heute.* Bielefeld: transcript.

Teubner, G. (1989). *Recht als autopoietisches System.* Frankfurt am Main: Suhrkamp.

Turk, A. T. (1976). Law as a Weapon in Social Conflict. *Social Problems*, 23(3), 276–291.

Voithofer, C. (2013). *Frau & Mann im Recht: Eine Kritische Diskursanalyse zum Unterhalt bei aufrechter Ehe.* Münster: LIT.

Wacquant, L. (2009). *Punishing the Poor: The Neoliberal Government of Social Insecurity.* Durham, NC: Duke University Press.

Weber, M. ([1913] 1985). Über einige Kategorien der verstehenden Soziologie. In: M. Weber, ed., *Gesammelte Aufsätze zur Wissenschaftslehre.* 6th edn. Tübingen: Mohr, 427–474.

7 A SKAD ethnography of educational knowledge discourses

Anna-Katharina Hornidge and Hart Nadav Feuer

Introduction

The topic of higher education (HE), particularly in international development, has always been contentious and multi-faceted because it lies at the convergence of a wide array of discourses and, furthermore, often serves as a political arena. Indeed, as the World Bank (2005: 64) has suggested, HE is "linked more directly to the emergence of a broad development vision for the society", which suggests that there is a strong parallel relationship between HE and social and political development. In responding to this dynamic, analysis has often defaulted to topics such as the relationship between the labour market and HE, quality of instruction, accreditation and internationalisation, and the university as a place of social learning. Although somewhat less mainstream, the *political dimension* of HE has also turned out to be a salient discourse for various social sciences, directing debates toward topics such as peace-building, reconstruction, and economic growth (Kohoutek, 2013). Here, common issues include the politics of curriculum development, selection of language of instruction, accessibility of education, culture of extra-curricular activities, and inclusion of minority sects/ethnicities (Tomlinson and Benefield, 2005). Since the 1990s, however, these various dimensions of HE have been joined increasingly by a discourse surrounding the term *knowledge*. The popularity and dynamism of this term has allowed it to achieve the status of something one might call a *super-discourse*, because it is easily injected into pre-existing discourses and can easily come to dominate them. In fact, the influence of *discourses of knowledge* as captured under the notions of *knowledge society*, *knowledge hubs* or *knowledge for development* quickly outgrew academia and – even though their popularity has subsequently decreased – they continue to guide policy-making all over the world. The enthusiasm behind these discourses of knowledge has perhaps even allowed for a false sense of global unity despite the fact that contestation over HE persists unabated (Hornidge, 2014a, 2014b). This contribution outlines how a number of individual studies of the emerging discourses conducted by the authors eventually came to use the Sociology of Knowledge Approach to Discourse (SKAD) to inform and combine these analyses.

While the studies that we drew into the broader SKAD analysis were carried out over a period extending from 2005 to 2014 by different groups of scientists (always involving at least one of the two co-authors of this chapter) and cover a range of alternate forms of these *knowledge* discourses, they shared a number of overlapping trends: the context of a steady globalisation of western/northern academy, an increasingly technology-based shaping of social reality, and a regional focus on Southeast Asia. Individually, the study foci range from ideals of human resource-driven development and national adaptation to the global competition in HE (Evers and Hornidge, 2007; Feuer and Hornidge, 2015; Hornidge, 2007, 2010) to the normative, factual and hegemonic character-traits of globally communicated images of knowledge-based futures visible in policy-making in Southeast Asia (Hornidge, 2014a, 2014b).

In many respects, this research has grown with, and alongside, the development and fine-tuning of SKAD as an analytical and methodological framework. While our earlier work was more grounded in Berger and Luckmann's (1966) original treatise on the sociology of knowledge and, to some degree, on its later offspring (e.g. Knoblauch, 1995, 2001b; Law, 1986), our convergence in methods and analysis coincided discretely with the further elaboration of SKAD by Reiner Keller (2011a, 2011b, 2013). Thematically, we also developed our ideas to match trends in education research, which have included methodological concerns in critical ethnography (Rogers, 2011), historical-evolutionary views on education (Ricken, 2006) and the question of internal learning or reflexivity in education (Wrana, 2006). The result is, in many ways, a guided tour or lesson in how SKAD can be incorporated into ongoing studies and (with some limitations) retroactively applied to past data sets and modes of analysis. In this sense, this chapter is useful for both readers hoping to gain the benefit of a more tailored approach to studying discourse, and for readers revisiting pre-existing work from a more cutting-edge perspective. We elaborate the development of our SKAD methods and framework for studying discourses of knowledge using an unfolding narrative approach that highlights those elements that we identified as having evolved our approach. In the next section, we open with the current positioning of SKAD in our research on HE and, in subsequent sections, trace the experiences that progressively filled out our approach.

How SKAD came to fit: chasing the dynamism of higher education

From the late 1980s and early 1990s (in the USA, European Union, and Japan), the power and scope of the discourses of knowledge have come to comprise a potent set of rules and practices for shaping and directing (mostly technological) development while engendering a dual sense of enthusiasm and urgency for action. Variously, these come under the banners of *knowledge society, higher education integration, internationalisation of higher education,* and other related formulations. These strands of discourse, especially for countries newly exposed to them (we reviewed, among others, Myanmar, Cambodia, as well as Malaysia and Singapore), have since become such dominant prevailing *realities* that excavating their basis requires a comprehensive set of methodologies. While the topical field of *knowledge,* as an evolving discourse in global education, is unrelated except by name to the *sociology of knowledge approach to discourse,* the analytical tools of SKAD have proven to be a useful anchoring point for the multi-level and multi-project education studies we have undertaken in the previous decade.

It is important to point out directly that the field of education is not new to discourse analysis of different stripes – quite the contrary. It has long been a pivotal field of study, with discourse analysts focusing on high-profile topics such as *human development,* censorship and curriculum control, (official) textbook narratives, education and innovation, and the debate over the priority of STEM (science, technology, engineering and mathematics). In many cases, and particularly in developing countries, various discourses of knowledge have subsumed these topic areas by repackaging politically sensitive issues in new, more palatable ways. For example, broad political support can be built around promoting a *knowledge society* or *innovation society* that would be difficult to achieve if the associated interventions, such as giving up sovereignty over HE content, providing secular instruction, or devaluing social sciences, were debated separately. The advent of a new *layer* of discourse on top of the predominant set of education discourses presented us with an analytical challenge that we incrementally, and eventually resolved by adopting a SKAD approach. This was facilitated by the fact that the relatively new discourses of knowledge often referred to initiatives with relatively little physical substance (in Keller's terms, non-discursive practices), in contrast to the divisive, tangible issues they comprised (particularly the high-profile topics listed above). SKAD has thus been useful for structuring the ethnographic methods to help with both our ongoing analysis of the more superficial structure of ideas (such as *knowledge society*) as well as with excavating the discursive under-structures.

For ethnographically documenting, assessing and understanding the practices (both discursive, non-discursive and model) associated with meta-discourses such as *knowledge society,* it is important to draw upon the usual range of etic data sources (documents, speeches, reports, news, etc.) as well as to create viable circumstances for emic types of "discovery" (in the Grounded Theory tradition) (Strauss and Corbin, 1994). This need arises because education manifests simultaneously as a lay discourse (most people confidently relate what they believe education is and does) as well as an expert, special discourse, encapsulating the governance, institutions, business orientation, and diplomacy of the sector at large. To understand what those who we study (i.e. the diversity of actors and their practices) are motivated by and what they can achieve in a given local context, Knorr-Cetina's (1999) suggests posing questions such as, "how do they know what they know?" and "how do the epistemic cultures of those under study reject, adopt, modify the two global discourses of knowledge studied?". Keeping these overarching questions in mind retains the focus on the actors' perspective, while reflecting on the actors' position in the relation to the discourses and other institutional structures. A useful feature of Knorr-Cetina's concept of "epistemic culture" is that local and scientific knowledge cannot be clearly separated, meaning that each epistemic culture is localised. The specific blend of explicit scientific knowledge and other forms of knowledge differs from one epistemic culture to another and has a lot to do with the history of each culture. An inclusive etic and emic approach to data gathering is a useful precedent for integrating such forms knowledge.

For studying actors and their embedding in, and co-construction of, various education sub-discourses, the sociology of knowledge approach to discourse has been useful for several reasons. First, unlike other forms of discourse analysis, SKAD does not encourage or discourage the adoption of any normative assumptions (Keller, 2012: 51), which leaves the researchers the space to tailor the starting point to the *audience* and the project – a useful tool when combining disparate project data or contributions. Second, SKAD is geared for assessing different discourses by looking at (1) their socio-historical embeddings; (2) their construction as normative, social imaginaries of a better future (here, revolving around the idea of *knowledge* and education as being increasingly crucial to development); (3) the social and material resources for action to be mobilised; as well as (4) some of the (un)intended power effects. In doing so, the focus is on both the actors guided by, and the actors determining the discourses, with emphasis on human, everyday practices – discursive, non-discursive, and model practices. The concept of model practices perhaps requires some elaboration here: they are activities positioned discursively to be intrinsic to a certain discourse. They differ from other types of practices outlined in SKAD, such as discursive practices (employed to maintain discursive coherence) and non-discursive practices (everyday institutional and economic processes). The integrated focus on discursive, non-discursive and model practices turned out to be important in data gathering as – especially in non-Western, (semi-)authoritarian contexts – non-discursive practices play a key role in constituting the social processing of a discourse, while model practices (i.e. templates for action) are strongly formulated and communicated in and through discourse.

An additional useful, but less explicit, component of the SKAD vocabulary that we put to use in our running analysis is the concept of *infrastructures* of discourse production (what Keller (2011a) refers to as "dispositifs"), which are established by social actors in order to resolve or guide a particular situation. Discourses of knowledge can be understood as *dispositifs of discourse production*, in that they constitute strong framing infrastructure for recruitment into a discourse, while underlying debates, such as those about STEM, can be considered *dispositifs from a discourse* (in this case, the discourses about the productivity of science and positivism in education performance). Defined in this way, it is easier for analysts to explore the basis upon which discourses are created *and maintained*. Keller (2005: 6) suggests how more specifically, noting that dispositif structures typically offer (1) normative orientations and rules for saying things; (2) rules of attesting to the constitution of meaning; and (3) social and material resources for action. With these dimensions in mind, progressing a few steps in a discourse analysis of knowledge is relatively straightforward. For example, the term *knowledge* aggressively applies a positive connotation to anything it is attached to, sidesteps critiques of component practices, and suggests its indispensability for governments wishing for economic growth and higher education institutions striving for recognition.

Assembling a SKAD ethnography

While it is important to recognise that SKAD is not a method (Keller, 2011a, 2011b), there are various tools and methods that are likely to prove useful in gathering data in preparation for SKAD's mode of analysis and those that, in our case, coincidentally fit in hindsight. As an overall guiding point of the research framework, it is therefore helpful to return to Berger and Luckmann's distinction between *subjective* and *objective reality* and Foucault's conceptual development of the exigencies of power, which have spawned considerable methodological treatment concerning how to excavate layers of discourse and render power relations more visible. It would also be advisable to add to this overarching framework research methods developed within the field of study itself (here, comparative education, development, and globalisation). In our case, as the research field itself evolved rapidly over the preceding decade of the research, we shifted research priorities to match at each step. The research adopted a case study approach, yet without aiming for a direct micro-level comparative analysis between the different projects from Malaysia, Indonesia and Singapore, Myanmar and Cambodia.

The projects, which were conducted over a period of a decade, represented a sequential investigation into the nature and evolution of *knowledge* discourses in Southeast Asia. In each case, the general topic of *glocal* accommodation to multi-lateral HE governance was situated both domestically (development, reconstruction, censorship, etc.) and regionally (trade integration, cultural exchange, economic inequalities, competitiveness, etc.). The range of methods, both before and after integrating SKAD, drew largely from the ethnographic toolbox: fieldwork with a case-study approach that applied methods suited to the degree of complexity (generally, the more complex, the more embedded types of fieldwork). The "focused ethnographies" (Knoblauch, 2001a) approach was particularly useful for the assessment of the reciprocal interdependence between dispositifs of discourse production and everyday practices (Keller, 2003; Wundrak, 2016; in line with this, suggests a Sociology of Knowledge Approach to Discourse Ethnography. As SKAD became more of a central feature of the research orientation, both data gathering and analysis were geared to track up and down SKAD's discursive hierarchy (see Figure 7.1), and, in abstract terms, lock together constellations of dispositifs and different types of practice with various discursively relevant findings.

More precisely, and as elaborated further in Hornidge (2013), in researching the *knowledge society* dispositif with its mainstream international presence, representational discourse mapping included secondary sources (in SKAD terms, *discourse fragments*), such as academic and pseudo-academic publications, conference/event papers and talks from the wider international community, strategy papers, policy briefs, event documentation from international and multi-lateral financial/donor institutions, as well as national level action plans, and strategic plans from individual countries of interest. Primary data collection of a qualitative nature was aimed precisely at the issue of *local activities and consequences*, and included semi-structured interviews with national level policy-makers and implementers, participant observation, surveying of physical infrastructure (transect walks), as well as focus group discussions with interactive exercises. Quantitative data gathering methods in support of the qualitative SKAD data aimed at capturing the nature of global discursive communication with the method of tracking: usage of key utterances in secondary literature (newspaper and academic) of terms such as *knowledge society, information society, knowledge-based economy, creative industries, cultural industries, knowledge for development, innovation development*. Quantitative data on

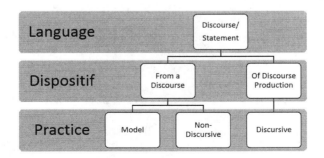

Figure 7.1 SKAD's discursive hierarchy.
Source: figure made by authors.

national level non-discursive practices were also collected, including statistics on R&D budgets, research and science-industry staffing, high-tech product output, publication indices, conferences and exhibitions organised, and patent applications.

For assessing the *knowledge for development* dispositif, similar methodological ground was covered but the focus was shifted toward key actors and locations where the development perspective is more prominent, such as development agencies, poorer countries, and conflict areas. Discourse fragments came more often in the form of strategy papers, policy briefs and event documentations from multilateral institutions such as the World Bank, International Monetary fund (IMF), United Nations Educational, Scientific and Cultural Organization (UNESCO), and European Commission; this also included documents written on behalf of aid-receiving countries. Comparing these texts with those ostensibly prepared by national government committees provides a particularly fruitful area of research. Given the inherent power issues in the relationship between donors and recipients, we conducted participant observation at events where HE models are brokered internationally as well as events where relations are more equalised, such as Southeast Asia regional meetings. Researching local practices, in contrast, entailed more direct, often more embedded, approaches suited to some of the challenging fieldwork areas. While we generally aimed at implementing a broad set of qualitative methods, including semi-structured interviews and focus-group discussions, site visits and participant observation, as well as more unique methods such as *follow-the-innovation*, it must be stated up front that research access and censorship were not always simple, particularly in post-conflict and transition areas. This often necessitated longer visits with more extended and careful periods of building rapport, participant observation, and careful training of local staff. Quantitative data was gathered for understanding the flows of resources unique to the development aspect of the knowledge discourse, including various project funding arrangements, employments, R&D budgets with development goals, and other state activities organised under the banner *knowledge for development*. To some degree, quantitative data on the more general aspects of the knowledge discourse, such as the usage of key terms and coding of documents, were applicable to analyses of both the *knowledge society* and *knowledge for development* dispositifs.

As with most research scoping endeavours, deciding what methods to employ and how many resources to devote to the effort was an evolving process. Initially, the scope of the data gathering methods was connected to the potential prevalence of the discourse; planning requires an open and flexible view toward the functional boundaries of the studied discourse. A period of piloting is likely necessary in preparation for quantitative data collection, but we found that most qualitative approaches could be adjusted in an ad-hoc manner. As research progresses, a particular challenge in this type of research is to remain contemporary with the shifting and fluid nature of various discourses. This is especially critical because it can lead to reflexive observations about the divergences between public discourses and special discourses nested within the public domain, as well as to help highlight strategic manoeuvring of actors and discourse coalitions. For example, model practices and discursive practices from within-EU initiatives about HE integration (corresponding to the specific discursive field) vary in important ways from the way the EU represents HE integration when dealing with different audiences in a diplomatic function abroad. Because the discursive field has been, and always is, in a constant state of flux, coding discourse fragments (texts, meeting minutes, legislation, etc.) by time and context is an essential element of excavating the storyline of a discourse and maintaining ongoing relevance. In general, steps to render data transparent across extended periods (of research) and between researchers is indispensable in maintaining and building up a strong discourse analysis.

Leveraging past and ongoing research from a range of projects

Research into the workings of a particular discourse is often part of a broader endeavour to understand a more general phenomenon. In our case, it was within the scope of a larger set of research projects, within which discourse analysis comprised only one of several components. Within such broader studies, non-discourse related research bears the potential to complement, substantiate, or contest discourses or underlying dispositifs using the toolbox of the respective qualitative research approach. Nevertheless, we found that discourse analytical training and the general openness for assessing the workings of the discourses in a particular research field became a central anchor for data gathering and analysis for most project components. Fortunately, because methods suitable for SKAD overlap with those of other qualitative approaches, they can be retroactively adapted even as late as the analysis stage of an existing project, although preferably earlier. Several of the research methods that we outlined above were therefore not chosen specifically with SKAD in mind; many methods, such as integrating stocks of natural data, and conducting open-ended interviews or embedded fieldwork, were basically employed because of their inherent transferability among techniques of organising data and conducting analysis. As the data were collected in the course of several different research projects and parts of projects, their analysis has taken – and continues to take – place in different steps, sometimes in isolation from the other data, sometimes interlinked. Nevertheless, each analysis explicitly or implicitly builds on the one before.

The data collected in these separate research projects capture the "real social practices" constituting a discourse (Keller, 2011b: 48). They comprise speech, text, discussion, visual images, and the use of symbols, as well as modes of adherence to social norms and values. Data on social practices are complemented by data on the organisational, institutional and social consequences of their related discourses. Furthermore, these were data collected in several different countries, and thus in several different languages and cultural backgrounds. While a sizeable proportion of this body of data was translated into English, the emic perspective on particular concepts is crucial and often captured better in the terms of the local languages than in translations. This is of methodological relevance for studying processes of perceiving, attaching meaning to, and interpreting aspects of communicated discourses and sub-discourses.

The studied individual and collective actors ranged from representatives of Western academia, international organisations, and national governments to large-scale farmers under a state plan for cotton and wheat, small-scale subsistence farmers and water users, males and females, old and young, highly educated and illiterate, as well as those with strong state connections and those without, just to name some of the distinctions. Despite these vast differences, relevant as they all are for certain research questions, a commonality in their actions and practices can be traced to the global discourses on *knowledge* – for development and poverty alleviation, but also for the construction of knowledge societies.

The study of the duality of actors and institutional structures in non-Western contexts highlighted the need to reflect on the common distinction of *formal* (i.e. the status-quo; often but not always represented by the state) and *informal* (i.e. traditionally grown, customary) institutions in ordering and guiding everyday life. Especially in contexts of *weak* states with ambiguously implemented *formal* regulatory frameworks and institutions, the *informal* sphere, or more specifically the *rules of the game* developed over centuries, underlines that many more logics exist additional to those officially enacted by the state, which guide actors in their practices. The research from Indonesia, Cambodia and Myanmar illustrated how this layering of the institutional frameworks guiding actors' practices contributes to complexity. In addition, it pointed to the limitations of working with Western conceptual thought in non-Western contexts. For example, the common practice of working with strict typologies turns out to be too simplifying when patterns of society–state interaction are characterised by functional differentiation rather than segmentary and hierarchical differentiations along the lines of patron–client relationships, gender, age, state connections etc. In such a context, a strict framework can easily overlook important determinants of the system under study. Similarly, Keller's distinction of discursive, non-discursive and model practices of discourse production (2005, 2011b) does not readily match emic categorisations of practices, a problem we found particularly in Eastern Indonesia. Instead our experience suggests differentiating further by, for example, studying more in-depth how *non-discursive* practices follow institutional frameworks, rules and norms of behaviour. Nevertheless, it is useful to keep in mind that even seemingly non-discursive *formal* and *strategic* practices, used often for ensuring access to resources or making oneself heard, can also be explicitly discursive (a reflexive expression of agency).[1]

While it is generally true that a larger body of data and wider set of analytical frameworks are helpful in understanding a discourse's profile, forming long-term habits of data collection around the thorough documentation and organisation of data – or the implementation of reliable and well-systematised data collection policies – can optimise eventual analysis. A similar "organisational ethos" can be found in the literature surrounding the grounded theory approach (Charmaz, 2000) and other research-practice oriented academic discussions. These often not only articulate methodological toolkits, which can be readily (and non-exclusively) integrated into most social science research including SKAD, but also suggestions for data management. Particularly suitable are tools borrowed from research-practice oriented discussions on discourse research as well as ethnographic approaches of data analysis, as they are mainly employed to answer *why* and *how come* questions with regard to actors' behaviours. When aiming for the most direct analysis of an actual discourse constituting and communicating practices, the selection of documents, speech acts or visual images to be analysed requires substantial care. In particular, the discourse fragments to be included should be similar in type and substance. For example, a final report from a national-level committee after years of research and deliberation should not be directly compared with a newspaper blurb. Ensuring that the body of data contains discourse fragments of comparable stature, as well as covers the discourse both topically and over-time, is important.

However, it is also important to fill out the *interpretive repertoire* (in SKAD terms) of a discourse in an even manner so that the weight of the storyline does not shift in favour of, for example, the bulk of more easily accessible documents. This is particularly important when – and this is often the case – representative statements that more simply actualise the discourse are more readily available (and more succinct) than more substantial (and perhaps more subtle or abstract) document sources. Through a process of theoretical sampling not dissimilar to that of the Grounded Theory approach, some rigor can be added to the selection of data to be assessed. With the aim of identifying the outer borders as well as the inner structure of the discourse, maximal and minimal contrasting can be pursued. In this, weighing data that are widely contrasting in terms of the content of the discourse offers insight into the outer borders of a discourse. The comparison of quite similar data (again with regard to the content of the discourse) offers insights into the subtle differences and connotations within a (sub-)discourse. The analysis of the inner structures of the different sub-discourses, their borders and relationships to other sub-discourses within one main discourse, offers insight into the phenomenal structure of the discourse. Each analysed discourse fragment offers a building block of the overall discourse and, with some retroactive organising of the data, can help build toward possible patterns of interpretation and fill out the main storyline of a discourse. The analysis of one (sub-)discourse is basically complete once the analysis of additional data contributing to it does not offer further insight (a SKAD version of data *saturation*).

Particularly for cases such as ours, in which SKAD was not chosen from the beginning of the research as a conceptual and methodological research framework, the stability of a conclusion from discourse analysis can be cross-checked by making use of the different analytical methods and data types at hand. In our case, this included verifying or discovering qualitative data through transect walks, network mapping, database searches, Q-Sort surveys, etc. Another way to validate data of unknown utility is to experiment with re-coding the data to see if conclusions are robust enough under different categorisation regimes. Additionally, discourse results can be substantiated or contextualised by linking them to quantitative data expressing background information of various types (demographic, sectoral, international, etc.). In general, the results of a SKAD-inspired analysis can benefit in terms of robustness and significance from a range of different research perspectives and, in turn, can help to corroborate or refute other analyses. For analysis at the micro-level, it is particularly important to be able to evaluate the applicability and scope of the results; this is the topic we turn to next.

Recognising *realities* and scoping strategically

For a researcher, the first sign of a pervasive discourse is that certain words or phrases that would otherwise be used more judiciously, become conspicuously present in documents, dialogue, and academic forums. In the nascent stages of the development of a discourse, terms such as *knowledge* are still employed with a certain measure of reflexivity, which is to say that everyday commentators are still aware of the phenomenological attribute of what they are saying (i.e. they bracket the word). The climax of a discourse is reached when not only a certain phrase, but also rules and pressures for employing that phrase, become taken for granted. In other words, the discourse becomes a lived reality, understood readily and freely employed to various ends. In line with Keller (2011b: 4), the discourses become "concrete and material" in character, shaped by and shaping subjective perceptions and framings, likewise influenced by and influencing organisations, institutions and (social) facts. Consequently, they also have to be assessed endogenously: as being shaped and at the same time shaping *realities*. Doing so requires data capturing the multitude of subjective realities and framings, as well as the objective realities and factual effects. Yet, since not all discourses necessarily reach this climax, from a methodological perspective, it is important to determine the extent and pervasiveness of the studied discourse.

To this end, it is imperative to stake out a suitable field of discourse (Keller, 2013: 91) – one that is analytically robust (with high potential for cross-checking and triangulation) and discursively relevant (in terms of theoretical contribution). While the projects that we included in our SKAD analysis were all individually selected because of their contribution to an emerging discourse of knowledge, we had to revisit their scope and look for connections, divergences, and shared data for validation. In general, we followed Keller's (2005: 6) endogenous approach to scoping by explicitly addressing the capacity of our combined projects to: (1) analyse historical events in the sense of "emerging problematisations of established regimes of practices"; (2) consider these events "as unintended (power) effects of heterogeneous practices performed by social actors trying to solve concrete problems of everyday routine"; (3) assess the "heterogeneous and not necessarily connected fields of practices behind such surface effects in order to explain historical shifts of transformations of knowledge/power regimes"; and (4) elaborate theoretical concepts based on empirical data.

To begin with, we observed that the discourse under the notion of *knowledge society* has long reached its climax, and in fact, has proceeded through a number of further mutations meant to render it applicable to more domains than science-focused HE, information and communication technology (ICT), and research and development (R&D). Indeed, our most recent work (Feuer and Hornidge, 2015) outlines how dominant HE consortia are using the knowledge discourse to break down barriers of national sovereignty and exert hegemonic control over other regions and countries. This meant that we had to expand our scope considerably to cover an adequate field of discourse. However, this was also a lesson in evaluating relevance/significance so as not to overwhelm the data gathering. When encountering a discourse as pervasive as the range of different discourses of *knowledge* (captured under the notions of *knowledge society*, *knowledge hub*, but also *creative city* or *cultural industries*), it was important to strategically select case studies that were representative of the width (diversity) and depth (complexity) of the discourse. In the case of HE standing in as a representative for studying the globalisation of western/northern academy, for instance, case studies from Southeast Asia allow for the assessment of parallels between the Bologna process in Europe and standardisation attempts of HE within the Association of Southeast Asian Nations (ASEAN).

Ideally one would select case studies that most efficiently unpack the discourse and help readers to make the intellectual leap into reflexivity and objectivity. In practice, however, one often sets out like we did, namely to study certain thematic issues (in our case, the construction of knowledge societies, ICTs, innovation policy, cultural industry developments or post-conflict HE reconstruction) and only latently discovers the embeddedness of these issues in the dispositifs of the discourses. Subsequently, by tracing our way through the structure of the discourse (i.e. from practices on through dispositifs of discourse production), we began to see useful starting points from which to launch a more targeted analysis and presentation.

In our case, studying national-level responses to several globally communicated discourses of knowledge eventually led us to circle back to the non-discursive practices rooted at the national level (e.g. new policies, standardisation initiatives, infrastructure projects, etc.). To begin with, we found the highest churn and strategic deployment of readily "identifiable ensembles of cognitive and normative devices" (Keller, 2005: 7) at the level of multilateral HE consortia, although we also found shadows of power emanating from the expansionist policy of regional blocs (such as the EU, North America, Japan and Australia) (Figueroa, 2010; Naidoo, 2011). Although it became apparent that the international agents were the (latent) source of the most active innovation and aggressive translation of the knowledge discourse, the dispositifs and practices were being continuously reconfigured and disseminated by national agents (governments, universities, students/families) to accommodate and/or resist the internationalisation efforts of dominant HE domains (Feuer and Hornidge, 2015; Hornidge, 2013: 405; Shahjahan and Kezar, 2013). What remained constant was the seemingly unshakable normative view that initiatives attached to the word *knowledge* were good for society and the economy. As a container, *knowledge* operates as, in SKAD terms, a *discourse strategy*, serving to veil otherwise provocative combinations of practices from direct, individual scrutiny.

The mainstream prevalence of various dispositifs, such as *knowledge for development*, *knowledge society* and *knowledge-based economy* in Southeast Asia (and elsewhere), is an indicator that, methodologically speaking, the research sites with the greatest potential for highlighting strategic discursive shifts will be those in which rather normative views of *knowledge* (in SKAD terms, the audience, primarily from policy-makers) meet with powerful agents of discourse shaping (in SKAD terms, actors in a discourse coalition, primarily diplomats and HE emissaries/consortia) (Keller, 2013: 72–74). The discursive cachet of an initiative about *knowledge for development*, for example, can generate the necessary legitimacy for gathering university leaders and education ministry leaders to meet with European standard-setting agencies. The triad of cooperation, international exchange and standard-setting in HE lend themselves to good publicity, just as do infrastructure interventions ("knowledge hubs") (Evers and Hornidge, 2007) that imply a linear movement towards a more technological future, often associated with being *more modern*.

Understanding interdependent and highly glocalised discourses of knowledge: concluding reflections

Over the course of more than a decade, and including many analytical and reflexive leaps among the evolving discourses of knowledge, the sociology of knowledge approach to discourse (Keller, 2013, 2011a, 2011b, 2005, 2003) has helped us in various ways to render transparent strategic manoeuvrings and shifts in HE and science and innovation policy. The studied discourses of knowledge were constituted and legitimised through the continuous communicative and instrumental action of individual and collective actors and their practices. Spanning numerous countries and research projects, our research eventually found a critical foundation on the question of whether the negotiations over the role of *knowledge* in society and development policy, which are usually rendered in an optimistic public discourse of global integration and technological modernity, are ultimately a veil over the power-laden special discourses that are present in the fraught negotiations between university consortia, national actors in science policy, multi-lateral development agencies, and other *knowledge* stakeholders.

In answering this on the basis of qualitative ethnographic research that was, at least initially, not explicitly targeted at this question, we discussed how SKAD can both guide research methods and become a heuristic tool in subsequent analysis. In this, we both draw upon and widen the SKAD tradition in regard to qualitative, ethnographic methods for long-term empirical field research, while also offering insights and guidance on how to analyse pre-existing data within the SKAD-frame and cross-validate findings by leveraging different components of project research. The primary lesson that we draw here is that the open-ended, explorative nature of general ethnographic inquiry can be complemented and enhanced by SKAD from the outset or integrated progressively or iteratively as the demand builds for critical social theory. In general, research projects or other initiatives with a wide scope, involving multiple researchers, locations, depths of field, and periods of data collection, can therefore work to integrate SKAD into their workflow and analysis if comparable approaches and data collection are already being employed. This allows for analysis that is both useful for project members in their individual capacities and for integrating findings in a manner suitable for cross-thematic critical analysis and theory building. To conclude on a practical note, a sample of such an integrated SKAD evaluation of this topic reads something like the text below.

Our findings highlight how the dominant dispositifs of discourse production centre around the optimistic conceptual progression of *integration* (i.e. the inevitability of globalisation), building a *knowledge society* (Western-oriented constellation of academic competition), and *reform* (i.e. the social imaginary of a better future inscribed in the dispositif *knowledge for development*). The arena of HE and science policy in the ASEAN is (historically) populated by countries that variously prioritise certain discourses and domains that tendentially leverage certain discourses or have pre-existing structures of symbolic and practical power. The competitive atmosphere of higher education globally, however, is increasingly defined by struggles to re-arrange the existing symbolic order in Southeast Asia, especially in light of the increasing assertiveness of the European HE system. The different domains are equipped differently to manage these processes. Europe is highly centralised, ordered and transparent but the USA and Australia have, respectively, strongly anchored model practices (i.e. templates for action) and regional embeddedness. Achieving broader success in ASEAN means that both international and regional actors have to simultaneously tie the dominant discourse of internal (economic) integration and development to their practice of *external* (higher education) integration while avoiding the perception of effecting politically unpopular contradictions to national sovereignty.

The strident regionalist-culturalist discursive field in Southeast Asia complicates the typical *knowledge society* dispositif of implementing programs that align the region's model practices (e.g. credit system, exchange programs, patent protection, and innovation policy) with those of dominant actors. Actors such as university consortia, standardisation agencies, and historical trends in academic mobility are thereby re-cast as a continuation of an important type of international diplomacy (namely HE *integration*) that appears to naturally parallel globalisation and economic integration. However, integration has proven to be a far more contentious process, balanced around dual processes of building strategic partnerships and defending sovereignty. And yet, even as the hegemonic tendencies of the *knowledge* discourse, as deployed by powerful agents, becomes increasingly clear in practice, the discourse strategy of maintaining the unassailable normative position of furthering modernity, quality education, and economic growth remains strongly anchored as ever.

Note

1 A similar argument has been made with regard to practices in water management in Uzbekistan (see: Hornidge, Oberkircher and Kudryavtseva, 2013; Hornidge, 2017).

References

Berger, P. L. and Luckmann, T. (1966). *The Social Construction of Reality: A Treatise in the Sociology of Knowledge*. New York: Penguin Books.

Charmaz, K. (2000). Grounded Theory: Objectivist and Constructivist Methods. In: N. K. Denzin and Y. S. Lincoln, eds., *Handbook of Qualitative Research*. Thousand Oaks, California: Sage, 509–536.

Evers, H.-D. and Hornidge, A.-K. (2007). Knowledge Hubs along the Straits of Malacca. *Asia Europe Journal*, 5(3), 417–433.

Feuer, H. N. and Hornidge, A.-K. (2015). Higher Education Cooperation in ASEAN: Building Towards Integration or Manufacturing Consent? *Comparative Education*, 51(3), 327–352.

Figueroa, F. E. (2010). The Bologna Process as a Hegemonic Tool of Normative Power Europe (NPE): The Case of Chilean and Mexican Higher Education. *Globalisation, Societies and Education*, 8(2), 247–256.

Hornidge, A.-K. (2007). *Knowledge Society. Vision and Social Construction of Reality in Germany and Singapore*. Münster, Germany: Lit-Verlag.

Hornidge, A.-K. (2010). An Uncertain Future – Singapore's Search for a New Focal Point of Collective Identity and Its Drive towards 'Knowledge Society'. *Asian Journal of Social Sciences*, 38(5), 785–818.

Hornidge, A.-K. (2013). 'Knowledge', 'Knowledge Society' and 'Knowledge for Development'. Studying Discourses of Knowledge in an International Context. In: R. Keller and I. Truschkat, eds., *Methodologie und Praxis der Wissenssoziologischen Diskursanalyse, Band 1: Interdisziplinäre Perspektiven*. Wiesbaden, Germany: Springer VS Verlag, 397–424.

Hornidge, A.-K. (2014a). Wissensdiskurse: Normativ, Faktisch, Hegemonial. *Soziale Welt*, 65, 7–24.

Hornidge, A.-K. (2014b). *Discourses of Knowledge: Normative, Factual, Hegemonic. Post-doctoral Thesis* (Habilitation), Philosophische Fakultät, University of Bonn.

Hornidge, A.-K. (2017). Mid-Range Concepts—The Lego Bricks of Meaning-Making: An Example from Khorezm, Uzbekistan. In: K. Mielke and A.-K. Hornidge, eds., *Area Studies at the Crossroads: Knowledge Production after the Mobility Turn*. New York: Palgrave MacMillan, 213–230.

Hornidge, A.-K., Oberkircher, L. and Kudryavtseva, A. (2013). Boundary Management and the Discursive Sphere – Negotiating 'Realities' in Khorezm, Uzbekistan. *Geoforum*, 45, 266–274.

Keller, R. (2003). *Zum möglichen Verhältnis zwischen Diskursanalyse und Ethnographie. Conference Paper*. Workshop 'Ethnographie der Arbeit – die Arbeit der Ethnographie, Berlin.

Keller, R. (2005). Analysing Discourse. An Approach From the Sociology of Knowledge. *Forum Qualitative Sozialforschung/Forum: Qualitative Social Research*, 6(3), Article 32.

Keller, R. (2011a). The Sociology of Knowledge Approach to Discourse (SKAD). *Human Studies*, 34, 43–65.

Keller, R. (2011b). *Wissenssoziologische Diskursanalyse. Grundlegung Eines Forschungsprogramms*. Wiesbaden, Germany: Springer VS Verlag.

Keller, R. (2012). Entering Discourses: A New Agenda for Qualitative Research and Sociology of Knowledge. *Qualitative Sociological Review*, 8(2), 46–75.

Keller, R. (2013). *Doing Discourse Research: An Introduction for Social Scientists*. London: Sage Publications.

Knoblauch, H. (1995). *Kommunikationskultur. Die kommunikative Konstruktion kultureller Kontexte*. Berlin, New York: de Gruyter.

Knoblauch, H. (2001a). Fokussierte Ethnographie. *Sozialer Sinn*, 1/2001, 123–141.

Knoblauch, H. (2001b). Diskurs, Kommunikation und Wissenssoziologie. In: R. Keller, A. Hirseland, W. Schneider and W. Viehöver, eds., *Handbuch Sozialwissenschaftliche Diskursanalyse, Band 1: Theorien und Methoden*. Wiesbaden, Germany: Springer VS Verlag, 207–223.

Knorr-Cetina, K. D. (1999) *Epistemic Cultures – How the Sciences Make Knowledge*. Cambridge, Massachusetts: Harvard University Press.

Kohoutek, J. (2013). Three Decades of Implementation Research in Higher Education: Limitations and Prospects of Theory Development. *Higher Education Quarterly*, 67(1), 56–79.

Law, J., ed. (1986). *Power, Action and Belief: A New Sociology of Knowledge*. London: Routledge.

Naidoo, R. (2011). Rethinking Development: Higher Education and the New Imperialism. In: R. King, S. Marginson and R. Naidoo, eds., *Handbook on Globalization and Higher Education*. Cheltenham, UK: Edward Elgar, 40–58.

Ricken, N. (2006). *Die Ordnung Der Bildung. Beiträge Zu Einer Genealogie Der Bildung*. Wiesbaden, Germany: Springer VS Verlag.

Rogers, R., ed. (2011). *An Introduction to Critical Discourse Research in Education*. 2nd edn. London: Lawrence Erlbaum.

Shahjahan, R. A. and Kezar, A. J. (2013). Beyond the 'National Container' Addressing Methodological Nationalism in Higher Education Research. *Educational Researcher*, 42(1), 20–29.

Strauss, A. and Corbin, J. (1994). Grounded Theory Methodology. In: N. K. Denzin and Y. S. Lincoln, eds., *Handbook of Qualitative Research*. Thousand Oaks, California: Sage, 273–285.

Tomlinson, K. and Benefield, P. (2005). *Education and Conflict: Research and Research Possibilities Draft Report*. The Mere, England: National Foundation for Educational Research.

World Bank (2005). *Reshaping the Future: Education and Post-Conflict Reconstruction*. Washington, D.C.: World Bank.

Wundrak, R. (2016). Verschleierung und Vereinnahmung alltäglicher Geschichte/n. Eine wissenssoziologische Diskursethnographie (WDE) narrativer Interviews in Rumänien und in Israel. *Journal for Discourse Studies*, 01/2016, 71–91.

Wrana, D. (2006). *Das Subjekt Schreiben. Reflexive Praktiken Und Subjektivierung in Der Weiterbildung – Eine Diskursanalyse*. Baltmannsweiler: Schneider Verlag Hohengehren.

8 Using SKAD to study Chinese contemporary governance
Reflections on our research process

Shaoying Zhang and Derek McGhee

Our research problem

In our study *Social Policies and Ethnic Conflict in China* (Zhang and McGhee, 2014), we find the existing literature on China's social policy, policy discourse and policy implementation processes predominantly focus either on the texts of policies, or the perspectives of the governed population on those policies. However, as we argue, the former approach often excludes "the analysis of struggles and conflicts, shifts in the balance of power, changes of opinion and the formation of political alliance" on the ground, and thus can result in the conflation of thought and practice and in the neglect of the politics of resistance (Zhang and McGhee, 2014: 6). For the later approach, as we argue, although the "unintended consequences" approach can provide a rich understanding of the relationship between China's policies and the dissidences of the governed population, many of these scholars have simplified episodes of dissidence to being products of the resistances against state policies (Zhang and McGhee, 2014: 12). Thus, the main problem of existing literature in studying Chinese policies, discourses, and policy implementations, we argue, is that it lacks a sustained engagement with the perceptions of communist officials (Zhang and McGhee, 2014: 12–13).

As we argue, communist officials as governmental agents are not simply puppets who are only acting as instruments of government (Zhang and McGhee, 2014: 14). In a communist country, local leaders play significant roles not only in implementing central governmental policies, but also in introducing associated policies locally (even if in discretionary ways). As such, the *messy actualities* of social relations, political processes and policy-making must be seen as constitutive of the "creative agencies of governance in their own right" (Stenson, 1998: 349). These processes generate shifting alliances and contestations at different sites, and always involve negotiations between central government policies and local agents (Clarke, 2008: 17). As we demonstrate, there are numerous cases of selectively and distorted interpretation of state policies among local officials in China.

By focusing on the interpretation of policy "texts" by officials, we reveal the site and extent of the "resistances" among officials. Since socialism lacked an intrinsic governmental rationality, it relied heavily on the conformity to texts. Ways of reading and interpreting these texts defined their ways of doing things and ways of governing (Foucault, Burchell and Davidson, 2008: 93–94). Thus most governing activities in China are based on writing, reading, discussion, and dissemination of texts (Van de Ven, 1994: 5). This discourse making process can be seriously undermined. For example, the means of accomplishing prescribed targets can be very diverse in different *local* settings. Furthermore, local official's individual interpretation, discretion, and prioritisation of policies can also be different. Officials' reflexive and practical interpretations of the structural conditions (policies in this case) can also cause structural transformations (Keller, 2011: 54) leading to the evolution of policies.

Thus, we advocate moving beyond "the analysis of pure texts" to instead empirically investigate how communist officials subjectively problematised specific issues. We propose not only to focus on the examination of "problems" that are to be "tackled", but on the dispositif itself that is to do the "tackling" (Zhang and McGhee, 2014: 13). This is to say our focus is principally on examining the "operation" of dispositif (Ferguson, 1990: 17) in a particular setting (Xinjiang Uygur Autonomous Region in our case) and to find out how officials impact on the effectiveness of government policies. In other words, our study not only addresses discourses contained in policies, but also examines the interpretations of these discourses by officials in order to examine: (1) how discourses were constructed by macro-structures (the central government); (2) how officials perceive these discourses in a multi-layered government structure; (3) the key discourses that the officials use, and whether they replicate fully the official discourses; and (4) to what extent, the local officials transform, mediate, distort or resist these discourses (Zhang and McGhee, 2014: 14).

We designed these questions for the purpose of examining our overarching research questions: are communist officials both governing agents and the governed subjects? What is the relationship between the policy discourses and the communist officials? How are they governed within the Communist Party in terms of implementation of policies? The questions, in turn caused further reflections on our approach to this research, for example, what are the possible data corpuses relevant to this research and how should we build them up? How should we interpret data? What should we expect from empirically engaging with those officials? It is against this background that we started looking for an alternative approach that can account for the roles of communist officials in a discursive field and can systematically guide our concrete empirical research step by step.[1] We found that *The Sociology of Knowledge Approach to Discourse* provides us with a framework, especially for understanding the role of communist officials in discourse making within the Communist Party, and enables us to systematically engage with our research questions.

In the next section, we will demonstrate how SKAD has helped us in clarifying the role of communist officials in discourse making and their relations with discourses, in the context of examining the dual-processes (the governed and governing) of China's governmentality, which has been rarely understood in contemporary literature.

Three-fold relationship between discourse and actor: understanding it through parrhesia

The Sociology of Knowledge Approach to Discourse recognises the dialectics between the production of discourses and role of social actors, while keeping faithful to Foucault's important contribution on power/knowledge. Practically, it presents a systematic methodology for how to do discourse analysis by employing some research strategies proposed by grounded theory. SKAD starts from social construction of reality, following Berger and Luckmann, to link Foucault's concepts on discourse to explore detailed "processes of institutionalization and transformation of symbolic orderings" (Keller, 2011: 48). It can be said that Keller was trying to *inject power* contained in discourse formations (developed by Foucault) into the more or less static *social bodies*, both as *objective reality* and *subjective reality* (developed by Berger and Luckmann). In other words, it asserts that knowledge is socially objectified and subjectively adopted by subjects (Keller, 2011: 45).

Particularly, SKAD prescribes a three-fold relationship between discourses and actors. The first is the relationship between speaker positions of the social actor and discourses. For each discourse, there must be relevant actors occupying statuses (for example, the leader of Communist Party) to utter discourse. Speaker position is the "material *foundation* of the utterance production" of discourse (Keller, 2011: 57). In this case, certain communist officials are first of all the speakers of public discourse. Second, speakers are also subjectified by discourses. In this relationship speakers as individuals can also reveal how they themselves are "subjectified" by discourses (Keller, 2011: 55). For example, in our interviews, officials engaged in confessional interaction with the interviewer, by which they self-reflected on their roles in the communist system and sometimes were critical of official discourses. As a result, our interviews had become a political theatre, by which the participants' self-censorship was negotiated and defocused and they were encouraged to tell their own truth. Third, social actors occupy a multi-faced position within discourses, based on complex positions and identities. They "accept, effect, translate, adopt, use or oppose discourses, and therefore *realise* them in a versatile way which should be empirically investigated" (Keller, 2011: 55).

Having clarified this three-fold relationship between discourses and actors, first, we find Foucault's study on parrhesia is a paradigm that can illustrate this three-fold relationship in a particular setting. We will use this notion to reflect our fieldwork experiences in the next section. According to Foucault, parrhesia (free-spokeness) is the public and risky expression of a personal conviction (Foucault, Davidson and Burchell, 2010: 379–380). It is the *true* discourse of the person who courageously commits his speech in order to defend his point of view on the common interest (Foucault, Davidson and Burchell, 2010: 382). The subject who practices parrhesia is called a "parrhesiast". In an autocratic polity, it is the specific advisor of the ruler who can practice parrhesia (Foucault, Davidson and Burchell, 2010: 196). Parrhesia is associated with the game of the right to speak and the game of truth in an autocratic form of government (Foucault, Davidson and Burchell, 2010: 189). Thus, only those social actors occupying certain organisational positions (officials and in-system scholars in China's case) can practice political parrhesia. This is what Keller calls "speaker position".

Second, as suggested by SKAD, the speakers of discourses are also subjectified by discourses. Similarly, parrhesiastes are not only the part of the *machine* or functionaries, but are also individuals, who constitute themselves as universal subjects (Foucault, Davidson and Burchell, 2010: 35–36). Thus they can also speak the truth about oneself. In speaking *truth* to the listener, they are objectivised as the subject by a dividing practice, by which the subject is either divided within himself or to be separated from others (Foucault, 2002: 326). In telling the *truth*, one becomes a *confessing subject* who is subject to the judgment of the listener. In this relationship, parrhesiastes reveal how they are *subjectified* through technologies of the self (Keller, 2011: 55) that can be "avowal, confession, or examination of conscience" (Foucault *et al.*, 2011: 3–4). The listener to whom the parrhesiast confesses does not need *institutional authority as with the Christian church*, nor like psychoanalyst-like professionals (Flynn, 1994: 214). Parrhesia in this sense acts as a means by which "interpersonal relationships and an aesthetics of existence of self" are tied together (Simpson, 2012: 109).

Third, the connection of the knowledge of truth and practice of the subjects is fulfilled by parrhesiastes' dialectic and psychagogy (Foucault, Davidson and Burchell, 2010: 336). On the one hand, parrhesiastes have to diagnose the polity's illness, seize the opportunity of intervention, and restore the order to things (Foucault, Davidson and Burchell, 2010: 232–233). On the other hand, parrhesiastes have to epistemologically reflect on the self in the course of defying existing power relations and instituting a new experience of reality (Simpson, 2012: 106). By employing SKAD, we examine how subjects are positioning themselves and being positioned within the phenomenal structure (Keller, 2011: 59). Parrhesiastes are acting as a dialectician and a psychagogue that reveals the divisions existing within them and educates the ruler or the listener. In this sense, parrhesiastic practice is a set of educational practices toward the self and others (Peters, 2003: 217), or the practices of "government of self and government of other" (Foucault, Davidson and Burchell, 2010: 6). Similar to the SKAD approach which connects the regime of truth and subjectivity, parrhesia is the study of "the relations between truth, power, and subject without ever reducing each of them to the others" (Foucault et al., 2011: 9).

In the next section, we will illustrate how we built up our data corpus, especially through interviews, and power relations established during the interviews. More importantly, as SKAD suggests, social actors, under specific positions, spatial and temporal environments must employ the art of telling the story (Keller, 2011: 59). As will be shown in the next section, the participants and the interviewer both adopted several techniques to avoid risks, in which officials engaged in a confessional interaction with the interviewer. Interviews are thus used as risk-sharing techniques to convey the *truth*. However, we also realised on added dimension, that the interviews were also perceived to be a vehicle for participants to indirectly impact on policies and advise the Communist Party through their involvement in the production of *scientific findings* associated with our research project. The assumption being that the interviewer in the process of disseminating their research would take on the role of being an "informant to rulers". In return, the interviewer used participants as data carrier for constructing critical knowledge. Finally, interviews had become a political theatre, by which the participants are encouraged to act as specific intellectuals through participating parrhesia in the contexts of an authoritarian country where free-speech is risky.

Building up our data corpus

As SKAD recognises the "materiality" of discourses, thus either discursive or non-discursive practices can always be realised through social actors' communicative actions (Keller, 2011: 53). They are real, manifest, observable, and describable social practice in oral or written languages or images (use of sign). Thus, actual speakers, texts, speeches, discussions, things, etc. can all be seen the way discourses exist in the societies. These different types of *real* existences of discourses can then be selected as *possible empirical data* (Keller, 2011: 53). These data are bearers of "actualisation" process of discourse structure into a real event and the process of modification or adoption of discourses into existing discursive fields (Keller, 2011: 53). Thus, our targeted population is those officials who are working or have worked in relevant issues and their discussions with us in the context of relevant policy texts are chosen as our data sources. The primary research tool we used was "expert" face-to-face interviews. Alongside these interviews, we also examined a number of documents and reports.[2,3] These texts were essential for our examination of how *problems* related to Xinjiang were constructed by policymakers.

Political sensitivity of doing field research in China

In China many, if not all, research topics dealing with social and political issues can be regarded as sensitive, depending on the timing and framing of the research (Heimer and Thøgersen, 2006: 263–264). Research related to Xinjiang is classified as highly *sensitive*. The sensitive statuses of participants (communist officials) in this research further complicated the interview situation, where state politics and interpersonal politics collided and became intertwined (Smith, 2006: 132). The general political environment and the individual's political situation have a significant impact on the process of conducting research related to Xinjiang. From the beginning of our study to the final interview, participants were constantly concerned with the political implications of discussing Xinjiang issues. This was not only the case for officials working in the government, but also for scholars (academics) who are generally considered to be more open and possessing greater freedom of speech.

Sensitivities (risk of telling the truth) and reservations (participants' willingness or unwillingness to tell the truth) can alter with time and participants may change their mind during or after interviews. Certain discourses in China can be greatly influenced by China's temporary political situations. For example, China attaches a great deal of importance to the discourse on *keeping strong stability* at certain times.[4] Moreover, officials, especially those associated with "sensitive issues" are encouraged and formally trained to *keep secrets*. They are periodically educated by "Secret Leak Warning Cases Training" in their departments whereby their consistent self-scrutiny further discourages them from revealing the truth.

Individuals' personal sensitivity can also alter in different periods. An example of this shifting dynamics is the case of a leading academic figure in Chinese minority issues who had initially agreed to become a participant in our research in his office in Beijing. However, at the time of our study, his political situation had been significantly affected by the WikiLeaks's exposition owing to his previous conversations with US diplomats in 2011 where he revealed that the Chinese government would take strong measures to suppress unrests within Xinjiang in the course of 18th Conference of Central Committee of Chinese Communist Party in the autumn of 2012.[5] According to an informer close to senior officials, leaders were enraged about his comments. Consequently, the interviewer was unable to conduct a face-to-face interview with him.

Furthermore, doing fieldwork in China is mostly a matter of the researchers' *guanxi* (connections) (Finley, 2008: 173). Zhang in particular has built good relations with some officials in China, and they supported the research through either becoming participants or helping us to recruit participants. Apart from getting access to participants, another prerequisite of conducting successful interviews in China is to create a sense of openness between the researcher and participants. As Callahan, along with many other Western scholars, have experienced in interviewing Communist officials: "most interlocutors, for understandable reasons, either tell me what they think foreigners want to hear or tell me what the party-state wants outsiders to hear" (Callahan, 2013: 4).

This is the major problem of trust. Western scholars' positionalities, their potential pre-defined ideological obstacles, and their ways of asking questions all contributed to the distrust of Communist officials. As one Chinese official argues:

> Westerners are always holding colonist views and with *colour glass* to see China's minority problems, you think those problems existing in Xinjiang do not exist in whole of China? ... We agree we have problems, but which country, the US, Canada, France, do not have similar minority problems with us?

For what we understood, participants' political sensitivity was always related to those whom they considered to be "political enemies". If the researcher is vigilant enough to ensure a harmonising atmosphere with the participants though maintaining a focus on *keeping the state united* (see below), so that there will be less discernible political divisions between interviewer and participant, it is possible to circumnavigate some of the interview challenges. In the next section, we will introduce our techniques of building rapport and openness during our interviews, in order to create a sense of trust between the interviewer and interviewees.

Building rapport

In order to conduct research on a sensitive topic in an authoritarian country such as China, it is sometimes necessary to employ a range of data collection methods, in order to be able to triangulate data and cross-check what they really mean. During our fieldwork, we adopted a defocusing tactic by communicating our research topic in the following way: our study could increase the state's energy security and help to solve the problems of Xinjiang's insecurities. Moreover, our research will also be a good opportunity for officials to express their consideration about China's minority policies and to respond to external critics and evil forces.

In order to build rapport, create openness and confidences in interviews, we also employed a few techniques such as quoting what decision-makers and high-ranking officials have said before in order to show that the interviewer would by expressing certain already held opinions, and will not make him a *betrayer* of government's policies. In so doing, we were able to portray existing problems (as being) unavoidable social realities from a historical materialist's point of view.

In terms of building trust, a number of our informants were introduced to us by some senior officials, which means that this sort of introduction has already established in itself a certain initial trust between the referee and the interviewer, in order to conduct the interviews (Lee, 1993: 113). Likewise, when Zhang introduced himself as a former official, it is also conveying that he is not only a researcher, but a politically reliable person. However, Zhang's disadvantage here, as a Chinese diplomat who politely responded is that Zhang is now studying outside of China and no longer formally *in-system*. Therefore, Zhang also had to rely on the introducers'/ gatekeepers' political influence and their guarantees to ascertain about his reliability when he failed to convince the interviewees of his trustworthiness.

In this regard, a senior official working in Beijing played a critical role during our fieldwork. The official acted in three different ways to assist us in this research. First, as a gatekeeper, allowing us access to participants; second, as an introducer who helped us to snowball from some participants; last, as a guarantor of Zhang's political reliability. As a guarantor, he accompanied Zhang in every interview he facilitated, in order to ensure that interviewees will hold no doubts about him. For his third role, there are some similarities with William F. Whyte's *Doc* story in his famous book *Street Corner Society*, in which the *Doc* becomes an *inside-ally* to the researcher (Lofland and Lofland, 2006: 60–61), for whom he is not there just to *open the door*, but also to *keep the door open*. As the "snowballing" method was adopted as one of our ways of approaching participants, however, during the fieldwork, the interviews resulting from "snowballing" were not productive. This may imply that de-sensitivity only works between the researchers and the participants, and was not extendable to indirect relationships through snowballed "contacts".

Defocusing the interview environment – speaking truth in a private situation

In order to avoid *too formal* interviews (as spoken in public) and protect themselves, the "defocusing interview situation" technique has also been frequently employed by eligible participants who have assistants or subordinates, especially those high-rank on-duty officials. Some participants brought along their reliable assistants or "underlings" working in their units to listen or to accompany them during the interview. Their assistants will also act as witnesses, just in case problems arise after the interview. As one participant said, "I brought one of my underlings with me; he can supplement some points in case I would not be able to talk". Therefore, in this interview we had two voices responding to the same questions. They were like a team whose players were mutually helping each other to complement, add to, or supplement each other's perspectives. In this case, the higher official was the main speaker, while the assistant's role is to provide some accurate figures and clauses of relevant policies regarding Xinjiang. In contrast, another participant reacted almost like the supporter of his assistant and was introduced in the following manner: "Ms. H knows our policies and plans for assisting Xinjiang very well; she is an expert in this field. Therefore, I will let her be the main speaker. For some rationalities decided by the higher level, I can supplement".

Apart from defocusing the interview situation, bringing assistants or "underlings" may also denote their monopoly of truth and power. Their assistants are symbols of their possessing truth (as they are senior officials who are making the discourse) about questions we asked (Foucault, Davidson and Burchell, 2010: 320). Third, there is also the power relation between participants and their assistants, for some participants the interview was seen as an opportunity to educate the assistant. This case can be observed in the interview with the official in Beijing. He directly introduces his assistant as "Little L is my assistant, I brought him to be here to be acquainted with our interview and I think this might also be a good opportunity for him to learn some good theories". Throughout the interview, Mr. L kept silent and sometimes filled our teacups for us. In this case, the confession of an official in telling the truth not only targeted the researcher, but also their assistants who are also listeners.

Similarly, tape-recording was also a serious concern for all the interviewees taking part in this research. There was a direct relationship between the sensitivity of the research topic and a reluctance to take part in a *formal* tape-recorded interview. The data we collected from participants on the basis of trust could, through the process of doing our research, conflict with participants' interests (Lee, 1993: 111). For example, participants in this research may fear that the information they provided is traceable to them (Wiles *et al.*, 2007: 10). Thus, both the sensitivity of participants' positions and the sensitivity of the topic were the two major factors that combined to determine whether the interview should be tape-recorded or not. (That is, based entirely upon the participant's political status and their own perceptions of their positions.)

Moreover, participants, who perceived themselves as not being in an *official position* to speak (or the right to speak as parrhesiastic practices requires), were less likely to accept being tape-recorded. For example, we thought officials working in central government would be more conservative than those working in regional government, however, during the fieldwork, we found this assumption to be incorrect, and the reverse was to be the case. On reflection, we also reacted differently with regards to tape-recording depending on the political position of the participants. For instance, when we interviewed senior officials, we just brought out the tape recorder and asked whether we could use it, and they would immediately reply: "go ahead" without any hesitation. However, when we interviewed middle ranking officials, we had to first ask for their permission to record before actually taking the recorder out. On the whole, these participants attempted to inject a sort of *informality* into the interviews, and part of this strategy was to suggest that recording would be unnecessary: for example, when we asked a middle-level official working in the local party whether we could tape-record, the official said: "You know, you are introduced by F, we are good friends, we can just freely chat, and there is nothing important to record". We then had to explain again about the usage of recording and measures we would take to ensure his safety.

Tape-recording can also have a significant influence on the quality of the interviews in terms of what the interviewee is willing to say to the researcher. When we started interviewing a military official, we first asked whether we could tape-record the conversation. In response he said:

> I know that researchers need to record in order to do the analysis afterwards, but you should also know that the tape-recorder is like a time bomb, you never know who could listen to it. It is not a matter of trust; it is the matter of danger.

The official's assistant then followed up:

> Y is a very important figure in terms of strategy research, his perspectives are normally reserved for top leaders, it has been our honour to have him at this table, but if you tape-record this conversation, Y may feel restricted, cannot be more open.

As a consequence, we decided not to use the tape-recorder during this interview.

In the occasion where the issue of tape recording was both subtly and unsubtly negotiated, some participants also interrupted us to stop recording for a while especially during the interview when we talked about *negative things about the government* and also when they made policing suggestions, for example, that *some harder measures should be taken*. Moreover, a power imbalance can also be caused by the researcher-selected interview locations. For instance, interviewees in this research project are relatively influential people in Chinese society, therefore the interview locations should correspond to their self-recognised status. As a result, we tried to organise interviews with participants especially those who did not want to be interviewed in their own offices, in quiet and luxurious places in order to get them on board.

Interview as everyday parrhesia and evaluation of data integrity

In this section, we will suggest participants' way of telling the truth can be seen as a parrhesiastic practice. For a truth telling practice to be regarded as a parrhesiastic practice, it must satisfy three conditions: (1) the parrhesiastes must have adequate resources to guide individuals (such as political office or profession, or in our case they are officials who are working on Xinjiang issues); (2) they use conditions of risk to generate trust as the condition of truth telling; (3) the power of interrogation in parrhesiastic practice is in contrast to modern *confessional speech*, parrhesiastic speech reverses the rule of speakers and listeners (Luxon, 2004: 465–472). In the following, we will illustrate how the interviews can be regarded as officials' practices of everyday parrhesia. But we should be aware that "Foucault's paradigmatic instances of parrhesia are those in which an uncompromising orator or counsellor states an unvarnished truth to a powerful person. This scene is only one of parrhesiastic occasions (Walzer, 2013: 3). There are techniques for parrhesiastes to minimise risks engendered in this truth telling. This is to say that there can be techniques partnering parrhesia (such as rhetoric) in offering frank criticism effectively and safely (Walzer, 2013: 6).

First, participants of this study are political elites working on Xinjiang and who have specific knowledge. In our interview, they were provided with opportunities to speak the truth in an everyday situation. The truth told by them that are critical to official discourses in the interviews can then be considered as the product of specific intellectuals telling the truth in an everyday situation (the informal interview). Thus, parrhesia is a form of criticism, directed either towards oneself or another (Peters, 2003: 213). Thus, one part of "officialdom" in China becomes:

> … (their) role is no longer to place himself "somewhat ahead and to the side" in order to express the stifled truth of the collectivity; rather, it is to struggle against the forms of power that transform him into its object and instrument in the sphere of "knowledge", "truth", "consciousness" and "discourse".
>
> (Foucault *et al.*, 1996: 75)

They are not only the *bearer of universal values*, but are gradually linked to the functioning of a dispositif of truth (Foucault, 2002: 131). Second, the risks of truth telling that generate trust between participants and the interviewer (Luxon, 2004: 465), were somewhat minimised. Bringing assistants into the interviews also conjures a certain degree of distrust from participants towards the researcher. All techniques used either by the researcher or by participants as discussed above, were to build trust. Thus, the interviews reinvented a political theatre for participants who are inscribed within an order of discourse (Foucault, Bonnefoy and Artières, 2013: 4–5) to practice parrhesia. Rapport between the researcher and participants can dismantle social rules and created a game of politics. They employed interview risk-sharing, truth speaking and/or using the researcher as a potential informant (to power) to convey their truth on an attempt to "educate" the central government.[6] Third, in telling the truth about themselves, they become *confessing subjects* who were subjected to the judgment of the researchers. In this case, the interviewer to whom the officials confessed is devoid of power. The interviewer as a trusted listener, their confessor, had an intersubjective intervention to those officials. Through this intersubjective intervention, officials reflected on issues and educated themselves as critical *specific intellectuals* possessing *autonomy* (Luxon, 2004: 465). The interviewer also acted as risk-sharer and informant to the ruler, while the participants act as parrhesiastes who are telling the truth. In this game of telling truth, the interviewer was also affected, since this truth telling often "threatens a comfortable position in life and demand new responsibility" to the listener (Simpson, 2012: 101) since the researcher takes on the burden and risks as they have become the bearer of "sensitive data".

To conclude, we brought Foucault's notion of parrhesia (compromised version) to examine ethical practices of participants in telling the truth (or the arts of telling the story in SKAD) during the interviews. This is to say, by using parrhesia as a paradigm to make the three-fold relationship more intelligible, we find that our fieldwork experiences can retrospectively enrich the understanding on the power relations among discourses, actors and the interviewers. We argue that SKAD's actors' art of telling the story is dialectically dependent on how the interviewer has constructed the scene for them.

Through their art of telling the story, we were able to collect their critical views on the issue. Thus, there is another question needing to be addressed: what is the relationship between the art of telling stories (how they say, for example) and the stories been told? In other words, how should we address the question of "integrity of data" in SKAD? As we always confront a question from academic colleagues: "how could you know what they told you are what they really think"? To address this question, we would quote what Foucault has said in his Louvain lectures – the truth was manifested in the establishment of a valid, just, and legitimate procedure of interrogation (Foucault *et al.*, 2014: 50). In other words, the integrity of our data is manifested by our investigating procedures. We are concerned not with revealing what was hidden inside the subjects, but with exposing what they can say under certain circumstances.

Doing data analysis and our findings

SKAD assumes that a particular document of discourse only articulates some (not all) elements of discourse or maybe appear as a crossing point of several discourses (Keller, 2011: 62). This is to say, it is to break up the unity of original data and then reconstruct a discourse based on researcher's interpretation (Keller, 2011: 62). In the process of the reconstruction of our research narrative, we generated interpretations, conceptual schemata, and so on out of the data around research questions, and in so doing it generates types of statements that were not in the actual data as such and could not have been (Keller, 2011: 63). Below, we will illustrate how we analysed our data, how we created our narratives, and presented our findings.

First, in our analysis, we first examined the construction of "problems" by addressing how Han officials at different levels perceive the significance of Xinjiang to China, and the problems in Xinjiang. Using SKAD prescription, these questions were addressed by the construction of participants' *interpretive schemes* such as Xinjiang's significance to China's economy, energy, military and political securities by looking at Buzan *et al.*'s notion of cross-sectorial securities in order to see how actors at different levels weigh and aggregate different types of security concerns (Buzan, Wæver and De Wilde, 1998: 168). We also examined *classifications* of problems (such as Xinjiang's social, economic and *separatist* problems, and, more importantly, the problems of communist officials) and the *phenomenal structures* of their discourses (such as causal relations between economic development and Xinjiang's problems, the responsibilities of various actors and how officials should act concerning Xinjiang's problems and so on).

We found that although many mainstream constructions of problems found in texts are shared by communist officials at different levels, there are many problems left "unsaid" in the "texts" but addressed in government practices, such as policy selection, target maximisation, distrust of Uygurs and avoidance of potentially unpredictable interventions. This implies that the empirical study of "problems" is as sociologically and methodological important as pure "texts" analysis approach. Through empirical research with officials on the front-line, we have also been able to get beneath the "official" problematisation to begin to observe issues that are left un-prescribed in state policies.

Second, following the un-prescribed problems, we used SKAD's two types of dispositif to analyse how the government practice in China really works. As Keller identifies, there are two types of dispositif: (1) "the institutional foundation, the total of all material, practical, personal, cognitive, and normative infrastructure of discourse production", for example, discourse making within the Communist system, and (2) "the infrastructures of implementation emerging out of discursively configured problematisations of fields of practice" for example, new policies to help addressing specific "problems" (Keller, 2011: 56–60). Having clarified these two types of dispositif, we were able to examine how the infrastructure of implementation is to be constructed by China's newly launched programs and how communist officials are to be governed by the infrastructure of implementation.

At first glance, some newly established policies, such as the Han official exchange program, might be perceived as technical solutions to the problems identified in the "texts". However, from the perspectives of our participants', the Han officials in Xinjiang are often problematised as "irresponsible", "unable to understand and implement minority policies" and possessing liberalised identities. Thus, these "problems" that are left unproblematised in official "texts" in actual fact lay the ground for the critical analysis of Han official exchange program.

We then find that in many ways the governing of the party is fulfilled in the course of governing people, which is the dual process of China's governmentality. This is to say, the governmentality of a socialist country in actual fact "could be called a governmentality of the party" (Foucault, Burchell and Davidson, 2008: 191). The governmentality of the Party is hiding behind the governing practice towards minority people. In SKAD's words, "the infrastructures of implementation" are de-politicised into technical problems in the name of improving the efficiency of implementation. It is similar to what Ferguson has found in "anti-politics machine", by which the fundamental effects of programmes are to de-politicalise "the problems of officials" and "political unification" (Ferguson, 1990: 256). Through these processes we can observe that a particular art of governing through "taking what is essentially a political problem, removing it from the realm of political discourse, and recasting it in the neutral language of science", ensures the enhancement of normalisation power (Dreyfus and Rabinow, 1982: 196).

Third, having discussed the problematisation and China's dual-process governmentality, we then addressed the institutional foundation of the Communist Party in discourse making. We do this in order to understand and analyse how the Communist Party produces discourses and how power relations evolve within this system. We have illustrated how different discourses compete with each other, in the context of the "fragmented" hierarchical and complex Communist Party. By so doing, we provided an empirical analysis of how communist officials resist central government's policies related to Xinjiang through evidence of their resistances. As also revealed, in many cases, "programs" are either in the form of "papers without power" (official policies) or "programs exist in implementation" (governing from below). Thus, we proposed that programs in China should be examined in a more pragmatic way. That is to say although social actors are dialectically constructing and constructed by the society, it is the adaptation of the "strategic reasons" of actors amongst various discourses that makes the social practices possible.

Fourth, having separately addressed the construction of problems, dispositif, and the effects of discourses, we then proceeded to articulate the complex power relations revealed within these three themes. For example, by taking metaphors from Foucault's study of the abnormal, we showed that the construction of Xinjiang's problems is actually the process of diagnosing the "serious diseases of the child" through advocating the importance of the "child" together with a critique of the "irresponsible parents" who are unable to look after the "child". Thus to cure the diseases of the "child", the central government has taken measures to ensure unification, not only in relation to its minority population, but also towards its communist officials who are the instruments of the Communist Party. However, as we demonstrated, the construction of problems and associated practices are seriously challenged within the party, since there are many problems within the process of discourse building, circulating and implementation at different levels.

Foucault's political analogy of the triadic relationship between doctors, parents and children can also be enriched by this empirical study. For example, doctors can become parents in some cases, parents are sometimes also patients, but the child is always the child. More actors can be also brought into this evolving relationship that also includes other family members (uncles and aunts), which means that the problem of power will become fundamentally the problem within the governing mechanism. Thus, linear resistances between the governing and the governed have little purchase if the child cannot fundamentally challenge the role of doctors and that of parents. In this regard, SKAD, by distinguishing between actors and speakers, "may identify silent or silenced voices". In our case, international actors who are silenced in China. Thus, we propose to examine the role of international actors, through which Foucault's paternalism framework can then be enlarged into power relations across certain polities in the globalisation era, during which time normative discourses have been empowering the "Child" to revolt. This can also enable us to see whether SKAD can be adopted to study power relations between internal actors and external actors and how the use of SKAD can be horizontally expanded into what Keller calls "transnational discourse space".

Concluding remarks

As Keller (2011: 61–62) argues, the analysis according to *The Sociology of Knowledge Approach to Discourse* is a

> sequential analysis of textual data directed towards its own research questions, to give an account of discursive claims and statements beyond the single utterance or discursive event: line by line, step by step development, debate and choice of interpretations, in order to build up a socially accountable analysis.

From this point of departure, we would discuss the challenges we faced in using it in order to produce a socially accountable discourse. We find, in many ways, Keller's "step by step development, debate and choice of interpretations" is in actual fact a paradigm-seeking process in every step of our reflection, by which numerous "stories" developed in different spaces and times are collected and partly used in service of compiling our own research narrative.

For example, in our case, we used SKAD's framework as a paradigm to make discourse building in China intelligible; we used Foucault's parrhesia as a paradigm to make officials' art of telling story knowable; we used Buzan *et al.*'s securitisation as a paradigm to understand China's crack down on unrests in Xinjiang; we used Stenson's governing from below as a paradigm to appreciate officials' resistances. In the end, we used Foucault's paternalism as a paradigm to articulate the sub-paradigms listed above. Therefore, our big story contains many small stories. It does not mean that Foucault's paternalism is necessarily more important than Buzan *et al.*'s securitisation. The division of big and small can interchange depending on different research questions. That is to say using a paradigmatic approach does not necessitate the comparison of predefined examples, rather it calls into question dichotomous oppositions, the objective is to transform the dichotomy's terms into indiscernible entities (Agamben, D'Isanto and Attell, 2009: 19).

The theoretical ground of the paradigmatic approach lies in, first of all, that paradigms establish a broader problematic context that they both constitute and make intelligible and go from a particular case to another particular case. It obeys not the logic of the metaphorical transfer of meaning but the analogical logic of the example (Agamben, D'Isanto and Attell, 2009: 17–18). It can be theoretical frameworks, case studies, and so on. For example, the "panoptic modality of power" can function as a paradigm of the societies of control by exposing the power relations of modern disciplinary society, in which it is a paradigm (Agamben, D'Isanto and Attell, 2009: 17). It is isolated from its context only insofar as, by exhibiting its own singularity, it makes intelligible a new ensemble, whose homogeneity it itself constitutes (Agamben, D'Isanto and Attell, 2009: 18).

Second, the paradigm is never already given, but is generated and produced through "placing alongside", "conjoining together", "showing", and "exposing" by the researchers. Thus the paradigmatic relation occurs between the singularity (which thus becomes a paradigm) and its exposition (its intelligibility) (Agamben, D'Isanto and Attell, 2009: 23). Thus, similar with what SKAD sees social reality as both objective and subjective, the discovery of social reality is thus a double-sided activity (Foucault *et al.*, 2014: 59). On the one hand, the discovery must bring to light the event itself; on the other hand, the discovery of the relationship between the researcher and event (Foucault *et al.*, 2014: 59). In other words, no fact emerges without giving rise to the emerging of the knowing subject itself (Agamben, 2009: 217). What is in question here is the epistemological paradigm of inquiry itself (Agamben, D'Isanto and Attell, 2009: 89). For SKAD, this means the effectiveness of using SKAD can be evaluated through examining the researcher's capacity to recognise and articulate paradigmatic cases. The ways in which a research identifies a paradigm is significant as belonging to a paradigmatic group and whether this is exemplary and singular. In SKAD's terminology, convincingly telling a story requires the researcher to recognise other well-known stories, wherever and whenever they are developed.

In this sense, SKAD can be seen as both a general and a particular approach. It is general as it allows researchers to analyse cases across different spaces and times. It is particular as what SKAD scholars produce are always particular narratives. Thus, it is a remnant produced by the opposition of subjective and objective that does not fit into dialectical thought (De la Durantaye, 2009: 299). The notion of *remnant* regards the impossibility for the part and the all to coincide with themselves or with each other (Agamben, 2005: 55). Remnant exists as a heterogeneous multiplicity and the homogeneous medium of countability (Safranski, 1999: 62–63). In this sense, SKAD is a paradigm, by which the whole of social bodies that are both objective and subjective is exposed from SKAD's paradigmatic exposition (Agamben, D'Isanto and Attell, 2009: 27) by Keller. SKAD stands for all social bodies from the fact that it is one case among others (Agamben, D'Isanto and Attell, 2009: 20). In this sense, the remnant is a paradigm and the paradigm is the remnant. In our case, the manipulation of "problems" by officials, or their positive resistance, can be seen as a remnant of the division between official policy and unofficial policy, or a paradigm of Chinese contemporary governance.

Moreover, we also find that drawing many stories or paradigms in constructing our own story would never fully satisfy what we were looking to understand. There are always problems left un-tackled. For example, we find the role of interviewer cannot be fully included by parrhesia's framework and Foucault's paternalist framework cannot expose how the child is able to revolt and so on. Thus, the paradigm-seeking process is more about posing more questions than giving answers that need our endless effort to know other stories, articulate them into new research plans and produce more paradigms.

Notes

1 We discussed three approaches: discursive approach to governmentality study, realist approach to governmentality study, and critical realist approach. For details, please see Zhang and McGhee (2014: 18–19).
2 Before commencing our fieldwork, we consulted an experienced politician in Beijing about whom we should approach to ask about minority policy-making. China's minority policy-making is a very complicated process, involving a large number of the Communist Party's organisations and relevant governmental departments. Influenced by the suggestions of the politician, we reorganised the participants list that we had previously prepared in the UK to include additional officials. As a result, we interviewed twenty-three participants during the fieldwork.
3 For example the compiled minority policy handbook edited by the Central Ethnic Committee. We have also analysed several government documents, reports and communications dealing with Xinjiang issues, Xinjiang's education and Xinjiang's economic development reports.
4 For example, political conferences convened by the Central Committee of Chinese Communist Party every year.
5 www.wikileaks.ch/cable/2009/12/09BEIJING3314.html [Accessed 08 September 2011].
6 Many participants expressed that the researchers should disseminate the "scientific findings" of our research to higher leaders or relevant central department in order to let them "know" how the "problems" should be solved.

References

Agamben, G. (2005). *The Time That Remains: A Commentary on the Letter to the Romans*. Stanford: Stanford University Press.
Agamben, G. (2009). Philosophical Archaeology. *Law and Critique*, 20(3), 211–231.
Agamben, G., D'Isanto, L. and Attell, K. (2009). *The Signature of All Things: On Method*. New York: Zone Books.
Buzan, B., Wæver, O. and De Wilde, J. (1998). *Security: a new framework for analysis*. Boulder: Lynne Rienner Publishers.
Callahan, W. A. (2013). *China Dreams: 20 Visions of the Future*. Oxford: Oxford University Press.
Clarke, J. (2008). Governing the Local? A Response to Jevin Stenson. *Social Work and Society*, 6(1), 15–20.
De la Durantaye, L. (2009). *Giorgio Agamben: A Critical Introduction*. Stanford: Stanford University Press.
Dreyfus, H. L. and Rabinow, P. (1982). *Michel Foucault: Beyond Structuralism and Hermeneutics*. Chicago: The University of Chicago Press.
Ferguson, J. (1990). *The Anti-politics Machine: 'Development', Depoliticization and Bureaucratic Power in Lesotho*. New York: Cambridge University Press.
Finley, J. S. (2008). Review of Doing Fieldwork in China. *The China Journal*, 59, 172–174.
Flynn, T. (1994). *Foucault as Parrhesiast: His Last Course at the Collège de France (1984)*. London: Routledge.
Foucault, M. (2002). *Power: The Essential Works of Michel Foucault 1954-1984*. London: Penguin Books.
Foucault, M., Burchell, G. and Davidson, A. I. (2008). *The Birth of Biopolitics: Lectures at the Collège de France, 1978–1979*. New York: Palgrave Macmillan.
Foucault, M., Davidson, A. I. and Burchell, G. (2010). *The Government of Self and Others: Lectures at the Collège de France, 1982–1983*. New York: Palgrave Macmillan.
Foucault, M., Bonnefoy, C. and Artières, P. (2013). *Speech Begins After Death*. Minneapolis, MN: University of Minnesota Press.
Foucault, M., Brion, F., Harcourt, B. E. and Sawyer, S. W. (2014). *Wrong-Doing, Truth-Telling: The Function of Avowal in Justice*. Chicago: University of Chicago Press.
Foucault, M., Lotringer, S., Hochroth, L. and Johnston, J. (1996). *Foucault live: Collected Interviews, 1961–1984*. New York: Semiotexte/Smart Art.
Foucault, M., Gros, F., Ewald, F., Fontana, A., Davidson, A. I. and Burchell, G. (2011). *The Courage of Truth: The Government of Seld and Others 2: Lectures at the Collège de France 1983–1984*. New York: Palgrave Macmillan.
Heimer, M. and Thøgersen, S. (2006). *Doing Fieldwork in China*. Honolulu: University of Hawaii Press.
Keller, R. (2011). The Sociology of Knowledge Approach to Discourse (SKAD). *Human Studies*, 34(1), 43–65.
Lee, R. M. (1993). *Doing Research on Sensitive Topics*. London: Sage.
Lofland, J. and Lofland, L. (2006). *Analyzing Social Settings: A Guide to Qualitative Observation and Analysis*. Belmont: Wadsworth/Thomson Learning.
Luxon, N. (2004). Truthfulness, Risk, and Trust in the Late Lectures of Michel Foucault. *Inquiry*, 47(5), 464–489.

Peters, M. A. (2003). Truth-telling as an Educational Practice of the Self: Foucault, Parrhesia and the Ethics of Subjectivity. *Oxford Review of Education*, 29(2), 207–224.

Safranski, R. (1999). *Martin Heidegger: Between Good and Evil.* London: Harvard University Press.

Simpson, Z. (2012). The Truths We Tell Ourselves: Foucault on Parrhesia. *Foucault Studies*, 13, 99–115.

Smith, J. N. (2006). Research Report: Maintaining Margins: The Politics of Ethnographic Fieldwork in Chinese Central Asia. *The China Journal*, (56), 131–147.

Stenson, K. (1998). Beyond Histories of the Present. *Economy and Society*, 27(4), 333–352.

Van de Ven, H. J. (1994). The Power of Words: The Emergence of the Text-Centered Party. In: T. Saich and H. J. Van de Ven, eds., *New Perspectives on the Chinese Communist Revolution.* Armonk: M. E. Sharpe, 5–33.

Walzer, A. E. (2013). Parrēsia, Foucault, and the Classical Rhetorical Tradition. *Rhetoric Society Quarterly*, 43(1), 1–21.

Wiles, R., Crow, G., Charles, V. and Heath, S. (2007). Informed Consent and the Research Process: Following Rules or Striking Balances? *Sociological Research Online*, 12(2).

Zhang, S. and McGhee, D. (2014). *Social Policies and Ethnic Conflict in China: Lessons from Xinjiang.* London: Palgrave Macmillan UK.

9 Using SKAD to analyse classification practices in public health

Methodological reflections on the research process

Hella von Unger, Penelope Scott and Dennis Odukoya

Introduction

In qualitative research, there is no "golden standard" methodology and no single methodological practice is per se privileged over another (Denzin and Lincoln, 2011: 6). Given the wide variety of methodological traditions and approaches in the interpretive paradigm, the question arises as to how we choose an appropriate methodology. This chapter shows how the Sociology of Knowledge Approach to Discourse Analysis (SKAD) provides a good methodological *fit* for a qualitative research project that pursues an interest in health discourses and ethnicity classification from a sociological point of view. Any discourse analysis entails prior assumptions about what constitutes a "discourse", and given that multiple theoretical approaches exist, the theoretical position, i.e. the specific discourse theory basis, should be clarified early in the research process (Keller, 2013: 69). In the project described here, we chose discourse theory as conceptualised in SKAD given the fruitful combination of Foucauldian thought and the sociology of knowledge with its unique attention to the role of actors and its fitting conceptualisation of categorisation that matched our research interests.

We first describe some of the theoretical concepts (such as *categorisation* and *classification*) and approaches (such as *discourse theory*) that inform our perspective and research question before we outline the specific project and study design. We then discuss some of the practical challenges we encountered in the course of the research process as well as the benefits of integrating aspects of neighbouring methodologies such as Grounded Theory (Charmaz, 2014) and Situational Analysis (Clarke, 2005; Clarke, Friese and Washburn, 2015), which have been described as compatible with SKAD methodology (Keller, 2012: 72–73).

Theoretical approaches to categorisation and classification

Categorisation and classification practices have traditionally been key issues in sociology – especially in the sociology of knowledge tradition (Berger and Luckmann, [1966] 1975; Douglas, 1986; Durkheim and Mauss, [1903] 1969) as well as in the field of Science and Technology Studies (STS). Classification, including scientific and administrative classifications, have also been a central concern in the works of Michel Foucault (1970, 1972). In SKAD, which integrates these strands of thinking, Reiner Keller (2011b: 243–244) suggests that the analysis of classifications may in fact serve as a main point of entry for analysing discourses. From a social constructivist point of view, classification constitutes a relatively formalised and institutionally stabilised form of social typification. Through analysing the genesis and function of classification processes, we are able to reveal their performative effects: classifications do not give an order to a *pre-existing* reality by sorting it into fitting categories (as a perspective of *representation* would suggest), instead classifications *enable* the experience of any reality and form the *basis* for its interpretation (ibid.).

Sociological perspectives typically frame processes of categorisation as *social* processes and examine the social aspects of the genesis and workings of classification systems. Tendencies of *naturalising* and *essentialising* classification systems (for example through common sense, biological or psychological explanations) are thus questioned – independent of whether human or non-human phenomena and objects (such as plants or animals) are concerned. In their seminal work on basic forms of classification, Émile Durkheim and Marcel Mauss ask how categories come about: "Every classification implies a hierarchical order for which neither the tangible world nor our mind gives us the model. We therefore have reason to ask where it was found". (Durkheim and Mauss, [1903] 1969: 5). Their answer points to the centrality of society: categories are collective imaginations of reality; they derive not from the "natural", nor the individual, but from the social – and they reproduce existing social hierarchies. Following up on this line of work, Mary Douglas took a closer look at the role that institutions play in providing us with the categories we use. She notes: "Our minds are running on the old treadmill already. How can we possibly think of ourselves in society except by using the classifications established in our institutions?" (Douglas, 1986: 99). This perspective on categorisation as an outcome of existing social orders and as a product of social institutions highlights an important aspect of the phenomenon. However, it is only one part of the story and it should not be (mis)understood in an overly schematic and simplified fashion. First of all, *multiple* social hierarchies and institutions exist in any social world. Furthermore, more recent works on social categorisation by state institutions point to the "political conflicts that arise over the choice and use of categories" (Starr, 1992: 266) thus stressing the work, struggle and negotiation over social categories in modern societies. The classifications provided by institutions vary and change and their uptake is not always straightforward – in fact, the way actors *use* them can be subversive and the meaning of the categories can change. It is thus necessary to take a closer look at how social categories come about and what happens with the categories provided by institutions.

In the sociological literature, the terms *categorisation* and *classification* are used more or less interchangeably. However, for the purposes of the current project, we call the basic act of identifying, defining, sorting and naming *categorisation*. The units thus created are categories. These tend to relate to one another. The system of how specific categories relate, the order they constitute, we call a system of *classification*.

Epidemiological classifications in public health

Our research interest focuses on categorisations and classifications in health reporting and epidemiology. Epidemiology is a sub-discipline of medicine concerned with explaining, monitoring (*surveilling*) and controlling the spread of diseases in populations. Health reporting is an applied part of epidemiology – carried out by public health institutions in charge of generating administrative statistics about the spread of diseases within a specified population. Many sociological studies have explored classification systems in administration, science and medicine (Bowker and Star, 2000; Epstein, 2007; Friese, 2010; Hacking, 1982, 1986; Jasanoff, 2004; Starr, 1992). The work of Geoffrey Bowker and Susan Leigh Starr (2000) is particularly pertinent to the current study. In their analysis of the international classification system of medical diseases (ICD-10), they show how this system is based on socially situated understandings of disease. The classification system is the product of various processes of contention and negotiation, and the categories are not neutral descriptors. Instead, they reflect and enable specific perspectives: "… each category valorises some point of view and silences another" (Bowker and Star, 2000: 5). Categories thus reflect the perspective of their creators – an aspect of classification also called "partiality" (Polzer, 2008: 480).

This conceptual understanding of categorisation processes and classification systems underscores a basic tenet of the sociology of knowledge, namely that knowledge is socially and historically contingent. In the area of knowledge on infectious diseases, Ludwik Fleck ([1935] 1979) showed in an early study on syphilis how "scientific facts" about the disease were shaped by the specific social, historical and institutional contexts in which they were generated. His notion of "thought collectives" predates similar theoretical concepts such as the "episteme" developed by Michel Foucault (1970) and "epistemic cultures" described by Karin Knorr-Cetina (1999).

The current study focuses on migration and ethnicity-related categorisation in public health discourses of infectious diseases. Michel Foucault

(1984) showed how the measurement of the health, illness and mortality of a "population" became a central feature of power and bio-politics in modern societies. Since the eighteenth century, public health surveillance systems have been developed to generate statistical and epidemiological knowledge for the purpose of governing the health of the population. Categories were introduced to divide the population in sub-populations and to describe characteristics of individuals and groups at increased risk of certain diseases.

As stated before, these categories and classification systems are closely related to issues of power – they both produce and reproduce specific power constellations. For example, ethnicity classifications used by state authorities for administrative purposes unfold power effects as discursive practices with structuring and performative effects (Keller, 2011b: 247). In terms of their structuring effects, the categories provide tools to give meaning, sense and order to the world thus influencing how phenomena are experienced as reality. Performative effects occur for example when administrative ethnicity categories become the basis for the self-descriptions and identity politics of the groups thus described. Similarly, other sociological approaches to theorising ethnicity classifications draw our attention to the interdependent relationship between "social categorisation" (for example through state actors for administrative purposes) on the one hand and "group identification" (i.e. the processes of self-identification of the groups thus described) on the other (Jenkins, 2000). Furthermore, in the field of public health, epidemiological categories serve the practical purpose of generating knowledge that can be used for interventions aimed at limiting the spread of a disease to improve the health of the population. Further power effects of the categories can thus be expected in the field of public health interventions, for example through the definition of *target groups* in disease prevention measures or in testing and screening policies.

Thus, the theoretical perspective described here involves the twofold assumption that the categories and classifications derive from existing social structures and power hierarchies, and at the same time, they unfold power effects and thus contribute to the sociality they are embedded in.

Aim and study design: the "changing categories" project

The project aims to understand the genesis and function of epidemiological categories specifying ethnic groups and migration-related characteristics of populations in health reporting. In the epidemiology of infectious diseases such as HIV/AIDS and Tuberculosis (TB), different categories are used in Europe in different places to describe im/migrants and ethnic groups. For example, the most striking difference between the categories used in the UK and Germany relates to ethnicity categories, which are used in the UK rather extensively but not at all in German health reporting. In both countries, the categories have undergone tremendous change since the 1980s. Thus, the "Changing categories" project pursued the following research questions:

- How – with which categories and classifications – is public health knowledge about im/migrants and infectious diseases produced, stabilised and changed (using the example of HIV and TB health reporting)?
- How are the epidemiological categories socially constructed – within specific sociohistorical contexts (in Germany and the UK)?
- Which statements, speaker positions, and interpretive schemes (*in German: Deutungsmuster*) characterise the discourses?
- How do the epidemiological categories display power effects, e.g. through public health interventions such as prevention and screening/testing policies?

With regard to the methodology, we applied SKAD conceptualised by Reiner Keller (2011a, 2011b, 2013). This research program seemed a good methodological fit. SKAD specifically aims to "account for the sociohistorical processing of knowledge and symbolic orderings in larger institutional fields and social arenas" (Keller, 2012: 51), which is appropriate to our interest in reconstructing the meaning and function of epidemiological knowledge in public health. SKAD integrates discourse theory in the tradition of Michel Foucault with sociological theory in the tradition of the sociology of knowledge and is thus particularly well equipped to consider the role of institutions and other actors in the discourse. SKAD pays close attention to language and signs and involves an interpretive approach to analysing the data (in the hermeneutical tradition described by Hitzler and Honer, 1997), but it does not constitute a linguistic approach to discourse analysis. Furthermore, in contrast to other approaches to discourse analysis (such as Critical Discourse Analysis) it eschews prior normative assumptions, e.g. about certain "ideologies" at work in the discourses under investigation, in order to increase the chances of finding new, unexpected results instead of generating "reductionist proof" of an ideology that was known beforehand (Keller, 2012: 51). As we will describe in more detail below, eschewing prior knowledge (e.g. in our case about racism in health discourses) proved to be a challenge in the course of the project as the specific topic of the research (i.e. racialised ethnicity classifications) lends itself to critical interpretations and positions including postcolonial theories of racism and othering.

SKAD involves an iterative, interpretive approach to data collection and analysis that is inspired by and compatible with various elements of Grounded Theory (Keller, 2012: 71–73). We were thus able to integrate elements of Grounded Theory (GT) in the constructivist tradition of Kathy Charmaz (2014) as well as Situational Analysis, the post-structural approach to GT developed by Adele Clarke (2005). For example, we integrated the

174 *Hella von Unger* et al.

GT procedures of theoretical sampling, constant comparisons, coding and memo writing (Charmaz, 2014). We also used the mapping techniques of Situational Analysis, i.e. we created situational maps, social arena/social world maps and positional maps (Clarke, 2005; Clarke, Friese and Washburn, 2015). These helped us deal with the complexity of the discourses by visualising various elements of the research situation, the institutions, social worlds and arenas and the different speaker positions regarding controversial issues. For example, to better understand the main actors and discourse coalitions that shaped the UK discourse on ethnicity categories in health reporting, we drew a social arena map (Figure 9.1).

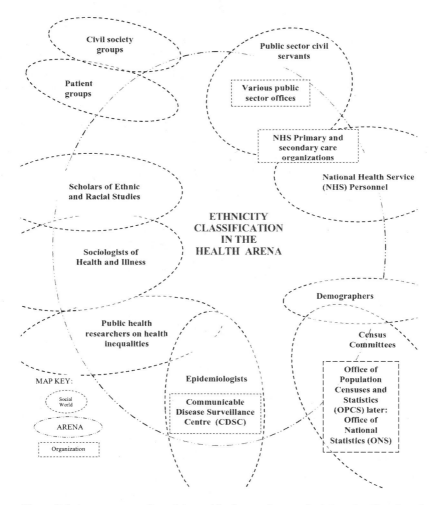

Figure 9.1 Arena map of social worlds focused on ethnicity classification in the health arena in the UK.

This visualisation technique supported the process of group interpretation and facilitated the in-depth analysis (and country comparison) through analytic questions. For example, this specific type of mapping raised questions of where to place certain social worlds and institutions on the map (and why), which in turn raised questions about the relationships among the actors and organisations and the proximity of their positions in this specific arena – thus aiding the process of identifying discourse coalitions.

The study used comparisons as a heuristic tool and incorporated comparative elements into the foundation of the study design. Three dimensions of comparison were included from the beginning: (1) Country (UK and Germany); (2) Disease (HIV/AIDS and Tuberculosis) and (3) Time (different points in time, roughly since the 1980s) (see Figure 9.2).[1]

At the outset, every SKAD project needs to define the discourse it aims to explore (Keller, 2013: 91). We started out with the assumption that we might be looking at one discourse – especially given the shared disciplinary background in epidemiology, the seeming similarity of the two infections, and the importance of international discourses and forms of cooperation in health reporting and epidemiology (especially vis-à-vis global epidemics such as TB and HIV). However, due to the different languages (English and German) used in the health reporting systems, given the different legislative frameworks and institutional settings for health reporting in Germany and the UK, and also the striking differences in categorisation practices, we quickly realised that we were dealing with at least two separable discourses. Furthermore, over the course of the study, we learned that there are considerable differences in the history and discursive construction of the two infectious diseases. Thus, we realised that we were in fact dealing with four discourses: the discourses of health reporting on TB and the one on HIV in the UK and the discourses of health reporting on TB and HIV in Germany – and how they change over time. These discourses are connected (symbolised in the overlap of the circles in Figure 9.2), but they also have their distinct histories, patterns and classifications.

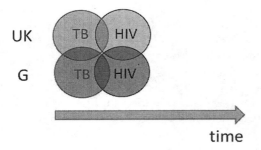

Figure 9.2 Comparative study design: exploring four discourses over time.

Creating a data corpus

In many qualitative studies, the researcher's experience of entering the field (or being kept out) provides ample information about the patterns and processes that characterise the field. This is also the case when analysing discourses that are still ongoing. In order to illustrate this point, it is worthwhile describing how we proceeded in collecting empirical material and creating our data corpus. The empirical part of the discourse analysis begins by "determining the field(s) of knowledge or discourse to be investigated" (Keller, 2013: 91). In our case, this was the field of knowledge relating to health reporting on migrants and infectious diseases in the case of HIV/AIDS and TB in two public health systems (Germany and UK). We formulated the research questions and refined them further over the course of the investigation. We chose methods of data collection and analysis that seemed a promising methodological fit between our theoretical assumptions, our research questions and the material and resources at hand. First, we needed to locate documents and other "utterances" (or statement-events, i.e. the concrete materialisations of the discourses we were interested in) that belonged to the respective field/s of knowledge. So how did we start with identifying appropriate material? Keller (2013: 91) notes:

> At the beginning of the practical part of the research there is initially a collection of accessible information of the research object. This is done through the reception of appropriate scientific and non-scientific literature, and possibly also in the context of exploratory interviews with experts in the field. Following this, a start is made [...] with the collection of data, i.e. the assembly of the data corpus. The analysis of the data can begin, even if a corpus is not yet considered to be "concluded".

Treating data collection and analysis as an iterative, interlocking process fits the procedures of Grounded Theory very well and provides an opportunity for applying the principles of theoretical sampling whereby the criteria for selecting the data depend on the developing theory and hypothesis. We thus started to collect material including the publications of the institutions in charge of health reporting (e.g. reports of the Public Health Laboratory System, the Health Protection Agency and later Public Health England in the UK as well as reports from the Robert Koch Institute and other organisations in Germany; we also collected documents from the European Centre for Disease Prevention and Control in Stockholm). Most of these reports (especially documents since the 1990s) were digitally filed and more or less easily accessible on the internet through the websites of the institutions.[2] Reports from the 1980s had to be attained in paper from the institutions, libraries and other archives.

Given that we were interested not in a public discourse mediated by the mass media, but in a "special discourse" (i.e. a discourse within a partially public social domain including scientific contexts) (Keller, 2013: 73), we also searched medical and public health databases (such as PubMed) for relevant scientific publications. We conducted expert interviews with representatives of the institutions in charge of health reporting as well as other epidemiologists, social scientists, activist and representatives from civil society. We conducted these interviews both for exploratory purposes and guidance through highly complex discourses as well as – later on – for probing purposes, i.e. answers to specific questions about the internal workings of the reporting system institutions (*in German: Betriebswissen*) as well as information on the broader political and social context of the different time periods (*Kontextwissen*) (Meuser and Nagel, 1991). We also used the expert interviews as an opportunity to discuss certain patterns we identified in the data through our analysis. The experts provided their informed consent and the interviews were audiotaped and transcribed verbatim. Further documents included prevention material and policy papers. Given that the project explored discourses that were still ongoing, it was also possible to gather data about "observable social practices" (Keller, 2013: 93), for example in conferences and meetings that addressed the topics of interest which we captured by writing fieldnotes. Last but not least we tried to get access to the actual forms and questionnaires used in the surveillance systems, some of which we were able to locate (mainly through the experts, since they are usually not publicly accessible).

Our data corpus was managed as a Citavi data base.[3] Initially, we planned to restrict the time frame or our analysis to the years 1980–2014, but as mentioned before (see endnote 2) we found that we needed to include some material from the 1960s and 1970s to better understand the history of TB reporting. In the end, the data corpus contained several hundred documents including the following data:

- Documents of health reporting (e.g. yearly reports of public health institutions as well as weekly and monthly reports, for example the British Communicable Disease Reports and articles in the German Epidemiological Bulletin);
- Scientific articles (e.g. in medical and public health journals including *Tubercle*, *The Lancet*, and *Gesundheitsförderung und Prävention*);
- Epidemiological forms and questionnaires used to collect the data in the public health system;
- Policy papers, laws and regulations (e.g. the Infectious Disease Law (IfSG) in Germany, the Race Relations Act in the UK, testing and screening regulations);
- Prevention Material (e.g. flyers, posters);
- Transcripts of expert interviews with epidemiologists, social scientists, activists, practitioners;

- Fieldnotes about the process of data gathering and topic-related meetings, events and conferences.

The Citavi database helped us organise the large data corpus, and paper-based material was scanned and digitalised to be included. In Citavi it is possible to categorise the documents according to a classification system that fits the project's needs. In our case, we categorised the material according to disease (HIV, TB, both) and country/region (Germany, UK, EU). This information was used for overviews, to double check if relevant data had been included and to make informed decisions about time management and the selection of texts for detailed analysis (see p. 180). This perspective on our own data generated many questions that aided the analysis. For example, at some point we noticed that we had many more (i.e. twice as many) scientific articles relating to the UK as compared to Germany in our database. This raised the question whether we had collected more articles from the UK (i.e. distributing our efforts unevenly) or whether there were more articles to be collected on the UK discourse. The latter turned out to be the case – there is a more lively and intense debate in the health sciences about HIV and TB and in particular about the use and validity of ethnicity categories in the UK as compared to Germany.

When managing our data corpus in Citavi, we also tried to distinguish between *material* and other *literature*. This distinction, however, proved very problematic and raised the important question of what constitutes *data* in our discourse analysis.

What counts as data?

When conducting an empirical study, in particular when applying for research funding, the researcher usually consults the scientific literature to describe what is known (and not known) about the topic in the respective thematic and disciplinary field, how it has been studied, how terms are defined – the literature acts as a background and starting point for the empirical project. After collecting and analysing empirical data, when presenting the results, the findings are discussed again in light of the literature, and thus the circle closes – the (new) empirical findings can be compared with and contrasted to other findings, thus contributing to the field of academic knowledge. In qualitative research, there have been debates on whether and when scientific literature should be consulted in the research process. For example, in GT one discussion has centred on whether or not literature should be consulted at the beginning, or not at all, or more towards the end. For example, Barney Glaser (2001) insists that researchers should consult the literature only at the very end while approaches in the constructivist tradition of GT on the other hand propose that scientific literature and sensitising concepts can aid the research process (Ramalho *et al.*, 2015). However, what happens when the basic distinction between empirical data vs. scientific literature dissolves?

Based on constructivist positions, some qualitative scholars argue that the empirical and the theoretical are closely intertwined so that it is impossible to clearly separate empirical data on the one hand from theoretical perspectives on the other (Kalthoff, Hirschauer and Lindemann, 2008). Furthermore, arguments have been made that empirical material only becomes *data* in the course of the analysis, i.e. through processes of interpretation and theorisation (Hirschauer, 2014). Nevertheless, these debates still assume that it is possible to clearly identify what constitutes the empirical *material* or *data* of the study on the one hand, and the published literature on the other. This was not the case in our study.

In the "Changing Categories" project, it was possible to view and treat some literature as scientific (background) literature in the usual sense: these include for example the sources (from the sociology of science and discourse theory fields) cited in the first section of this article. Also, some empirical material could be clearly identified as *data*, for example the health reports we collected, the interviews we conducted and the fieldnotes we wrote. There was however, a third group of documents which met the criteria of both: these included scientific literature which at first we read as background literature, but in the course of our analysis became *material* and thus was read and treated differently, i.e. analysed more thoroughly and in more depth. Examples of documents of this third group include publications by health and social scientists who analysed the issues of ethnicity classifications and migrant-related categorisations in social and health statistics (e.g. Bhopal, 2014). These documents contain "utterances" and "statements" (Keller, 2013: 73–74) that clearly belong to the discourse we aimed to understand. Even though they were not (or not always) reporting on HIV and TB, they were commenting on such reports, citing from them and providing arguments regarding the relevance of a topic and/or the usefulness and validity of a certain category. Very often, these were publications of authors who were directly or indirectly involved in the debates and decisions about the use of certain categories in health reporting.

As the scope of our analysis widened to explore the broader social and historical factors influencing the development and introduction of certain categories and classifications in public health, even more scientific publications joined this third group of documents, i.e. *material* formerly known as *literature*. Now, even publications from our own discipline became empirical data as these documents contained statements relating to the larger discourse of migration- and ethnicity-related categories in the social sciences, which influences the discourse in the health sciences, epidemiology and health reporting. These provided important answers to the question why a certain category was introduced, stabilised or changed – and not another. This expansion of our empirical material and the different treatment of scientific literature was slightly overwhelming and raised a few questions, such as *how can we quote this literature/material? Can we quote it in the background sections of our publications, or only in the "results"?* These struggles reminded us of the basic tenet of SKAD that the term discourse "refers to a construct of social researchers" (Keller, 2013: 89). Whether or not any material could be included into the data corpus as data depended on our research questions. Thus, the focus and scope of the analysis determine what becomes – or more precisely what is treated as – data.

This realisation points to a related methodological assumption of SKAD: "Discourse research is characterised by an essential reflexivity of which it should be aware: it does not produce truth, but 'statement-events' which are themselves part of a (social science) discourse" (Keller, 2013: 89).

If a SKAD project analyses a scientific discourse that is still ongoing, and that connects to the social science discourse, the empirical data can be found rather *close to home*. In some way, we were reminded of the Glaser dictum "all is data" (2001: 145) even though we do not share his objectivist stance towards data (Glaser, 2002: 2) nor his exclusion of scientific literature from the research process. From our point of view, the constructivist stance which views data as co-constructed by the researcher/s is much more plausible (Charmaz, 2014). The lesson thus learned from our difficulty of dealing with the dissolving boundaries between *literature* and *material* can be summarised more aptly as *all may become data* – depending on the focus of the research question which may change, sharpen and widen over the course of the research process as a result of the analysis.

Analysing the data

In our analysis of the material (including the various health reports and transcripts of the expert interviews), we did not focus on the (inter-) actions or intentions of individual actors. Instead, we searched for patterns that cut across different texts and material. We asked, *who produces a statement, how, where and for whom?* We interpreted the texts and images – thus reconstructing implicit meaning patterns and interpretive schemes that go beyond what the individual actor or organisation might intend to say or do.

Given the large amounts of data, we did not follow line-by-line open coding as suggested by Charmaz (2014). Instead, as is suggested in SKAD (Keller, 2013: 98–99) we selected some texts and text passages for detailed analysis. In order to do so, we followed the principle of theoretical coding as described above and analysed the data similar to the approach outlined by Emerson and colleagues (1995) who suggested for extensive ethnographic data corpuses a procedure of coding in two rounds: first, after reading the material, larger text units are open coded and in a second round of coding, a more thorough line-by-line coding occurs with selected passages of the texts and tables.

In this fine-grained analysis of selected passages, we did ask the material the classical GT question "What is happening in the data?" (Charmaz, 2014). When interpreting examples of categorisation in specific parts of health reports containing text, tables and graphs, we asked the data the following questions, which were informed by our theoretical assumptions and borrowed from other studies on classification (Bowker and Starr, 2000; Jenkins, 2000; Polzer, 2008):

- Which categories and classifications are used?
- What is their logic? How logical are they?
- What do the categories highlight, what do they ignore?
- Who is defining the category – from what perspective?
- What is the purpose of defining the categories at a particular point in time?
- How does the categorisation relate to the self-identification of the groups targeted by the category?

We interpreted the data both individually as well as in group data sessions as a team. In line with GT, we wrote memos about the process and results of these interpretations and constant comparisons.

As mentioned above, we also applied the mapping techniques of Situational Analysis (Clarke, 2005; Clarke, Friese and Washburn, 2015). The mapping exercises proved very helpful for "engaging with the complexity" of the discourses (Clarke and Keller, 2014), for visualising social worlds and arenas that connected and separated institutions and actors, and for understanding different positions that characterise the discourse, including positions that do not exist. The latter was particularly helpful for the country comparison. As mentioned at the beginning, in the German discourse categories of *race* and *ethnicity* have not been explicitly addressed and used in social and health statistics since World War II. This became very clear when we first mapped the positions in the individual countries. When drawing a map integrating the positions from the two discourses, more differences and similarities became clear including that certain anti-*ethnicisation* positions, which were clearly expressed in the German discourse, were missing or marginal in the UK discourse (in public health, not in the social sciences). As mentioned above, when interpreting racialised ethnicity categories as well as when interpreting the silences about *race* and racism in the German health discourse, we struggled with the question of whether or not to refer to theories of racism and othering, including those developed by Foucault and scholars of Cultural and Postcolonial Studies (e.g. Hall, 1996, 1997). We tried to resolve this problem by not starting from the assumption that we would necessarily find racism, but by not closing our eyes to the possibility either. Thus, we cultivated the recommendation to increase the validity of our qualitative analysis by asking ourselves "How could we be wrong?" (Maxwell, 2005) in all phases of the research process. With this approach, we did not interpret racialised ethnicities (e.g. "White", "Black African", "Black Caribbean") as necessarily *racist* and *bad*, but tried to understand how the labels came about, what they connote, what function they have and how they contribute to interpretive patterns of im/migrants and ethnic minorities as both *a risk* (i.e. dangerous) and *at risk* (i.e. vulnerable, in need of services they deserve) in the context of discourses on migration and infectious diseases (Scott, von Unger and Odukoya, 2017; von Unger, Odukoya and Scott, 2016).

Challenges when publishing the results (legal and ethical issues)

As described in the aims and research questions above, the project aimed to explore the power effects of epidemiological categories. One possible field in which power effects might unfold is the field of prevention policies and practices. We thus analysed posters distributed as part of World-AIDS-Day and World-TB-Day campaigns. Here we had to come to terms with the meaning, function and role of images in discourses (Keller, 2013: 103–105; Maasen, Mayerhauser and Renggli, 2006). However, a big surprise came when we were preparing to submit this analysis for publication in a peer reviewed journal – here we encountered legal problems: even though the material was freely available in the internet, we did not manage to attain the rights to reproduce the posters in our publications. The institutions that had produced the images (usually with state funding) were either unwilling to agree to a scientific evaluation of their material and/or had signed contracts with the persons depicted on the posters (such as public celebrities) that excluded additional uses of the images.

Another challenge in terms of research ethics and data protection concerned the expert interviews. German data protection law, as well as the ethics code of the German Sociological Association (DGS, 2014), requires the anonymisation of the interview data that we collected. However, given that the experts were also prominent actors in the field with a specific education and training, unique expertise and a publicly available professional and publication record, this anonymisation can easily be undone. Even more problematic: how can we anonymise the name of an expert whose publications we might cite as it corresponds, contradicts or illustrates a point that was made in an interview? Furthermore, even trying to anonymise the institutional affiliations of the experts raises methodological issues given that these may be – from a SKAD perspective – quite important for understanding their specific speaker position in the discourse.

Conclusion

These methodological reflections on the research process aimed to show not only how a SKAD project is conceptualised in theory, but also how it is done in practice. We stressed the methodological "fit" between the theoretical assumptions that inform the research question and the specific characteristics of the discursive field requirements of approaching the field in a flexible and open manner, adjusting the methods and the procedures to the opportunities, problems and tasks at hand. Regarding the challenges we encountered, some proved to be very insightful (e.g. when reflecting on the problems of accessing the material, and what counts as data) while others remained unresolved, open questions (e.g. the legal and research ethics issues).

Acknowledgements

We would like to thank the editors and especially Reiner Keller who provided helpful advice over the entire course of the research project. We are also very grateful to Adele Clarke for her inspiring feedback during her visit in Munich in 2015. Many thanks also to our student workers Dimitra Kostimpas, Simon Starz and Sabrina Tschiche for maintaining the Citavi database and their contributions to the interpretation of the data. The project received funding from the Deutsche Forschungsgemeinschaft (DFG UN 263/4-1).

Notes

1 In the case of TB, to better understand the specific history of the disease in both countries in the second half of the twentieth century, we extended the time frame of the empirical material (health reports) to the 1960s and 1970s (e.g. Scott, von Unger and Odukoya, 2017).
2 Accessing the reports through the internet was not so easy in the British case study due to institutional changes: the institutions in charge of health reporting on HIV and TB changed more than once during the time frame of interest, e.g. first the Public Health Laboratory System (PHLS) was in charge of regular health reporting, then the Health Protection Agency (HPA) which was later transformed into Public Health England (PHE). The difficulties in locating and accessing the material drew our attention to the country specific differences regarding the institutional actors and responsibilities as well as to the dramatic changes in technological infrastructure since the 1980s. On reflection, the difficulties (which we documented in field notes and analysed in our team meetings) thus proved rather insightful.
3 For information on the Citavi software and its functions see www.citavi.de/en/index.html (accessed: 17 December 2015).

References

Berger, P. L. and Luckmann, T. ([1966] 1975). *The Social Construction of Reality: A Treatise in the Sociology of Knowledge.* Garden City, NY: Doubleday.

Bhopal, R. S. (2014). *Migration, Ethnicity, Race, and Health in Multicultural Societies.* 2nd edn. Oxford: Oxford University Press.

Bowker, G. C. and Star, S. L. (2000). *Sorting Things Out: Classification and its Consequences.* Cambridge, MA: MIT Press.

Charmaz, K. (2014). *Constructing Grounded Theory: A Practical Guide Through Qualitative Analysis.* 2nd edn. London: Sage.

Clarke, A. E. (2005). *Situational Analysis: Grounded Theory After the Postmodern Turn.* Thousand Oaks: Sage.

Clarke, A. E. and Keller, R. (2014). Engaging Complexities: Working Against Simplification as an Agenda for Qualitative Research Today: Adele Clarke in Conversation with Reiner Keller. *Forum: Qualitative Social Research*, 15(2), Art. 1.

Clarke, A. E., Friese, C. and Washburn, R. (2015). *Situational Analysis in Practice.* Walnut Creek: Left Coast Press.

Denzin, N. K. and Lincoln, Y. S. (2011). Introduction: The Discipline and Practice of Qualitative Research. In: N. K. Denzin and Y. S. Lincoln, eds., *The Sage Handbook of Qualitative Research.* Thousand Oaks: Sage, 1–19.

DGS (2014). *Ethik-Kodex der Deutschen Gesellschaft für Soziologie (DGS) und des Berufsverbands Deutscher Soziologen (BDS).* [online] Available at: www.soziologie.de/de/die-dgs/ethik/ethik-kodex.html [Accessed 14 August 2017].

Douglas, M. (1986). *How Institutions Think.* Syracuse, NY: Syracuse University Press.

Durkheim, E. and Mauss, M. ([1903] 1969). *Primitive Classification.* London: Cohen & West.

Emerson, R. M., Fretz, R. I. and Shaw, L. L. (1995). *Writing Ethnographic Fieldnotes.* Chicago: University of Chicago Press.

Epstein, S. (2007). *Inclusion: The Politics of Difference in Medical Research.* Chicago: University of Chicago Press.

Fleck, L. ([1935] 1979). *The Genesis and Development of a Scientific Fact.* Chicago: University of Chicago Press.

Foucault, M. (1970). *The Order of Things.* Oxon, NY: Tavistock/Routledge.

Foucault, M. (1972). *The Archaeology of Knowledge.* London: Tavistock.

Foucault, M. (1984). The Politics of Health in the 18th Century. In: P. Rabinow, ed., *The Foucault Reader.* New York: Pantheon, 273–289.

Friese, C. (2010). Classification Conundrums: Classifying Chimeras and Enacting Species Preservation. *Theory and Society*, 39(2), 145–172.

Glaser, B. G. (2001). *The Grounded Theory Perspective: Conceptualization Contrasted with Description.* Mill Valley, CA: Sociology Press.

Glaser, B. G. (2002). Constructivist Grounded Theory? *Forum: Qualitative Social Research*, 3(3), Art. 12.

Hacking, I. (1982). Biopower and the Avalanche of Printed Numbers. *Humanities in Society*, 5(3 and 4), 279–295.

Hacking, I. (1986). Making Up People. In: T. C. Heller and C. Brooke-Rose, eds., *Reconstructing Individualism: Autonomy, Individuality, and the Self in Western Thought.* Stanford: Stanford University Press, 161–171.

Hall, S. (1996). The Question of Cultural Identity. In: S. Hall, D. Held, D. Hubert and K. Thompson, eds., *Modernity: An Introduction to Modern Societies.* Cambridge: Blackwell.

Hall, S. (1997). The Spectacle of the 'Other'. In: S. Hall, ed., *Representations: Cultural Representations and Signifying Practices*. London: Sage, 223–279.
Hirschauer, S. (2014). Sinn im Archiv? Zum Verhältnis von Nutzen, Kosten und Risiken der Datenarchivierung. *Soziologie*, 43(3), 300–312.
Hitzler, R. and Honer, A. (1997). Einleitung: Hermeneutik in der deutschsprachigen Soziologie heute. In: R. Hitzler and A. Honer, eds., *Sozialwissenschaftliche Hermeneutik: Eine Einführung*. Opladen: Leske & Budrich, 7–27.
Jasanoff, S. (2004). Ordering Knowledge, Ordering Society. In: S. Jasanoff, ed., *States of Knowledge: The Co-production of Science and Social Order*. London, New York: Routledge, 13–45.
Jenkins, R. (2000). Categorization: Identity, Social Process and Epistemology. *Current Sociology*, 48(3), 7–25.
Kalthoff, H., Hirschauer, S. and Lindemann, G., eds. (2008). *Theoretische Empirie: Zur Relevanz qualitativer Forschung*. Frankfurt am Main: Suhrkamp.
Keller, R. (2011a). The Sociology of Knowledge Approach to Discourse Analysis (SKAD). *Human Studies*, 34(1), 43–65.
Keller, R. (2011b). *Wissenssoziologische Diskursanalyse: Grundlegung eines Forschungsprogramms*. 3rd edn. Wiesbaden: Springer VS.
Keller, R. (2012). Entering Discourses: A New Agenda for Qualitative Research and Sociology of Knowledge. *Qualitative Sociological Review*, 8(2), 46–75.
Keller, R. (2013). *Doing Discourse Research: An Introduction for Social Scientists*. Los Angeles, London: Sage.
Knorr-Cetina, K. (1999). *Epistemic Cultures: How the Sciences Make Knowledge*. Cambridge, MA: Harvard University Press.
Maasen, S., Mayerhauser, T. and Renggli, C. (2006). Bild-Diskurs-Analyse. In: S. Maasen, T. Mayerhauser and C. Renggli, eds., *Bilder als Diskurse – Bilddiskurse*. Weilerswist: Velbrück Wissenschaft, 7–26.
Maxwell, J. A. (2005). *Qualitative Research Design: An Interactive Approach*. Thousand Oaks: Sage.
Meuser, M. and Nagel, U. (1991). ExpertInneninterviews – vielfach erprobt, wenig bedacht: ein Beitrag zur qualitativen Methodendiskussion. In: D. Garz and K. Kraimer, eds., *Qualitativ-empirische Sozialforschung: Konzepte, Methoden, Analysen*. Opladen: Westdeutscher Verlag, 441–471.
Polzer, T. (2008). Invisible Integration: How Bureaucratic, Academic and Social Categories Obscure Integrated Refugees. *Journal of Refugee Studies*, 21(4), 476–497.
Ramalho, R., Adams, P., Huggard, P. and Hoare, K. (2015). Literature Review and Constructivist Grounded Theory Methodology. *Forum: Qualitative Social Research*, 16(3).
Scott, P., Von Unger, H. and Odukoya, D. (2017). A Tale of Two Diseases: Discourses on TB, HIV/AIDS and Im/migrants and Ethnic Minorities in the United Kingdom: Social Theory & Health. *Social Theory and Health*, 15(3), 261–284.
Starr, P. (1992). Social Categories and Claims in the Liberal State. *Social Research*, 59(2), 263–295.
Von Unger, H., Odukoya, D. and Scott, P. (2016). Kategorisierung als diskursive Praktik: Die Erfindung der „Ausländer-Tuberkulose". In: S. Bosančić and R. Keller, eds., *Perspektiven Wissenssoziologischer Diskursforschung*. Wiesbaden: Springer VS, 157–176.

10 Self-positioning of semi-skilled workers

Analysing subjectification processes with SKAD

Saša Bosančić

Introduction

Poststructuralist theories are decentring the subject insofar as they claim that the knowledge about the subject is a highly contingent outcome of socio-historic processes. Furthermore, poststructuralist theories underscore that the scientific "games of truth" (Foucault) starting in the sixteenth and seventeenth century and lasting until today, which claim to gather the somehow situated but still more or less objective "facts" about the human condition, are in fact producing these conditions at the same time. The theories of the decentred subject in postmodern and poststructuralists theories, like in Michel Foucault's or Jacques Derrida's work, were followed by debates about how qualitative research could be conducted without referring to an essentialist conception of the "knowing subject" (Lather, 2013; St. Pierre, 2013; MacLure, 2013). Elizabeth Adams St. Pierre criticises for instance, that there are many qualitative studies "that claimed to use post-structural theories of the subject but then in the methodology section included description and treatments of people as humanist individuals with unique 'voices' waiting to be set free by emancipatory researchers" (St. Pierre 2014: 10).

But how do we start a qualitative inquiry that can meet the requirements of the perspective of a decentred subject? Should we refuse qualitative methods completely because they are a "trap for those who want to do new empirical inquiry" (St. Pierre, 2015) and because the poststructuralists and postmodern ontologies and epistemologies are not compatible with the ones that have guided the established methods like the qualitative interview? How can we even interview people and use the transcripts as "data" when Foucault said that he was not interested in the "thinking, knowing, speaking subject" (Foucault, [1969] 2002)?

In this chapter I will argue, bearing on the *Sociology of Knowledge Approach to Discourse* (SKAD), (Keller, 2005, 2011, 2012, 2013) that the alleged differences or even incompatibilities between some poststructuralists theories and some theories of the Interpretive Paradigm of Sociology, which underlie the methodologies of "conventionalist" qualitative research, are rather to be overcome than they are located on an ontological or epistemological level. Drawing on SKAD, I propose a concept of *subjectification* that includes Foucault's understanding of power/ knowledge regimes and the concepts of the self in the works of George H. Mead, Herbert Blumer, Anselm Strauss, Erving Goffman and others. Before that, I will demonstrate how I used the actor categories of SKAD in doing so. Furthermore, I will argue that it is necessary to adapt and extend these categories in order to examine how and if discourses can influence actual human subjectivities. Finally, I am going to refer to my empirical data gained in the twenty interviews conducted with semi-skilled workers in order to demonstrate how I applied a heuristic model of subjectification and I will argue that it is possible to apply "conventionalist" qualitative methods without getting "trapped" in the essentialist perspective of the "knowing subject".

Methodological groundings in the SKAD frame of reference

SKAD is a research program that situates Foucault's concepts of discourse, power and knowledge in the pragmatist tradition of the Chicago School of Sociology, Symbolic Interactionism and the European tradition of the Sociology of Knowledge. Regarding Foucault's conceptions of the subject, it becomes clear that he has been misunderstood insofar as he is associated with having proclaimed the "death of the subject". This "death" thesis is underpinned mostly by referring to Foucault's *The Order of Things* and the famous quote that the human subject may disappear "like a face drawn in sand at the edge of the sea" (Foucault, [1966] 1994) if the arrangements of the power/knowledge regimes that "invented" the subject in the first place change. Keller (2005) points out that Foucault of course denies an empathic understanding of the subject as an autonomous and sovereign instance in the sense of Enlightenment. Nevertheless, Foucault's interest in the subject can be compared with Max Weber's (Keller, 2012): both were studying the socio-historical processes of the social constructions of knowledge about the subject (that could be described as religious or scientific power/knowledge regimes) and the possible impacts of these symbolic orders on the actual subjectivities of the embodied individuals and their everyday living practices in a given historical period. So Foucault is not at all proclaiming a "death of the subject" which would imply that all attempts to refer to a "classical" sociological actor concept must fail. On the contrary, going through the works of Foucault, it is more than evident that he was concerned with the question of how we have become what we are and he described that his goal is "to show people that they are much freer than they feel, that people accept as truth, as evidence, some themes that have been built up at a certain moment during history, and that this so-called evidence can be criticized and destroyed" (Foucault 1988: 10).

And to be more precise and refer back to Max Weber's studies on how the protestant messages of salvation influenced peoples' everyday practices and how this was *situated in* and at the same time *pushing forward* a capitalist formation of society, Foucault describes his engagement with the subject in a similar way as follows:

> What are the games of truth by which man proposes to think his own nature when he perceives himself to be mad; when he considers himself to be ill; when he conceives of himself as a living, speaking, laboring being; when he judges and punishes himself as a criminal?
> (Foucault 1990b: 7)

Foucault's "games of truth" can be understood as social practices of the discursive construction of symbolic orders and his historic-empirical analyses of madness, of the penal system or of sexuality were centred around the questions of how the life sciences[1] have constructed specific subjects, mostly within division practices of normal/deviant subjects, and how these "truths" were imposed on individuals and populations with different power/knowledge technologies like the disciplines or bio-politics (Foucault, 1990a).

According to Keller and as it will be further developed in this chapter, Foucault's thoughts came close to classical sociological thinkers like Durkheim or Weber (Keller, 2011), and close to symbolic interactionism when addressing discourses as "battle fields, as power struggles around the legitimate definition of phenomena" (Foucault, 1990a). Turning back to the subject, Keller argues that the misunderstanding concerning the already mentioned "death of the subject" could also be due to Foucault's misleading uses of the notion subject. In order to clarify this usage, Keller differentiates different actor categories taking up the similarities of sociological and Foucauldian thought (Keller, 2012). In the SKAD frame of reference social actors are related to discourses mainly in two ways:

- Speaker positions depict positions of legitimate speech acts within discourses which can be taken on and interpreted by social actors under specific conditions (for instance, after the acquisition of specific qualifications) as role players (Keller, 2011: 55).
- Subject positions/Identity offerings depict positioning processes and "patterns of subjectification" which are generated in discourses and which refer to (fields of) addressees. Technologies of the self are understood as exemplary elaborate, applicable and available instructions for subjectification (ibid.).

The subject positions as identity templates and "instructions for subjectification" are addressed to individuals (and/or collectives), but these "interpellations" by the discursive construction of truths should not be confused with how the living, speaking and embodied human individuals are reacting to them. But if one wants to analyse how discourses actually influence the self-relations of individual actors, this means asking how discursively constructed knowledge systems and symbolic orders are affecting our selves and identities, one is on the "edge" or "border" of a classical SKAD perspective. Since SKAD is embedded in the Sociology of Knowledge and uses Foucault to broaden the micro-perspective inherent in the tradition of Sociology of Knowledge and Symbolic Interactionism, the research programme is focused on the investigation of the discursive construction of typified knowledge and the social practices of the construction of symbolic orders. This means that SKAD rather aims to analyse the social relations of knowledge and the politics of knowledge on a meso-level of institutions, organisations and social actors, than the influences of subject positions on living human individuals. But even though the connection between discourses and actual self-relations of individuals are not the primary interest of SKAD, Keller criticises nonetheless the more or less deterministic assumptions in poststructuralist contexts and in the field of governmentality studies. In contrast to these theories and research programs Keller (2011, 2012) points out that the way "interpellations" are adopted by addressees merits empirical analyses of their own instead of assuming implicitly strong impacts or influences – an issue that I will address later.

Whereas the studies of subjectification with a close Foucault orientation shift their perspective to the programmes and strategies that produce subject positions on the discursive level, many researchers of the Interpretive Paradigm of Sociology do not take the discursive production of truth and knowledge into account in their empirical works on human subjectivities and self-relations. In other words, most of these empirical studies of selves and subjective self-relations remain on the micro-perspective of the actors. Adele Clarke (2005) refers to this micro-perspective in the elaboration of her *Situational Analysis* in so far as she applauds the new developments in qualitative methods like auto-ethnography, interpretive ethnography, new biographies and life stories which contribute valuable individual-centred empirical data. But nevertheless she insists that the postmodern turn is challenging us to broaden our perspectives and to go beyond the "knowing subject". With regard to analysing identities and subjectivities she notes that "we and the people and things we choose to study are all routinely both producing and awash in seas of discourses" (Clarke, 2005: 145). In this respect St. Pierre (2014) also points out, that one main aspect of getting beyond the conventional humanist qualitative methodology perspective is to stop privileging some texts over others. For her it is not just an empirical question but an ontological statement, that it makes no sense "to separate our analysis of words 'collected' in existing documents into a section of the research report called the 'literature review' from our analysis of words 'collected' in interview transcripts and fieldnotes in a section called 'findings'" (St. Pierre 2014: 12).

Bearing on Keller and Clarke, it is clear that this kind of "literature review" belongs in the section "findings", because in a Foucauldian sense they are discursive practices that "systematically form the objects of which they speak" (Foucault, [1969] 2002); and as such they produce and construct "truths" that influence us and – what is more important – they also do have an impact on the contexts of our interviewees, the surroundings and situations where we take our field notes. On the groundings of such an epistemology one has to take into consideration that the empirical analysis of human subjectivities and identities should not just focus on the classical contexts such as racial, ethnic, gendered, religious and subcultural identity templates which can be experienced in the lifeworld and in everyday face-to-face interactions. These are still very important elements one has to take into account, but in postmodern "societies of spectacle" – to use an expression by Guy Debord like Clarke (2005) does – most of these classical factors are mediated through discourses in mass media from television to the internet, in self-help literature, lifestyle magazines and so on. All these elements can be understood as a kind of discursive *venues* (Bosancic, 2014), where subject positions and identity templates are negotiated and where these negotiations can have an influence on actual human self-relations.

To summarise, in the SKAD frame of reference subjectification is a two-sided process: on the one hand, there are *subject positions*. As described above, these are understood as identity templates and role expectations which are generated in discourses and which refer to addressees. On the other hand, these subject positions are instructing addressees to shape their self, but one has to keep in mind that the process of the actual self-shaping is not determined by the subject positions. On the contrary, the actor concept of the Sociology of Knowledge and the theories of self in the Interpretive Paradigm consider that human actors are *more or less free* when they are adopting or referring to subject positions. And more or less free means in a Foucauldian sense that individuals and groups are never just passive or reactionary forces in the powerful "games of truth" – if it were so, Foucault (1990a) says, power would not be needed in the first place. And bearing on Keller (2011, 2012) it is clear that possible reactions to interpellations have a wide range from affirmative adaption, adaption in parts, to misinterpretation or ignoring the interpellation. But in order to examine how individuals actually refer to the "interpellations" of the subject positions, it was necessary to extend the SKAD, as will be shown in the next chapter.

The extension of the SKAD-based concept of subjectification

In order to conduct research, one has to start with theories and concepts and not with methodology, as post-qualitative researchers advise

(St. Pierre, 2015); and so in the initial step it is necessary to specify what subjectification means on the level of the actual embodied individual. Before that, some ontological remarks need to be made. First of all, in addition to Foucault, there are many different notions used when addressing this level of subjectification, including self-formation, self-relation, actual subjection, self-interpretation or technologies of the self (Butler, 1997; Bührmann/Schneider, 2008; Keller, 2012 and Reckwitz, 2006). Despite the differences of the notions, most of the theorists invoke a concept of identity[2] in some way when they talk about the processes on the level of lived subjectivities. But the term is used without any further explication. Considering the assumptions on the decentred subject, I argue that the non-essentialist concept of identity in the tradition of the Interpretive Paradigm of Sociology can be a useful tool to understand subjectification processes. But "the tool" needs to be grounded as a concept, which I will do in exploring the similarities of Foucault and the Interpretive Paradigm. Foucault's concept of subjectification can be "translated" or reshaped according to the way identity is conceptualised in the Interpretive Paradigm because the ontologies are rather comparable than different. One of the major references for the later works of Blumer, Goffman, Strauss and others is Mead's concept of the self, which I will briefly sketch out to show the similarities. According to Mead, the self is a social structure in the sense that it is developed in interaction and communications processes based on significant symbols which are part of a socio-historically and interactively generated "universe of discourse" (Mead, [1934] 1972). Mead's conception of the self therefore, does not refer to an autonomous and sovereign subject since its mind is always bound to the socio-symbolic order in a given historical time. Foucault enables us to understand more deeply how these symbolic orders produce truths about the subject and how the power/knowledge regimes as outcomes of "games of truth" are binding it to specific individualised identities. Hence Mead's and Foucault's ontologies[3] are compatible insofar as they both underscore the necessity to comprehend the subject as a changeable "code" (Goffman, 1971) which is produced by the social and cultural systems of knowledge and meaning. And both theorists do show us that these contingent but still powerful symbolic orders do not determine human action and the ways we relate to ourselves: Foucault (1988, 1990a) for instance, by showing that power always produces resistance and opposition and that we are freer than we think we are; and Mead is referring to the "free" subject when stating that the self consists of the inseparable instances of the "I" and the "me" and the "I" as the process, which can never be fully controlled by "society" or even oneself:

> It is because of the "I" that we say that we are never fully aware of what we are, that we surprise ourselves by our own action. It is as we act that we are aware of ourselves. It is in memory that the "I" is constantly

present in experience. We can go back directly a few moments in our experience, and then we are dependent upon memory images for the rest. So that the "I" in memory is there as the spokesman of the self of the second, or minute, or day ago. As given, it is a "me," but it is a "me" which was the "I" at the earlier time. If you ask, then, where directly in your own experience the "I" comes in, the answer is that it comes in as a historical figure. It is what you were a second ago that is the "I" of the "me." It is another "me" that has to take that role. You cannot get the immediate response of the "I" in the process. The "I" is in a certain sense that with which we do identify ourselves. The getting of it into experience constitutes one of the problems of most of our conscious experience; it is not directly given in experience.

(Mead, 1972: 174–175)

This quotation illustrates that the "I" is a kind of black box which we cannot fully be aware of. Related to this conception of the "I" is Judith Butler's theory of subjectification because she assumes that the produced and powerfully subordinated subject is always "haunted by an inassimilable remainder" (Butler, 1997); and she uses psychological terms like melancholia or concepts of desire to describe and explain the composition of this "remainder". But as Charles W. Mills notes in his analysis of *vocabularies of motive*: "There is no need to invoke 'psychological' terms like 'desire' or 'wish' as explanatory since they themselves must be explained socially" (Mills, 1940); and Foucault also argues that psychology as a discipline is more a technique of controlling and subordinating the self and therefore their "games of truth" should be analysed and not used as explanations. Ultimately, and despite all the differences, Mead's, Butler's and Foucault's ontologies are compatible insofar as they assume that the human self, the mind or in general this kind of "inner space" is an instance of self-reflexivity which is bound to "outer" symbolic orders, materialities and time and space relations.

Since the compatibility of the ontologies is given when the subject is conceptualised as a socio-historic situated entity that is constantly interpellated, which can be understood as permanently being bound to identities, we can now return to the question of how this "inner space" of the human subject and self-reflexivity can be described; in other words, how subjectification processes can be conceptualised on the level of the actual empirical embodied individual in a heuristic model. One major insight from the preoccupation with the questions of the self and identity in the tradition of the Interpretive Paradigm is a concept which can be described as *self-positioning* (Bosancic, 2014). The groundings for this derived from Mead's ([1934] 1972) and Goffman's (1974) work and their understanding of identity as an ongoing process; and this process is – to quote Anselm L. Strauss – "open-ended, tentative, exploratory, hypothetical, problematical, devious, changeable, and [has] only partly-unified character" (Strauss,

1959). Beside the important notion of *identity as a process* it is furthermore possible to argue with Goffman (1961, [1963] 1986) that groups, institutions and organisations confront individuals with identity expectations. Goffman points out that the participation in social situations is always tied to identity expectations and not just behavioural expectations like classical role theory assumed. Therefore, Goffman notes that social situations are not just characterised by prescribed activity but more by prescribed being: "Now if any social establishment can be seen as a place where implications about self systematically arise, we can go on to see it as a place where these implications are systematically dealt with by the participant" (Goffman 1961: 187).

Additionally, it can be pointed out that individuals are identified by social constructed facts like gender and race and by personal facts such as our looks or the stories we tell about ourselves; people collect, attach and entangle these facts around us like "candy floss" as Goffman ([1963] 1986) puts it in Stigma. Considering Goffman's concept of *role distance* ([1961] 2013/1961) and *secondary adjustment* (1961) another basic process can be identified as a reaction to the permanent pressures of identification that come out of human and non-human entities surround the individual, people usually tend to adapt, to some degree, to the expectations and demands of the situation in order to keep "the action" going, but they reject the identity expectations which are implied in these "performances", for instance, by making jokes or exaggerating oneself's subordination gestures. Cohen and Taylor take up these thoughts and show that identity in (post)modern times is being subordinated by the rules and routines of everyday life and that people try "to escape the press of paramount reality" (Cohen and Taylor, [1979] 1992). Dissociating from different pressures is a way of keeping a feeling of autonomy – but the individuals do not "really" escape the pressures, they just react to another cultural and discursive produced pressure and that is to be an autonomous and sovereign subject with an "inner core".

These analyses are showing that subjectification processes on the level of the embodied human individuals can be conceptualised as *self-positioning processes*. Like Herbert Blumer (1958), who has shown that we are being identified by and as members of groups (racial or religious groups), emphasises that these positioning processes are not so much dependent on lifeworld face-to-face interactions but on the negotiations about the groups in the "public arena" (Blumer, 1958); with the concept of self-positioning which is situated within SKAD, I want to push the "classical" self and identity analysis towards a discursive perspective. As I have illustrated, humans are being positioned by groups, organisations and institutions and they are positioned in their everyday practices and in their private or professional lives. More important, it seems however, that they are positioned by subject positions and identity templates which process in discourses, because in postmodern societies these everyday identity expectations in more or less organised social contexts or in the lifeworld in general are strongly influenced by discursive formations. Furthermore I argued, that these numerous processes of identification and the identity expectations surrounding us in almost every sphere have a certain degree of pressure for adaptation, and this *positioning pressure*, as one could call it – however slight it might be – forces us to react in some way: either we do accept the identity expectations or ignore them, or we choose a middle ground like Goffman analysed with the concept of role distance or secondary adjustment; or as can be said referring to SKAD, there are also other forms of reactions possible like misinterpretations, adaptation in parts and so on. Finally, I underscore the fact that the adaption of subject positions or whatever kind of reaction to discursive constructed identity templates on the level of the actual self-formation and the subjective self-relations is a permanent, precarious, tentative, dynamic and ongoing process of self-positioning. With this understanding of subjectification, I am now turning to empirical data in the last chapter in order to demonstrate how this heuristic can be applied.

How to apply a heuristic model of subjectification?

Before turning to the empirical data, it is necessary to elucidate that the previously suggested concept of subjectification does not claim to be a "new" or "better" theory of subjectification making all other concepts obsolete. Rather, it should be taken as a *sensitising concept*: according to Blumer (1954), an approach in this sense is open towards the "messiness" (Law, 2004) of the empirical world and it is changeable during the process of inquiry. Using the suggested subjectification and self-positioning concepts as sensitising concepts helps to avoid imposing theoretical assumptions on the empirical world or fitting the phenomena we purport to study in the theoretical framework in some or another way – instead, sensitising concepts "merely suggest directions along which to look" (ibid.). Besides the twenty qualitative interviews with semi-skilled male workers from the industrial sector,[4] another important direction in my research in the context of the subjectification concept was to analyse how the semi-skilled workers are being positioned through discourses and – more generally – it was also important to look at the history of the working class and the economic transformations that took place and lead to the current social status of the workers. For collecting this data, it was possible to rely on the findings from empirical discourse studies about economy, work and qualifications (Boltanski and Chiapello, 2005).

So in the first step of my research, based on other discourse studies, I reconstructed the *story line* (Keller, 2011) about semi-skilled workers as follows: semi-skilled workers have been marginalised on a cultural and economic level due to globalisation and de-industrialisation processes whilst their jobs were transferred to so-called low-wage countries. The main message in the discourses is always: if you are not qualified, you can only work in precarious jobs in the low-wage sector. Another important issue that is discussed is the marginalisation of the unions and that their loss of power in the last decades disables them to provide positive identity templates for the workers like they did in the past. Besides that the working class neighbourhoods also transform due to selective mobility processes: the middle class workers moved out and the vacant places were then occupied by migrants with low qualifications; since then, these neighbourhoods only appear as "problematic quarters" in the public arena. All these marginalisation processes are accompanied by a new hegemonic discourse that has come up in Europe: the ongoing and permanently repeated proclamation of the *knowledge-based society*. The main storyline here is that a knowledge-based economy only needs high-skilled workers and semi- or low-skilled workers are no longer necessary. If the semi-skilled workers are still mentioned in public discourses it is mostly in the context of unemployment, low-wages or their unwillingness to accept the necessity of life-long learning.

In the end, the findings in the discourses analysis clearly show that there are no positive identity templates for semi-skilled workers. The next task was then to work through the discourse analysis again to reconstruct the dominant subject positions and identity templates. The findings show three main subject positions: the entrepreneurial self, the creative self and the flexible self. These dominant subject positions hardly provide any identification possibilities for semi-skilled workers and taking this and the marginalisation processes into account, the question guiding the interviews was whether, and what consequences it had on the self-positioning processes, there are only unreachable or negative identity templates for the semi-skilled workers.

One outcome from the interviews was that neither the subject positions of the creative nor the entrepreneurial self are influencing the self-positioning of the workers – a finding that is not very surprising. But for the flexible self, there are indications that the identity templates from these discourses do have a kind of impact on the workers' self-positioning. The kind of impact or influence I am referring to can be shown with the data. The following extract is from an interview with Lothar, who has been working in a logistic department of an automotive factory for over fifteen years:

> I can do almost everything that's needed. I am responsible for the incoming goods as well as for the outgoing goods. I check what is needed for the production department and do many more things. And if one of my colleagues is ill, I'll just jump in and take his place – that's no problem at all. For me it's normal, I can work everywhere in the warehouse. Most of my colleagues have their own sector – I mean, that is also a lot of work, too. But for me, there is not just one thing,

I can work anywhere in the logistics department. Ingoing goods, outgoing goods, processing orders, packaging, just everything.

(Lothar, 48 years old)

Like Lothar, some of the workers were telling typical stories that could be interpreted as *internal flexibility*: this group of workers was talking throughout the interviews about their special abilities to do all the jobs in their working section and they also made it clear that they can adapt to new tasks quickly and that this is the reason why "the boss" or the company needs them. These workers often added that being a semi-skilled worker enables them to apply for many different jobs – if they had completed an apprenticeship they would be limited to the specific occupation they had been trained in. They also pointed out that they have an advantage over high-skilled workers because they have already worked in many different jobs. These typical stories can be interpreted as a kind of *external flexibility*, which means that they position themselves as having advantages on the labour market.

But why are these reconstructed self-narratives influenced by the identity templates and subject positions of the flexible self and how could it be made plausible that these self-positioning processes are actually influenced by identity templates in discourses of flexibility? There are two main reasons. The *first* indication is the similarity of the storylines in the discourses and the self-narratives: the workers' ways of positioning themselves imply that they are able to do many different jobs, that they can quickly adapt to new demands, work extra hours and so on – and these are exactly the attributes and qualifications which are highlighted in the discourses of the flexible self. So even without any of the interviewees using the term "flexible" in their self-narratives they *appear* flexible in their self-narratives. The *second* reason has to do with the self-narratives of the other workers who did the same jobs but told completely different stories. So it was typical that one worker would tell me about the many abilities that are needed to do the job and how flexibly he can adapt to the demands of the job and so on. But another worker doing the same job would tell me how boring the job was or that he was sorry that he was not to able to tell me anything interesting because his job was the same every single day; or they would talk about how easy it is to learn the job and that one does not need any skills to do it. The question to be asked at this point is why the workers at the same workplace tell these completely different stories? My interpretation of this is that people do not just react to the actual conditions of the workplace – this is an assumption that was often made in the sociology of work. On the contrary, the theoretical framework of SKAD clearly outlines that the structural conditions are always mediated through the symbolic order which in some cases can be analysed as discourses. And the findings of this empirical study referred to in this chapter show that people are able to use different resources to make sense of their workplace and labour market situation. For example, one group of the workers, which I called "domestically situated" because all they seemed to care about was their family, their house and their back garden, lead a withdrawn life without any interests other than their near social environment and so their interpretation of the workplace is more or less indifferent.

The other group of workers who position themselves as flexible are more open to the demands of the world at large, which for instance means that they are active in unions or they followed the news and wanted to talk to me about the current financial crisis, unfair wages, the "useless politicians" and "greedy managers" and so on. So this group clearly had more resources to present themselves, but maybe they presented their selves in a way they thought the interviewer expected? Or maybe this could have been just facework or identity politics in Goffman's ([1963] 1986) sense? This possible alternative interpretation of the finding points to an important methodological question and that is, how can a researcher be sure, that the interviewees are telling the truth and that they are not just trying to keep a positive self-image in the interview situation? If we take Goffman's insights seriously, then this distinction between a "true" or "false" self-presentation becomes less important and in the end, one can even assume that it does not matter at all if a self-presentation is true or if it is "just" facework.

The question of true and false would imply that there is a kind of unchangeable "inner core" of the subject and this would undermine all attempts to go beyond the knowing subject. But if the self-narratives are considered in the already outlined sense of the subject as a *changeable code*, in the perspective of subjectification a self-presentation then can be understood as an indication for the way the interviewees perceive the normative order – which in postmodern societies is mostly the outcome of the discursive constructed realities and the subject positions that are interpellating the individual and collective actors. This is a perspective in which the question of true and false becomes obsolete and one has to analyse the data in a different way insofar as the researchers should not be trying to find some kind of "deeper truth" of the self, a truth that even the interviewees themselves are not aware of. Instead, the researcher has to turn to the questions of the vocabularies of motive (Mills, 1940) which are invoked by the interviewees; one has to look after the legitimations the interviewees are using when they talk about their thoughts and actions and ask oneself why someone seems to feel the necessity or thinks that it is normatively required to position themselves like this in the interview situation.

So coming back to the self-positioning processes of the workers, a possible and plausible interpretation of the findings, taking these considerations into account, is that the workers do know about their precarious situation as semi-skilled workers – not just through media discourses but also through the downsizing[5] processes they experienced in their workplaces. Positioning themselves as flexible could be a *fictional security strategy*, as I have called it. By that I mean that workers do know what the labour market is demanding and that is: to be flexible – these discourses are absolutely dominant. And with the self-attribution of being flexible they are able to feel secure that they will not lose their jobs – at least to some degree.

Conclusion

With the latter exemplary interpretation of the findings, it can be seen that I suggest a new strategy of interpreting the data rather than to request giving up "classical" methods or re-invent new ones in order to go *beyond the knowing subject*. Of course it still is and will be interesting to find out about the trustworthiness of interviewees or to search the self-narratives for incidents and events in the past of the interviewees that would explain their way of self-positioning like it is often done in biographical research. But this way of conducting research remains in the "trap" of the knowing subject as do most of the studies of social justice, studies in the field of the sociology of work and studies based on the habitus concept of Bourdieu. These are often assuming that individuals in similar social status groups and milieus have similar self-relations and that all of this can be explained by referring to some "inner capital" that is formed by social and economic structures in basic socialisation processes. Again, I am not arguing that this is a false assumption, but what has to be taken into account in a SKAD framework is that we need a more differentiated perspective on human self-relations. My findings in this chapter clearly indicate that workers with a very similar habitus, with the same workplace and even similar family lives, can nevertheless have different ways of positioning themselves as working beings – as a flexible self or as the domestically situated selves. And what can also be shown is that the self-positioning as a flexible subject cannot be explained by the biographies of the workers, the milieu, the workplace or the structural conditions of the labour market or the society in general. This way of self-positioning can be understood and analysed in a more elaborate way by reconstructing discursively constructed storylines and subject positions and comparing them with the stories and narratives the interviewees use to present themselves in the interview situation.

So by embedding the subjectification heuristics in the SKAD framework, I argue that subjectification has to be understood as a complex positioning process: on the one hand, an external positioning through discursive constructed identity templates and on the other hand, the actual self-positioning processes on the level of the individuals. This kind of subjectification research does not understand the human individual as the centre of meaning-making and an absolute free individual in an empathic sense nor does it imply a fully determined actor. Taking the complexity of subjectification processes seriously it would be misleading to speak of subjectification in cases where researchers just make simple comparisons of discourses and interviews and find matching keywords. In such cases the researcher is analysing how people refer to discourses or in what way they are doing that. But the subjectification concept embedded in SKAD is rather useful when *identities as changeable codes* are at stake and when people are being positioned as flexible selves, as responsible or caring, political or sustainable selves. The concept of self-positioning is then useful in exploring how and if these identity templates in discourses do actually influence human selves and subjectivities. To close with Adele Clarke (2005: 145): "Like it or not", she writes, "we are constantly awash in seas of discourses". In addition to that I want to point out the following: as my research concept follows the footsteps of SKAD and SKAD is following Foucault, like Clarke, I want to underscore that the so-called decentred subject needs to be integrated more deeply into empirical research. And the concept of subjectification discussed here can be understood as a move towards a broader perspective on the *discursive situatedness of human subjectivity*. And with this move, I want to underscore that it is still possible to use classical methods which have been developed in qualitative research if the ways of conducting the interviews and – more importantly – the ways of interpreting the data is instructed and guided by the theoretical insights about the decentred subject. The epistemological and methodological standpoint of a SKAD-based subjectification concept presented in this chapter considers empirical research as an interconnected process of co-constructing realities by the researcher as a situated being, the method, the research subject and the materialities involved instead of just "finding" something "out there" or representing something that *is* in the data somehow.

Notes

1 Foucault (1990a: 142) describes them as "different fields of knowledge concerned with life in general".
2 Judith Butler (1997: 130) for instance, assumes that the "lure of identity" is the reason for individuals to accept or adapt injurious interpellations.
3 See also Keller (2011, 2012) and Clarke (2005) for other possible connections of Foucault and the Interpretive Paradigm. Stanley Cohen's and Laurie Taylor's Goffman-based work on identity in (post)modern times also remarks on the fruitfulness of Foucault's ideas in their second edition of *Escape Attempts* (1992), which was originally published in 1976 without references to Foucault.
4 The interviews were conducted with male workers aged between thirty-five to fifty. The interviewees have been working for at least ten years for the same company and the interviews took place in three different companies during working hours. The workers were semi-skilled, which meant that in this case it just takes a few hours or days to learn the necessary job skills. It is important to mention that I use the category "semi-skilled worker" just as an analytical category in Goffman's (2013: 83) sense for the purpose of the study. I have carefully avoided imposing these categories on the Interviewees. Furthermore, I explicitly do not intend to qualify their qualifications in any way – so

"semi-skilled" only refers to the job description and not to actual abilities and skills of the interviewees.

5 For instance, all the workers have seen many workmates lose their jobs and being replaced by temporary workers; and these temporary workers are earning lower wages in spite of doing the same jobs as they are.

References

Blumer, H. (1954). What is Wrong with Social Theory? In: *American Sociological Review*, 18, 3–10.

Blumer, H. (1958). Race Prejudice as a Sense of Group Position. In: *The Pacific Sociological Review*, 1(1), 3–7.

Boltanski, L. and Chiapello, E. (2005). *The New Spirit of Capitalism*. London and New York: Verso.

Bosancic, S. (2014): *Arbeiter ohne Eigenschaften. Über die Subjektivierungsweisen angelernter Arbeiter*. Wiesbaden: VS.

Bührmann, A. and Schneider, W. (2008). *Vom Diskurs zum Dispositiv. Eine Einführung in die Dispositivanalyse*. Bielefeld: transcript.

Butler, J. (1997). *The Psychic Life of Power. Theories of Subjection*. Standford: Standford University Press.

Clarke, A. (2005). *Situational Analysis: Grounded Theory After the Postmodern Turn*. Thousand Oaks: Sage.

Cohen, S. and Taylor, L. ([1976] 1992). *Escape Attempts. The Theory and Practice of Resistance to Everyday Life*, 2nd edition. London and New York: Routledge.

Foucault, M. (1988). Truth, Power, Self: An Interview with Michel Foucault, October 25 1982". In: Martin, L. H., Gutman, H. and Hutton, P. H., eds. *Technologies of the Self: A Seminar with Michel Foucault*. Massachusetts: University of Massachusetts Press, 9–15.

Foucault, M. (1990a). *The History of Sexuality. Volume 1: An Introduction*. New York: Pantheon.

Foucault, M. (1990b). *The Use of Pleasure. Volume 2 of The History of Sexuality*. New York: Pantheon.

Foucault, M. ([1966] 1994). *The Order of Things: An Archaeology of the Human Sciences*. New York: Random House.

Foucault, M. ([1969] 2002). *The Archeology of Knowledge*. London: Routledge.

Goffman, E. (1961). *Asylums. Essays on the Social Situation of Mental Patients and Other Inmates*. Graden City/New York: Anchor Books.

Goffman, E. (1971). *Relations in Public. Microstudies of the Public Order*. New York: Basic Books.

Goffman, E. (1974). *Frame Analysis. An Essay on the Organization of Experience*. New York: Harper Colophon Books.

Goffman, E. ([1963] 1986). *Stigma. Notes on the Management of Spoiled Identity*. New York: Touchstone.

Goffman, E. ([1961] 2013). *Encounters. Two Studies in the Sociology of Interaction*. Mansfield Centre: Martino Publishing.

Keller, R. (2005). *Wissenssoziologische Diskursanalyse. Grundlegung eines Forschungsprogramms*. Wiesbaden: VS.

Keller, R. (2011). The Sociology of Knowledge Approach to Discourse (SKAD). In: *Human Studies*, 34(1), 43–65.

Keller, R. (2012). Entering Discourses: A New Agenda for Qualitative Research and Sociology of Knowledge. *Qualitative Sociology Review*, 8(2), 46–75.

Keller, R. (2013). *Doing Discourse Research. An Introduction for Social Scientists.* London and Thousand Oaks: Sage.

Lather, P. (2013). Methodology-21: What Do We Do in the Afterward? *Qualitative Studies in Education*, 26(6).

Law, J. (2004). *After Method. Mess in Social Science Research.* London: Routledge.

MacLure, M. (2013). Researching Without Representation? Language and Materiality in Post-qualitative Methodology. *Qualitative Studies in Education*, 26(6).

Mead, G. ([1934] 1972). *Mind, Self, and Society. From the Standpoint of a Social Behaviorist.* Chicago: The University of Chicago Press.

Mills, C. W. (1940). Situated Actions and Vocabularies of Motive. *American Sociological Review*, 5(6), 904–913.

Reckwitz, A. (2006). *Das hybride Subjekt. Eine Theorie der Subjektkulturen von der bürgerlichen Moderne zur Postmoderne.* Weilerswist: Velbrück.

St. Pierre, E. A. (2013). The Posts Continue: Becoming. *International Journal of Qualitative Studies in Education*, 26(6), 646–657.

St. Pierre, E. A. (2014). A Brief and Personal History of Post Qualitative Research. *Journal for Curriculum Theorizing*, 30(2), 2–19.

St. Pierre, E. A. (2015). Practices for the "New" in the New Empiricism, the new Materialism, and Post Qualitative Inquiry. In: Denzin, N. K. and Giardina, M. D., eds., *Qualitative Inquiry and the Politics of Research.* Walnut Grove, CA: Left Coast Press, 75–95.

Strauss, A. (1959). *Mirrors and Masks: The Search for Identity.* Glencoe: The Free Press of Glencoe.

11 Dangerous or endangered?
Using the sociology of knowledge approach to discourse to uncover subject positions of sex workers in South African media discourse

Carolin Küppers

Introduction

Before the FIFA World Cup 2010 in South Africa, the national and international media reported that sex workers[1] were about to "flood" the country. This prognosis seems to be a recurring phenomenon. This compares to the expectations voiced leading up to the FIFA World Cup 2006 in Germany (as well as prior to the Olympic Games 2004 in Greece and 2012 in London), where likewise a "flood" of sex workers were expected. As mega events, major sporting events seem to precipitate attention to the issue of sex work and media discourses increase. Since none of these forecasts came true, as actually a cutback in the demand for sexual services was reported afterwards, it may be assumed that this is a purely discursive event, an occurrence, which has no empirical reality but is being exploited politically and in the media. This recurrent discursive event can be regarded as a transnational, global phenomenon and serves as the starting point of the discourse analysis I will present in this article. The research question is, which subject positions of sex workers are visible in media discourses on sex work and how the different subject positions vary or resemble with regards to the political intention of the various authors and newspapers.

Using SKAD I aim to uncover the subject positions of sex workers in the South African media discourse around the FIFA World Cup 2010. My data sample consists of 221 newspaper articles from fifty-five South African daily and weekly newspapers published during the year of the FIFA World Cup 2010 itself. To analyse the data I used sampling and coding strategies from Constructivist Grounded Theory, which harmonise well with the research programme SKAD offers (Keller and Truschkat, 2012).

Theoretically I am drawing from queer, postcolonial and intersectional theories, to reflect on the gendered and sexualised positions of sex workers and the particular societal context in South Africa. Focusing on a country-immanent discourse places the debate inside South Africa and shifts the centre of analysis to the global South. Within this context, three subject positions could be ascertained – the "magosha" ("whore"),[2] the "victim" and the "mother". These subject positions must be interpreted within the context of heteronormative, post-colonial and intersectional power relations. SKAD offers a useful toolbox for this purpose, as it allows combining deconstructivist theoretical approaches with discourse analytical methodologies.

Methodological frame and analytical tool-box

This chapter draws from the research findings of my PhD-Thesis "Dangerous or endangered? Discourses on sex work during the men's Soccer World Cup in South Africa".[3] In my work I chose an adaptation of *critical discourse analysis* (CDA) (Lazar, 2005; Wodak, 2001) and the *sociology of knowledge approach to discourse analysis* (SKAD) (Keller, 2005, [1998] 2009) as the methodological framework. The principal aim of CDA is to unmask the discriminatory use of language in e.g. the mass media (Keller, 2016: 1–2) which is fruitful for the analysis of metaphors and verbal images that occur in the discursive intersection of sex work and the FIFA World Cup. SKAD enables an examination of the discourse actors and their relationship to the discourse, thus expanding the linguistic perspective of CDA. The combination with SKAD makes it possible to determine in which subjective positions sex workers become visible in media discourse – the question I present in this chapter. Consequently, I will focus on the analysis with SKAD in the following section.

Methodologies can be seen as a form of negotiation between theoretical assumptions and methodological processes (Truschkat, 2012: 70). Within this context, the discourse research perspective chosen for this chapter is to be understood as a methodology; it negotiates between discourse *theory*, which deals with the systematic analysis of the importance of discourses in the social construction of reality (Keller, 2005: 16) and the corresponding application of practical research in the form of a discourse *analysis* as the basis for empirical research.

The sociology of knowledge approach to discourse analysis is concerned with reconstructing "the processes which occur in social constructions, objectification, communication, and the legitimisation of meaning structures or, in other words, of interpretation and acting structures on the institutional, organizational or social actors' level" (Keller, 2011: 49). In conjunction with the queer, post-colonial, and intersectional perspectives applied in the analysis, this enables a focus on aporias and dimensions of re-construction as the formation of subject positions, structural and political contexts as well as sense making and speakability (Hark, 2006: 371).

SKAD takes up Michel Foucault's (1976: 53) frequently cited assertion that his books are "a kind of tool-box", which others can and should use for their own research purposes. Since each research project focuses on different topics and within various contexts and discourse analysis is not a uniform method, it must be partially "redefined" (Keller, 2004: 9) for each project.

In the following, I examine the subject positions of sex workers that emerge in the discourse on sex work during the World Cup or, more precisely, the *medial discourse on the projected increase of sex work during the 2010 World Cup in South Africa*. From a *discursive* point of view, this is an example of the *intertwining* of two *events* with one another: a *real event*, the World Cup, and a *discursive event*, the projection of an increase in sex work. A *discursive event* is an event that is heavily discussed by the media and extensively debated, it must not necessarily be a real event of the same magnitude. To a certain degree, discursive events are a discourse *about* specific events that have had a large impact on politics and the media and thus influenced the direction and quality of the discourse and they "create the typifiable material form of utterances, in which a discourse appears" (Keller, 2011, 53). The description of discursive events constitutes the horizon for the examination of a discourse (Foucault, 1981: 41).

As already mentioned, discourses do not speak for themselves, they are rather realised by actors and exist solely in speech acts or the production of texts. Social "actors" are always "bound up in many ways in discursively structured symbolic battles about definitions of reality" (Keller, 2012: 70) and "formulate the communicated components out of which discourses unfold" (Keller, 2012: 62). In other words, they create the corresponding material, cognitive, and normative infrastructure of a discourse and orientate themselves in their (discursive) practices to the rules of the particular fields of discourse, in this paper, to the rules of publication for media coverage (Keller, 2012: 62). In this study, various newspapers, the authors of numerous articles, and the experts quoted in these articles are the corresponding actors in the discursive intertwining of sex work and the FIFA World Cup, because they are responsible for stating, quoting, publishing, and reproducing various discourse fragments. Frequently, these actors are clearly defined, e.g. certain stakeholders; in the discourse analysed here, they are often NGOs such as the Sex Workers Education and Advocacy Taskforce (SWEAT) or the Embrace Dignity Campaign. They represent conflicting discourse positions and shape the various discursive strands.[4]

In contrast to discourse actors whose positions shape a discourse, the *discourse protagonists* – in this chapter, sex workers – are addressed and discussed in a specific manner within the discourse and attributed specific *subject positions*. The discourse on sex work during the World Cup revolved particularly around these subject positions attributed to sex workers. By subject positions I mean *discursive identity offerings*. Subject positions "depict positioning processes and 'patterns of subjectification' which are generated in discourses and which refer to the addressed" (Keller, 2011: 55). Discourses position social actors and offer more or less fixed subject positions (Keller, 2007: 26), while subjects are generally located at the intersection between a number of different, partially competing discourses and subject positions (Keller, 2005: 163). It thus becomes apparent that each of the subject positions visible in a discourse are social and historical products that are only conceivable within the context of the dominant discourses and are therefore in no way "natural" categories. The subject positions created within a discourse must not be confused with real processes of interpretation, action, and appropriation carried out by intelligible subjects in everyday life.

In her reflections on subject theory, Paula-Irene Villa (2013: 66) explains how individuals become intelligible subjects by being woven into the discourse.[5] Accordingly, subjects represent socially inhabitable zones that are created by discursive semantics. These are the linguistic categories that allocate representations of people, which are either worthy of recognition or intelligible (ibid.). These allocations are made from a position of power, because only certain subject positions are considered worthy of recognition within specific constellations and the discourse regulates what role a person can assume or *who* a person can be within a social constellation (ibid.: 67). Butler (1997: 11) refers to this process of becoming a subject as "subjectification". Subjectification is connected with an interpellation, in which an individual is hailed as a concrete subject and turns around in response, thereby submitting to this interpellation and accepting the conferred identity category (ibid.: 95–97). Subjectification thus defines the "process of becoming subordinated by power as well as the process of becoming a subject" (ibid.: 2).

This chapter, however, analyses *media* discourses, in which the process of becoming a subject can only be understood to a limited extent. Focusing on discursive subject positions circulated by mass media forces the analysis to remain on the level of interpellation or allocation. All of the subject positions that are visible in the discourse analysed here are allocated a subject status – although they often inhabit fringe areas located on the periphery of the matrix – because they have been named and can thus be "articulated". I therefore use subject positions in this chapter as a discursive tool to determine the various articulated representations of sex workers. I aim to discover how specific attributions and their linguistic manifestations constitute the subject positions of sex workers within a discourse. In addition to this, SKAD allows one to take a closer look at the interrelation of subject positions in a discourse with specific political positions or discourse generated model practices.

Situating South Africa

Based on the approach of SKAD, I propose to examine sex work discourses at the time of the World Cup 2010 in South Africa as part of the more general socio-historical sex work discourse. Since the latter, however, can by no means be assumed to be universal, localisation is called for.

South Africa's socio-historical discourse is informed by both the country's specific history and its current situation.

Even though South Africa is known for its liberal constitution and its extensive anti-discrimination laws, sex work is still prohibited under the Sexual Offences Act from the Apartheid Era (Gardner, 2009). This led to the foundation of a Law Reform Commission on Prostitution in 1997. Yet without resulting in a legal change so far. There have been various suggestions for draft laws, but none of these was approved and implemented by parliament. Four alternative legal options that might be employed in South Africa are discussed:

- *total criminalisation*, which is the existing legislation in South Africa that completely criminalises commercial sex – the seller and the buyer;
- *partial criminalisation*, also known as the Swedish model, which criminalises the purchase of sexual services;
- *legalisation* and *regulation*, which legalises the selling and purchasing of sexual services in specific areas and under regulated conditions;
- and *decriminalisation*, which completely legalises commercial sex and only regulates sex work in terms of labour legislation.

These options as well as the work of the Law Reform Commission is frequently addressed in South African print media and discussions on which legal framework would be suitable for the country lead to quite inappeasable debates between abolitionists, moralists and the sex workers rights movement. The subject positions of sex workers in the analysed media discourse also differ across these political divides. They are part of competing feminist positions on which legislation caters to the needs of women in the sex industry the most as well as on a more general debate on gender relations in South Africa.

All in all, gender relations in South Africa are highly contradictory on both the structural level and the level of everyday experience. While the fight against discrimination by "race" is indeed, and with tangible results, implemented on the political level, the same is not true for gender justice. There is no programme targeting the still unequal and gendered distribution of economic resources. In this respect, it is obvious that the progressive constitution and the Bill of Rights' list of fundamental liberties are at odds with their political implementation and social reality (van Zyl, 2009: 364).

On the one hand, South Africa is one of the countries with the highest proportion of females in parliament worldwide. Currently, 41.5 per cent of parliamentary seats and 35.2 per cent of seats in the Senate are held by women (Inter-Parliamentary Union, 2017). Moreover, of the thirty-five ministries in President Zuma's cabinet fifteen are currently headed by women. On the other hand, the proportion of feminised poverty is particularly high, and gender continues to be a decisive marker for access to education and resources (May and Govender, 1998; May, 2000, Seekings and Natrass, 2005).

What is more, the reality of women's everyday life is informed by sexualised and domestic violence (Frenkel, 2008; Moffett, 2009; Moolman, 2009). Thus, 42.4 per cent of all male respondents in a study conducted by the Medical Research Council reported having committed acts of intimate partner violence (Jewkes *et al.*, 2009: 2). South Africa is considered one of the countries with the highest incidence of rape (Hirschowitz *et al.*, 2000: 12). These contradictions and the climate of violence are part and parcel of the specific historical context of South Africa and attest to the continuities between the apartheid era and present-day society (Frenkel, 2008: 2).

To understand the dimensions of gender relations in post-apartheid South Africa we need to take into account the various socio-historical discourses that inform the debates about gender and sexuality. Here, Western and indigenous discourses continuously confront each other:

> In South Africa, the persistent history of hegemonic whiteness together with postcolonial globalisation has resulted in the dominance of westocentric meanings of sex and sexuality. Indigenous southern African meanings have largely been silenced by the violence of the colonising project [...], and the practice of sacralising knowledges and philosophies of sexualities within the secret domains of traditional healers. [...] Contemporary discourses shaping South African sexualities, then, are a complex mix of the dominant western discourses, both the contemporary global strands and the often still colonial local inflections, and the tensions in postcolonial African heteropatriarchies as they formulate re-imagined African national identities.
>
> (Steyn and van Zyl, 2009: 5)

Discourses that are conceived of as Western are informed by Christian values as well as recent trends (such as the growing emancipation discourse in terms of women's and LGBT rights). These are the discourses that prevail in the representations of sexuality and gender. They also resonate with the colonial discourse about the allegedly hypersexualised and "animal-like" African sexuality as opposed to the allegedly "civilised" European sexuality (Osha, 2004: 92). On the other hand, there also are traditional and indigenous gendered practices that are widespread and visible and have their share in shaping the understanding of gender and sexuality. South Africa is characterised by various indigenous as well as Western discourses and practices, and it is often impossible to clearly distinguish between "what is "European" and what is "African" (Mokoena, 2015: 176). Given the background of social inequality that results from colonialism and apartheid and, as shown above, always comes with a gendered aspect it appears useful to examine sex work discourses in South Africa from both a post-colonial perspective and a perspective that is critical of heteronormativity.

Data sampling and analysis

Newspaper articles represent "natural" data, or statements and utterances that are produced within the field of research (Keller, [1998] 2009: 55). Newspapers can be understood as mass media and therefore constitute a public sphere for discourses (Keller, 2010: 211). Texts that are reproduced in print media are both the stage and the actor in discourses, because they publish and comment on the related speeches of the discourse actors (Keller, [1998] 2009: 52; Smith, 2009: 2). Print media thus provide a stage for the formation and expression of opinions, but they do not solely *in*form people, they also form a consciousness (Jäger and Jäger, 2002: 15). In other words, they participate in the social construction of reality and influence what can be said and debated about an issue at a particular time in a society.

The use of newspaper articles for empirical data proved to be fitting because, among other reasons, print media play an important role in South Africa due to both the current and historical situation. Even though South Africa is one of the most technologically advanced countries in Sub-Saharan Africa, the majority of the population does not have reliable internet access (Deegan, 2001: 116). For this reason, daily newspapers in particular, which are sold on every street corner, are an important source of information, as well as the free newspapers that are generously distributed in the communities and districts of the cities. Furthermore, newspapers play an important role in the fight against illiteracy, which is still prevalent in the country, and are also inexpensive reading material for schools (Mathews, 2000). Therefore, analysing the media discourse in printed newspaper articles allows one to draw conclusions to the societal discourse prevalent in South African society.

The data collection followed three major criteria: a temporal focus on the year of the World Cup 2010, a spatial focus on South Africa and a topical focus on sex work in relation to the major sporting event. The temporal focus is explained by the discursive event of an assumed rise in sex work through the World Cup. The spatial focus follows aspects of research ethics and politics. Taking postcolonial demands into account, it seemed appropriate to focus on the discourse immanent to the host country instead of on the gaze from the global North. As SKAD suggests using established strategies of interpretive research (e.g. some elements of grounded theory) in data sampling and analysis, the topical focus follows the concepts of minimal and maximal contrast in structuring data collection (Strauss and Corbin, 1998: 201–216). In order to capture a specific stock of data entirely the concept of minimal contrast required to collect all articles that were published on sex work in the year of the World Cup. Following the concept of maximal contrast the entire South African print media landscape was taken into account.

Consequently my empirical basis for the reconstruction of the discourse on sex work during the 2010 World Cup consists of newspaper articles from all major English daily and weekly South African newspapers as well as most free and social project papers. While quality newspapers are mostly important for academic and political elites (mainly readers of LSM-categories[6] 6–10), it's tabloids that play a major informative and social role for readers from LSM-categories 1–5. Consequently tabloids had to be included into the sample as well.

To collect the data I spent eight months in South Africa, volunteering for the Sex Workers Education and Advocacy Taskforce (SWEAT). I scanned the eight newspapers with the highest circulation myself[7] – searching for all articles that thematised sex work/prostitution or trafficking in relation to the World Cup. For all other newspapers SWEAT provided the services of *Media Monitoring SA*, who scanned all nationwide newspapers for the keywords *sex work* and *prostitution*. In the end, my data sample consisted of 415 newspaper articles from 71 South African daily and weekly newspapers published in 2010.

Via selective sampling, that took region, circulation and the reference to sex work into account, I selected 221 newspaper articles from fifty-five South African daily and weekly newspapers as my sample.[8]

Selective sampling, as introduced by Leonard Schatzman and Anselm Strauss (1973) means to define criteria beforehand – e.g. circulation or readership of a newspaper – which in my opinion matches the discourse analytical research programme (especially when it is dealing with natural data like print media articles) better than *theoretical sampling* as it was introduced by Grounded Theory Methodology (Charmaz, 2006; Strauss and Corbin, 1998). My first criteria was the circulation of a newspaper – the

Table 11.1 Number of published articles on sex work in South African print media 2010[9]

Month	Articles
February	45
March	55
April	47
May	94
June	78
July	39
August	22
September	14
October	21
Total	415

circulation had to be at least 10,000 or higher otherwise their range was considered too small. The newspapers with the highest circulation are tabloids,[10] followed by the so-called "quality newspapers" (Wasserman; 2010: xi) which include daily papers of the major cities und national papers. The second criteria was to map the nationwide media discourse. Thus I included some regional papers despite their smaller circulation to cover less populated areas and twenty-five regional free papers because of their easy access for everyone. The third criteria was that the intersection of sex work and the World Cup had to be discussed in at least one paragraph of the article.

To analyse the data, I applied, again according to methodological principles of SKAD (see Keller, 2012: Chapter 3), strategies from grounded theory, here in particular the two coding phases of *initial* and *focused* coding suggested by Constructivist Grounded Theory (Charmaz, 2006: Chapter 5).[11] In the phase of initial coding it's important to stay close to the data (*line-by-line*) and to be open to any suggestion and direction, the data will offer. Nevertheless the researcher is always part of the process of analysis: "You act upon your data rather than passively read them" (Charmaz, 2006: 59). Thus constant self-reflection is called for at all times of the research process. Having a research group is incredibly helpful in this stage of the process and allows for rigor focused codes.[12]

Focused codes "are more directed, selective, and conceptual" (ibid.: 57) than initial codes and aim to explain larger segments of the data. I created my focused codes in accordance to the discursive frames that constitute the subject positions of sex workers in media discourse. Helpful for this purpose was asking which subjects are involved, what role they play in the discourse and what virtues, qualities or modes of being are ascribed to them. These questions enabled the codes to be condensed and focused into the narratives that constitute the subject positions of sex workers in the media discourse during the FIFA World Cup in South Africa.

Subject positions of sex workers in South African media discourse

In my empirical approach I was open to the idea, that commercial sex is not necessarily linked to specific gender roles or gendered bodies and that various forms of sexual services exist. However, the analysed data consistently addressed sex workers as female and their clients or pimps as male. Furthermore, media discourses on sex work mostly function through reproducing the binary of the "whore-stigma". Therein, sex workers are depicted as either victims or perpetrators, which can both be analysed as "abject" or "othered" subject positions, against which various female sexual identities are constructed. The term *othering* was coined by Spivak (1985). It describes the process by which a person or a group is placed outside of the norm, and constructed as abject. Othering plays a fundamental role in the history and continuity of racism as well as other forms of discrimination, whereby assumed characteristics of a group are used to distinguish them as different from the alleged norm.

That is also the case with the representation of female sex workers in the South African media discourse. Heteronormativity depends upon the spectre of unchastity and homosexuality in order to constitute itself. The "good wife" or the "innocent daughter" as a social category cannot exist without the position of the "whore" that reinforces the norm of procreative heterosexuality (Pendleton, 1997). In contrast to this hegemonic discourse, a shift from the representation of "other" to ordinary can be observed. There are still mostly othered subject positions of sex workers that manifest in media discourse, but there is also an appropriated subject position that portrays sex workers as mothers.

Empirically there are three subject positions through which sex workers manifest in the media discourse in South Africa. The first subject position I named the "magosha" (or "whore"). The "magosha" is an othered position through which sex workers are portrayed as dangerous to society. The second subject position is the "victim": an ambivalent position, through which sex workers are othered as endangered subjects without agency, but are sometimes discursively included in society when their occupational choice is legitimised as "prey to (economic) circumstances". The third subject position depicts the sex worker as a "mother", who is portrayed as an appropriated member of society since she is taking care of her children and therewith fulfilling her attributed gender role. In the following I will show how these subject positions manifest in media discourse and of which narratives they are constituted.[13]

Sex workers as "abamagosha"/"whores"

As mentioned above, the "magosha"/"whore" is an othered subject position. There are specific discursive narratives linked to it. One for example is the description of the locations, where sex workers work, as dirty and untidy:

> Another business owner said the women litter the streets by burning rubbish, which piles up on the pavements, especially on cold nights, and remains uncollected for days. Our streets are sometimes littered with used tissues and condoms, she said.
> (Ngqulunga, *The Witness*, 25.10.10)

> As I walked up the stairs at 8 pm I felt my shoes stick to the floor. The tiles are dirty and there are beer bottles lying everywhere.
> (Pongoma, *Sowetan*, 2.03.10)

In the first quote sex workers are held responsible for messing up the area. Remarkable is the wording "*our* streets". As a consequence sex workers ("*the* women"), who litter these streets are distinguished from "us". The traces of sex work in public spaces are problematised – something that is supposed to take place secretly now becomes obvious.

This attribution of being dirty or messy also manifests in the metaphor of a "spring clean", which is quite common in the analysed articles:

> In a belated spring-clean, police have stepped up their efforts to rid Pietermaritzburg's streets of the burgeoning sex trade.
> (Ngqulunga, *The Witness*, 25.10.10)

The term cleaning up the streets infers that sex workers are dirty. It also stands for something persistent – you can spring clean every year, there will still or again be dirt next spring. According to cultural anthropologist Mary Douglas (1966) dirt and untidiness is often associated with immorality and endangering social order. By the attribution of causing dirt or being dirty themselves sex workers are constructed as others.

This process of othering becomes even more obvious via narratives of being a vector of diseases, especially HIV:

> Sex workers know [...] they may be transmitting life-threatening diseases to their clients, who then may pass them on to trusting innocents, such as their wives. [...] the disease factor [of sex work], is extremely damaging to society.
> (Brann, *The Witness*, 11.03.10)

Embedded in the notion of being a vector is the accusation of being dangerous – to their clients as well as their wives. The clients are not addressed as the ones who transmit the diseases to their wives themselves. This has to be put into the historic context of World War I, in which sex workers were accused of being vectors of syphilis and endangering the military clout in Europe as well as in the colonies (Bashford, 2004; Levine, 2003). Being depicted as dangerous or "damaging to society", sex workers as "whores" are placed on the outside of society.

Even though the subject position of sex workers as "whores" can be found in various articles that have different political intentions, it is most common in articles that argue for the total criminalisation of sex work:

> A community member, speaking to the Rising Sun, said that prostitution [...] is totally immoral and that government should "never" legalise it.
> (Lepere, *Rising Sun Lenasia*, 14.04.10)

The attributed immorality of the activity functions to legitimise its criminalisation. But it also correlates with sex workers in othered positions, which is visible in quotes like:

> South Africa is a proud nation, not a whorehouse.
> (N.N, *Cape Argus*, 02.03.10)

So, the "whorehouse" is implied to be the opposite of proud and not part of the nation but rather placed on its outside. So being dangerous is – by implication – significant for the subjectification as abject others.

Sex workers as "victims"

The subject position of the "victim" is constituted by victimising interpellations. The central narrative for depicting sex workers as "victims" is the conflation of sex work and trafficking:

> The overwhelming majority of women and girls trafficked into South Africa are for prostitution. You cannot stop trafficking without stopping prostitution. Armed with these facts, it is inconceivable that any civilised nation will consider decriminalising prostitution when it is clear this policy will benefit organised crime the most.
> (Naidoo, *Cape Argus*, 10.06.10)

In this quote the political position of the author is obvious. The allegedly causal connection of sex work and trafficking is used to argue against decriminalisation. This is quite common and the subject position of the "victim" is mostly visible in articles that argue in favour of partial criminalisation or the "Swedish model". To prove their political point, authors often argue, that people in favour of decriminalisation would romanticise sexual freedom at the expense of sex workers:

> The privileged class romanticises "sexual freedom", "agency" and "choice", and argues for the law to be relaxed, supposedly to make life better for the prostituted women. What really happens, though, is that decriminalisation opens up the space for pimps and traffickers to expand their business and the bodies of predominantly black, poor women become re-enslaved and re-colonised.
> (Madlala-Routledge and Mayne, *Daily News*, 23.09.10)

The conflation of sex work and trafficking in media discourse plays a key role in promoting particular ideas about what victims of trafficking look like, where they come from, and what they're capable (or incapable) of. These pictures are usually highly racialised and gendered. There are also specific attributions towards the social position of these "victims": "poor black women", "re-enslaved and re-colonised" – who are specifically positioned as endangered. In narratives like these sex workers are depicted without agency, as if they would be completely controlled by others. This could also be interpreted as an othered position. Being immediately and directly threatened and vulnerable, can therefore be viewed as significant for the construction as "others" as well.

Specific vulnerabilities ascribed to sex workers are central to constructing the subject position of the "victim". These vulnerabilities manifest for example in metaphors from hunting:

> But the danger is that they [young girls, CK] might fall into the clutches of abusive pimps and end up trapped in a life of prostitution.
> (Naidoo, *City Press*, 21.02.10)

Young girls are represented as vulnerable to fall prey to pimps. With verbs as "targeted" and "trapped" girls are narrated as target-objects of a hunt, defenceless and unable to free themselves. By this attribution of defencelessness, agency is denied and othering takes place. This is a common narrative and in the same article, prospective prostitutes are sometimes even narrated as naive:

> The traffickers use various methods to lure victims such as offering them a better life or money when they don't have much. They often promise the victims high profile jobs and a chance to see the world.
> (Snyders, Tygerburger Eersterivier, 02.06.10)

On the other hand – describing the motives or reasons, why sex workers enter the industry, also enables solidarity. The hope for a better life, a good job, more money or to see the world is something many people can relate to. Therefore the subject position of the "victim" is more ambivalent than the subject position of the "whore". It is an othered position by means of missing agency, but as some reasons to join the sex trade are made plausible, solidarity is possible to some extent.

Sex workers as "mothers"

Surprisingly, there is one representation that alters from the othered subject positions of sex workers as "whores" and "victims". In some articles sex workers are portrayed as caring mothers,[14] who sell sex as a necessity to support their children and families:

> By day, she [Skye] is a clerk at Cape Town factory, earning less than R4,000 a month. With eight people to support her pay is simply not enough. My mom lost her job, and basically we're a big family. No one was working. I'm the only income, and I can't keep them. I have to support myself and my son. He is five.
> (Makwabe, *Sunday Times*, 30.05.10)

This quote is part of an article that portrays Skye, a sex worker from Cape Town. We get to know Skye as a person, her hopes, her fears and how she takes care of her son. In Skye's personal story, sex work is depicted as the only honest and reliable option for her to provide for her family. So being a caring "mother" enables sex workers to be appropriated in media discourse. This caters to a particularly normative understanding of female gender roles.

All in all there are four narratives that construct sex workers in the subject position of the "mother": responsibility, honesty, selflessness and innocence. The narrative of sex workers being responsible and caring mothers can be found in various articles:

> The Witness also spoke to some of the sex workers. [...] One sex worker said, I am pregnant and the father of my baby does not want to take responsibility for his action; being on the road is the only way I know that will help me save money for my unborn child.
> (Ngqulunga, *The Witness*, 25.10.10)

Though sex workers in the subject position as "mothers" do not only take *responsibility* for their children but for their parents as well:

> Her mother lives in rural KwaZulu-Natal and thinks the monthly remittance comes from her waiting on tables in the City of Gold.
> (Richter, *Mail & Guardian*, 29.01.10)

The sex worker in this quote is depicted as a mother who is also a daughter herself, who makes sure to spare her mother the truth about her occupation.

Another narrative that constitutes the subject position of the "mother" is, that sex work is an *honest* choice, especially in articles that promote sex workers rights and advocate for the legalisation or decriminalisation of sex work:

> We know that the basic source of life is money, yet we criticise sex workers for trying to make a living for themselves. These queens of the night are not making their money like thugs and murderers, [...].
> (Marawu, *Daily Sun*, 09.03.10)

In quotes like these, alleged reasons for entering the sex industry are made plausible, which is often the case in articles that promote legalisation. Here, the abject is being a murderer or a thief, so sex work becomes an honest choice and thus sex workers can be included as part of the poorer part of society. Linked to that is the narrative, that sex workers in the subject position of the "mother" need to be represented as *innocent* in media discourse. This becomes visible in narratives of a tragic story:

> Khoza, like most of her friends, turned to sex work to earn a living and support her six-year-old brother. "This has been my job for six

years. It is my first job. I dropped out of school after the death of my parents to take care of my brother".

(N.N., *Mail & Guardian*, 06.01.2010)

I have to support myself and my son. He is five. His dad died in a car crash when he was two. So a few times a week I come in (to the parlour) from 10 to two.

(Makwabe, *Sunday Times*, 30.05.10)

A huge tragedy, like the death of a guardian or partner, allows sex workers to make socially tabooed choices and yet remain "innocent" and maintain "moral integrity". Central is the hardship and that sex workers as "mothers" don't decide for egoistic reasons but responsibly for the sake of others. That a mother does whatever it takes to take care of her children is highly accepted in heteronormative discourse. The figurine of the "mother" seems to be so strong, that she enables recognition of sex workers despite their choice of money-making. What also stands out is the fact that sex workers as "mothers" are neither dangerous nor immediately endangered. This can therefore be regarded as constitutive for the construction of appropriated subject positions.

Conclusions

In summary, the attribution of dangerousness, as well as the attribution of being acutely in danger, both result in sex workers being constructed as "others" in media discourse. The only subject position through which sex workers are discursively accepted as part of majority society is being portrayed as "caring mother" – which usually includes the absence of dangers or threats of any kind. These subject positions also relate to the political positions in the newspaper articles. Especially in articles moralising sex work and advocating for total criminalisation, sex workers are othered and interpellated as whores (or abamagosha). Articles in support of the Swedish model feature sex workers mostly in the subject position of the vulnerable "victim", for example by constantly conflating sex work and trafficking. Articles in favour of legalisation or decriminalisation represent them more often as caring mothers, who sell sex as a necessity to support their children.

But in total it is certainly not that simple and the subject positions of sex workers in media discourse also share similarities across these political divides. The subject position "mother" should not be mistaken for an emancipatory figurine. All three subject positions must be interpreted within the context of heteronormativity and intersectional power relations. Sex work exists within a system of racialised and gendered labour markets and normative gender roles that includes all people and in which women (especially women of colour), experience unequal power. This leaves very limited representations for sex workers in media discourse – either affirmative, as "mother", ambivalent (and often racialised) as "victim" or as their abject counterpart – the "magosha"/"whore", who is mostly constructed as the "other" to procreative, monogamous heterosexuality. So all subject positions, affirmative or abject, draw from a heteronormative understanding of gender roles. For example, there was no media representation of an empowered sex worker in my sample.[15] In the subject position of the "mother" the institution of heteronormativity is particularly visible in "family" and "kinship" ideologies. The narratives that constitute the "magosha" create punitive rules for non-conformity. This shows, how the analysed media discourse leaves very limited gender representations for everyone.

SKAD enables to analyse subject positions and political positions of social actors in the discourse in relation to each other. So, in addition to the linguistic analysis of discourse-constituting narratives of CDA, SKAD focuses on the *relationship* between discourses and actors (Keller, 2011: 55). Moreover, SKAD as a methodological frame allows to analyse how discursive narratives and utterances constitute subject positions of discourse protagonists. Re-constructing the subject positions of sex workers in media discourse allows for baring speakabilities on sex work in context of major sporting events – and therewith pointing out the limitations of representations mentioned above. Social actors are discursively positioned in specific ways that limit and enable their positions in society. Discourse analytical work helps to reveal the contingency of these social positions:

> Constructivism, as the basic approach of a discourse-theoretical and analytical program, means focusing the analysis on the socially produced "order of things" in the medium of discursive knowledge politics, and so to make the contingency of the symbolic order the basis for the questions about those processes which it transforms into temporarily fixed crystallizations and structural contexts.
> (Keller, 2011: 62)

With these theoretical bonds, the methodological frame of discourse analysis resembles queer and postcolonial approaches. SKAD, as well as postcolonial and queer approaches emphasises the performative, constituting character of language and language use (Keller, 2004: 204–211 as well as the necessity of reflecting the contingency of every research topic. SKAD, by drawing from theories of sociology of knowledge, aims to work against processes of "reification" (Berger and Luckmann, 1966: 89) of assumed social realities, as it "is characterised […] by a relation of self-reflexivity" (Keller, 2011: 62). As constructivism and self-reflexivity are also crucial concepts in queer and postcolonial approaches, the Sociology of Knowledge Approach to Discourse coincides well with empirical analyses based on these theories. By analysing what can be said about a specific topic or specific social actors at a specific time, the limitations of (media) discourses can be shown. To dissect the contingency of these limitations means to expand what can be said about this topic and is a first step to open the arena for new subject positions and new stories.

Notes

1 In this chapter I adopt the term sex work, to emphasise that I'm speaking of a consensual, commercial sexual service.
2 "Magosha" (magosha/umagosha (singular), abomagosha/abamagosha (plural)) is a pejorative isiZulu/isiXhosa term to designate sex workers. The literal translation is "those who sell sex" or "these sex worker(s)". It is widely used colloquially as well as in media discourse and can be regarded as the South African equivalent of the term "whore". While "whore" is used as a derogatory term as well as a reappropriated self-designation, "magosha" lacks the part of reappropriation. Self-designations would rather be "abothengisi bocansi" in isiZulu and "abathengisi besondo" in isiXhosa, which means "people who sell sex" ("abathengisi" = "people who sell", and "-cansi"/"-sondo" = "sex". The prefix "bo-"/"be-" means "of" – so the literal meaning would be "sellers of sex"). For that reason it subserves to label the othered subject position of sex workers.
3 See Küppers (2017): "Gefährlich oder gefährdet? Diskurse über Sexarbeit zur Fußball-Weltmeisterschaft der Männer in Südafrika".
4 SWEAT is a Cape Town based NGO that advocates for sex workers' rights and the total decriminalisation of sex work, while the Embrace Dignity Campaign lobbies for the prohibition of buying sexual services.
5 In accordance with Butler (1997: 5), Villa (2013: 66) defines subject as a linguistic category and a structure in formation as well as a socially inhabitable zone that is created by discursive semantics.
6 LSM stands for *Living Standards Measure* which is the most widely used marketing research tool in South Africa. It divides the population into ten LSM groups, with ten being highest and one lowest. The LSM is a unique means of segmenting the South African market as it cuts across race and other outmoded techniques of categorising people. Instead it groups people according to their living standards using criteria such as degree of urbanisation and ownership of major appliances (South African Advertising Research Foundation, 2012).
7 The daily papers *Cape Times, Cape Argus, Daily Sun, Sowetan, The Citizen, The Star*, the weekly *Mail & Guardian* and the tabloid *Daily Sun*.
8 E.g. *Atlantic Sun, Big Issue, Business Day, City Press, Daily Voice, The Herald, The Mercury, North Coast Courier, Sunday Tribune, Weekend Argus*, etc.
9 The last articles that linked sex work to the World Cup were published on 23 October.
10 The tabloids with the widest circulation are the *Daily Sun* (circulation 433,000 and a readership of 4.7 million, the *Sunday Times (circulation* 462,000, readership 3.9 million). All circulation figures were verified by the Audit Bureau of Circulations of South Africa (ABCSA) and are the average for the year 2010. All readership figures were verified by the All Media Products Survey (AMPS) of 2007.
11 It should be noted, that using some such elements of GT does not imply doing a GT research. GT approaches have been particularly helpful to explain analytical features which are widely used in qualitative research.

12 On this occasion I'd like to thank Imke Schmincke, Gabriele Fischer, Anna Buschmeyer, Tina Denninger and Eva Tolasch-Marzahn for manifoldly discussing my data with me.
13 Due to the limitations of a chapter, I can only present a small part of all narratives that constitute one subject positon. For a more detailed description see Küppers (2017).
14 As this subject position is only visible in seven articles it can be regarded as part of a counter discourse to the hegemonic subject positions shown above.
15 Therein the media discourse has to be distinguished from self-descriptions of sex workers, who of course inhabit empowered subject positons that differ tremendously from the limited ones in media discourse.

References

Bashford, A. (2004). Medicine, Gender, and Empire. In: Levine, P., ed. *Gender and Empire*. Oxford: Oxford University Press, 112–133.
Berger, P. L. and Luckmann, T. (1966). *The Social Construction of Reality: A Treatise in the Sociology of Knowledge*. New York: Anchor Books.
Butler, J. (1997). *The Psychic Life of Power: Theories in Subjection*. Chicago: Stanford University Press.
Charmaz, K. (2006). *Constructing Grounded Theory: A Practical Guide Through Qualitative Analysis*. London: Sage.
Deegan, H. (2001). *The Politics of the New South Africa. Apartheid and After*. Harlow, New York: Longman.
Douglas, M. (1966). *Purity and Danger: An Analysis of Concepts of Pollution and Taboo*. London and New York: Routledge.
Foucault, M. (1976). *Mikrophysik der Macht. Michel Foucault über Strafjustiz, Psychiatrie und Medizin*. Berlin: Merve.
Foucault, M. (1981). *Archäologie des Wissens*. Frankfurt am Main: Suhrkamp.
Frenkel, R. (2008). Feminism and Contemporary Culture in South Africa. *African Studies*, 67 (1), 1–10.
Gardner, J. (2009). Criminalising the Act of Sex. Attitudes to Adult Comercial Sex Work in South Africa, In: Steyn, M. E. and van Zyl, M. eds, *The Prize and the Price. Shaping Sexualities in South Africa*. Cape Town: HSRC Press, 329–340.
Hark, S. (2006). Feministische Theorie – Diskurs – Dekonstruktion. Produktive Verknüpfungen. In: Keller, R., Hirseland, A., Schneider, W. and Viehöver, W., eds., *Handbuch sozialwissenschaftliche Diskursanalyse. Band 1, Theorien und Methoden*. Wiesbaden: VS Verlag, 357–376.
Hirschowitz, R., Worku, S. and Orkin, M. (2000). *Quantitative Research Findings on Rape in South Africa*. Pretoria: Statistics South Africa.
Inter-Parliamentary Union (2017). *Women in National Parliaments. World Classification*. IPU. [online] www.ipu.org/wmn-e/arc/classif010617.htm. [Accessed 06 July 2017].
Jäger, M. and Jäger, S. (2002). Medienanalyse zur Berichterstattung über den NATO-Krieg in Jugoslawien. Eine Einleitung. In: Jäger, M. and Jäger, S., eds. *Medien im Krieg. Der Anteil der Printmedien an der Erzeugung von Ohnmachts- und Zerrissenheitsgefühlen*. Duisburg: DISS, 11–27.
Jewkes, R., Sikweyiya, Y., Morrell, R. and Dunkle, K. (2009). *Understanding Men's Health and Use of Violence. Interface of Rape and HIV in South Africa. Medical Research*

Council. Pretoria. Policy Brief. [online] www.mrc.ac.za/gender/violence_hiv.pdf [Accessed 12 June 2018].

Keller, R. (2004). Der Müll der Gesellschaft. Eine wissenssoziologische Diskursanalyse. In: Keller, R. Hierseland, A.; Schneider, W. and Viehöver, W., eds. *Handbuch sozialwissenschaftliche Diskursanalyse.* Vol. 2: Forschungspraxis, Wiesbaden: VS Verlag, 197–232.

Keller, R. (2005). *Wissenssoziologische Diskursanalyse. Grundlegung eines Forschungsprogramms.* Wiesbaden: VS Verlag.

Keller, R. (2007). Diskurse und Dispositive analysieren. Die Wissenssoziologische Diskursanalyse als Beitrag zu einer wissensanalytischen Profilierung der Diskursforschung. [online] *Forum Qualitative Sozialforschung.* www.qualitative-research.net/index.php/fqs/article/view/243/538 [Accessed 21 February 2014].

Keller, R. ([1998] 2009). *Müll. Die gesellschaftliche Konstruktion des Wertvollen.* 2nd edn. Wiesbaden: VS Verlag.

Keller, R. (2010). *Diskursforschung. Eine Einführung für SozialwissenschaftlerInnen.* Wiesbaden: VS Verlag.

Keller, R. (2011). The Sociology of Knowledge Approach to Discourse (SKAD). *Human Studies,* 34, 43–65.

Keller, R. (2012). *Doing Discourse Research: An Introduction for Social Scientists.* London, Thousand Oaks, New Dehli, Singapore: Sage.

Keller, R. (2016). Has Critique Run Out of Steam? On Discourse Research as Critical Inquiry. *Qualitative Inquiry,* 1–11.

Keller, R. and Truschkat, I. (2012). Einleitung. In: Keller, R. and Truschkat, I., eds. *Methodologie und Praxis der wissenssoziologischen Diskursanalyse.* Wiesbaden: VS Verlag, 9–23.

Küppers, C. (2017). *Gefährlich oder gefährdet? Diskurse über Sexarbeit zur Fußball-Weltmeisterschaft der Männer in Südafrika.* Wiesbaden, VS Verlag.

Lazar, M. (2005). Politicizing Gender in Discourse. Feminist Critical Discourse Analysis as Political Perspective and Praxis. In: Lazar, M. M., ed. *Feminist Critical Discourse Analysis. Gender, Power, and Ideology in Discourse.* Basingstoke: Palgrave Macmillan, 1–28.

Levine, P. (2003). *Prostitution, Race, and Politics. Policing Venereal Disease in the British Empire.* New York: Routledge.

Mathews, J. (2000). *The Role of the Print Media in Education Division in South Africa.* [online] www.mediaclubsouthafrica.com/component/content/article?id=110:the-media-in-south-africa [Accessed 04 April 2017].

May, J. (2000). *Poverty and Inequality in South Africa. Meeting the Challenge.* Cape Town: Zed Books.

May, J. and Govender, J. (1998). Poverty and Inequality in South Africa. *Indicator South Africa,* 15(5), 53–58.

Moffett, H. (2009). Sexual Violence, Civil Society and the New Constitution. In: Britton, H., Fish, J. N. and Meintjes, S., eds. *Women's Activism in South Africa. Working Across Divides.* Scottsville: University of KwaZulu-Natal Press, 155–184.

Mokoena, H. (2015). The Black Interpreters and the Arch of History. In: Xolela, M., ed. *The Colour of Our Future. Does Race Matter in Post-apartheid South Africa?* Johannesburg: WITS University Press, 169–183.

Moolman, B. (2009). Race, Gender and Feminist Practice. Lessons from Rape Crisis Cape Town. In: Britton, H., Fish, J. N. and Meintjes, S., eds. *Women's*

Activism in South Africa. Working Across Divides. Scottsville: University of KwaZulu-Natal Press, 185–210.
Osha, S. (2004). Unravelling the Silences of Black Sexualities. *Agenda,* 62(2), 92–98.
Pendleton, E. (1997). Love for Sale. Queering Heterosexuality. In: Nagle, J., ed. *Whores and Other Feminists.* New York: Routledge, 73–82.
Schatzman, L. and Strauss, A. (1973). *Field Research. Strategies for a Natural Sociology.* Englewood Cliffs: Prentice Hall.
Seekings, J. and Nattrass, N. (2005). *Class, Race, and Inequality in South Africa.* New Haven: Yale University Press.
Smith, M. (2009). The Right to Respond. A Meta-Review of the Role of the South African Media's Coverage of Xenophobia and the Xenophobic Violence Prior to and Including May 2008. In: *Report: South African Civil Society and Xenophobia.* [online] www.atlanticphilanthropies.org/sites/all/modules/filemanager/files/14_Media_c.pdf [Accessed 02 April 2017].
South African Advertising Research Foundation (2012). *Average Issue Readership of Newspapers and Magazines. All Media Products Survey.* [online] www.saarf.co.za/lsm-presentations/2012/LSM%20Presentation%20-%20February%202012.pdf [Accessed 07 July 2017].
Spivak, G. (1985). The Rani of Sirmur. *History and Theory,* 24(3), 247–272.
Steyn, M. E. and van Zyl, M., eds. (2009) *The Prize and the Price. Shaping Sexualities in South Africa.* Cape Town: HSRC Press.
Strauss, A. and Corbin, J. (1998). *Basics of Qualitative Research.* London: Sage.
Truschkat, I. (2012). Zwischen interpretativer Analytik und GTM – Zur Methodologie einer wissenssoziologischen Diskursanalyse. In: Keller, R. and Truschkat, I., eds. *Methodologie und Praxis der wissenssoziologischen Diskursanalyse.* Wiesbaden: VS Verlag, 69–87.
van Zyl, M. (2009). Beyond the Constitution: From Sexual Rights to Belonging. In: Steyn, M. E. and van Zyl, M., eds. *The Prize and the Price. Shaping Sexualities in South Africa.* Cape Town: Human Sciences Research Council Press, 364–390.
Villa, P. (2013). Subjekte und ihre Körper. Kultursoziologische Überlegungen. In: Graf, J., Ideler, K. and Klinger, S., eds. *Geschlecht zwischen Struktur und Subjekt. Theorie, Praxis, Perspektiven.* Opladen: Budrich, 59–78. (Reprint of Villa 2010 In: Wohlrab-Sahr, Monika ed. *Kultursoziologie. Paradigmen – Methoden – Fragestellungen.* Wiesbaden: VS Verlag, 251–274.)
Wasserman, H. (2010). *Tabloid Journalism in South Africa. True Story!* Bloomington: Indiana University Press.
Wodak, R. (2001). What CDA is About – A Summary of Its History, Important Concepts and its Developments. In: Wodak, R. and Meyer, M., eds. *Methods of Critical Discourse Analysis.* London: Sage, 1–13.

Quoted newspaper articles/data

Bamford, H. (2010). Uphill battle to help sexworkers and their families. In: *Weekend Argus,* 26.06.10.
Brann, C. (2010). Beyond the sex worker. In: *The Witness,* 11.03.10.
Isaacson, M. (2010). No sex for sale – prostitution is slavery. In: *The Sunday Independent,* 28.02.10.
Lepere, B. (2010). Prostitutes flock to SA? In: *Rising Sun Lenasia,* 14.04.10

Madlala-Routledge, N. and Mayne, A. (2010). Poverty's sex bonds. In: *Daily News*, 23.09.10

Makwabe, B. (2010). Sex workers hope for World Cup bonanza. In: *Sunday Times*, 30.05.10.

Marawu, V. (2010). Hands off SA's sex workers! In: *Daily Sun*, 09.03.10.

N.N. (2010). FIFA sidesteps World Cup sex worker debate. In: *The Witness*, 02.03.10.

N.N. (2010). Sex workers set sights on 2010. In: *Mail & Guardian*, 06.01.10.

Naidoo, E. (2010). Prostitution not "work" like any other vocation. In: *Cape Argus*, 10.06.10

Naidoo, Y. (2010). Teen hookers flood streets ahead of Cup. In: *City Press*, 21.02.10

Ngqulunga, T. (2010). City's red light spring clean. In: *The Witness*, 25.10.10.

Pongoma, L. (2010). Sex workers up for World Cup. In: *Sowetan*, 02.03.10

Richter, M. (2010). Dressing down sex work. In: *Mail & Guardian*, 29.01.10

Seaman, J. (2010). SA is a proud nation, not a whorehouse. In: *Cape Argus*, 02.03.10

Snyders, L. (2010). Trafficking in humans. In: *Tygerburger Eersterivier*, 02.06.10

Viljoen, C. (2010). "Angels" are volunteers. In: *Mail & Guardian*, 29.01.10.

12 Guidance on transitions

Reconstructing the rationalities of the European discourse on career guidance services using the sociology of knowledge approach

Inga Truschkat and Claudia Muche

Introduction

In reaction to the diagnosed increase, expansion and condensing of life course transitions, as people pass between life stages or positions regarding their profession or status (see Blossfeld *et al.*, 2005; Heinz, 1991, 2000; Heinz *et al.*, 2000; Mayer, 2001; Stauber, Walther and Pohl, 2007; Walther, 2008; Helsper, 2013), European policy on the concept of lifelong learning (within the economics of education) has forced what are known as "career guidance services", i.e.

> [...] services intended to assist people, of any age and at any point throughout their lives to make educational, training and occupational choices and to manage their careers. Career guidance helps people to reflect on their ambitions, interests, qualifications and abilities. It helps them to understand the labour market and education systems, and to relate this to what they know about themselves. Comprehensive career guidance tries to teach people to plan and make decisions about work and learning.
>
> (OECD, 2004: 19)

By promoting individual career management skills, career guidance services aim to affect labour market policy by accompanying allocation and matching processes on the labour market, and to affect social policy by creating and maintaining equality of opportunity (avoiding unemployment; improving the social integration of disadvantaged groups) (see Schober and Jenschke, 2006). In our research project, which is founded by the German Research Foundation (DFG), we are interested in these career guidance services in different fields of transition. In special we see that this propaganda of politics forces new forms of managing transitions in society. By giving more attention on such services, transitions become more and more influenced by pedagogical logics. In our research we follow this assumption and we investigate if and how transitions are processed through this form of services and if and how transitions become processed in a pedagogical way.

As part of the triangular design of our research we used a Sociology of Knowledge Approach to Discourse (SKAD) to investigate the European education policy discourse on career guidance services. This article will present how we applied SKAD during this analysis and the theoretical and methodological concepts we picked up on and made additional use of, as well as offering insights into our initial analyses. To this end, our first step will be to explain how we used the concept of the interpretive scheme to reconstruct inherent rationalities. We will then reveal how we used the raised questions as a basis for narrowing down the corpus of data and how we began to interpret that corpus by analysing the discursive context and reformulating a storyline. Another section will offer an example of sequential analysis. The article finishes with an identification of a first interpretive scheme, a look forward to further steps in our analysis and a reflection on the significance of SKAD in the process of analysis.

Tracing rationalities: the heuristic concept of the interpretive scheme

For the investigation of the European education policy discourse on career guidance services, the project used SKAD and here in special the central heuristic approach of interpretation pattern as it is taken up in SKAD under a discourse analytical perspective (on the use of the interpretive scheme in SKAD see Keller and Truschkat, 2014). Keller connects his approach to a sociology of knowledge perspective by Lüders and Meuser (1997: 64) who locate this approach to the level of collective cultural concepts. With this they define it as a knowledge on the societal level and distinguish their approach from the concept by Oevermann (2001) who sees it related with the problems of action in everyday life. Also Plaß and Schetsche (2001) emphasise that the concept not only refers to the tensions of practical action problems, but that interpretation patterns are also constructed and reconstructed through expert knowledge. As the concept of the interpretive scheme is one of the central analytical perspectives of SKAD, this method was used to investigate the "processes by which structures of interpretation and action (regimes and politics of knowledge) are constructed socially at the level of institutions, organisations and collective actors, and the social effects of such processes" (Keller, 2011: 27).

As we mentioned above, our research focus lies on the questions if and how transitions are processed through forms of career guidance services and if and how transitions become processed in a pedagogical way. In accordance with the concept of heuristic pragmatic research, this analysis is initially based on a loose understanding of the term "pedagogical". Current findings on how society is becoming pedagogised have a sensitising effect in this context. Pedagogisation is discussed in terms both of how pedagogy guides society (with regard to the pedagogisation of social problems, see Müller and Otto, 1984; Schelksy, 1961) and of how pedagogy is diffusing into society as an integral aspect of how subjects and institutions see themselves (see Kade, Lüders and Hornstein, 1993; Lüders, Kade and Hornstein, 1998; for an overview of discourses see Proske, 2002). In this context, new approaches mainly concentrate on investigating pedagogical rationalities in terms of the theory of the subject and the theory of power (see Höhne, 2004; Ribolits and Zuber, 2004).

With this research focus we extended the perspective of analysing interpretive schemes by the concept of rationalities. Social interpretive schemes are seen to have specific criteria of *reason* and *validity* which correlate with a systematic judgement of what is right or not. These criteria of reason and validity we understand as rationalities; as legitimate knowledge used to deal with a dilemma requiring action. Here, the term "rationalities" does not refer to any transcendental reasoning.

> One isn't assessing things in terms of an absolute against which they could be evaluated as constituting more or less perfect forms of rationality, but rather examining how forms of rationality inscribe themselves in practices or systems of practices, and what role they play within them.
> (Lemke, Krasmann and Bröckling, 2000: 20)

From the point of view of rationalities, the main interest focuses on how boundaries are drawn between truth and falsity, reality and illusion, scientific rigour and neglect etc., which all establish specific things as rational, and thus legitimate (see also Kessl, 2011; Karl, 2014; Truschkat, 2008). In our research the assumption was made that such rationalities are contained in interpretive schemes, and describe the boundaries drawn between the true and the false.

Altogether, with SKAD and in special with the concept of interpretation patterns we can investigate the regimes and politics of knowledge on the political level of the European education policy discourse on career guidance services and can ask how these interpretation patterns relates to (e.g. pedagogical) rationalities.

From question to corpus. Strategies for narrowing down the subject

In the next step it was important for our research to make our research design more precise. Accordingly, the subject of the investigation needs to be further narrowed down (see Keller, 2008, 2012). One important step was thus to define a more precise corpus of data for further analysis. To do so, theoretical sampling (see Strauss and Corbin, 1996; Truschkat, Kaiser-Belz and Volkmann, 2011) was initially used to define actors of probable theoretical and analytical relevance to the theory being developed. The preliminary research ahead of the project already showed clearly that the career guidance services are mainly policy-driven, hence an initial focus on political actors. This went on to reveal that though there are policy-related arguments on both EU level and on national level, the main impetus comes from the EU. In view of this, the decision was made during the research process to start out primarily from the relevant EU papers. Initial research led to the following central actors being selected on EU level as they are repeatedly referred to in EU documents: the European Commission (EC), CEDEFOP (European Centre for the Development of Vocational Training), the ETF (European Training Foundation) and Eurydice (European information network). Other actors at a higher level, which stood out as relevant and were also included in the research, were the UNESCO (United Nations Educational, Scientific and Cultural Organization) and the OECD (Organisation for Economic Cooperation and Development). The next step was to identify central documents by means of Internet research. The documents were selected and added to the corpus of data using the search term "guidance". By this means, a corpus of data was compiled including documents from a period lasting from the 1990s until the current day. Overall, the first aspect which stands out is the variety of the papers. For example, for CEDEFOP the search came up not only with many reports and studies well over 100 pages long but also with shorter brochures, guidelines, strategy papers and manuals.

The main terms used with regard to guidance in the documents are "lifelong vocational guidance", "lifelong educational and vocational guidance", "lifelong guidance systems", etc. The term is thus used as a counterpart to or similarly to the term "lifelong learning". The terms "career guidance" and "career services" are also used occasionally (apparently increasingly frequently as time goes by). In the texts, educational and vocational guidance are usually described or framed as a central strategy for implementing the European policy of lifelong learning.

Initial data breakdown. Context analysis and storyline

In a second step, the corpus of data thus gathered required further analytical focusing to prepare for the theoretical sampling of documents prior to the third step: sequential analysis. This was achieved by using and combining two approaches. First, the discursive context of the documents was analysed (see Keller, 2011). To do so, the documents were listed chronologically in a table with brief descriptions pertaining to each regarding the year of publication, editor(s), length, document type and a summary of the contents. This was used to *scan* the documents for an initial impression of the events which appeared over the course of the discourse, the political developments which were relevant at different times and how the discussion developed as a whole. The aim of this step was to work out a heuristic storyline for the discourse. With SKAD, this concept is mainly used to describe synchronous links between different interpretive representation and/or diachronic updates to such representations. For the selected corpus of data it was thus possible to build a heuristic storyline, the main points of which are set out below.

The diachronic view on the data corpus shows that we can trace different phases of dealing with career guidance in the EU discourse. The emergence of career guidance can be situated in the years before 2000. Some European Union activities from the 1990s can already be identified as important points of reference in the discourse on career guidance services. For example, in this context, the European Commission's White Papers on "Growth, Competitiveness, Employment" (1993) and "Teaching and Learning – Towards the Learning Society. White Paper on Education and Training" (1995) contain descriptions of challenges regarding the future shape of guidance services and transitions to work as a whole. Various other European papers of the time call for work and jobs to be supported and, especially, the field of occupational integration to be redesigned, or identify this as an important basis for European action. Career guidance is here introduced as a response to the crisis, which is equated with the employment situation in the EU. The problem of unemployment is interpreted as an endless spiral that needs to be permanently negotiated. The solution to secure economic competitiveness is ensured by continuous reforms. This is accompanied by a shift of responsibility from central to decentralised levels. The member states, their vocational and educational system and finally everyone is addressed. Career guidance is able to grant a permanent processing of the crisis and therefore seems to be the method of choice.

While career guidance is introduced in the 1990s as a reactive instrument through which a method in dealing with barely controllable crisis phenomena is found, the political feasibility and controllability of social change and transformation processes through career guidance was given priority since the 2000s. In March 2000 a broad political aim of EU was given by the European Council's Lisbon Strategy for growth and jobs. This was intended to make Europe by 2010 "the most competitive and dynamic knowledge-based economy in the world, capable of sustainable economic growth with more and better jobs and greater social cohesion" (EU Council, 2000). Within the Lisbon process, education and training are named as central fields of action for the European Union. Following on from this, one key agreement reached during the discourse was the European Commission's "Memorandum on Lifelong Learning", also from the year 2000 (EU Commission, 2000). This generally describes lifelong learning as a central strategy to deal with the challenges posed by a knowledge-based society. In these significant papers, central patterns already come to light, aiming at a wider range of guidance becoming more easily accessible to everyone.

Career guidance should no longer be promoted only through political measures, the medium of career guidance has rather set itself as a key policy instrument. In December 2002, the European Commission went on to implement an expert group on "Lifelong Guidance" made up of various members (such as the OECD). Another important point of reference is a Council Resolution on guidance throughout life in May 2004, calling for a fundamental realignment of guidance in policy and practice (EU Council, 2004). During the reform process, special importance was placed on access to guidance services, strengthening quality assurance processes, enabling citizens to manage their educational and occupational paths in a logical way, and improving guidance service coordination (see CEDEFOP, 2008: 1). In these papers, guidance increasingly shifts towards the centre of Europe's development as a knowledge-based society. In 2008 another "Council Resolution on better integrating lifelong guidance into lifelong learning strategies" (EU Council, 2008) followed with direct reference to the topic of transitions. From about 2008 there was stronger focus on setting up national policy forums on lifelong guidance, with CEDEFOP playing a key role. Altogether, at first glance the CEDEFOP documents reveal the familiar topics of extension and accessibility, but these are then accompanied by increased discussion on quality. They are concerned with a dynamic process of development and improvement by the guidance services and systems in each European country. The titles of the CEDEFOP publications alone suggest that guidance services should be developed and implemented following a certain process: in 2004 there is thus a synthesis report entitled "Guidance policies in the knowledge society. Trends, challenges and responses across Europe". This sets out the status of guidance practice and its current challenges in twenty-nine countries (see CEDEFOP, 2004). A subsequent document from 2005, "Improving lifelong guidance policies and systems", presents three common European reference tools for educational and vocational guidance (see CEDEFOP, 2005). Other papers (e.g. the document "From policy to practice. A systemic change to lifelong guidance in Europe" from 2008) list the advances made in the European countries since the Council's initial decision on lifelong guidance, etc. On the whole, the central aspect seems to be building on the existing guidance services, or linking in with what already exists in the context of guidance. The idea of a *common programme* still stands out: central guidelines are to be set down at a European level and implemented at a national level, with the idea of constant comparison or comparability being conveyed.

From about 2009/2010, there is a renewed change in the discourse on lifelong guidance. After the resolution in 2008, the EU (Council and Commission) published no more specific publications on career guidance. Instead, the discourse about career guidance is continued by the accompanying actors – especially CEDEFOP and the European Policy

Network of lifelong guidance (ELGPN). At the same time, a rhetoric of crisis resurfaces in the documents.

Starting from this diachronic description of the storyline (see Keller, 2011) text sequences for detailed analysis could be selected in a next step. First contrastive criteria for this theoretical sampling were the year of publication, the editor or author and the typology of the documents.

From big to small. Examples of sequential analysis

Using SKAD the data are broken down in a next step by sequential analysis. Sequential analysis means deconstructing the text in an extremely reflective, transparent and well-explained manner (see Keller and Truschkat, 2014). This occurs through systematic variations on the interpretation of sequences of meaning, going along the order of the document, whereby – in a manner of SKAD – formal units of meaning (such as the article as a whole case) being broken down analytically. A document does not need to be consistent or coherent. It can appear (though it does not have to) as a field or arena for widely differing discourses. Sequential analysis is used to identify interpretive schemes and dimensions of a discursive a phenomenal structure (see Keller, 2008). It is a methodological means of breaking through everyday interpretive habits and, by slowing down the process, leading to a causal demultiplication of readings (Foucault, 2005). Because of this, this step of analysis can be understood as a form of "open coding" (see Strauss and Corbin, 1996; Keller and Truschkat, 2014; Truschkat, 2012). "Open coding connotes just that data are open to multiple simultaneous readings or codes" (Clarke, 2009: 7).

In the following, the sequential analysis of an extract from the corpus of data will be presented as an example. For this we refer to documents from CEDEFOP which implement the EU's strategy of decentralisation and which take up the new rhetoric of crisis as we described in the storyline.

The first phrases are taken from the document "Career guidance in unstable times: linking economic, social and individual benefits" published by CEDEFOP in 2014. The document takes the form of a short six-page report and contains descriptions of current challenges in the context of guidance, and brief case examples of career guidance from different European countries. The document begins as follows:

> Career guidance in unstable times: linking economic, social and individual benefits. Economic crisis, social exclusion and uncertain career prospects: lifelong guidance can help us respond to this triple challenge.[1]
>
> (CEDEFOP, 2014: 1)

Straight away, in the first sentence (the main heading) a division is made between three levels: the economic, the social and the individual levels.

This division is set against guidance, seen as a way to overcome that separation, at the same time creating benefits on several levels. This threefold division is repeated in the subheading (second sentence), identifying the problems in each field, then again pointing to guidance as the solution to the existing challenges. Looking at these headings to the report, one aspect already becomes clear: rhetoric is used to describe a crisis ("economic crisis, unstable times"), which is contrasted with guidance, as a type of safe entity. The suggestion is that the instrument of guidance could be used to create forms of safety and linearity. The reference to "us" constitutes a collective speaker position which either delineates an explicit group of people responsible for responding to the challenge, or addresses a collective distress with regard to the challenges.

> The economic crisis that peaked in 2009 sent shockwaves that will be felt for a long time to come. Businesses were affected, social risk increased for many people, and job and career prospects were destabilised.
>
> (CEDEFOP, 2014: 1)

The rhetoric of crisis continues the moment the text starts, and is intensified ("shockwaves"). The metaphor of shock suggests an inability to take action and to plan due to exceptional circumstances. However, as it mentions waves, this indicates that there will be recurring exceptional circumstances. The paper from 2014 predicts that this future prospect will be due to the crisis persisting ("for a long time to come"). This perpetuates the idea that the crisis will be long-term or lasting, perpetuating the ambivalent logic of long-term exceptional circumstances. Once again there is an emphasis on the division into the market ("Businesses"), social aspects as structural uncertainty of institutionalised pathways ("job and career prospects") and individuals, who are directly affected by risks ("people"). All in all the basic feeling of instability is underlined.

> In response, European Union (EU) countries have devised several education, training and labour market policies. In all of these strategies, vocational and career guidance plays an increasingly central role as it helps develop the right skills and attitudes people need for successful careers.
>
> (CEDEFOP, 2014: 1)

As the text goes on, the collective inability to act due to instability continues to be contrasted with the solution of guidance. Here, the countries of the EU are introduced as central, active actors devising and implementing strategies to cope with the crisis. These affect the fields of education, vocational training and employment policy, with vocational and career guidance being ascribed a central role in all these fields, thus making it a central entity. In this context, guidance itself is involved in a dynamic process of development ("plays an increasingly central role"). Guidance is also aimed at all people. No distinction is made between people who are in need of guidance or not, between different age groups or social situations. Guidance is thus interpreted as a fundamental driving force for human development. This involves ensuring that the "right skills and attitudes" are developed, giving guidance a highly normative function.

> Although centred on individuals, benefits of vocational and career guidance go much wider. Guidance links individuals' agendas, enterprises' and governments' economic and social goals. Being flexible, guidance can help individual citizens realise their aspirations, by giving them better information about their career prospects and individual learning and training needs. This can be used in enterprises, local communities or schools to improve learning outcomes, knowledge transmission, productivity and innovation. In short, vocational and career guidance can help citizens and organisations to adapt and be productive under new and atypical economic and social conditions.
> (CEDEFOP, 2014: 1)

Again it is made clear that guidance starts out with the individual, though *working on* that individual serves the interests of the other two entities: the market and the social system. Guidance is constituted as a *new* social element linking the system together: it connects various social fields and maintains individual's connectivity as a member of society. Guidance is thus also ascribed a great deal of flexibility. It conveys information to those being guided, i.e. rational knowledge about themselves ("information about their career prospects and individual learning and training needs") which is, however, also made available to the other entities: the market and the social system. Here, too, norms are brought into play such as "better information" or the goals of adaptation and productivity. Altogether, one aspect which stands out is that, in the descriptions, guidance always remains without any actors, and is thus constantly constituted as a kind of superior entity.

The image of the social ubiquity of counselling can also be found in other documents of the CEDEFOP, for example in the strategy paper of the CEDEFOP "Improve policies and systems of lifelong guidance. Using common European reference tools" from the year 2005. This paper describes the principles of lifelong guidance:

- Independence: The free choice of employment and personal development of the citizen or the user is respected in counselling;
- Objectivity: The provided guidance is solely based on the interests of the citizen, is not influenced by provider-specific, institutional or financial interests and does not discriminate on grounds of sex, age, ethnicity, social origin, skill levels, individual skills etc.;

- Confidentiality: The citizens have the right of protection of personal data they disclose in the guidance process;
- Equal opportunities: The provided guidance promotes equal opportunities for all citizens in education and in the workplace;
- Holistic Approach: The personal, social, cultural and economic context in which the citizen makes his or her decision is taken into account in the counselling process.

(CEDEFOP, 2005: 13)

It is striking that here nearly unquestionable assumptions and certainties are expressed which are ultimately rooted and accepted in the sense of general fundamental rights. One might expect under this point other, more specific discussion – for instance about how counselling itself acts independently. By circumferential positioning of citizens as citizens of counselling, they are initially designed as dependent on the medium of counselling. A citizen without counselling is hardly conceivable – but then in a next step their rights of liberties as citizens must be emphasised clearly. In this sense the fundamental rights are negated by creating a citizen through counselling, in order to reconstruct these rights through counselling in a next step. This is done through the emphasis of rights such as independence. In the other points legal and socially legal and social rights are shown (for example anti-discrimination, privacy and equal opportunities). Herein counselling appears as an incontestable and necessary medium from which the citizens are dependent. Consequently they have to be produced again as free citizens in order to match the logic of self-responsibility and self-control.

From small to big. Further analytical steps

These brief insights into sequential analysis show clearly some initial interpretive hypotheses (see Keller and Truschkat, 2014) about the strategy of decentralisation and reactualisation of the rhetoric of crisis which we have found in the storyline.

While the crisis was based on the processing of unemployment in the 1990s, it gains a much fuller extent in these documents. On one hand, the crisis is comprehensive in a temporal way, by being constituted as long-term exceptional circumstances. On the other hand, it also acts in a socially comprehensive manner, because it leads to instabilities on the levels of the market, the social system and the individual level. Their consequences are constructed as a collective inability to act. We therefore find here a specific pattern of legitimacy of counselling.

This is accompanied by a specific speaker position in the discourse. It is rather a collective inability to act which is stressed, than a status of expertise which allows a processing or control of the crisis. The situation is not interpreted in the light of expert knowledge. It rather seems to be a pure description of reality, which all have to cope with in the same way. Counselling is stylised as its own entity which makes the crisis workable.

Counselling as an instance gains a normative power. Counselling is accompanied by specific expectations of normalisation. Guidance is used to adapt people for developing the right skills and attitudes, the right information and the right way of being productive.

This goes hand in hand with specific subject positions. Human beings are generally in need of guidance. There is no distinction made between groups of people. The citizens only exist in the context of counselling. The residents are formed to be active and empowered citizens only by counselling. Counselling makes the person become a responsible citizen and is thus constituted as an authority of socialisation and education. In this way counselling seems to be all-encompassing because it guarantees basic social rights (for example, anti-discrimination, privacy and equal opportunities). Therefore counselling represents a fundamental element of the social world.

Based on the short analyses we can show some interpretive hypotheses about elements of a phenomenal structure (see Keller, 2008) and their characteristics: legitimacy, speaker position, normalisation strategies and subject positions. Looking at these elements in their entanglement, a specific typology of coherent expressions emerges: Counselling seems to be the ideal tool for processing a permanent crisis. For this purpose, on the one hand counselling functioned as an instance of socialisation and education and with this creates responsible citizens. On the other hand counselling constitutes fundamental social rights for these citizens. Thus, we see in this entanglement of expressions a type which we may call the interpretation pattern *counselling as brave new world*. As part of the comprehensive analysis of the project, we were able to further densify this interpretation pattern. We can show that it is gradually asserted in a diachronic perspective in discourse.

As we mentioned in the beginning, this analysis is embedded in a wider research project. In this project we are interested in how transitions are processed through career guidance services and how these processes are influenced by pedagogical rationalities. With SKAD we can show that on the level of institutional knowledge within the interpretation pattern *counselling as a brave new world* pedagogical rationalities of processing of transitions emerge. In further analysis we will take into account concrete practices of counselling in different fields. We do this by analysing conversation in counselling settings, biographical interviews and interviews with experts and ethnography. The analysis will show whether the main expressions of the interpretation pattern *counselling as a brave new world* and their pedagogical rationalities also have dispositive effects on the level of the concrete practices.

234 *Inga Truschkat and Claudia Muche*

Note

1 In the study, the German version of the texts are analysed whenever they are available. The documents are mostly also available in English. In this article, the extracts were translated from German to English, as the versions in different languages may not be exactly the same.

References

Blossfeld, H.-P., Klijzing, E., Mills, M. and Kurz, K. (2005). *Globalization, Uncertainty and Youth in Society.* London: Routledge.

CEDEFOP (2004). *Guidance Policies in the Knowledge Society: Trends, Challenges and Responses Across Europe. A Cedefop Synthesis Report.* Luxembourg: Office for Official Publications of the European Communities, Available at: www.cedefop.europa.eu/en/publications-and-resources/publications/5152 [Accessed 12 April 2015].

CEDEFOP (2005). *Verbesserung der Politik und Systeme der lebensbegleitenden Bildungs- und Berufsberatung. Anhand von gemeinsamen europäischen Bezugsinstrumenten. (english version: Improving Lifelong Guidance Policies and Systems. Using Common European Reference Tools).* Luxembourg: Office for Official Publications of the European Communities, Available at: www.cedefop.europa.eu/en/publications-and-resources/publications/4045 [Accessed 12 April 2015].

CEDEFOP (2008). *From Policy to Practice – A Systemic Change to Lifelong Guidance in Europe.* Luxembourg: Office for Official Publications of the European Communities, Available at: www.cedefop.europa.eu/en/publications-and-resources/publications/5182 [Accessed 12 April 2015].

CEDEFOP (2014). *Laufbahnberatung in unsicheren Zeiten. Wirtschaftlichen, sozialen und individuellen Nutzen verbinden. Kurzbericht. (english version: Career guidance in unstable times. Linking economic, social and individual benefits.)* Available at: www.cedefop.europa.eu/en/publications-and-resources/publications/9094 [Accessed 12 April 2015].

Clarke, A. E. (2009). *Situational Analysis: Grounded Theory After the Postmodern Turn.* Thousand Oaks, CA: Sage Pub.

EU Commission (1993). *Growth, Competitiveness, Employment: The Challenges and Ways Forward into the 21st Century.* Brussels: Commission of the European Communities, Available at: http://europa.eu/documentation/official-docs/white-papers/pdf/growth_wp_com_93_700_parts_a_b.pdf [Accessed 12 April 2015].

EU Commission (1995). *White Paper on Education and Training: Teaching and Learning: Towards the Learning Society.* Commission of the European Communities, Available at: http://europa.eu/documents/comm/white_papers/pdf/com95_590_en.pdf [Accessed 12 April 2015].

EU Commission (2000). *A Memorandum on Lifelong Learning (SEC 1832).* Brussels: Commission of the European Communities, Available at: http://arhiv.acs.si/dokumenti/Memorandum_on_Lifelong_Learning.pdf [Accessed 12 April 2015].

EU Council (2000). *Lisbon European council 23 and 24 march 2000 presidency conclusions.* European Parliament, Available at: www.europarl.europa.eu/summits/lis1_en.htm [Accessed 12 April 2015].

EU Council (2004). *Draft Resolution of the Council and of the Representatives of the Governments of the Member States Meeting within the Council on Strengthening Policies, Systems and Practices in the Field of Guidance Throughout Life in Europe (EDUC 109*

9286). Brussels, Available at: http://register.consilium.europa.eu/doc/srv?l=EN &f=ST%209286%202004%20INIT [Accessed 12 April 2015].
EU Council (2008). *Resolution of the Council and of the Representatives of the Governments of the Member States, Meeting within the Council of 21 November 2008 on Better Integrating Lifelong Guidance into Lifelong Learning Strategies (C 319/4).* Brussels, Available at: www.consilium.europa.eu/ueDocs/cms_Data/docs/pressData/en/educ/104236.pdf [Accessed 12 April 2015].
Foucault, M. (2005). Diskussion vom 20. Mai 1978. In: M. Foucault, ed., *Schriften in vier Bänden – Dits et Ecrits 4: 1980–198.* Frankfurt am Main: Suhrkamp, 25–44.
Heinz, W. R. (1991). *The Life Course and Social Change: Comparative Perspectives: Vol II.* Weinheim: Deutscher Studien Verlag.
Heinz, W. R. (2000). Übergänge: Individualisierung, Flexibilisierung und Institutionalisierung des Lebensverlaufs. *Zeitschrift für Soziologie der Erziehung und Sozialisation,* 3rd supplemental.
Heinz, W. R., Marshall, V., Krüger, H. and Verma, A. (2000). *Restructuring Work and the Life Course.* Toronto: University of Toronto Press.
Helsper, W. (2013). Die Bedeutung von Übergängen im Bildungsverlauf. In: S. Siebholz, E. Schneider, A. Schippling, S. Busse and S. Sandring, eds., *Prozesse sozialer Ungleichheit.* Wiesbaden: VS Verlag für Sozialwissenschaften, 21–28.
Höhne, T. (2004). Pädagogisierung sozialer Machtverhältnisse. In: E. Ribolits and J. Zuber eds., *Pädagogisierung – Die Kunst Menschen mittels Lernen immer dümmer zu machen.* Wien: Studien Verlag, 30–44.
Kade, J., Lüders, C. and Hornstein, W. (1993). Die Gegenwart des Pädagogischen: Fallstudien zur Allgemeinheit der Bildungsgesellschaft. In: J. Olkers and H.-E. Tenorth eds., *Pädagogisches Wissen.* Weinheim: Beltz, 39–65.
Karl, U. (2014). Rationalitäten des Übergangs als Rahmenkonzept: Diskursive Verortungen und Erkenntnisinteresse. In: U. Karl, ed., *Rationalitäten des Übergangs in Erwerbsarbeit.* Weinheim/Basel: Beltz Juventa.
Keller, R. (2008). *Wissenssoziologische Diskursanalyse: Grundlegung eines Forschungsprogramms.* Wiesbaden: VS Verlag für Sozialwissenschaften.
Keller, R. (2011). Zur Praxis der wissenssoziologischen Diskursanalyse. In: R. Keller and I. Truschkat, eds., *Methodologie und Praxis der Wissenssoziologischen Diskursanalyse: Vol. 1: Interdisziplinäre Perspektiven.* Wiesbaden: Springer VS Verlag, 27–68.
Keller, R. (2012). *Doing Discourse Research: An Introduction for Social Scientists.* London: Sage.
Keller, R. and Truschkat, I. (2014). Angelus Novus: Über alte und neue Wirklichkeiten der deutschen Universitäten: Sequenzanalyse und Deutungsmusterrekonstruktion in der Wissenssoziologischen Diskursanalyse. In: J. Angermüller, M. Nonhoff, E. Herschinger, F. Macgilchrist, M. Reisigl, J. Wedl, D. Wrana and A. Ziem, eds., *Diskursforschung: Ein interdisziplinäres Handbuch.* Bielefeld: Transcript, 294–328.
Kessl, F. (2011). Die Analyse von Rationalisierungspraktiken als Perspektive sozialpädagogischer Forschung. In: B. Dollinger and M. Schabdach, eds., *Zugänge zur Geschichte der Sozialpädagogik und Sozialarbeit.* Siegen: universi – Universitätsverlag Siegen, 31–43.
Lemke, T., Krasmann, S. and Bröckling, U. (2000). Gouvernementalität, Neoliberalismus und Selbsttechnologien: Eine Einleitung. In: T. Lemke, S. Krasmann and U. Bröckling, eds., *Gouvernementalität der Gegenwart: Studien zur Ökonomisierung des Sozialen.* Frankfurt am Main: Suhrkamp, 7–40.

Lüders, C. and Meuser, M. (1997). Deutungsmusteranalyse. In: R. Hitzler and A. Honer, eds., *Sozialwissenschaftliche Hermeneutik*. Opladen: Leske + Budrich, 57–79.

Lüders, C., Kade, J. and Hornstein, W. (1998). Entgrenzung des Pädagogischen. In: H. H. Krüger and W. Helsper, eds., *Einführung in die Grundbebriffe und Grundfragen der Erziehungswissenschaft*. Opladen: Leske + Budrich, 207–216.

Mayer, K. U. (2001). The Paradox of Global Social Change and National Path Dependencies: Life Course Patterns in Advanced Societies. In: A. Woodward and M. Kohli, eds., *Inclusions and Exclusions in European Societies*. London: Routledge, 89–111.

Müller, S. and Otto, H.-U. (1984). *Verstehen oder kolonialisieren: Grundprobleme sozialpädagogischen Handelns und Forschens*. Bielefeld: Kleine.

OECD (2004). *Career Guidance and Public Policy: Bridging the Gap*. Organisation for Economic Co-operation and Development, Available at: www.oecd.org/education/country-studies/34050171.pdf [Accessed 04 April 2013].

Oevermann, U. (2001). Zur Analyse der Struktur von sozialen Deutungsmustern. *Sozialer Sinn*, 1/2001, 3–33.

Plaß, C. and Schetsche, M. (2001). Grundzüge einer wissenssoziologischen Theorie sozialer Deutungsmuster. *Sozialer Sinn*, 3/2001, 511–536.

Proske, M. (2002). Pädagogisierung und Systembildung: Das Pädagogische im gesellschaftlichen Umgang mit dem Dritte-Welt-Problem. *Zeitschrift für Erziehungswissenschaft*, 5(2), 279–298.

Ribolits, E. and Zuber, J. (2004). *Pädagogisierung: Die Kunst, Menschen mittels Lernen immer dümmer zu machen!* Innsbruck: Studienverlag.

Schelksy, H. (1961). *Anpassung oder Widerstand?* Heidelberg: Quelle & Meyer.

Schober, K. and Jenschke, B. (2006). Zukunft der Beratung und Bildung: Beruf und Beschäftigung in Europa. In: P. Faulstich and M. Bayer, eds., *Lernwiderstände: Anlässe für Vermittlung und Beratung*. Hamburg: VSA-Verlag, 123–135.

Stauber, B., Walther, A. and Pohl, A. (2007). *Subjektorientierte Übergangsforschung*. Weinheim and Munich: Juventa.

Strauss, A. and Corbin, J. (1996). *Grounded Theory: Grundlagen Qualitativer Sozialforschung*. Weinheim: Beltz.

Truschkat, I. (2008). *Kompetenzdiskurs und Bewerbungsgespräche: Eine Dispositivanalyse (neuer) Rationalitäten sozialer Differenzierung*. Wiesbaden: VS Verlag für Sozialwissenschaften.

Truschkat, I. (2012). Zwischen interpretativer Analytik und GTM – Zur Methodologie einer wissenssoziologischen Diskursanalyse. In: R. Keller and I. Truschkat, eds., *Methodologie und Praxis der Wissenssoziologischen Diskursanalyse: Vol. 1: Interdisziplinäre Perspektiven*. Wiesbaden: VS Verlag für Sozialwissenschaften, 69–87.

Truschkat, I., Kaiser-Belz, M. and Volkmann, V. (2011). Theoretisches Sampling in Qualifikationsarbeiten: Die Grounded Theory Methodologie zwischen Programmatik und Forschungspraxis. In: G. Mey and K. Mruck, eds., *Grounded Theory Reader*. Wiesbaden: VS Verlag für Sozialwissenschaften, 353–379.

Walther, A. (2008). Die Entdeckung der jungen Erwachsenen: eine neue Lebensphase oder die Entstandardisierung des Lebenslaufs? In: T. Rietzke and M. Galuske, eds., *Lebensalter und Soziale Arbeit, Vol. 4: Junges Erwachsenenalter*. Baltmannsweiler: Schneider Verlag Hohengehren, 10–36.

13 Using SKAD to investigate cooperation and conflict over water resources

Tobias Ide

Discourses, environmental conflict/cooperation and the added value of SKAD

The potential links between environmental stress, natural resource scarcity and (violent) intergroup conflict have been intensively debated in the scientific literature since the 1990s (Gleditsch, 1998; Homer-Dixon, 1999). This debate has attracted further interest after the publication of the 2007 report of the Intergovernmental Panel on Climate Change (IPCC, 2007), including concerns articulated by Barack Obama, Ban Ki-Moon, John Kerry, the UN Security Council, the G7 foreign ministers and the European Commission about future violent conflicts about natural resources (McDonald, 2013). An alternative literature has focused on the opportunities and incentives that resource scarcity provides for cooperation on shared problems, the creation of mutual benefits and the building of trust and understanding (Conca, Carius and Dabelko, 2005; Feil, Klein and Westerkamp, 2009). In this debate on conflict or cooperation about natural resources, water has received most attention (e.g. Selby, 2013; Weinthal, 2002; Tir and Stinnett, 2012; Brochmann and Gleditsch, 2012).

Recently, the literature on socio-environmental conflicts has been criticised for its often rationalist and positivist understanding of science,[1] nature and societal relations. Theoretically, nature is often conceived as a material entity which is perceived by human actors in an objective manner, while individuals and social groups are assumed to be rational utility maximisers (Ide, 2016). Methodologically, the research field is dominated by quantitative/statistical accounts, which are based on questionable assumptions and datasets and cannot include variables such as identities or threat perceptions (Selby, 2014).

Such theoretical and methodological assumptions have been strongly challenged by studies from various disciplines. Environmental sociology (e.g. Engels, 2008), integrative geography (e.g. Murtinho *et al.*, 2013) and poststructuralist environmental security research (e.g. Oels, 2013) highlight the intersubjective construction of environmental challenges, risks and threats. Constructivist conflict research (e.g. Kaufman, 2006) and identity studies (e.g. Chatterjee, 2012) point out the high relevance of worldviews, situation assessments, diacritica and identity markers for understanding intergroup conflict and cooperation. Similarly, political ecology (e.g. Wittayapak, 2008) and a small number of constructivist environmental security scholars (e.g. Fröhlich, 2012; Norman, 2012) emphasise the discursive/narrative dimensions of conflict and cooperation over natural resources.

I would like to suggest that the Sociology of Knowledge Approach to Discourse (SKAD) is helpful to analyse and understand the intersubjective dimensions of socio-environmental conflict and cooperation for three reasons. First, it combines insights of the Foucauldian approach widely resonated in constructivist and poststructuralist conflict studies (Evans, 2010) and environmental security research (Oels, 2013) with the sociology of knowledge and symbolic interactionism, which is a basis for many works in environmental sociology (Hannigan, 2006). This reduces theoretical incompatibilities when connecting to and incorporating insights from these academic fields. Second, Keller provides clear definitions for his key concepts as well as a set of helpful methodological tools, standards and criteria. This is still not the case for all discursive approaches utilised in peace and conflict studies (Milliken, 1999) or environmental security research (Detraz and Betsill, 2009) and increases the transparency of SKAD as well as its applicability in empirical research.

Third, research on socio-environmental conflict and cooperation clearly benefits from the incorporation of intersubjective factors (see pp. 248–249). But it would be misleading to deny the relevance of material factors, such as the links between harvests, food prices and malnutrition (Sternberg, 2012) or the transboundary nature of rivers like the Jordan, Nile or Mekong (Sayre, 2005). SKAD allows researchers to consider "the simultaneity of symbolic and material struggles over environmental resources" (Peluso and Watts, 2001: 30) by seizing a middle ground between linguistic idealism and materialism/objectivism. On the one hand, Keller (2013: 61) emphasises that reality is discursively constructed: "everything we perceive, experience, sense is mediated through socially constructed and typified knowledge [...]. We have no direct access to the world per se". But on the other hand, SKAD also allows the inclusion of material factors in the analysis:

> In this context, neither the resistant character of reality nor the existence of physical phenomena and processes that are independent from assignment of meaning are denied. Therefore, not everything can be *successfully* said and practically *done* in all kinds of ways about everything. However, the criteria for the evaluation of evidence and inconsistencies themselves are a part of discourses.
>
> (Keller, 2011: 62)

This ontological pragmatism allows taking into account the material characteristics of bio-physical and socio-economic systems, but highlights that discourses structure how the relevant actors perceive and act towards these systems.

In what follows, I will demonstrate the utility and applicability of SKAD for analysing socio-environmental conflict and especially socio-environmental cooperation. In order to do so, I will use my own study of Israeli-Palestinian water cooperation (see also Ide, 2017; Ide and Fröhlich, 2015). In addition, I illustrate how SKAD can be combined with field research in conflict-intensive environments. This chapter proceeds as follows: in the next section, the context and the goals of the study are discussed. Afterwards, I will describe in greater detail how I used SKAD to analyse water cooperation between Israeli and Palestinian communities before some central results of this study are briefly presented. Finally, a conclusion is drawn and some suggestions for future research are formulated.

Context: the Israeli–Palestinian water conflict and the Good Water Neighbours project

The water conflict is one among several intertwined dimensions of the Israeli–Palestinian conflict, which has not been resolved yet (Moore and Guy, 2012). There are three major manifestations, or expressions, of the water conflict: On the diplomatic level, no final agreement on the distribution and management of the shared water resources (mainly the Jordan River and two large underground water systems, the Mountain Aquifer and the Coastal Aquifer) could be reached yet. Only a highly contested interim agreement is effective at the moment. On the material level, shared water resources are distributed highly unequally in favour of the Israeli side. Both conflict manifestations are embedded in an institutional framework (including the Israeli occupation of the West Bank) which gives Israel far-reaching veto opportunities regarding Palestinian water policies and which is consequentially contested by the Palestinian side (Lautze and Kirshen, 2009; Selby, 2013; Zeitoun, 2008).

However, several authors have emphasised "that water is of only marginal significance within the political economy of the modern Middle East" (Selby, 2005: 331) and that the dominant and confrontational discourses of both parties are crucial to understand the ongoing water conflict. To summarise an extensive literature (Alatout, 2006; Feitelson, 2002; Fröhlich, 2012; Messerschmid, 2012), in the dominant Israeli discourse, water is considered as crucial for the creation of a Jewish homeland and a viable Israeli state, while the Middle East is conceived as a naturally water scarce region. This scarcity can be mitigated by efficient and technologically advanced water management, which is currently done by Israel, but not by the Palestinians, who thus have to be blamed for the water problems they face. Relinquishing control over the region's water resources is therefore strongly opposed. In the dominant Palestinian discourse, water is also constructed as crucial for the Palestinian identity and a (future) Palestinian state. However, the region's water resources are considered as sufficient for a major improvement of the living standard of most Palestinians, implying that water scarcity is not natural, but politically induced by Israel. Consequentially, increased control over the region's water resources is demanded.

But the fact that there is a protracted conflict over water resources on the international level should not obscure the existence of water-related cooperation between Israeli and Palestinian communities. One example of such cooperation is the Good Water Neighbours (GWN) project, which was initiated in 2001 by the NGO EcoPeace (formerly Friends of the Earth Middle East (FoEME)). In late 2013, seven Israeli and nine Palestinian communities engaged in various forms of cross-border collaboration on shared water resources.[2] Co-management or a more equitable sharing of water resources has not been achieved yet due to administrative obstacles and lack of high-level political support. However, GWN has conducted water-related education and awareness-raising projects, participated in development of cross-border conservation areas, initiated water infrastructure projects benefiting both sides and prevented construction works in ecologically and hydrologically sensitive areas, among others (FoEME, 2013; Djernaes, Jorgensen and Koch-Ya'ari, 2015).

Using SKAD to analyse water cooperation in Israel/Palestine: a research project

A significant literature deals with the discursive dimensions of the Israeli–Palestinian water conflict (e.g. Fröhlich, 2012; Feitelson, 2002; Harris and Alatout, 2010), while no discourse analysis of parallel processes of Israeli–Palestinian water cooperation exists. In general, few studies explore dominant discourses in the context of water cooperation (but see Norman, 2012). In order to fill this gap, the goal of my study was to analyse the dominant discourse of the GWN activists (volunteers and professional staff) in Israel and Palestine in order to answer the following questions:

- What does the phenomenal structure of the GWN discourse look like?
- What are the key differences between the dominant national discourses in Israel/Palestine and the GWN discourse?
- Does the GWN discourse facilitate more cooperative water interactions?

According to Keller (2013), the reconstruction of a discourse can be conceived as a six-stage process which encompasses the following phases:

- Definition of the discourse to be studied and the research question to be answered
- Development of a theoretical framework
- Choosing procedures to collect and analyse data
- Collecting data
- Analysing data
- Concluding interpretation of the discourse.

The discourse under investigation and the central research questions have already been introduced above. The theoretical framework cannot be discussed here in greater depth (see Ide, 2016). It basically claims that discourses are simultaneously:

- structured by human actions (through utterances and practices which (re-) produce or challenge existing discourses)
- structuring human actions (through providing taken-for-granted knowledge of the world)
- and constituting human actors (e.g. by providing subject positions).

In this sense, discourses enable and restrain, but never determine human action. With regard to (confrontative or cooperative) interactions between groups, it is particularly important how certain identities (Hansen, 2006) and situation assessments (Fröhlich, 2012) are constructed within the dominant discourses of these groups.[3] As a result of these discursive constructions, more or less confrontative or complementary interests emerge (Ringmar, 1996), which facilitate actions that in turn (re-)produce not only patterns of conflict and cooperation, but also (dominant) discourses (Kaufman, 2001).

In the next (third) step, the procedures for collecting and analysing data were chosen. These procedures are discussed in greater detail in the following paragraphs. To create the corpus for the discourse analysis (step four), three major strategies were deployed. First, I collected discourse fragments from the English-language homepage of GWN and from several project reports. However, it is possible that these utterances are not representative of the GWN discourse because they might be produced by a small number of professional activists that are fluent in English. Therefore, my second major strategy for corpus creation was the conduction of semi-structured interviews with GWN activists during two-months of field research in Israel and the West Bank.[4]

In a first step, professional staff from the national GWN offices in Tel Aviv and Bethlehem were contacted and interviewed. They served as key informants and provided valuable information as well as access to mailing lists and contact information of further GWN activists. Subsequently, the snowball sampling method was used to contact and interview further people involved in the GWN project (Cohen and Arieli, 2011).

The snowball sampling method is especially useful if external researchers enter conflict environments that are characterised by relatively low levels of trust. It also allows identifying a large number of interview partners within a short time period and accounting for potential contact biases.

In order to single out the relevance of discourses vis-à-vis other factors, the diverse case technique was used (Gerring and Seawright, 2007). In other words, the interviews were conducted in Israeli and Palestinian communities that greatly differed with regard to location, size, population structure, history, political affiliation and economic structure. Hence, the impact of other structural factors (e.g. predominately rural populations or very left electorates) on the occurrence of local-level water cooperation could largely be excluded. Altogether, thirty-eight semi-structured interviews with forty-four GWN activists from the national offices and five cooperating community-pairs were conducted. The number of Israeli (twenty-five) and Palestinian (nineteen) respondents was roughly equivalent. The interviews were mostly conducted in English and if necessary, a local translator fluent in German or English and Hebrew or Arabic was hired.[5]

The third major strategy for corpus creation was theoretical sampling as suggested by the Grounded Theory literature (Corbin and Strauss, 2008: 143–157). Theoretical sampling refers to the idea of choosing the data to be collected according to the data already analysed. More precisely, the researcher is supposed to collect and analyse some data fitting his or her research questions. When some crucial concepts, interesting hypothesis and potential blind spots begin to emerge, one can in the next step collect more data which allow for the elaboration of the relevant categories or the lightening of the blind spots discovered earlier.

Combining theoretical sampling with SKAD has another advantage. Before the actual analysis is carried out, one cannot verify the existence or identify the characteristics of a certain discourse (Keller, 2005b: 163). For instance, it would have been possible that no coherent GWN discourse exists, or that two or more very different, competing GWN discourses are identified (though this was not the case). Theoretical sampling allows the researcher to remain flexible in the face of such uncertainties. In the concrete research project, theoretical sampling implied that I adjusted the interview guidelines during my field research in order to account for unexpected aspects of the GWN discourse. Towards the end of the field research, I also gave preference to scheduling interviews with persons that were so far underrepresented in my sample, such as policymakers of activists from certain villages/cities. Since only one field visit was planned during the research project, the (preliminary) analysis of the interview data had to take place during the field research, e.g. in buses, taxis and ho(s)tel rooms.

Some scholars are sceptical about using primarily interview data for a discourse analysis because the material did not appear in its original context, but was intentionally created by the researcher through the conduction of interviews. This poses the risk that the material is biased, for instance because the interviewer asked explicit questions about some aspects of the issue under investigation, but not about others. I utilised several strategies to account for such potential biases, such as including non-interview data into the corpus or conducting member checks (see p. 245). As for the semi-structured interviews, I included narrative elements, that is, I asked several open questions to give the respondents the opportunity to develop their own perspectives and to raise topics previously not considered (Gläser and Laudel, 2010: 61–153). Examples of such open questions can be found in Table 13.1.

According to Keller's (2013) guidelines, analysing the data is the fifth step of reconstructing a discourse. For the analysis of the corpus, I drew on Keller's (2013: 93–94) distinction between a more general examination of the corpus (macro-analysis) and a more fine-grained analysis of selected utterances (micro-analysis). The macro-analysis was used to get an overview over the data and to formulate hypotheses. The micro-analysis was then used for an extensive examination of particular utterances in order to verify, falsify or modify the hypothesis developed during the macro-analysis, but also to formulate new hypotheses.

Since an intense analysis of all utterances would have been too time-consuming (especially given the fact that parts of the analysis took place during field research), single utterances were selected for the

Table 13.1 Examples of open questions (narrative elements) in the guidelines for the semi-structured interviews

Question	Possible follow-up questions
Could you please describe the most impressive, surprising, exciting or shocking experience since you are part of GWN?	
What was your motivation to join GWN?	(a) If not mentioned: Did the environmental situation motivate you to participate? (b) If mentioned: How would you describe the water situation in Israel and Palestine? Is there any difference between the overall situation and the situation of your local community?
Can you shortly describe the main achievements of the GWN project?	(a) If not mentioned: What are the main achievements in your region/community? (b) Who (which persons) profit from these achievements?

micro-analysis according to the principles of maximal and minimal contrast. That is, after the analysis of a (particularly interesting or representative) utterance, other utterances were chosen which were very similar (in order to analyse specific aspects of the GWN discourse as detailed as possible) and very different (in order to reconstruct the entire discourse) to the original utterance (Keller, 2013: 129–130). Phases of macro- and micro-analysis alternated because every hypothesis created during the macro-analysis has to be verified through the micro-analysis. And since a discourse is never completely represented by/in a single utterance, the results of the micro-analysis needs to be compared from a macro-perspective to the wider set of utterances.

For the micro-analysis, I utilised a coding procedure in the tradition of Grounded Theory (Glaser and Strauss, 1967: 101–115; Glaser, 1978: 82–92). In this context, coding means

> taking raw data and raising it to a conceptual level [...] deriving concepts to stand for those data, then developing those concepts in terms of their properties and dimensions. A researcher can think of coding as "mining" the data, digging beneath the surface to discover the hidden treasures contained within the data.
>
> (Corbin and Strauss, 2008: 66)

Each time a specific utterance was analysed, one or several codes were assigned to it. These codes were accompanied by memos, which are comments about why the specific code was assigned to a particular utterance, which alternative interpretations could be possible, how the respective code could relate to other codes and what blind spots in the analysis might exist (Corbin and Strauss, 2008: 159–193). At the beginning of the analysis, I kept the codes and memos as flexible as possible in order to remain open for alternative interpretations of the material (open coding). In order to move forward with the analysis, it was important to synthesise or specify codes to more robust and elaborated categories (axial coding) and relate them to each other in order to produce the final analysis of the discourse (selective coding) (Böhm, 2012). Codes therefore served as the building blocks for the final analysis of the discourse. Table 13.2 gives three short examples of utterances, codes and memos used in the analysis.

As explained above, the goal of the discourse analysis was to uncover the phenomenal structure of the GWN discourse. But the phenomenal structure was simultaneously used as a tool to structure the macro-analysis (and, at least partially, the micro-analysis as well). The phenomenal structure:

> includes cognitive devices like the concepts used to name an object, the relations between those concepts, the introduction of causal

schemes and normative settings, the dimensions, urgencies and legitimations for action, as well as the kind of practices considered to be suitable to a particular phenomenon.

(Keller, 2005a: 14)

In line with Keller (2013: 115–120), I first developed relevant categories (syntheses of various codes) and then verified and refined them through the micro-analysis. Examples of core categories of the phenomenal structure identified in the GWN discourse include in-group/out-group identities, water situation, causes of water problems or proposed solutions.

With regard to the last stage of a discourse analysis, the concluding interpretation of the GWN discourse, it was important to determine when the collection and interpretation of data is completed, that is, when the analysis is saturated. Keller (2013: 130) recommends to continue the analysis "until the point where the material has been exhaustively analysed and there are no further results with regard to the research questions". However, it always remains theoretically possible that the incorporation of the very next utterance allows the researcher to gain insights he or she was previously not aware of. For more specific advice, I therefore drew on the work of Corbin and Strauss (2008: 148), who tell us:

> Saturation is usually explained in terms of "when no new categories or relevant themes are emerging". But saturation is more than no new categories or themes emerging. It also denotes a development of categories in terms of their properties and dimensions, including a variation, and possible relationships to other concepts.

This means that a discourse analysis can be considered to be complete if it has first identified several categories of the phenomenal structure which provide deeper insights into the discourse under investigation, second spelled out several attributes and dimensions characterising these categories and third detected relationships between the central categories.

Once this was the case, I validated my findings and related them to the wider literature on environmental stress, water, conflict and cooperation. Since no other analyses of the GWN discourse were available, I used member checks as the primary validation strategy (Steinke, 2012). A discourse "that is grounded in data should be recognizable to participants" (Corbin and Strauss, 2008: 115). Hence, I summarised the goals and core findings of my analysis in a short report (six pages) and distributed it among my interview partners, asking them for feedback. I received extensive feedback from three of my interview partners (and short comments from several others) which I discussed with them before I reviewed my analysis in case of disagreement.

Table 13.2 Example from the coding process

Source	Utterance	Code(s)	Memo
Water Care Textbook, p. 6	"With the ability to think and reason, humans have succeeded in developing technology that allows them to alter the environment, as a means of controlling the source of existence, first and foremost – water. Developments in technology made it possible for people to store significant amounts of water and/or to transport it from place to place, thus paving the way for the Agriculture Revolution […]. In the desert and semidesert regions such as the Middle East, the development of water systems was crucial for the development and advancement of human culture" (p. 6).	importance technology	Water is not only "the source of existence", but also central for the development of civilisations, and thus a high and universal meaning is attributed to it. This stands in contrast to the more exclusive relationships between Zionism/Palestinian nationalism and water in the dominant discourses. However, it is not water alone, but the combination of water and technology that is key for human development. Furthermore, it is technology that distinguishes the "'intelligent' human being" from the "other living creatures" (animals) (p. 6). Technology is thus conceived positive here. Relationship to code "in-group, out-group" should be checked since Palestinian water management is technologically inferior to the Israeli water management.

Interview, Bethlehem, 09/05/2013	"And the other problem is that we still have, also because of the occupation and, and, and, we have less, unfortunately, less awareness about the environment [...]. Here, unfortunately, because of the Intifada and uprising time and occupation, there were no attention for such issues. And sometimes, there were no schools in the Intifada times. And we did not have resources, we are occupied."	water problems knowledge	Although internal problems (education, awareness) of water problems are mentioned, they are seen as caused by the Intifada and occupation, and thus, Israel is blamed for water problems in Palestine (and Israel?). However, this does not obscure the fact that knowledge about water issues in Palestine is considered to be low.
Interview, Hadera, 14/05/2013	"And therefore, any drop of water, of sewage or anything that going in in, untreated water, going into the rock find it's way into our water [...]. Our water. All the water is coming from the Westbank [...]. We will pay for this. We are paying already."	interdependence water problems	Water interdependence between Israel and Palestine is constructed. Could imply that water problems should be solved together, but could also legitimatise Israeli interference in Palestinian water affairs. Water quality is the major concern here. It relates to code "depolitisation". If Israelis are "paying already" and no adequate policy measures are implemented, this implies a negative image of politicians (or parliamentarians).

Research results

While I have discussed the results of the discourse analysis in greater length elsewhere (Ide, 2017; Ide and Fröhlich, 2015), I will give a brief summary of them here in order to illustrate the utility of SKAD in the research project described in the previous sections. When doing so, I focus on five particularly important categories of the phenomenal structure, namely the relevance of water, water problems, the water situation, solution for water problems and out- and in-group images.

The dominant national discourses in Israel and Palestine attribute a high relevance to water, mainly because (control over) water is conceived as an essential precondition for the establishment of a safe Jewish homeland or an independent Palestinian state (Fröhlich, 2012; Waintraub, 2009). The GWN discourse also highlights the relevance of water in the largely arid to semi-arid Middle East. However, water is considered relevant because it enables life, it is vital for a high quality of life and it sustains agricultural livelihoods. Framed in these terms, the relevance of water is not deduced from conflicting and potentially exclusive national projects, but is established via reference to universal norms that are applicable to all inhabitants of the region. This is frequently expressed by utterances of GWN activists such as "water is, *of course*, important to *all of us*" (Interview, Jerusalem, 13 May 2013, author's emphasis).

When it comes to water problems, the dominant Israeli and Palestinian discourses are quite confrontative. The Israeli discourse diagnoses bad water management in Palestine, which is described as a major reason for the water pollution problems Israel faces. In Palestine, the dominant discourse portrays the Israeli occupation and water appropriation as the by far most important cause of the significant water availability problems in the West Bank and Gaza (Waintraub, 2009; Alatout, 2006). These lines of tension also exist between Israeli and Palestinian GWN activists. Nevertheless, the GWN discourse is characterised by a strong consensus that the Middle East is suffering from water quality and water quantity problems and that climatic and geographic factors as well as Israeli policies are major drivers of these conflicts. In the words of an Israeli GWN activist:

> Then, unfortunately, we had 1967 another war. And this time, Israel occupied, or take, took over the West Bank, and occupied. And since then, Israeli had no, no intention of letting the Palestinian really survive in a proper, decent way [...]. To get the pump to a village, to pump water, it will be a procedure of paper work of half a year, or a year, and now the couple of years before they let you do it.
> (Interview, Hadera, 14 May 2013)

A further relevant characteristic of the GWN discourse is that it constructs strong water interdependence between Israeli and Palestine. GWN activists emphasised in nearly every interview that "water has no border" (Interview, Bethlehem, 26 May 2013) and that the crucial water resources of the region are shared between both parties. Therefore, common (or at the very least coordinated) water management is considered to be much more reasonable than separate, national-level water policies. In the dominant national discourses, by contrast, notions of water interaction as a zero-sum game prevail and national rather than transnational water management is preferred (Fröhlich, 2012). The claim that existing water resources should be shared more equally between Israelis and Palestinians is also uncontested in the GWN discourse, which is expressed by utterances like: "There is a need for a more equitable allocation of Israeli-Palestinian shared waters, including an immediate increase of fresh water to be made available to Palestinians" (GWN-Homepage, 2017). Such issues are strongly disputed between the dominant Palestinian (fairer water sharing is necessary) and Israeli (water sharing is already fair) discourses (Waintraub, 2009).

The depiction of the (Israeli or Palestinian) out-group by the GWN discourse is not unequivocally positive. The Israeli GWN discourse sometimes refers to Palestine as a corrupt, insecure and unorganised place, while Israeli water management is portrayed to be excellent. The utterances of Palestinian GWN activists are often characterised by a strong distinction between the Israeli public (which is described in the positive terms) and the Israeli government and settlers (who are judged very negative). But Israeli and Palestinian GWN activists still largely describe their respective counterpart in positive and empathic terms. In the dominant national discourses, negative images of the out-group are still far more common (Kaufman, 2009).

In sum, the main result of my analysis is that the GWN discourse is indeed much more cooperation prone that the dominant (water) discourses in Israel and Palestine. In combination with the fact that the communities selected for the interviews vary considerably with regard to their political, economic, ecological and geographic characteristics, this suggests that discourses are indeed important factors that can facilitate or impede water cooperation.

Conclusion

At latest since the 1980s, various scholars have suggested that phenomena such as conflict, mass violence, social movements, peace and cooperation can only be adequately analysed if the intersubjective construction of (social) phenomena is taken into account (Hansen, 2006; Kaufman, 2001; Wendt, 1992; Snow and Benford, 1988). Despite the still existing positivist-rationalist bias of the research field (Ide, 2016), some recent studies have productively used these insights in the research on socio-environmental conflicts (e.g. Fröhlich, 2012; Zeitoun, Talhami and Eid-Sabbagh, 2013; Simmons, 2014), while very few investigations focus on socio-environmental cooperation from a constructivist or post-structuralist perspective (Norman, 2012).

The research project described in this chapter highlights two points. First, it adds further empirical support to the claim that discourses are important drivers of socio-environmental conflict and cooperation. Supposedly natural *facts* such as water availability or the causes of water problems are discursively constructed and can be objects of intense political conflicts, but also drivers of cooperation. Second, SKAD is well-suited to analyse the dynamics of socio-environmental conflict and cooperation, especially if it is combined with Grounded Theory in terms of methodology and with constructivist environmental sociology and conflict research in terms of theory. SKAD is also useful for the research on human-nature interactions because it allows the consideration of the symbolic and material dimensions of nature and because it provides well-defined conceptual and methodological guidelines.

In this context, two tasks seem to be particularly promising for future research. Empirically, the symbolic dimensions of other socio-environmental conflicts and cooperation efforts should be studied in order to comparatively investigate characteristics of discourses which facilitate conflict or cooperation and to identify potentials for discursive conflict transformation (Buckley-Zistel, 2006). Theoretically, SKAD should be more thoroughly connected to the political ecology literature, which has also analysed the symbolic dimensions of socio-environmental conflict at various scales and could profit from SKADs solid theoretical underpinnings and transparent guidelines for the concrete analysis (Peluso and Watts, 2001; Allen, 2013).

Notes

1 While such conflicts are frequently termed environmental or climate conflicts, I prefer the term "socio-environmental conflicts" (Reboratti, 2012: 3) because both social and environmental factors drive their dynamics.
2 Jordanian communities participated in the project as well, but are not discussed here.
3 A discourse is considered to be dominant here if its core messages are accepted as valid knowledge by a large majority of the members of a social group.
4 The Gaza Strip was not visited because only one GWN community is located there, entry permits were hard to obtain, and the security situation was critical.
5 I express my deep gratitude to my interview partners, who shared their time and insights with me, as well as to Abdallah Taha and Amina Nolte, who supported me during my research stay. I also thank the German Environmental Foundation (DBU) for a grant enabling this research.

References

Alatout, S. (2006). Towards a Bio-territorial Conception of Power: Territory, Population, and Environmental Narratives in Palestine and Israel. *Political Geography*, 25, 601–621.

Allen, M. G. (2013). Melanesia's Violent Environments: Towards a Political Ecology of Conflict in the Western Pacific. *Geoforum*, 44, 152–161.
Böhm, A. (2012). Theoretisches Codieren: Textanalyse in der Grounded Theory. In: U. Flick, E. Flick Von Kardorff and I. Steinke, eds., *Qualitative Forschung: ein Handbuch*. Reinbek: Rowohlt.
Brochmann, M. and Gleditsch, N. P. (2012). Shared Rivers and Conflict: A Reconsideration. *Political Geography*, 31, 519–527.
Buckley-Zistel, S. (2006). In-between War and Peace: Identities, Boundaries, and Change After Violent Conflict. *Millenium*, 35, 3–21.
Chatterjee, I. (2012). How Are They Othered? Globalisation, Identity and Violence in an Indian City. *The Geographic Journal*, 178, 134–146.
Cohen, N. and Arieli, T. (2011). Field Research in Conflict Environments: Methodological Challenges and Snowball Sampling. *Journal of Peace Research* 48, 423–435.
Conca, K., Carius, A. and Dabelko, G. (2005). Building Peace Through Environmental Cooperation. In: Worldwatch Institute, ed., *State of the World 2005: Redefining Global Security*. Washington DC: Worldwatch.
Corbin, J. and Strauss, A. L. (2008). *Basics of Qualitative Research: Techniques and Procedures for Developing Grounded Theory*. London: Sage.
Detraz, N. and Betsill, M. M. (2009). Climate Change and Environmental Security: For Whom the Discourse Shifts. *International Studies Perspectives*, 10, 303–320.
Djernaes, M., Jorgensen, T. and Koch-Ya'ari, E. (2015). Evaluation of Environmental Peacemaking Intervention Strategies in Jordan–Israel–Palestine. *Journal of Peacebuilding and Development*, 10, 74–80.
Engels, A. (2008). Local Environmental Changes and Global Sea-level Rise: The Case of Coastal Zones in Senegal. In: M. J. Casimir, ed., *Culture and the Changing Environment: Uncertainty, Cognition and Risk Management in a Cross-cultural Perspective*. Oxford/New York: Berghahn.
Evans, B. (2010). Foucault's Legacy: Security, War and Violence in the 21st Century. *Security Dialogue* 41, 413–433.
Feil, M., Klein, D. and Westerkamp, M. (2009). *Regional Cooperation on Environment, Economy and Natural Resource Management: How Can It Contribute to Peacebuilding?* Brussels: Initiative for Peacebuilding.
Feitelson, E. (2002). Implications of Shifts in the Israeli Water Discourse for Israeli-Palestinian Water Negotiations. *Political Geography*, 21, 293–318.
FoEME (2013). Community Based Problem Solving on Water Issues: Cross-border "Priority Initiatives" of the Good Water Neighbours Project. Amman/Bethlehem/Tel Aviv: FoEME.
Fröhlich, C. (2012). Security and Discourse: The Israeli–Palestinian Water Conflict. *Conflict, Security and Development*, 12, 123–148.
Gerring, J. and Seawright, J. (2007). Techniques for Choosing Cases. In: J. Gerring, ed., *Case Study Research: Principles and Practices*. New York: Cambridge University Press.
Glaser, B. G. (1978): *Theoretical Sensitivity*. Mill Valle: Sociology Press.
Glaser, B. G. and Strauss, A. L. (1967). *The Discovery of Grounded Theory: Strategies for Qualitative Research*. New York: Aldine de Gruyter.
Gläser, J. and Laudel, G. (2010). *Experteninterviews und qualitative Inhaltsanalyse als Instrumente rekonstruierender Untersuchungen*. Wiesbaden: VS.

Gleditsch, N. P. (1998). Armed Conflict and the Environment: A Critique of the Literature. *Journal of Peace Research*, 35, 381–400.

GWN-Homepage, (2017). *GWN-Homepage*. [online] Available at: http://foeme.org/www/?module=projects&record_id=201 [Accessed at 30 January 2017].

Hannigan, J. (2006). *Environmental Sociology*. New York: Routledge.

Hansen, L. (2006). *Security as a Practice: Discourse Analysis and the Bosnian War*. London: Routledge.

Harris, L. M. and Alatout, S. (2010). Negotiating Hydro-scales, Forging States: Comparison of the Upper Tigris/Euphrates and Jordan River Basins. *Political Geography*, 29, 148–156.

Homer-Dixon, T. (1999). *Environmental Scarcity and Violence*. Princeton: Princeton University Press.

Ide, T. (2016). Towards a Constructivist Understanding of Socio-environmental Conflicts. *Civil Wars*, 18, 69–90.

Ide, T. (2017). Space, Discourse and Environmental Peacebuilding. *Third World Quarterly*, 38, 544–562.

Ide, T. and Fröhlich, C. (2015). Socio-environmental Cooperation and Conflict? A Discursive Understanding and Its Application to the Case of Israel/Palestine. *Earth System Dynamics*, 6, 659–671.

IPCC (2007). *Climate Change 2007: Synthesis Report*. Geneva: IPCC.

Kaufman, S. (2001). *Modern Hatreds: The Symbolic Politics of Ethnic War*. Ithaca/London: Cornell University Press.

Kaufman, S. (2006). Symbolic Politics or Rational Choice? Testing Theories of Extreme Ethnic Violence. *International Security*, 30, 45–86.

Kaufman, S. (2009). Narratives and Symbols in Violent Mobilization: The Palestinian-Israeli Case. *Security Studies*, 18, 400–434.

Keller, R. (2005a). Analysing Discourse: An Approach from the Sociology of Knowledge. *Forum: Qualitative Social Research*, 6, 1–18.

Keller, R. (2005b). Wissenssoziologische Diskursanalyse als interpretative Analytik. In: R. Keller A. Hirseland, W. Schneider and W. Viehöver, eds., *Die diskursive Konstruktion der Wirklichkeit*. Konstanz: Universitätsverlag: Konstanz.

Keller, R. (2011). The Sociology of Knowledge Approach to Discourse (SKAD). *Human Studies*, 34, 43–65.

Keller, R. (2013). *Doing Discourse Research: An Introduction for Social Scientists*. London: Sage.

Lautze, J. and Kirshen, P. (2009). Water Allocation, Climate Change, and Sustainable Water Use in Israel/Palestine: The Palestinian Position. *Water International*, 34, 189–203.

McDonald, M. (2013). Discourses of Climate Security. *Political Geography*, 33, 42–51.

Messerschmid, C. (2012). Reality and Discourses of Climate Change in the Israel-Palestinian Conflict. In: J. Scheffran, M. Brzoska, H. G. Brauch, P. M. Link and J. Schilling, eds., *Climate Change, Human Security and Violent Conflict: Challenges for Societal Stability*. Berlin/Heidelberg: Springer.

Milliken, J. (1999). The Study of Discourse in International Relations: A Critique of Research and Methods. *European Journal of International Relations*, 5, 225–254.

Moore, D. and Guy, A. (2012). The Israeli–Palestinian Conflict: The Sociohistorical Context and the Identities it Creates. In: D. Landis and R. Albert, eds., *Handbook of Ethnic Conflict: International Perspectives*. New York: Springer.

Murtinho, F., Tague, C., De Bievre, B., Eakin, H. and Lopez-Carr, D. (2013). Water Scarcity in the Andes: A Comparison of Local Perceptions and Observed Climate, Land Use and Socioeconomic Changes. *Human Ecology*, 41, 667–681.

Norman, E. S. (2012). Cultural Politics and Transboundary Resource Governance in the Salish Sea. *Water Alternatives*, 5, 138–160.

Oels, A. (2013). Rendering Climate Change Governable by Risk: From Probability to Contingency. *Geoforum*, 45, 17–29.

Peluso, N. L. and Watts, M. (2001). Violent Environments. In: N. L. Peluso and M. Watts, eds., *Violent Environments*. Ithaca/London: Cornell University Press.

Reboratti, C. (2012). Socio-environmental Conflict in Argentina. *Journal of Latin American Geography*, 11, 3–20.

Ringmar, E. (1996). *Identity, Interest and Action: A Cultural Explanation of Sweden's Intervention in the Thirty Years War.* Cambridge: Cambridge University Press.

Sayre, N. F. (2005). Ecological and Geographical Scale: Parallels and Potential for Integration. *Progress in Human Geography*, 29, 276–290.

Selby, J. (2005). The Geopolitics of Water in the Middle East: Fantasies and Realities. *Third World Quarterly*, 26, 329–349.

Selby, J. (2013). Cooperation, Domination and Colonisation: The Israeli-Palestinian Joint Water Committee. *Water Alternatives*, 6, 1–24.

Selby, J. (2014). Positivist Climate Conflict Research: A Critique. *Geopolitics*, 19, 829–856.

Simmons, E. (2014). Grievances Do Matter in Mobilization. *Theory and Society*, 43, 513–536.

Snow, D. A. and Benford, R. D. (1988). Ideology, Frame Resonance, and Participant Mobilization. *International Social Movement Research*, 1, 197–217.

Steinke, I. (2012). Gütekriterien qualitativer Forschung. In: U. Flick, E., von Kardorff and I. Steinke, eds., *Qualitative Forschung: ein Handbuch*. 9th edn. Reinbek: Rowohlt.

Sternberg, T. (2012). Chinese Drought, Bread and the Arab Spring. *Applied Geography*, 34, 519–524.

Tir, J. and Stinnett, D. M. (2012). Weathering Climate Change: Can Institutions Mitigate International Water Conflict? *Journal of Peace Research*, 49, 211–225.

Waintraub, N. (2009). Water and the Middle East Peace Process. *Potentia*, 1, 23–35.

Weinthal, E. (2002). The Promises and Pitfalls of Environmental Peacemaking in the Aral Sea Basin. In: G. Dabelko and K. Conca, eds., *Environmental Peacemaking*. Baltimoore: Johns Hopkins University Press.

Wendt, A. (1992). Anarchy is What States Make of It: The Social Construction of Power Politics. *International Organization*, 46, 391–425.

Wittayapak, C. (2008). History and Geography of Identifications Related to Resource Conflicts and Ethnic Violence in Northern Thailand. *Asian Pacific Viewpoint*, 49, 111–127.

Zeitoun, M. (2008). *Power and Water in the Middle East: The Hidden Politics of the Palestinian–Israeli Water Conflict.* London: Tauris.

Zeitoun, M., Talhami, M. and Eid-Sabbagh, K. (2013). The Influence of Narratives on Negotiations and Resolution of the Upper Jordan River Conflict. *International Negotiation*, 18, 293–322.

14 Studying discourses ethnographically
A sociology of knowledge approach to analysing macro-level forces in micro-settings

Florian Elliker

Introduction

This chapter is based on an ethnographic case study that examines the process of increasing diversity in South African student residences that were formerly segregated along racial population categories. This university-wide transformation process – launched at the beginning of the 1990s – was met with dedicated resistance by the students well into the first decade of the twenty-first century. Why would students continue to oppose such an integration process (or at least experience it as difficult) over a decade after the abolishment of formal segregation legislation? Conventional explanations draw on notions of racial formation (Omi and Winant, 2014): in a society shaped by racial segregation policies for decades, deep cleavages between racial population categories do not disappear overnight. Students continue to be socialised in 'mono-racial' environments (in schools, families, neighbourhoods, leisure associations, and religious organisations) and inherit, to some extent, a feeling of being separated. For some of them, that means wanting to be separated from individuals categorised differently in terms of race or ethnicity (Jansen, 2009).

During my encounter with students living in these residences, I was able to observe modes of experiencing and articulating that corroborate such explanations, namely the use of a discourse of culture and cultural differences (Elliker, Coetzee and Kotze, 2013). However, my participation in residence life also demonstrated that the local reality was not only (more or less strongly) shaped by enduring macro-level structures, such as the racial formation and discourse of cultural difference, but by a set of complex idiocultural elements from which students not only develop specific stakes but also derive the capacity to create a sense of commonality and groupness along other identificational categories than the widespread racial ones.

Social action, as student life in the residences demonstrated, is not only shaped by one or more singular macro-level force; rather, local and resilient micro- and meso-level contexts mediate and co-structure action and the social outcomes of macro-level phenomena and processes. For the case study, I have conceptualised this distinction as one between local groups (Fine, 2010; Fine, 2012) and discourses (Keller, 2011) (see Elliker, Coetzee and Kotze, 2013; Elliker, 2015). The ethnographic research approach to studying the residences demonstrated that considering all social reality a priori as shaped by discourses – and sometimes, by only one discourse – did not do justice to the complexity of the local group cultures that formed resilient contexts on their own. Discourses are mediated by local action, and substantial parts of local action seem not to be discourse-related at all, but shaped by other social forces on the meso- or macro-level.

In this chapter, I argue that reconstructing and analysing macro-level forces ethnographically may provide us with important insights into how such forces play out in, and are intertwined with, local contexts on the micro- and meso-levels of analysis. As I will suggest, a sociology of knowledge approach to discourse (SKAD) seems particularly well suited to such an endeavour, as it shares an interpretive epistemological framework that underpins much of sociological ethnographic research. My aim is thus to further develop a sociology of knowledge approach to discourse ethnography departing from Keller's initial suggestions (Keller, 2003, 2011: 260) and partially drawing on a recent contribution to such an approach (see Elliker, Wundrak, and Maeder, 2017; Akbaba, 2017; Maeder, 2017 and Wundrak, 2017 in the thematic issue on discourse ethnography of the *Journal for Discourse Studies*).

This chapter unfolds in four steps: after this introduction, in section 2 I introduce the aforementioned empirical case study that analyses the transformation processes in a South African university, focusing on the highly contested transformation process in the student residences. In section 3, I further conceptualise a sociology of knowledge approach to discourse ethnography with the aim of developing a research strategy that enables consideration of the different ways in which the micro-, meso-, and macro-levels are entangled in the construction of specific social realities. Section 4 draws upon the case study introduced in section 2: after a short methodological account, I will show how an ethnographic research strategy allows a differentiated study of how external constraints become relevant in social situations, focusing on the meso-level of group culture and on discourses as phenomena on the macro-level. This chapter concludes with a summary of the main epistemological premises and their methodological implications.

The case study: increasing diversity in student residences

This case study examines the so-called integration process of student residences at a South African university. Situated in a formerly racially segregated education system, the university is considered to be a historically white Afrikaans institution to which only individuals categorised as Whites had access, and which used Afrikaans as language of instruction (the language of the then-ruling political elite).

Students deemed to belong to the three other major race-related population categories still in widespread use today (Coloured, Black, and Asian) became allowed for admission from the end of the 1980s onwards. Beginning with the transition to a democratic political dispensation, the number of students in these categories steadily increased parallel to considerable growth in the overall number of students. Although the growth of student numbers has transformed the university from a residential to a commuting institution, the student residences remain an important part of what is locally called "university culture". Many of the "cultural" activities on campus, such as theatre and singing competitions and sport events, are performed by members of the student residences, in addition to events through which the university becomes visible to a wider public, such "rags" (events to collect funds for charity, consisting partly of a carnival parade through town) or national competitions of university sports teams covered by mass media. These residences form relatively resilient, bounded groups with their own idiocultures (Fine, 1979, 2010), internally hierarchically structured and reciprocally related through ties of competition and cooperation in a university-wide status hierarchy.

In addition to opening the university to students (and academic staff) attributed to the Black, Asian, and Coloured population categories, the university administration decided that the student residences should become racially mixed and started integrating the residences in 1995. These efforts were, however, met with dedicated resistance by the established (white) student population in the residences, culminating in sometimes violent protests on campus, first resulting in segregation within the residences, and then in White-only and Black-only residences (from the year 1999 onwards). After several attempts to integrate the residences, it was only in the year 2011 that the transition process from "historically white" and "historically black" residences to residences for all racialised population categories (with certain goals set in terms of percentages) was implemented, based on a revised residence diversity policy and newly created institutional capacity to oversee the process.

This case study set out to understand why the integration processes in the student residences were met with resistance. Based on a previous study that employed focus-group discussions (Elliker, Coetzee and Kotze, 2013; Coetzee and Kotze, 2014), it adopted an ethnographic research strategy that included participant observation and ethnographic interviews in the student residences, as well as recorded in-depth interviews that were held outside the student residences. As socially bounded settings with idiocultures of their own, the residences constitute what could be termed a fairly common setting for sociological ethnographers to explore. As shown below, however, the fieldwork demonstrated that despite the widely present and readily available common-sense infrastructure of racialised population categories and racialised everyday theories, far from all social situations and activities in the residences were framed in racialised terms, and not all practices that led to segregation along racial categories were viewed as problematic by black and white students alike. Only in some circumstances were these racialised practices and views contested, negotiated, and experienced as (deeply) problematic.

Instead of presuming the omnirelevance of race and ethnicity (cf. Brubaker, 2002), this case study aimed at studying how, when, and why racial and ethnic notions became salient; to what ends they were employed; how they were intertwined with processes of generating, maintaining, and dissolving feelings of groupness (Brubaker and Cooper, 2000); and how race and ethnicity were implied in categorisation, membership, social organisation, and (everyday) politics (Brubaker, 2009: 26). This allows, at least analytically, the possibility that settings may become more or less racialised, that practices based on racialised categories may be used to negotiate and claim more equality, and that practices that arose within a mono-racial setting may be slowly reappropriated and may become "deracialised" to some extent, so as to serve as common ground (although this is a contested position, cf. section 4).

In terms of discourse analysis, the corollary analytical implication is that not every aspect of a given social setting of interest is structured by a specific discourse; rather, everyday action and experience are structured by multiple discourses and by other, meso- and micro-level processes. As I aimed at such a differentiated analysis of everyday settings, it would not have been sufficient to consider only the conventionally used data source in those strands of discourse analysis that conceive of discourse as macro-level structures (such as institutional documents, mass-media reporting, documentation of political processes). With the purpose, then, of better understanding why the student integration processes were met with resistance, I embarked on the case study and what is described below as discourse ethnography, aiming to analyse how racialised practices play out in everyday life and how they intersect with other structuring moments such as the idiocultures of the student residences.

A sociology of knowledge approach to discourse ethnography

In contrast to classical ethnographic studies, discourse ethnography is not concerned with studying small life-worlds and communities as such in their entirety, but rather discourse-related types of action and communication. Keller (Keller, 2003, 2011: 260) introduced such an approach as early as 2003, referring to the concept of "focused ethnography" as presented by Hubert Knoblauch (see Knoblauch, 2001). Knoblauch argued for the use of audio-visual data collection via video etc. allowing for an ethnographic approach that is focused on particular situations and constellations. According to Keller, however, focused ethnography could also be understood as ethnography directed towards a particular research interest – in this case, the making of discourses and the discursive intervention into social fields of practices (also see the chapter by Hornidge and Feuer, Chapter 7). This implies, for example, that one would not be interested in studying an organisation in its entirety, its members' practices, its hierarchies, its cultural leitmotivs, etc. Rather, the ethnographic fieldwork and research interest would focus on those actors, things, practices, resources, etc. that are used and combined to make up a discursive contribution, e.g. a text, a report, a leaflet. In this example, the focus would be on the means and processes of making contributions to discourses. A second focus underlined by Keller would consist of studying discursive interventions, techniques, objects, and symbolic ordering devices which – as effects or outcomes of discursive meaning making – intervene in a concrete field of practice. A good example is classification forms used in health services, school testing, etc. to create rankings or – more generally speaking – to produce differences between people, with the concomitant different treatments that follow the criteria of discursive meaning-making. One might call these two types of sites – sites of discursive production and sites of discursive performance – the two "ends" of discursive meaning-making. Concrete situations of discursive performance in between these two ends would then constitute a field for discourse ethnography. In order to account for these two types of sites, Keller used the Foucauldian term "dispositif", and often conceived of discourse ethnography as "ethnography of dispositifs" (Keller, 2016), whereby "dispositifs" are understood (in the pragmatic French tradition implied in Foucault's use of the term) as "infrastructures of discourse production and discursive world interventions" (Keller, 2016, 5) – that is to say, all the resources that enable the production of discourses and all those means and instruments that are geared towards handling action problems in discourse-related ways (for the term dispositif, see also Keller, 2007). Such a dispositif ethnography may entail:

> (1) a detailed analysis of discursive and non-discursive practices of discourse production; (2) a detailed analysis of the establishment, composition and use of dispositifs; (3) a detailed analysis of the practical reception, appropriation, examination and effects of discourses; [and] (4) an analysis of the interplay between situated contexts and practices with discourses [and the] constitution of contexts through discourses.
>
> (Keller, 2016: 9)

This is premised on the conceptual distinction between discursive and non-discursive practices as well as discourse-related and discourse-external practices (Keller, 2011: 255). While non-discursive practices refer to the material, non-linguistic reproduction of discourses, discourse-external practices refer to the notion that discourses are but one amongst many other structural elements that shape everyday social settings. These settings may form more or less resilient and autonomous local contexts or fields of practice that are *co*-shaped by discourses.

While I fully agree with Keller's ideas about such an ethnography of discourses and dispositifs, my own research aims at extending the sociology of knowledge approach to discourse ethnography by adding another focus and demonstrating its analytical potential: how discursive meaning-making shapes local settings, interactions, and practices of meaning-making in sites which are not the main sites of serious speech acts and discursive meaning making (Foucault, 1972), which make up the core discourse production. Such a version of discourse ethnography furthermore addresses the complex ways discourses enter the stage of daily life. The strengths of such an approach, I suggest, are two-fold. On the one hand, this approach retains the analytic concern with a macro-level of analysis, but it examines, with an ethnographic research strategy and in a differentiated manner, how discourses structure local social settings and how such settings are connected through the discourse-specific structural connection (cf. Keller, 2011: 260). The analytical distinction between discourses and discourse-external contexts prevents the assumption of a "direct", unmediated effect of discourses on everyday life, but instead warrants an empirical examination of how discourses are intertwined with local settings and knowledge forms that are structured by other social forces. On the other hand, as indicated below and argued elsewhere (Elliker, 2017), a phenomenological sociology of knowledge (Berger and Luckmann, 1966; Schütz, 1967; Schütz and Luckmann, 1974, 1989) provides an epistemological and theoretical basis differentiated to integrate analytical categories of discourse analysis and ethnographic research. Importantly, the corresponding notion of "discourse" as developed within the sociology of knowledge approach provides a concept adequately suited to providing a link between external social forces and the micro-settings of social action.

Discourses as external contexts of and in social situations

Ethnographic research strategies involve participant observation, a practice in which the researcher joins the actors in the social domains and fields of interest and observes the corresponding social situations and (inter)actions. Such an experience is constrained to what Schütz and Luckmann (1974, 1989) have called "the world in actual reach". If employed to study macro-level processes and phenomena that structure social situations but lie beyond the world in actual reach of the actors, we must address the question of how such a link between social situations and macro-level structures can be conceptualised. From a (radical) situational perspective, there is no such external context. In her discussion of notions such as "condition" and "context" in the field of Grounded Theory, Adele Clarke critically remarks that the:

> *conditions of the situation are in the situation.* There is no such thing as "context". The conditional elements of the situation need to be specified in the analysis of the situation itself as *they are constitutive of it*, not merely surrounding it or framing it or contributing to it. They "*are* it".
> (Clarke, 2005: 71 emphasis in the original)

The fundamental question must hence be: "*How do these conditions appear – make themselves felt as consequential – inside the empirical situation under examination?*" (Clarke, 2005: 72 emphasis in the original). In any given situation, conditions are manifest as elements that influence and affect other elements in that situation – that is to say, they are "mutually consequential". According to Clarke, such elements may *inter alia* be sociocultural and symbolic elements or organisational and institutional elements, but also discourses (Clarke, 2005: 73). These elements, however, are not confined to any specific situation, and raise the aforementioned question of how the structuring effect of elements "larger" than the situation can be conceived of.

As I have argued elsewhere (Elliker, 2016), a sociology of knowledge approach in a phenomenological tradition may provide an epistemological framework to conceptualise how "external" processes may have a structuring effect within any given situation. Such a perspective considers relevant not only what is perceptible to the actors through their senses directed at phenomena outside their bodies (implied above by being "manifest" in the situation), but also meaningful sensory "inner" experience. If we distinguish analytically between manifest action and behaviour on the one hand and meaningful sensory experience on the other, and consider both dimensions, this has several implications with regard to the conditions that structure social situation. It implies, first, that not just manifest action may be socially relevant, but also specific motivational, thematic, and interpretive systems of relevance that are not externalised in the interaction situation. Second, social action may be motivated to generate specific experiential qualities that are, again, not necessarily externalised. Thus, conditions may become socially relevant in ways that remain implicit in social situations. And third, this implies that the externality of conditions – *seen from "within" any given social situation* – becomes relevant on the level of meaningful experience. On the one hand, externality is established by generating a trans-situational connection; on the other, conditions in a given situation are external if the typical structuring effect of the knowledge employed by actors has been produced, objectified, and institutionalised "outside" – that is to say, before the given interaction situation. Hence, external conditions become relevant in a given interaction situation as constraints introjected into the actors' knowledge (Fine, 1991).

The structuring influence of discourses as macro-level phenomena is manifest in the discourse-related typicality of statements, constituting the typicality of the "introjected constraints" (Fine, 1991). These discourse-related constraints operate in two ways: (1) on the one hand, they shape the knowledge that underpins the perception, experience, interpretation, and (social) action of the participants involved in any given social situation; (2) on the other, discourse-related knowledge may serve as a basis for meaning constitution. These two structuring effects may not, however, coincide or be coherent: while the situated meaning of manifestations of discourse-related action may be constituted with reference to knowledge that is not discourse-related, action that is otherwise not related to discourse may come to be interpreted in the light of a specific discourse. The structuring effects differ with regard to whether discourse-related constraints operate on an implicit and routine level or in a reflective, explicit manner.

Of particular importance for a discourse ethnography is the distinction between discourses as macro-level structures and other resilient local contexts on the micro- and meso-level of analysis. In taking up a concern in Foucault's later work, Keller (2011: 138) underlines the importance of separating "discourses form discourse-external practices or fields of practice and the study of the relations between the two". Potentially, both actors and local contexts are endowed with a degree of autonomy and resilience in relation to discourses: "Practices established in institutional settings or social fields of practices [...] have a specific routinized meaning for the involved actors, a meaning that is often not in line with expectations set by discourses" (Keller, 2011: 138). If discourses not only constitute specific speaker positions and distribute speaking and interaction rights unevenly, but also effectively silence certain actors, then their subjectivities are likely to be articulated with reference to alternative knowledge conglomerates, either framed by other discourses or lodged in more or less resilient local contexts. Discourse ethnography is particularly well suited, through first-hand experience of social settings, to identifying and distinguishing discourses and local contexts alike, and to investigating how actors are subjected to and resist discourses by drawing on alternative knowledge resources to conceive of themselves and to shape their actions – that is to say, to articulating those aspects about which the actors themselves remain silent (Hirschauer, 2001).

An ethnographic approach to analysing discourses

As a research strategy, ethnography has become a wide field of approaches, methods, and methodologies that are almost too diverse to survey (for overviews and introductions, see e.g. van Maanen, 1988; Adler and Adler,

2008; Atkinson *et al.*, 2001b; Hammersley and Atkinson, 2007; Gobo and Molie, 2017). There are, however, two key features of many ethnographic approaches that render it particularly suitable to studying discourses (see Elliker, 2017). The first is the methodological commitment to experiencing social reality in a more or less unmediated manner – that is to say, to studying social reality based on "first-hand experience and exploration" (Atkinson *et al.*, 2001a: 4). The second characteristic feature of many ethnographic research approaches is a concern with meaning and knowledge, namely with reconstructing the explicit and implicit knowledge that underpins and shapes perception, experience, interpretation, and (social) action in the social setting of interest (see e.g. Spradley, 1979; Frake, 1980; Quinn and Holland, 1987; Geertz, 1973). Leveraging the strengths of the classic ethnographic data collection instruments such as participant observation and interviews, as well as document and artefact analysis, a discourse ethnographic approach is particularly well suited to considering the complexity that shapes the ways in which discourses as macro-level phenomena are reproduced through, are intertwined with, and co-structure contexts and situations on the micro- and meso-levels.

In particular, an ethnographic research strategy has the potential to:

- Investigate the specific modes in which discourses structure everyday action as introjected constraints in implicit or explicit ways or embedded in routines or used reflexively, indicating the degree to which discourses appear as objectified and obdurate to the involved actors.
- Reconstruct the typical ways in which discourses enfold their structuring effects in everyday life.
- Explore what other macro-, meso- and micro-level processes (conceived of as discourse-external practices) structure local action and how discourses are intertwined with them in competing or complementary ways. The distinction between discourse-related and discourse-external practices has an additional important consequence – it makes it possible to:
  - Consider the possibility that some discourses may, in any given setting, become more or less salient and relevant – that is to say, the empirical possibility that the influence of discourses is not static but constituted in processes in the course of which the structural impact of discourses may be waxing or waning.
  - Provide a good basis, through (extended) participation in the local field and building a rapport with the actors involved, for an ethnographer to study the dynamics through which actors are situated with regard to specific discourses. This includes to what extent actors remain resilient or adapt to discourses, how far they are endowed with a sense of (autonomous) agency with regard to positioning themselves in and being subjected to discourses, how

they use discourses for specific purposes, and how discourses shape the local "allocation" and resulting "distribution" of speaking and interaction rights.
- To study – through participant observation – discourses not only as *discursive*, but also as *non-discursive* practices. If corporeal, sensory experiences and sign-based processes of meaning constitution are *analytically* distinguished, there are varying degrees to which they may become relevant: while some modes of action and experience are primarily focused on handling one's body, on using material artefacts, on engaging with others in a physical sense, and on interacting with the built and natural environment, other modes of action and experience focus primarily on sign-based processes of meaning constitution, as well as internalising and externalising meaning in processes of communication. While the former refers to the discursive realm, the latter refers to non-discursive realms. The former may entail writing text messages, posting entries on social media platforms, reading news websites, taking notes, and engaging in conversations with others; while the latter may include handling one's body during sports exercises and stage appearances, moving around physically in informal group conversations, engaging in protest marches, attending lectures, etc. Both modes do not, however, imply that the other mode is completely absent; rather, they refer to a different primary focus of action and experience, and there may be many forms of practices in which the focus rests equally on both. A discourse ethnographer is positioned to experience first-hand all those fleeting and evanescent non-discursive activities involved in discourse reproduction, being able to use his or her own experience to study the affective and sensory (i.e. corporeal and material) dimension of how discourses affect and intervene in the daily lives of the actors (cf. the various life-world analytic ethnographic approaches, e.g. Honer, (1993) and Hitzler and Eberle (2004)).
- Finally, in terms of the evanescence and fleetingness of the discourse-related construction of social reality, an ethnographer is well positioned to experience and register all those elements of everyday life that either go unnoticed by the actors or are never solidified into tangible artefacts. Discourse ethnography thus provides a window on all those aspects that are lost in the naturally occurring data of conventional discourse analyses that consist predominantly of recorded artefacts of a discursive nature or of mediated representations of non-discursive actions.

Analytic purposes and methodological considerations

Situated within an interpretive-qualitative research tradition, the analytical task of discourse analysis may encompass on the one hand, in terms of *understanding*, a hermeneutic analysis of single utterances to reconstruct typical discourse statements (see Keller *et al.*, 2005). Based on such a reconstruction, an analysis aims at demonstrating how specific discourses construct reality and the phenomena, processes, practices, and subjectivities involved therein. Through the analysis of contrasting settings or cases, a discourse ethnography can thus reconstruct the structural connection of any given discourse of interest, and provide a differentiated interpretation of the extent to which local settings are structured – or *not* structured – by discourses. In terms of *explanation*, it may involve developing hypotheses with regard to what social conditions gave rise to the formation and socially complex organisation of discourse-related practices of constituting and intervening in social realities. This entails studying the organisational complexity with which a diverse range of situations and contexts are interlinked and shaped in discourse-specific ways.[1]

More specifically, a discourse ethnographic research strategy may be used for two broadly distinguishable analytic purposes that warrant (to some extent) different methodological considerations: (1) to reconstruct and analyse a specific discourse in various settings, and (2) to examine a specific setting with regard to the various discourses that co-structure that setting. In terms of methodology, I briefly discuss and focus on some of the main differences and commonalities of both analytical purposes with regard to the sampling process and the type of data warranted for discourse ethnographies. As shown in the discussion on the relationship between the micro- and macro-level, the notion of organisational complexity does imply a difference in the number of settings considered, as well as the ways in which the interconnectedness of these settings constitutes specific types of organisational complexity. Thus, discourse ethnography is set apart from other forms of discourse analysis and ethnography, particularly (but not only) in terms of the specific sampling and types of data it considers.

(1) For a discourse ethnography with the aim of reconstructing and analysing a particular discourse, Collins' (1981, 1988) metaphor of the "film still" that Jepperson and Meyer (2011) critically discuss adequately captures the basic methodological challenge, namely the sampling of various micro-instantiations of the discourse of interest. Each of these instantiations represents one "film strip" of the entire "film" – the discourse. These micro-settings are likely to be structured by other macro- and meso-level processes, and might constitute relatively resilient micro-contexts themselves. To capture the typicality of the structural connection of a discourse, a sampling strategy should ideally not only include situations of the same kind, but a range of different situations, so

the structuring effect of the situation can be distinguished from the typical yet different ways in which any given discourse may operate in such settings.

In the context of the case study introduced in section 2 on how contemporary notions of race and ethnicity shape interactions in a tertiary education context, the ethnographer was able to observe relatively anonymous public social situations on campus, such as client–customer interactions in the cafeteria, how students interact with administrative staff, student council discussions, the various large sports and cultural events on campus, etc. Evidently, any of these micro-instantiations cover only a small segment of an entire discourse. To cover the entire range of typical elements in the discourse-related repertoire of statements and interventions, a theoretical sampling strategy as developed by the Grounded Theory tradition (see e.g. Corbin and Strauss, 2008) provides an adequate procedure: situations are chosen step by step, maximising and minimising contrast with regard to how the typical discourse-related statements affect everyday practices, proceeding with additional sampling and analysis to the point of theoretical saturation.

(2) If the central aim is to reconstruct how a specific setting is shaped by various discourses, a discourse ethnography needs to consider how these situations form resilient contexts on their own. This entails the study of all the different social situations of a setting and how these situations are interlinked to form a local context (warranting the use of a conceptual framework that makes it possible to analytically identify the type of local context). In addition, discourse ethnography needs to consider that other macro-level forces shape this local setting. While this provides a starting point for empirically distinguishing discourse-related phenomena from other (particularly local) phenomena, this distinction is a process based on the empirical specificities of each case.

For both analytical purposes, the main challenge for discourse ethnography is the reconstruction of the overall structural connection of the discourse. As mentioned above, the use and influence of discourses might in some ways be explicit and thus be traceable through communicative action by the actors in the social setting that is observed. All those elements of discourses that remain implicit or are embedded in routines must, however, be reconstructed by the researcher based on his or her field experiences. The demonstration of the externality of these elements must be based on material that demonstrates the higher organisational complexity that in turn warrants a demonstration of how discourses structure more than the local micro- or meso-level context that is studied ethnographically. There are two principle ways of collecting such additional data: through participant observation in other contexts, and through the use of existing, naturally occurring artefacts from other contexts. As additional participant observation is resource-intensive, covering typical situations is not feasible. Both types of discourse ethnographies thus have to be complemented with naturally occurring data that demonstrate how discourses operate in other fields – namely, data from domains that are conventionally conceived of as particularly relevant to macro-level processes, such as the mass media, the political field, the education system, organised religion, or the various fields of scientific research – all relevant in distributing, generating, inculcating, and formally regulating specific discourse-related knowledge conglomerates.

Both of these methodological procedures are what could be called a "parallel" analysis – that is to say, a reconstruction and study of similar patterns in different fields that are attributed to the same structural connection based on their typical core elements. However, a parallel occurrence of similar patterns in different fields may not necessarily indicate that they are part of the same structural connection. To establish such a connection, three strategies may be employed. A first strategy entails the tracing of references in everyday actions to other contexts (on all levels of analysis): references to political party programmes, mass media reporting, literature and art – in principle, to any other field. To the extent to which such references are traceable in everyday interactions, an ethnographic research strategy can identify such links and thus plausibly reconstruct a structural connection through which patterns of action and interpretation in several contexts are tied to each other, based on actually existing current unilateral or reciprocal relationships between domains. A second strategy may involve the identification of common sources that are used in both the social settings examined ethnographically and the other additional domains from which naturally occurring data are drawn. The third option is linked to the second one: a historical analysis of how specific rules, patterns, and so on have entered a specific social domain, or how discourse-related domains have been created. This strategy too goes beyond the assumption that present elements are "somehow" linked to a discourse, but reconstructs the actual formation of discourse-specific elements.

The case of student residences: discourses in local contexts

Having outlined a sociology of knowledge approach to discourse ethnography in the previous sections, I now discuss the case study introduced at the beginning to demonstrate the analytical potential of analysing discourses ethnographically. I approached the setting with an ethnographic research strategy in an ethnoscience tradition (Spradley, 1979, 1980; Werner and Schoepfle, 1987). Such an approach seemed particularly suited to the context, as it shares the basic interpretive premises of a sociology of knowledge approach to discourse: both aim at reconstructing and studying knowledge – cultural in one case, discourse-related in the other – that forms the basis for experience, interpretation, and social action. Based on a Grounded Theory sampling procedure (Corbin and

Strauss, 2008), the hermeneutic methods in both approaches aim at reconstructing the typical relevant structuring principles through an analysis of language (see Spradley (1979, 1980) on domains and cultural themes and Keller (2013: 110) on phenomenal structures and meaning patterns).

In terms of data collection, I participated in and observed, during several months, the daily activities of historically white male residences. This entailed taking part in house meetings and informal tea break meetings in the morning and afternoon, as well as informal conversations and ethnographic interviews with residence members. Additionally, I observed campus-wide activities in which residences were involved, such as the diverse cultural competitions held throughout the semester. These observations and experiences were recorded as field notes (consisting of condensed and expanded accounts) and complemented with photography. In addition to these participant observations, I held in-depth, problem-centred interviews (Witzel, 1982: 66, 1995; Witzel and Reiter, 2012) with students of male and female residences. These interviews focused on the students' experience of life in the residences and of the transformation process thereof. The data collection was complemented with artefacts from the residences such as leaflets, blackboard messages, residence symbols on display, etc. and with administrative data concerning the composition of the residence population.

Students who enter a residence in their first year are immediately enmeshed in a net of diverse identifications that are embedded in an internal residence hierarchy and that come along with different interaction rights. The most prominent categorical identifications are the ones of *first year* and *senior*, constituting the main categories on which the internal hierarchy in the residence is built. The use of these residence-related identifications is, however, paralleled by the use of the conventional racial classifications. These racial categories of identification are embedded in a large array of social domains from everyday life: amongst others, in legal texts, in organisational regulations, and in mass media. As a *potentially* available set of identifications, they are implicitly present in virtually every social situation. Residences thus constitute "tiny publics" (Fine and Harrington, 2004) in which practices can always also be interpreted as "banal" ethnicity, race, or nationalism (Billig, 1995), and in which negotiations pertaining to relations between racially categorised individuals may come to be seen as representative of South African society at large. Whether practices and symbols are perceived, experienced, and interpreted as racially or ethnically specific, however, depends on the situation and context; and when they are indeed seen as racially or ethnically specific, they are not always perceived as problematic. The following paragraph illustrates this situational use and problematisation of racial categories and associated practices, as well as the intersection of that use with residence-related categorical identifications.

Everyday conversations in the residences that refer to racial categories are underpinned by a basic and vague notion of categorical difference. As noted above, the existence of individuals categorised racially and the associated notion that these individuals are "somehow" different in ways that go beyond the classificatory attributes remain largely implicit in everyday life, thus constituting a relevant macro-level context on the meaning level. Practices associated with these categories are, however, explicitly thematised by the students when they become engaged (either by the researcher or by fellow students) in discussions on when, how, and which different practices distributed along racial categories are legitimately enacted. Differences in such practices become relevant in two ways: they structure everyday life either "within" the residence-related category boundaries (e.g. *first years* negotiate how to proceed in an interaction ritual reserved for *first years*), or they structure practices "across" residence-related categories, such as informal segregation practices during the so-called *tea kan* ritual (a popular morning and afternoon tea break open to all residence members) that involves *first years* and *seniors* alike. When engaged in such discussions, students of all categories typically employ a discourse of culture or cultural difference (Elliker, Coetzee and Kotze, 2013).

During the *tea kan* ritual, an informal segregation takes place: two small groups are formed, one consisting predominantly or only of white students, and the other one of black students (with a single or a few coloured student(s) in each of the groups). These two groups each gather around one of the two benches placed within the passageway in which the *tea kan* ritual takes place (the tea container is placed between the two groups). There is neither a formal regulation nor stipulation that would require the formation of these two groups, nor is the usage of the passage infrastructure for this purpose regulated. The usage of the benches is structured by the divide between *first years* and *seniors*: only *seniors* are allowed to sit on the benches, an informal but firmly entrenched rule observed by all students. When talking about the informal segregation practices along racial lines, students of all racial categories refer, first, to the qualities that motivate participation in the *tea kan* ritual: seen as a break from studying, they expect to relax and enjoy the presence of others by exchanging the latest news, gossiping, and having fun together (on the importance of fun in building group commitment, see Fine and Corte, 2017). In order to generate these experiential qualities, they second refer to the need to find common conversational topics, to share an implicit understanding of what may and should be thematised in these conversations, and express a wish to use a language in which they feel comfortable communicating and expressing themselves. In all of these aspects, the students draw on a discourse of cultural difference in describing how white "Afrikaner" individuals and black individuals typically differ: while black students converse in English, the white students use Afrikaans; while sports constitute an important topic in both informal groups, black students almost exclusively talk about soccer and find it difficult to engage in a meaningful conversation about rugby; the same applies in reverse for the Afrikaans-speaking students. Similarly, there are differences with regard to the propriety of what may be shared during such conversations, for example with regard to relationships with women. However, neither the difference in these practices nor the resulting informal segregation in the *tea kan* ritual is problematised by black or white students. The separation into two groups is predominantly seen as enabling the qualities students expect from such informal conversations and is neither experienced as racially undergirded exclusion nor as generating inequalities or particular hierarchies between these two groups.

This sharply differs from negotiations in the so-called "house meeting" in which all residence members assemble to discuss issues concerning the entire residence. A continuous complaint that black students bring forward concerns the support of the residence sports teams: a majority of residence members support the (multiple) internal rugby teams and not the soccer team. They provide symbolic support by appearing as a fan crowd at rugby competitions and vote in favour of channelling the financial resources of the residences into the rugby team (also reflecting a still uneven balance in terms of racial categories represented amongst residents). The discussions concerning the residence sports teams revolve around the notion of representation: the sports teams come to represent "what" and "whom" the residence stands for with regard to its campus-wide reputation and place in the status hierarchy, but also with regard to sports cups amongst universities that may generate considerable national media coverage, and during which a residence team is regarded as representative of the university. The argument of white students that supporting the rugby team is solely related to the historically established reputation of the residence (and to building on this pre-existing reputation) is contested by black students by framing the practices as culturally specific, and by implicating the resulting representation and reputation of the residence as culturally specific. In this context, the discourse of cultural differences is problematised, criticised, and interpreted as standing in a tradition that privileges white Afrikaans-speaking students in terms of reputation and status. Thus, the same practices as well as the discourse of cultural differences that are perceived as non-problematic in the context of informal segregation during the *tea kan* ritual come to take on problematised and contested meanings in the context of negotiations related to the reputation of the residence.

Conclusion

The presentation of a sociology of knowledge approach to discourse ethnography in this chapter has departed from an ambiguity in the premise that there is no context external to social situations. Based on a sociology of knowledge approach to discourse (SKAD) (Keller, 2011), I have suggested, first, that seen from any given social situation, the *externality* of conditional elements is constituted on the meaning level, the elements operating as introjected constraints in the socially derived, discourse-related stocks of knowledge of the involved actors. The approach is premised on the notion that not all experience and action is (structured by) discourse, but shaped by a diverse range of other processes on the micro-, meso- and macro-levels of analysis. An ethnographic research strategy makes it possible (based on first-hand experiences of social settings) to analyse *how* discourses shape social action, to reconstruct other relevant processes that co-structure the environment in which discourses operate, and to study in detail how discourses are intertwined with local contexts (contexts that may be more or less resilient) – and thus demonstrate how this entanglement is implied in producing specific social realities. Second, in addition to being able to distinguish between discourse-related and non-discourse-related experiences and actions, an ethnographer's first-hand encounters allow him or her to register the discursive as well as non-discursive ways in which discourses operate. That is to say, discourses are studied not only as linguistic, but also as embodied and material experiences and actions. By observing and participating, an ethnographer is well positioned to register what remains unarticulated in everyday practice but what may still be relevant: the implicit and routine ways in which discourse-related knowledge shapes local action, but also practices and voices that are marginalised, silenced, or suppressed. By building a rapport with the local actors and by personally experiencing the setting, the ethnographer gets a sense not only of how actors are subjected to discourse-related practices, but also how their agency and self-understanding are constituted, situated in the relation between discourse and context.

Note

1 See Elliker (2017) for a discussion of Jepperson and Meyer's (2011) argument that macro-level processes are distinguished from meso- and micro-level processes by their organisational complexity.

References

Adler, P. A. and Adler, P. (2008). Of Rhetoric and Representation. The Four Faces of Ethnography. *The Sociological Quarterly*, 49, 1–30.

Akbaba, Y. (2017). Discourse Ethnography on Migrant Other Teachers: Turn the Stigma into Capital! *Journal for Discourse Studies*, 5(3).

Atkinson, P., Delamont, S., Coffey, A., Lofland, J. and Lofland, L. (2001a). Editorial introduction. In: Atkinson, P., Delamont, S., Coffey, A., Lofland, J. and Lofland, L., eds. *Handbook of Ethnography*. London: Sage, 1–7.

Atkinson, P., Delamont, S., Coffey, A., Lofland, J. and Lofland, L., eds. (2001b). *Handbook of Ethnography*. London: Sage.

Berger, P. L. and Luckmann, T. (1966). *The Social Construction of Reality. A Treatise in the Sociology of Knowledge.* Garden City, New York: Doubleday.
Billig, M. (1995). *Banal Nationalism.* London, Thousand Oaks (CA), New Delhi: Sage.
Brubaker, R. (2002). Ethnicity Without Groups. *Archives Européennes de Sociologie/European Journal of Sociology,* 43(2), 163–189.
Brubaker, R. (2009). Ethnicity, Race, and Nationalism. *Annual Review of Sociology,* 35, 21–42.
Brubaker, R. and Cooper, F. (2000). Beyond "Identity". *Theory and Society,* 29, 1–47.
Clarke, A. (2005). *Situational Analysis. Grounded Theory After the Postmodern Turn.* Thousand Oaks, London, New Delhi: Sage.
Coetzee, J. and Kotze, P.C. (2014). Optimizing the Epistemological Potential of Focus Groups in Research on a Contested Issue. *Qualitative Sociology Review,* 10(2), 30–41.
Collins, R. (1981). The Microfoundations of Macrosociology. *American Journal of Sociology,* 85, 984–1014.
Collins, R. (1988). *Theoretical Sociology.* San Diego: Harcourt Brace Jovanovich.
Corbin, J. and Strauss, A. (2008). *Basics of Qualitative Research. Techniques and Procedures for Developing Grounded Theory.* Thousand Oaks, London: Sage.
Elliker, F. (2015). Transformation und Widerstand. Wie Mikrohierarchien und Emotionen die soziale Organisation interkulturellen Zusammenlebens stabilisieren. In: Brosziewski, A., Maeder, C. and Nentwich, J., eds. *Vom Sinn der Soziologie.* Wiesbaden: Springer VS, 79–97.
Elliker, F. (2016). Externe Kontexte als sinnhafte Strukturierung sozialer Situationen. Überlegungen zum Verhältnis von Diskurs und Interaktion. In: Raab, J. and Keller, R., eds. *Wissensforschung – Forschungswissen.* Weinheim, Basel: Beltz Juventa, 47–59.
Elliker, F. (2017). A Sociology Approach to Discourse Ethnography. On the distinction between local context and discourse. *Journal for Discourse Studies,* 5(3).
Elliker, F., Coetzee, J. and Kotze, P. C. (2013). On the Interpretive Work of Reconstructing Discourses and Their Local Contexts. *Forum Qualitative Sozialforschung/Forum: Qualitative Social Research* 14(3), article no: 4. [online] Available from: nbn-resolving.de/urn:nbn:de:0114-fqs130342. [Accessed 25 October 2017].
Elliker, F., Wundrak, R. and Maeder, C. (2017). Introduction to the thematic issue and programmatic thoughts on the Sociology of Knowledge Approach to Discourse Ethnography. *Journal for Discourse Studies,* 5(3).
Fine, G. A. (1979). Small Groups and Culture Creation. The Idioculture of Little League Baseball Teams. *American Sociological Review,* 44(5), 733–745.
Fine, G. A. (1991). On the Macrofoundations of Microsociology. Constraint and Exterior Reality of Structure. *The Sociological Quarterly,* 32(2), 161–177.
Fine, G. A. (2010). The Sociology of the Local: Action and its Publics. *Sociological Theory,* 28(4), 355–376.
Fine, G. A. (2012). Group Culture and the Local Interaction Order. Local Sociology on the Meso-Level. *Annual Review of Sociology,* 38, 159–179.
Fine, G. A. and Corte, U. (2017). Group Pleasures. Collaborative Commitments, Shared Narrative, and the Sociology of Fun. *Sociological Theory,* 35(1), 64–86.
Fine, G. A. and Harrington, B. (2004). Tiny Publics. Small Groups and Civil Society. *Sociological Theory,* 22(3), 341–356.
Foucault, M. (1972). *Archaeology of Knowledge.* New York: Pantheon Books.

Frake, C. O. (1980). *Language and Cultural Description. Essays by Charles O. Frake.* Stanford: Stanford University Press.
Geertz, C. (1973). *The Interpretation of Cultures.* New York: Basic Books.
Gobo, G. and Molie, A. (2017). *Doing Ethnography.* Los Angeles, London, New Delhi: Sage.
Hammersley, M. and Atkinson, P. (2007). *Ethnography. Principles in Practice.* London, New York: Routledge.
Hirschauer, S. (2001). Ethnografisches Schreiben und die Schweigsamkeit des Sozialen. Zu einer Methodologie der Beschreibung. *Zeitschrift für Soziologie,* 30(6), 429–451.
Hitzler, R. and Eberle, T. S. (2004). Phenomenological Life-World Analysis. In: U. Flick, E. von Kardorff, and I. Steinke., eds. *A Companion to Qualitative Research.* London, Thousand Oaks, New Delhi: Sage, 67–71.
Honer, A. (1993). *Lebensweltliche Ethnographie.* Wiesbaden: Deutscher Universitäts-Verlag.
Jansen, J. D. (2009). *Knowledge in the Blood. Confronting Race and Apartheid in South Africa.* Stanford: Stanford University Press.
Jepperson, R. and Meyer, J. W. (2011). Multiple Levels of Analysis and the Limitations of Methodological Individualism. *Sociological Theory,* 29(1), 54–73.
Keller, R. (2003). Zum möglichen Verhältnis zwischen Diskursanalyse und Ethnographie. Workshop "Ethnographie der Arbeit – Arbeit der Ethnographie", Berlin.
Keller, R. (2007). Diskurse und Dispositive analysieren. Die Wissenssoziologische Diskursanalyse als Beitrag zu einer wissensanalytischen Profilierung der Diskursforschung. *Forum Qualitative Sozialforschung/Forum: Qualitative Social Research* 8(2), article no: 19. [online] Available at: http://nbn-resolving.de/urn:nbn:de:0114-fqs0702198. [Accessed 25 October 2017].
Keller, R. (2011). *Wissenssoziologische Diskursanalyse. Grundlegung eines Forschungsprogramms.* Wiesbaden: VS Verlag für Sozialwissenschaften.
Keller, R. (2013). *Doing Discourse Research. An Introduction for Social Scientists.* London, Thousand Oaks, New Delhi: Sage.
Keller, R. (2016). *Die Untersuchung von Dispositiven. Überlegungen zur fokussierten Diskursethnographie der wissenssoziologischen Diskursanalyse.* Forschungsgespräch "Diskursethnographie", St. Gallen.
Keller, R., Hirseland, A., Schneider, W. and Viehöver, W., eds. (2005). *Die diskursive Konstruktion von Wirklichkeit.* Konstanz: UVK.
Knoblauch, H. (2001). Fokussierte Ethnographie. *Sozialer Sinn,* 1, 123–141.
Maeder, C. (2017). Wissenssoziologische Diskursethnographie (WDE)? Die Kombination von Diskursanalyse und Ethnographie als Suchbewegung zwischen Wahrheit und Wirklichkeit. *Journal for Discourse Studies,* 5(3).
Omi, M. and Winant, H. (2014). *Racial Formation in the United States.* New York: Routledge.
Quinn, N. and Holland, D. (1987). Culture and Cognition. In: Holland, D. and Quinn, N., eds. *Cultural Models in Language and Thought.* Cambridge, New York, Victoria: Cambridge University Press, 3–41.
Schütz, A. (1967). *The Phenomenology of the Social World.* Evanston, Ill.: Northwestern University Press.
Schütz, A. and Luckmann, T. (1974). *The Structures of the Life-World.* Vol. 1. London: Heinemann.

Schütz, A. and Luckmann, T. (1989). *The Structures of the Life-World.* Vol. 2. Evanston: Northwestern University.
Spradley, J. P. (1979). *The Ethnographic Interview.* New York, Chicago, London: Holt, Rinehart & Winston.
Spradley, J. P. (1980). *Participant Observation.* New York, Chicago, London: Holt, Rinehart & Winston.
van Maanen, J. (1988). *Tales of the Field. On Writing Ethnography.* Chicago: University of Chicago Press.
Werner, O. and Schoepfle, G. M. (1987). *Systematic Fieldwork.* Vol. I: Foundations of Ethnography and Interviewing. Newbury Park, Beverly Hills, London, New Delhi: Sage.
Witzel, A. (1982). *Verfahren der qualitativen Sozialforschung.* Frankfurt, New York: Campus.
Witzel, A. (1995). *Das problemzentrierte Interview.* In: Jüttemann, G., ed. Qualitative Forschung in der Psychologie. Grundfragen, Verfahrensweisen, Anwendungsfelder. Weinheim, Basel, 227–256.
Witzel, A. and Reiter, H. (2012). *The Problem-centred Interview.* Los Angeles, London, New Delhi: Sage.
Wundrak, R. (2017). "Welcome to paradise". Methodological accentuations to the Sociology of Knowledge Approach to Discourse Ethnography based on field notes from a refugees' shelter. *Journal for Discourse Studies,* 5(3).

15 From analysis to visualisation

Synoptical tools from SKAD studies and the entity mapper

Anne Luther and Wolf J. Schünemann

Introduction: the common challenge of visualisation

It is a similar question discourse researchers find themselves confronted with when the analytical work is done. After having analysed hundreds, sometimes thousands of documents or other sorts of material, they often struggle when they are asked to present the results of their research in an accessible manner. While this can be seen as a general problem of qualitative research it seems even bigger in the paper-based publication environment of today. While a monograph like a dissertation allows for the detailed documentation by quotation – it is another question of course who will be able to read it from cover to cover – this cannot work for an article or research paper of twenty pages' maximum as required by most academic journals. Moreover, as the proliferation of digital tools has made the creation of graphs and diagrams much easier, some kind of visual synopsis has even become a natural expectation of the usual reader of academic literature.

There is of course a supply for the demand even in qualitative social science. Leading software solutions for qualitative data analyses like *Atlas.ti* or *MaxQDA* include more and more sophisticated sets of visualisation tools that are easy to handle and transform coded data into colourful and fancy diagrams with a few mouse clicks only. While these tools might be of great help they should not be used without reflection, as they come with important side-effects and their more or less hidden conditions might not fit to fundamental assumptions of the interpretive analyses that they are meant to serve. In order to avoid the temptation of *creeping quantification*, as we call it, we would make a plea, on the one hand, for more original, hands-on visualisation conceived and sketched by the qualitative researcher him- or herself. On the other hand, with the new *Entity Mapper*, we would like to propose a particularly flexible tool for the visualisation of qualitative research data, which allows for intriguing visualisation without leaving qualitative grounds.

In the remainder of the chapter, we thus deal with visualisation as a major challenge of qualitative social science in general and discourse analysis (DA) research in particular. Presenting the results of discourse analysis in an illustrative way is far from being a trivial task. However, it is indispensable in order to make knowledge accessible. Although there is some available advice on using mapping strategies for conducting and presenting research (see, with reference to discourse, especially Clarke, Friese and Washburn, 2017), discourse research can still and by far be considered a waste land of visualisation. While discourse analyses tend to fill volumes with detailed documentation of findings by quotation more and more authors have presented innovative synoptical tools and instruments. This holds also true for SKAD research. In section 3, we present some of those tools and techniques and discuss their comparative advantages. Before that, in section 2 already, we reflect on the temptation of *creeping quantification* and its potential repercussions for qualitative research. In section 4, we introduce a more generally applicable software for data visualisation in qualitative research: the Entity Mapper.

Ready-to-use tools and the temptation of *Creeping Quantification*

Qualitative researchers in general and discourse researchers in particular do mostly have strong reasons for what they do. Based on the conviction that mainstream quantitative social science is not well suited for the analysis of the aspects of social reality that they are going to study they orient towards the interpretive paradigm. This commitment of course has a price as qualitative studies mostly mean to read and code masses of material and still only cover one or a little number of case studies. Large-n-designs are almost completely reserved for quantitative researchers. So seemingly are graphs and diagrams that are used to visualise the results of research in an allegedly accessible and impressive manner. While the quantitative researchers can choose between a never-ending selection of techniques and tools to present their results in colourful pictures there are certain limits for qualitative researchers to *sell* the results of their research accordingly. This at least holds true if tools are based on automation as automation has quantification as a precondition. Quantitative methods that are based on automated, statistical and algorithmical approaches follow certain hypotheses about relations and patterns in the datasets. Quantitative analysis is often extrapolated from an investigation of measurement and sorting, for example to frequency, which in the past resulted in a trend of the simplest and dated visualisation strategy of static images especially suited for paper-printed publications. Statistical classification and pattern recognition are quantitative methods that are used with deductive approaches, in the sense that researchers develop their analysis and subsequently test their hypothesis in accordance with existing theory on large datasets with certain similarities in already structured data.

However, the supply of Computer-Aided Qualitative Data Analysis Software has not changed significantly in underlying data structures and software development since the 1990s (Flick, 2002: 366–367), when the most prominent software tools today were first developed. It includes software applications that have transferred methodologies of qualitative social science and especially grounded theory methodology into a digital environment, thus made the qualitative research process (data administration, coding and retrieval) much easier than it had been before and have served generations of qualitative researchers well. Leading tools of this kind are Atlas.ti, MaxQDA (Diaz-Bone and Schneider, 2011) and NVivo. If one only looks at what newer versions of the software have on offer, it is especially the automated analysis and visualisation rubriques that have been considerably extended in recent years. MaxQDA for instance offers different kinds of statistics on code variables and codings, including tools to visualise code frequencies and collocations. Thus, interestingly, it is the same software applications that helped qualitative researchers to organise their work for many years that seduce a lot of them nowadays to potentially leave the grounds of consistency with their initial convictions. For, even in the best digital environments for qualitative social science, what we call creeping quantification is only a few mouse clicks away.

So what is the problem here? First of all, the ready-to-use character of the tools mentioned does not fit to the reflexive process of qualitative social science research in general and DA research in particular, because they mostly make researchers rely on – at least in many cases – non-transparent tools in exchange for impressive pictures. In more concrete terms, the static graph or picture by mouse click would not work if not for automation and quantification. The computer takes over part of the reflexivity without being able to understand the interpretive analytics that underlie the coding procedure. The researcher thus necessarily subjugates under some sort of counting or even scoring if variables are differentiated by their relative value. Moreover, some mostly non-transparent algorithm cares for the positioning of objects and their shape in the resulting graphs. Yet, all the decisions the machine makes for the researcher would need to be understood and reflected in order to avoid inconsistencies.

One only has to look into the software development to find illustrations for the fundamental problem. The first analytical and visualisation tools of MaxQDA for instance were built on codings as the sole unit for all sorts of quantification. This meant that the relative weight or relevance of a code was based on the frequency of codings only and presented accordingly in a suggestive manner (more codings = more relevant). Yet, at the core of qualitative research is the challenge to control the balance of corpora not only regarding the composition by relevant actors and groups (for instance from different camps in a political analysis) but also within the subsets by the number, kinds and dimensions of the material studied. When analysing political debates for instance, one quickly makes the observation that the political left is usually much more talkative and explicit than the right, which leaves remarkable traces in corpus composition. Because while actors on the left of the political spectrum might present their position on a certain issue in a higher number of treatises by different currents and splinter parties, actors from the right might be satisfied with a simplistic brochure. Not quantity counts but the quality (significance, influence or relevance) of what was said and researchers in their reflective position code the qualitative weight of certain words or paragraphs accordingly.

A similar uncontrollability can be observed in the coding procedure itself. As the sorts of material within the same corpus might be very diverse and the coding procedure might take a longer while with interruptions and resumptions it seems almost hopeless to control for a harmonised form of a single coding. While a code is ascribed to a whole paragraph in the one document, it might be only a sentence or even a word in the next one, let alone the single code that is ascribed to a picture, a poster or a meme. Software tools have partly met this latter challenge as the analyst can select the unit of counting between codings (How often has a code been ascribed?) and documents (In how many documents a code has been ascribed at least once?). However, the general rule should still be valid: If amount and range of the material studied cannot systematically be controlled in the first place it is difficult to build informative graphs out of it at the end, that are based on quantitative measurements.

Understanding the inevitable progress in qualitative research, that all textual, numeric, pictorial (static and moving images) and audio sources are digital or digitised for analysis processes makes a strong case for a paradigm shift in the use and presentation of these data forms in qualitative research. The recognition of a clear gap of analysis tools in qualitative research that are at the level of current possibilities in computational data analysis in other fields such as STEM fields (science, technology, engineering, and mathematics) with a focus in statistics or Natural Language Processing to name but a few. It becomes evident that we need to develop new tools that are specifically augmented to administer qualitative research methodologies and the analysis of new forms of digital data. The main challenges that we are confronted with when developing new tools for qualitative analysis is the shift from interactive, reflexive analysis to static presentation of results or in a material sense the shift from digital data analysis to a result presentation on material paper or Portable Document Format. Although current publications are digitally available the format of interactive data presentations as part of digital publications is still not a norm in current academic publishing. Other printed media, such as newspapers have adapted digital possibilities to present interactive maps, graphs and data stories based on data driven documents, D3.js, an open-source JSON library, developed amongst others by former New York Times Graphics employee Mike Bostock. The integration of media such as audio or video as raw data or hyperlinked data collections of articles, reports and video documentation of speeches is neither considered as an integral part when publishing results grounded in exactly these data sources. This means that we do not only have to initiate new forms of analysis that go beyond the possibility of tagging, assigning concepts, marking and commenting but also to find appropriate and creative ways to present results that go beyond synoptical or textual visualisations that became a standard in academic publishing due to the materiality of printed publications. The argument to find solutions for a digital materiality that provides the storage of digital publications without obsolete hyperlinks, code bases and media players is an argument that is part of this article but needs to be discussed in a different context.

Currently three differences that can be made in data visualisation are interactive (with e.g. the data, form or colour), dynamic (e.g. video in form of a documentation) and static representation (e.g. synoptical graphs). Currently static representation is the most commonly developed form to show results in qualitative research. The limitations that these forms of presentation offer comparable with the current state of the art in data representation are for example that an immersive exploration of hierarchies between the raw data (text files, images etc.), the analysis (ascribes codes) and results (paradigm or argumentation maps) is impossible. The transparency of the underlying data and analysis structure for every resulting report is missing in any static representation. The possibility to develop tools that give researchers the opportunity to dive deep into the data and analysis in parallel to the resulting textual report is an enlargement of the reflexivity that is inherent to qualitative research. The tool introduced in the following is the initiation of such computational methods for the representation of results that brings extensive solutions for collaborative, reflexive and transparent research.

Of course, all this criticism does not mean that it would not be helpful to try innovative ways of visualisation. Maybe they bring new insights during the research process; maybe they can really stand as a form of presentation of research results. However, they need to be applied in a transparent, competent and reflexive way. This is far too seldom the case when ready-to-use tools of leading software applications are applied. This is why we present the Entity Mapper as an alternative that avoids creeping quantification and is thus more compatible to qualitative social science research. Before we introduce the Entity Mapper though, we would like to also recommend a liberation from technology in the conception and design of synoptical elements – as static representations still – by giving some illustrative examples from SKAD research.

Static ways to present discourse research? Examples from SKAD studies

The actor or speaker dimension

The illustration of actors or speakers that are represented by documents or discursive events in a given corpus serves at least a triple function. First, it allows for the reduction of complexity both for the analysts and for the readers of a study. Second, actors can be positioned within their social settings, from which socialisation effects might be explained. This also helps the analyst as well as the readers to understand the basic architecture and dynamics of the social conflict at stake. Third, as a differentiation and selection of actors or speakers is mostly a precondition and filter method for corpus building, the mapping of actors also serves as a form of visual argument or proof for a balanced corpus. Some sort of mapping can best illustrate the analysis of actors or speakers in a given debate. This is also the visualisation that most discourse analysts intuitively choose.

For his comparative study of discourses on trash and recycling Keller (2009) chose sort of a map in order to summarise the respective policy publics in Germany and France as Figure 15.1 shows (for maps and further discussion on visualisation see Keller, 2012).

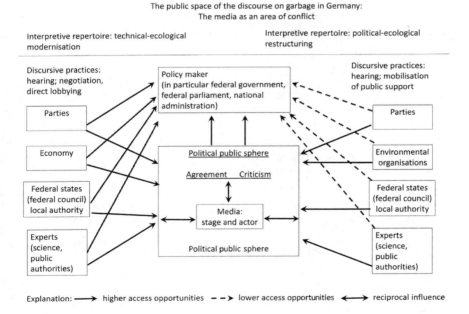

Figure 15.1 Policy publics on trash and recycling in Germany.
Source: Keller, 2009, translated by the authors.

This figure is a result of empirical research. It accounts for discursive strategies of involved actors and the thereby emerging structure of an issue-related public sphere of waste discourse as an empirical phenomenon at a given period and point in time (the 1980s and early 1990s in Germany). It therefore could be different for other issues or other time sequences. It can be read as follows: on the left, you see groups of actors performing the discursive position of technical-ecological modernisation (which in the study was coined the "structural-conservative discourse; see Chapter 4 by Keller on "the social construction of value"), on the right side those performing the discourse of political-ecological restructuring in a tone of cultural pessimism. The actor and actor groups on each side formed a particular discourse coalition in this discursive conflict. They used different ways of access to governmental institutions; direct lobbying only was available for the coalition on the left side of the figure; the actors on the right side mainly had to address government via the media (which was common for the other side too). The media itself worked as an arena for the presentation of agreement and criticism, particular media actors affiliated themselves to one of the discursive coalitions. The policymakers on the national level showed a slight tendency towards the left coalition, therefore they appear not exactly in the middle of the figure. The full content of this figure unfolds in contrast to the one presenting the French case, which had a much simpler structure: there was only one hegemonic discourse performed by governmental institutions and addressing civil society via the French media (see Keller, 2009). It is important to note that this is not a general model for the public sphere, but a presentation of the analytical results gained by an issue specific study of discourse. It could be rather different in other cases.

In Schünemann's work on EU referendum debates in different countries (Schünemann, 2014), so-called discourse maps are most explicit and detailed. They are used as a systematised tool for the comparison of discourses throughout his works. By colouring of areas (political left/political right; yes/no), shape and size of labels types of organisations (parties, interest groups, campaign organisations) are differentiated and the building of a balanced corpus is made more plausible. Although frequency is not a precise indication of weight within the debate, the absolute and relative weight of any actor/organisation by documents in the corpus (in absolute numbers and as a percentage of the respective camp) can be helpful for assessing the quality of a corpus. Figure 15.2 shows the discourse map for the first Irish referendum debate on the Lisbon Treaty in 2008.

The content dimension

Having presented tools for the illustration of speakers and speaker positions, in this section we present some synoptical tools for the content dimension of discourse analyses as well. Figure 15.3 proposes a spatial visualisation for all the arguments of both camps in the Dutch referendum campaign of 2005 on the EU Constitutional Treaty, again taken from Schünemann's study of the respective debates (Schünemann, 2014). Even though in his work there were no substantial comparative conclusions drawn from quantification, the size of the labels does nonetheless depend on the frequency of codings for the respective category.

The dimensions of actors and content or meaning can of course be presented in one figure as well. In his study on trash and recycling discourses for instance, Keller (2009) merges the two dimensions of discourse research when juxtaposing the two ideal-type discourses he identified in his research and ascribed the respective actors to them, as Figure 15.4 shows.

This figure presents the two opposing discourses and discourse coalitions in the German case of waste politics. The titles of the columns indicate the labels Keller attributed to these discourses. Moreover, the figure accounts for concrete political parties, economic actors, experts and newspapers which formed those coalitions. The presentation can be read as "ideal type": The more actors are situated to both extremes (right and left), the more pronounced was their engagement for the discursive position in question. The more they are situated in the middle, the more mixed was there discursive performance. Here again, the French case stands for a completely different structure of the discursive landscape. Please note again, that this figure is rather static. One surely could and maybe should do several mappings giving snapshots of different moments in the unfolding of discursive conflicts.

In her empirical, ethnographic study on discourses of knowledge, captured under the notions "knowledge society" and "knowledge for development", Hornidge (2014) assesses how these global discourses travel to and are picked up by governments in Southeast and Central Asia, legtimised by reference to developments within the field of information and communication technologies, creative industries and multi-media.

Hornidge argues, that these discourses do not only guide policy-making in countries such as Singapore, Malaysia, Indonesia, Uzbekistan and Tajikistan, but that the discourses tip, as she puts it, and defeat in many ways their actual purpose of "development" once some of the discourse inspired policies are being implemented in the local context (2014, 2013a, 2013b). Based on the empirical qualitative tracing of these two global discourses, how and what type of policy-making they inspire on the level of the selected nation states as well as what these policies, i.e. immense government investments into the building of a "Multimedia Super Corridor"

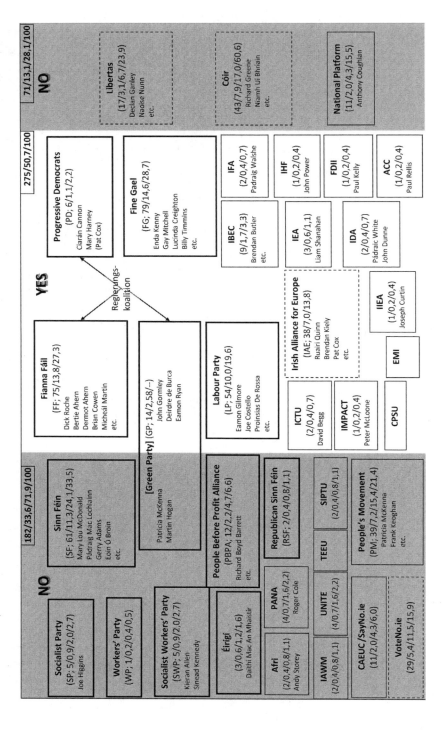

Figure 15.2 Discourse map for the first Irish referendum debate on the Lisbon Treaty in 2008.

From analysis to visualisation 283

in Malaysia or a "Biopolis" in Singapore, achieve in terms of facilitating social change towards a so-called "knowledge society" as development stage, Hornidge conceptualises "tipping points of discourse" as those points, where the intended, as communicated by a particular discourse, tips and in actual implementation of the discourse-inspired decisions taken, produce unintended consequences. It is here, according to Hornidge, where the normative and factual discourses of knowledge as captured under the notions of "knowledge society" and "knowledge for development" turn hegemonic.

While the illustrative examples above, all taken from different studies of the editors of this volume constitute original ways to present SKAD research and to not suffer from creeping quantification, they cannot overcome one central shortcoming of almost any visualisation made for printed publication: its static character. Thus, with complexity, which is meant to be reduced by visual tools, static illustrations always reduce reflexivity, as they do not allow readers to recapitulate the interpretive process from an empirical finding to its graphical representation. However, in the following section, with the Entity Mapper we want to present a more dynamic and interactive tool.

The entity mapper

The development of the Entity Mapper was initiated due to a certain frustration and limitation that current software tools for qualitative research offer in their usability and data representation. Managing data sets that are semi-structured or do not follow a clean data structure at all is a fundamental challenge in qualitative research and the complexity of multimedia can be an inherent part of the analysis process. Researchers access data with certain expert knowledge and previous study of technical literature but nevertheless build the analysis often in a reflexive, inductive character and therefore it is data that informs theory development. Although

---

Legend
"SP: Socialist Party; WP: Workers' Party; SF: Sinn Féin; SWP: Socialist Workers Party; PBPA: People Before Profit Alliance; RSF: Republican Sinn Féin; Afri: Action from Ireland; PANA: Peace and Neutrality Alliance; IAWM: Irish Anti-War Movement; TEEU: Technical Engineering and Electrical Union; UNITE: Unite the Union; SIPTU: Services, Industrial, Professional and Technical Union; CAEUC: Campaign Against the EU Constitution; PM: People's Movement; FF: Fianna Fáil; PD: Progressive Democrats; GP: Green Party; IAE: Irish Alliance for Europe; IBEC: Irish Business and Employers' Confederation; FG: Fine Gael; LP: Labour Party; EMI: European Movement Ireland; IEA: Irish Exporters Association; IFA: Irish Farmers' Association; ICTU: Irish Congress of Trade Unions; IIEA: Institute of International and European Affairs; IDA: Industrial Development Agency; IHF: Irish Hotels Federation; IMPACT: Impact Trade Union; CPSU: Civil Public & Services Union; FDII: Food and Drink Industry Ireland; ACC: American Chamber of Commerce in Ireland."

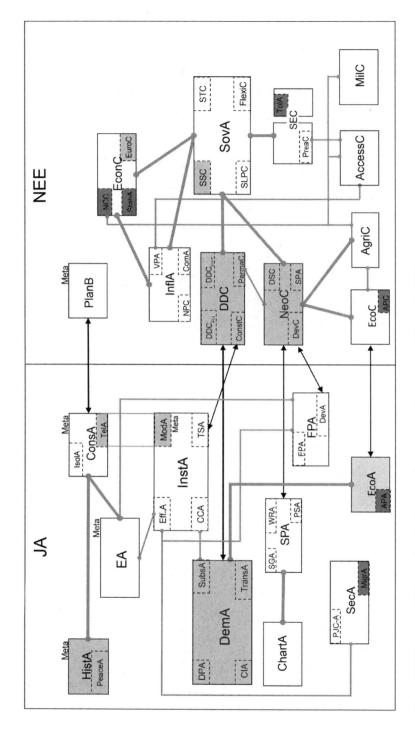

Figure 15.3 Structural Scheme for the Dutch debate on the Constitutional Treaty in 2005.

Actors	Structurally conservative discourse on garbage: technical-ecological modernisation	Culturally critical discourse on garbage: political-ecological restructuring
Politics/ administration (e.g.)	Discourse coalitions *Federal government (Ministry of economics) (Ministry of environment) *Federal States (Baden-Württemberg, North Rhine-Westphalia) *Parties *FDP *CDU/CSU *SPD *local authority	Discourse coalitions *Federal state governments (Lower Saxony, Hesse) *Parties *SPD *Die Grünen *PDS
Economy/ environmental organisations (e.g.)	*Trade associations (BDI, DIHT, VCI) *individual large companies *Disposal and utilisation industry (Initiative Sichere Abfallbehandlung, BDE, DSD) *Labour unions	*Environmental organisations (BUND, Greenpeace, Robin Wood, Das bessere Müllkonzept)
Experts (e.g.)	*Experts from public authorities and science *Federal environmental agency *Advisory council on the environment	*Experts from public authorities and science *Office for Technology Assessment of the German Federal Parliament *Environmental institutes
Media (e.g.)	*FAZ *Die Welt *Handelsblatt *Rheinischer Merkur *SZ *Wirtschaftswoche	*SZ *Der Spiegel *Die Zeit, DAS *FR *taz *nature, global garbage journal

⟵ Way of profiling ⟶

Figure 15.4 The public discourse arena (policy-specific) in Germany.
Source: Keller 2009, translated by the authors.

methodologies in qualitative research can differ immensely in their data collection methods, research design and analysis methods, it is important to understand that it is not the qualitative form of the data (e.g. reports, interviews) but the methods that allows researchers to develop theory in reflexive approaches which makes data analysis "qualitative". The qualitative approach allows to weight, mark and comprehend the quality of

---

Legend
"Sub-arguments (fig. 15.3): APA: Animal Protection Argument; APC: Animal Protection Critique; CCA: Competence Catalogue Argument; ChartA: Charter Argument; CIA: Citizen Initiative Argument; ComA: Commission Critique; ConstC: Constitutional Critique; DevA: Developmental Argument; DevC: Developmental Critique; DPA: Democratisation and Politicisation Argument; DSC: Dumping Social Critique; Eff$_2$A: Effectivity and efficiency Argument; EPA: Europe Puissance Argument; EuroC: Euro Critique; FlexiC: Flexibility Critique; IsolA: Isolation Argument; MigrA: Migration Argument; ModA: Modernisation Argument; NCC: Net Contributor Critique; NPC: New Posts Critique; PeacA: Peace Argument; PermaC: Permanency Critique; PJC-A: Police and Justice Cooperation Argument; PreaC: Preamble Critique; PSA: Public Services Argument; SGA: Social Goals Argument; SLPC: Supremacy and Legal Personality Critique; SPA: Services Publics Argument; SSC: Super State Critique; StabA: Stability Argument; STC: Sovereignty Trasfer Critique; SubsA: Subsidiarity Argument; TelA: Teleological Argument; TolA: Tolerance Argument; TransA: Transparency Argument; TSA: Treaty Simplification Argument; VPA: Voting Power Argument; WRA: Workers' Rights Argument."

286 *Anne Luther and Wolf J. Schünemann*

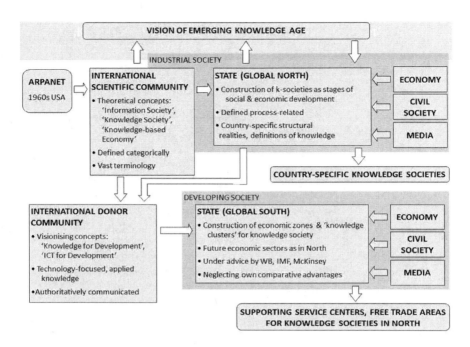

Figure 15.5 Emerging Knowledge Age.
Source: Hornidge, 2014.

what is said, written or shown in the data rather than quantify a data set by semantics, parsing or word counts. One example for a study about quantitative data interpreted with qualitative methods is Loukissas' *Life and Death of Data* (2014), a study on the technological and material history of the Arnold Arboretum with an understanding of local data design, telling a narrative about cultural and time historic contexts that created, collected and stored particular data with research queries in mind. The report also shows an interactive data visualisation of the data set corresponding to active hyperlinks in the written report, a fluid presentation between data, analysis and resulting theory. An outstanding example of current possibilities to narrate research results with a transparent connection to raw data, analysis process and results. The current state of the art in data visualisation of qualitative research is nevertheless mostly anchored in static data presentation (synoptical graphs, infographics, static maps and network views) and examples such as the above mentioned data driven research and visualisation *of Life and Death of Data* (Loukissas, 2014) and the following description of the Entity Mapper are momentarily exceptions to the aim to develop new software that is specific to methods in qualitative research and that allow a transparent connection between data and analysis without slipping into the corner of the described *creeping quantification*.

The Entity Mapper is a software that allows researchers analysing their data in Atlas.ti to visualise their full analysis as a node-link network. Atlas.ti was developed for a hierarchical data structure that is foremost built in Grounded Theory research. Figure 15.6. shows how the reflexive analysis process originates in a network between the raw text files (rtf), marked quotations, ascribed codes and concepts (code families). The hierarchy is developed in the manner that researchers first read the text files and mark quotations that seem relevant for the research question. Re-entering the text, asking what these quotations are about, show or relate to another narrative structure leads to codes that describe the data. The codes can be ascribed with an understanding of external technical literature, the expert knowledge of the researcher or directly quote language of the field. Theoretical concepts emerge from cross-referencing the descriptive codes. The simplified node-link network in Figure 15.6 shows this hierarchy to illuminate the underlying data structure for such analysis process.

Data structure

The network illustrated in Figure 15.6 is more complex in applied analysis because researchers usually use more than one text file and develop codes and concepts that are shared in a hermeneutic unit of multiple documents. The documents are linked through a code base that emerged grounded in the raw text files. Code families are linked through a complex and cross-referenced code base. In the same way that quotations can be dedicated to multiple codes, codes can also be found in multiple concepts

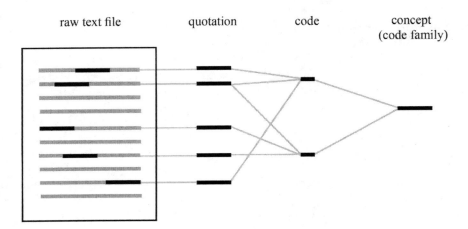

Figure 15.6 Node-Link Network of data structure developed in Atlas.ti.

(code families). The network that evolves shows that the data structure that grows is dependent on the analysis process and is structured by an inductive approach of the researcher. The complexity of the developed node-link network is inherent to the analysis process and it becomes important to develop new software that gives the possibility to clearly illustrate results without losing the underlying complexity and with the intention to give transparency to the coding choices of the researcher. Multi-level modalities, visibility, movability and a flow between text and visual form make it possible to understand the analysis in its full complexity without losing a sense for a result structure.

The dataset shown in Figures 15.7–15.11 is a demo of a partial data set of a field study about the contemporary art world in New York between 2014–2016. The figures show the analysis network resulting from ten semi-structured interviews with artists, curators, collectors, critics and art advisors. The entire data set and analysis is available (Luther, 2016) and shows the first application of the novel open-source software. In the following, the description of the modalities is described as part of the development and possible application of the software.

Visibility

Atlas.ti allows exporting the complex network of the entire hermeneutic unit in xml format, which can be uploaded in the software Entity Mapper, a web-based software, which was built in Angularjs (2017), D3js (2017), and Bootstrap (2017). Figures 15.6 and 15.7 show the web browser view. Once the xml file is uploaded the entities (rtfs, quotations, codes and concepts) are visible in its full complex relational node-link network. Figure 15.8 shows an example of a hermeneutic unit of ten raw text files and the data structures resulting from the analysis in Atlas.ti. In the lower left corner of Figure 15.8 the pop up window shows the entities in text form and gives the researcher the ability to enable or disable the visibility of the entities.

Figure 15.7 shows the visual network the researcher can interact with in their web browsers. The figures here are shown merely as references for the interactive web-based network that it always shows in colour. The bubbles of the raw text files of the analysed data set are yellow, the quotations in these rtfs are grey, the ascribed codes are green and the resulting concepts are pink. The more quotes are linked to a code the bigger the bubble becomes. The complexity of the network does not necessarily give the researcher the possibility to explore the data set in a presentable way. It was important to develop a feature in the tool that allows constructing a narration through interaction with the entities of the data analysis and to be able to abstract the complexity of the data set without losing access to the data. Figure 15.8 shows the same data set but the researcher "switched off" the entities quotations and rtf by clicking on the respective names in

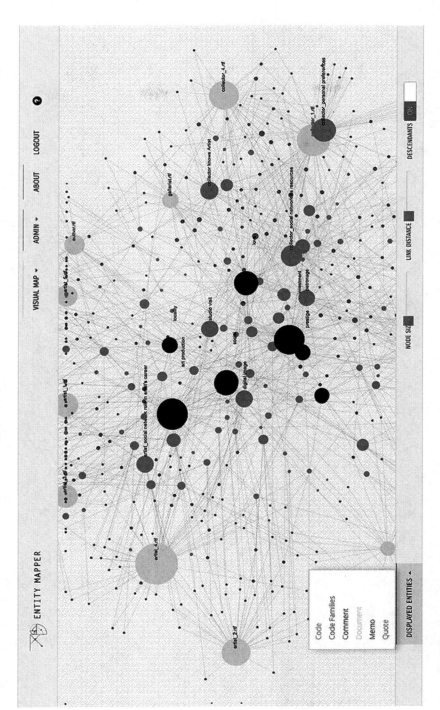

Figure 15.7 Display of all entities.

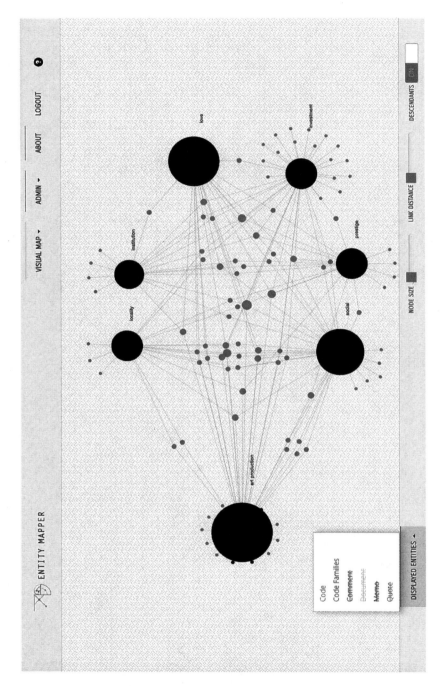

Figure 15.8 Display of codes and code families.

the pop up window "Displayed Entities". The enabled or displayed entities are code and code families in Figure 15.8. The network becomes cleaner and better accessible for the creation of a visual narration through the movability of entities.

Movability

The movability of entities is an important modality. It allows the researcher to interact with the data structures that they developed in their analysis. Figure 15.11 shows an arrangement of the entities according to a paradigm map constructed by Strauss and Corbin (1998). Art Production, a concept entity (pink) pinned to the left side of the network by pressing down the command key and moving the entity over the screen, is here titled as the cause for the network. Love and investment, pinned on the right side of the network are located as the consequence of the phenomenon that the network describes. Social and prestige, two entities at the bottom of the network are strategies for the existence for both the cause and consequences, and locality and institutions, two entities at the top of the network are context and intervening conditions between art production and love and investment. The paradigm map shows the codes (green) that are connected to the concepts that were developed in the analysis. The patterns or constellations of the codes that are visible by the movability of entities emerge from links of their responsive node-children. For example, on the left lower corner, the constellation of six codes between art production and social are codes that are linked to both concepts. Revealing which codes are visible in the network can be achieved through a flow between text and form.

Flow between text and visual form

Figure 15.9 shows that the interaction with the entities pops up a window on the right side of the screen, which shows the entities in textual form, codes that are connected to the concept. The researcher sees at the same time on the left side of the screen the highlighted links. By hovering over the name of a code in the text box, the code in the network is highlighted and the location of the code becomes clear. This allows understanding patterns between links that were constructed in the analysis. Quotations that are connected to codes can be accessed by clicking on the code name either in the network or in the text box. All quotations that are linked to the code will appear as text and can be copied and pasted into the resulting report, as shown in Figure 15.10. The text box also indicates linked codes of the quotation and allows clicking "back" to all linked quotations of the parent codes. The linked rtf that the quotation is taken from also pops up to show the researchers the data source. The rtf name indicates the role of the interviewee in the network in these figures. The interactive

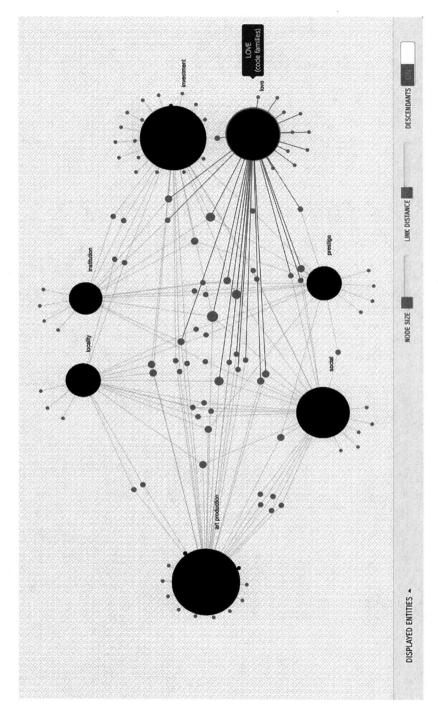

Figure 15.9 Hovering over entities.

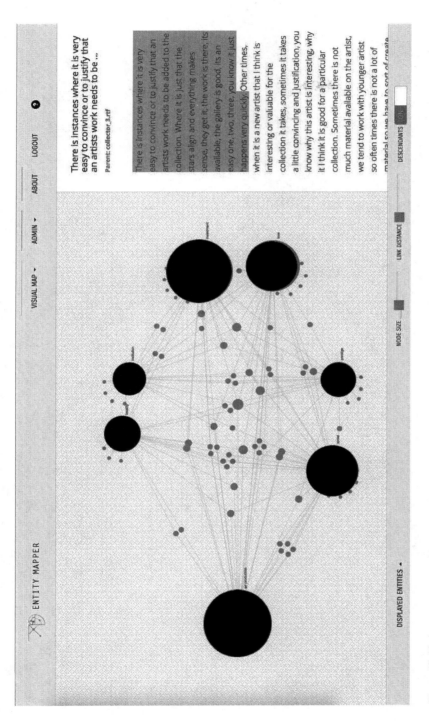

Figure 15.10 Access to quotations.

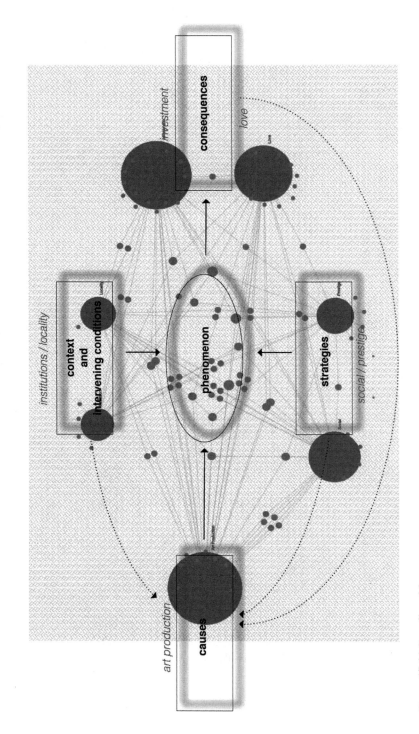

Figure 15.11 Paradigm Map.

flow between the visual map and the text box gives the researchers a reflective moment in the establishment of argument structures and theory development. The recursive question of what was said by the participants that are studied is inherent to any qualitative analysis and is a fundamental element to the developed interactive visualisation of the qualitative analysis. The described movements between text and visual form, and data and results are not achievable with static synoptical graphs.

Meta-data

Data that gives information about the collected and analysed data can be measured in quantities such as how many links are connected to certain concepts. Rather than displaying a numeric report and sorting textual codes alphabetically or according to the number of appearance, the Entity Mapper displays the information visually in size of the nodes. Linked entities are sorted alphabetically in the text box. The researcher can intuitively understand meta-data information as an integral part of the visual map. The choice to interpret a quantitative element of the analysis is therefore a choice of the researcher and can be used as a tool to understand missing data in the analysis. For example, in Grounded Theory research the comprehension of absent data or missing data is a process in the research design that can lead to follow-up interviews, a restructuring of the interview design or the scoping of participants that were not known to the researcher when first entering the field. The circular process of data collection and interpretation is reinforced by the visual display of meta-data. One example of the study that one of the authors has conducted with the Entity Mapper about the contemporary art market shows that the location of entities in the network in relation to the quantity display (size) can also build an argument. The code "studio visit" an entity that describes a place where roles of the art market (curators, collectors, critics etc.) that are external to the operations in an artist studio come to visit the artist in the place where art is often produced or conceptualised. The interviewees described different intentions, protocols and language. Although the code studio visit is not the largest in size it can be described as a code with a high significance due to the location of the node in the network shown in Figure 15.10. The code studio visit is located between art production and love and investment. As mentioned above, laid out, as a paradigm map art production is the cause for the resulting entities that lead to love and investment as a consequence. It becomes clear that the studio visit is a strategy on both the artist's and the collector's side to build prestige and is bound to a contextual locality (for example collectors who live in the same city as the artist are more likely to visit a studio in the same city). The code studio visit is also located between prestige as a strategy and locality as a context in the constructed visual map. The locality of entities results from links to their parent entities. The visual comprehension of place and size is dependent on quantity of links in the constructed node-link network. The quantitative information that the manual analysis shows can be described with a qualitative understanding of the field.

A main element of the software is design that leads to intuitive workflows, clean distinctions between elements such as text and visual form or the hierarchies of entities, and meta-data that is instantly comprehensible. Design is often dismissed in scientific presentations and especially in qualitative research despite the intention to present results visually. Aesthetic decisions about information management can be made by identifying distinctions between form and content, background and foreground, colour and form, location, interaction and workflow to name but a few. A comparison to the visualiser in Atlas.ti shows that the user interface and experience uses less steps to get to a similar result: In Atlas.ti it takes at least five steps and multi windows to show links (codes and code families) of one document, an interaction that is solved in the interface of the Entity Mapper by simply choosing to display the entity at the bottom of the screen. The described hovering or choosing of an entity to display its name and links was a choice to avoid that tags or text is crowding the visualisation to a degree in which tags are overlapping and are incomprehensible, a problem that we see for example in network views created with Graph Commons. The choice to highlight links only when an entity is selected gives a clear hierarchy between nodes and links and also leads to a clean visual image – the location of the nodes is more important than the location of links unless the researcher wants to consciously see the links for the construction of an argument. The differentiation between text and visual is highlighted by the coloured and structured background of the visualisation, a design choice that brings a certain visual depths to the interaction with visual elements. Rather than working with multiple screens or pop-up windows, the choice to flatten the interaction with the hierarchy of the networked dataset was also made with the intention to provide a clean and intuitive interface. Bringing design to interface and usability of new tools in qualitative analysis does not follow the argument to beautify research but rather has practical functions for the comprehension of the data set. The interdisciplinarity between humanities and social sciences, engineering and design is grounded in research processes and aims to illuminate the full complexity of datasets without losing qualitative roots.

Using the entity mapper for SKAD research

As SKAD researchers mostly apply elements of Grounded Theory Methodology, their studies could immensely profit from tools like the Entity Mapper. This can be illustrated with reference to the SKAD work of one of the authors on referendum debates on the EU Constitutional Treaty and the Lisbon Treaty in France, the Netherlands and Ireland in 2005 and

2008 respectively (Schünemann, 2014, Chapter 5). Therefore, arguments can be regarded as the code families or concepts in the language of the Entity Mapper. Sub-arguments which appear in reality when campaigners try to substantiate their claims are the codes. The network of codes and code families (Figure 15.9) would be of great help in order to get an overview of argumentation in one debate and compare this between the cases. As all nodes or bubbles remain movable, the researcher would be able to group concepts and codes according to the camp (yes/no) of the debate. Node size and position as well as link size would give indications as to how central or important a given pattern is for the debate. However, this quantitative weight does not need to be taken for granted but a reader can delve deeper into the data and recapitulate the interpretive analysis by opening codings/quotations and the original data material. Thus for instance, where we find the overall label Sovereignty Argument in one of the networks, we can easily see which elements this concept is composed of in that particular case. Then these codes could be checked again, as for the Sovereignty Transfer Argument, one could open a quotation from French FN Leader Le Pen and another one from the Dutch populist politician Geert Wilders and compare them directly. The same can be repeated so that coding within one case or the comparative analysis of several cases can be intersubjectively reproduced to a certain extent.

Please remember that SKAD research uses some strategies of grounded theory research (as do other approaches), but it is different in its interests and additional methodology (see Keller on SKAD, Chapter 2). It suggests, that the paradigm matrix as suggested by Strauss and Corbin is too formal in order to account for the heterogeneity of discourses. SKAD's concept of the phenomenal structure is more open: Remember that both the dimensions of a phenomenal structure as well as its concrete appearance are results of empirical analysis, that is they have to be constructed by the analyst during her or his empirical work. Therefore they are different for different discourses and discursive landscapes. The challenge would then be to replace the paradigm map by a map of phenomenal structures. The Entity Mapper would need to be modified accordingly.

Conclusion

The importance of design and engineering shows the distinction of the described software to a current trend in Digital and Computational Humanities to develop tools that undermine qualitative research processes through algorithmic or automated analysis processes. The need to make a clear distinction from the intention to develop new software for qualitative analysis with a computational approach from scientific fields that depend on mathematical interpretation is based in the argument that these approaches lead to a creeping quantification as argued in this article. Utilising interdisciplinarity in the realm of computer-aided analysis often comes with the prize to use computers as data processors rather than finding solutions that support qualitative methodology that depends on manual decision-making processes of researchers that have studied or participated in the field of study. The chapter has made a double and almost antithetic argument: on the one hand, we argue for more original handmade illustrations by the researchers themselves, as such visualisations can best illustrate the interpretations and reflections the analyst had during the research process while it avoids creeping quantification or other inconsistencies of many ready-made-tools in standard software. On the other hand or at the other end of the continuum, we would propose an innovative and much more dynamic tool for this visualisation of DA research (not only its results). The Entity Mapper is an example for the utilisation of design and engineering for software development that does not support automated analysis but rather helps to comprehend elements in qualitative analysis that researchers lay out with inductive, reflexive and interpretive approaches.

References

Angularjs.org (2017). *AngularJS – Superheroic JavaScript MVW Framework.* [online] Available at: https://angularjs.org [Accessed 28 August 2017].

Bootstrap (2017). [online] Available at: http://getbootstrap.com [Accessed 28 August 2017].

Clarke, A., Friese, C. and Washburn, R. (2017). *Situational Analysis.* 2nd edn. Thousand Oaks: Sage.

Diaz-Bone, Rainer, Schneider, Werner (2011). Qualitative Datenanalysesoftware in der sozialwissenschaftlichen Diskursanalyse – Zwei Praxisbeispiele. In Reiner Keller, Andreas Hirseland, Werner Schneider, Willy Viehöver, eds., *Handbuch sozialwissenschaftliche Diskursanalyse. Bd. 2 Forschungspraxis.* 3rd edn. Wiesbaden: VS, Verl. für Sozialwiss.

D3js.org (2017). *D3.js – Data-Driven Documents.* [online] Available at: https://d3js.org [Accessed 28 August 2017].

Flick, U. (2002). *An Introduction to Qualitative Research.* London: Sage.

Hornidge, A.-K. (2013a). Wissen-fokussierende Wirklichkeiten und ihre kommunikative Konstruktion. In R. Keller, H. Knoblauch and J. Reichertz, eds., *Kommunikativer Konstruktivismus – Theoretische und empirische Konturen eines neuen wissenssoziologischen Ansatzes.* Wiesbaden: Springer VS Verlag, 205–232.

Hornidge, A.-K. (2013b). 'Knowledge', 'Knowledge Society' and 'Knowledge for Development'. Studying Discourses of Knowledge in an International Context. In R. Keller and I. Truschkat, eds., *Methodologie und Praxis der Wissenssoziologischen Diskursanalyse.* Wiesbaden: Springer VS Verlag, 397–424.

Hornidge, A.-K. (2014). *Discourses of Knowledge: Normative, Factual, Hegemonic, Habilitation,* Fac. of Philosophy, University of Bonn: Venia Legendi: Development Res.

Keller, R. (2009). *Müll – die gesellschaftliche Konstruktion des Wertvollen. Die öffentliche Diskussion über Abfall in Deutschland und Frankreich.* 2nd edn. Wiesbaden: Springer VS.

Keller, R. (2012). Entering Discourses: A New Agenda for Qualitative Research and Sociology of Knowledge. *Qualitative Sociology Review* 8(2), 46–55.

Loukissas, Y. A. (2014). *The Life and Death of Data.* [online] Available at: www.lifeanddeathofdata.org [Accessed 01 March 2018].
Luther, A.-K. (2016). *Collecting Contemporary Art: A Visual Analysis of a Qualitative Investigation into Patterns of Collecting and Production.* PhD thesis, University of the Arts London.
Schünemann, W. J. (2014). *Subversive Souveräne: Vergleichende Diskursanalyse der gescheiterten Referenden im europäischen Verfassungsprozess.* Wiesbaden: Springer VS.